Gender and History

Series Editors
Amanda Capern
University of Hull
Hull, UK

Louella R. McCarthy
University of Wollongong
Wollongong, Australia

Gender and History is an important series of books that offers teachers and students lively and accessible surveys of the most recent research into the impact of gender and sexual orientation on the past. Exciting new methodologies and topics are covered using gender as a category of historical analysis. The series acknowledges the multiple cultural constructions and fluidity of gender and sexuality as well as intersectionality with race. Its titles aim to embed women's and LGBTQ+ histories in the curriculum while revealing some of the root causes of global inequalities of power. Culture, race, politics, economy and religion are all covered in books that use the lens of gender to excite interest in the lived and embodied experiences of people whose voices have been marginalized. Reimagining history for the twenty-first century, this series tackles questions of power and emotional life in ways that are highly engaging for the reader and that restore social justice to the historical narrative.

More information about this series at
https://link.springer.com/bookseries/14997

Paula Bartley

Women's Activism in Twentieth-Century Britain

Making a Difference Across the Political Spectrum

Paula Bartley
Stratford upon Avon, UK

Gender and History
ISBN 978-3-030-92720-2   ISBN 978-3-030-92721-9 (eBook)
https://doi.org/10.1007/978-3-030-92721-9

© The Editor(s) (if applicable) and The Author(s), under exclusive licence to Springer Nature Switzerland AG 2022

This work is subject to copyright. All rights are solely and exclusively licensed by the Publisher, whether the whole or part of the material is concerned, specifically the rights of translation, reprinting, reuse of illustrations, recitation, broadcasting, reproduction on microfilms or in any other physical way, and transmission or information storage and retrieval, electronic adaptation, computer software, or by similar or dissimilar methodology now known or hereafter developed.

The use of general descriptive names, registered names, trademarks, service marks, etc. in this publication does not imply, even in the absence of a specific statement, that such names are exempt from the relevant protective laws and regulations and therefore free for general use.

The publisher, the authors and the editors are safe to assume that the advice and information in this book are believed to be true and accurate at the date of publication. Neither the publisher nor the authors or the editors give a warranty, expressed or implied, with respect to the material contained herein or for any errors or omissions that may have been made. The publisher remains neutral with regard to jurisdictional claims in published maps and institutional affiliations.

Cover illustration: The cover photo is of Lilian Bilocca.
Cover credit: Mirrorpix / GettyImages

This Palgrave Macmillan imprint is published by the registered company Springer Nature Switzerland AG.
The registered company address is: Gewerbestrasse 11, 6330 Cham, Switzerland

For Réka and Dóra Dudley and to the memory of Carol Adams

Acknowledgements

First of all, thanks to my editor Emily Russell, who encouraged this project from its early beginning, discussed it at each stage and provided such great advice.

Thanks to my lovely women's group of activists, Jane Clarke, Joan McKenna, Sue Morley and Rachel Wiggans, for helping me to remember some of our joint political endeavours. Sadly, one of our group, Carol Adams, the country's first inspector for Equal Opportunities and champion of women's history, died some years ago, and this book is partly dedicated to her. Since 1982, individually and collectively my women's group have provided laughter, politics and love. Much of their spirit, I hope, is encapsulated in this book. Without the numerous women like them, often supported by sympathetic men, the women's rights we now enjoy would never have been achieved.

I would also like to thank my former colleagues at Lewisham Girls' School, Helen Leigh, Nicole Stone and Doug Thorburn, for devising one of the first women's history courses in the United Kingdom. Our collective educational activism provides the backbone of my writing, and I still draw upon our work in this area.

Thanks to my students who enrolled on my women's history courses at the University of Wolverhampton and gave me such great feedback. Colleagues and friends like Janis Lomas and Maggie Andrews were so supportive of my project—our discussions about women's history and politics more generally have all helped shape the book.

A number of other friends helped, and I would like to thank them too. Cathy Loxton, Dawn Rumley, Hilary Bourdillon, Jeanette Black, Rosie Keep and Rebecca Liebmann commented on various chapters; Janet Anslow, Diane Atkinson, Libby Bennett, Angela V. John, Hilda Kean and Kathy Stredder all helped in one way or another. I am indebted to Sue Morgan for all our conversations about women's history. Thanks to Vicky Robinson for early inspiration.

Thanks to Tom Kelly for putting me in touch with Margaret Fleck and Leah Strug. Thank you Margaret for sharing your amazing story about The Dolly Mixtures with me.

I was researching this book just as the pandemic began. Without the vast number of sources available online, this book could not have been written. I am therefore grateful to the British Newspaper Archive, the University of Warwick, the London School of Economics, the Women's Resource Centre and a number of feminist journals for putting their archives online. My special thanks to Christine Maloney and Amy Merriott at Stratford-upon-Avon library, Eddie Bundy at the British Library and Indy Bhullar at the Women's Library, LSE.

A number of people have helped with illustrations: Pat Bickerstaffe, Leah Strug and Margaret Fleck gave me private photographs; and Christine Hankinson and Rebecca Odell gave permission to use their images.

I am especially grateful to the Women's History Network and all those (mostly) female scholars who have reclaimed women from the obscurity of the past and in so doing reinterpreted history. I have referenced those who have helped in this particular project. Thank you to the anonymous readers who read my proposal and to the anonymous reviewer who read the finished manuscript for their comments on how to improve the book.

Huge thanks to Clare Short for helping me in countless ways: discussing the book right from its early stages, unearthing material for me to use, suggesting ways of improving the book and commenting on the entire manuscript. Her wisdom and insights were invaluable.

My greatest thanks, as ever, are to my husband Jonathan Dudley, whose love and care have been unsurpassable in these most difficult times. Always supportive, always encouraging, always fun to be with, he remains both my rock and my rocket. The book is dedicated to two special young women in our family as well as to Carol Adams.

Contents

1	Introduction: Themes and Debates	1
2	A New Age: 1900–1914	13
3	The Home Front: 1914–1918	37
4	The Not-So-Roaring Twenties: 1918–1929	63
5	The Hungry Thirties: 1930–1939	93
6	The Second World War: 1939–1945	123
7	The Post-War World: 1945–1960	151
8	The Less-Than-Swinging Sixties: 1960–1970	175
9	The Selfish Seventies?: 1970–1979	197
10	Margaret Thatcher's Age and After: 1979–2000	225
11	Conclusion: Change and Continuities	257
Bibliography		269
Index		279

List of Figures

Fig. 2.1	Olive Christian Malvery, 1904 (Courtesy of Rebecca Odell and the British Library)	14
Fig. 3.1	The Women Welders' School, from Ray Strachey *Women's Suffrage and Women's Service*, published by London and National Society for Women's Service, 1927 (Courtesy of author)	39
Fig. 3.2	Women ambulance drivers, from *The Great War*, 19 April 1919 (Courtesy of author)	47
Fig. 3.3	Women in the Land Army, spraying fruit trees, from *The Great War*, 19 April 1919 (Courtesy of author)	49
Fig. 3.4	WRAFS from *The Great War*, 19 April 1919 (Courtesy of author)	51
Fig. 4.1	Seven of the eight women: Dorothy Jewson, Susan Lawrence, Vera Terrington, Margaret Bondfield (L-R standing) Margaret Wintringham, Nancy Astor, Mabel Hilton Philipson (L-R sitting) (Courtesy of Christine Hankinson, Leeds Postcards)	69
Fig. 4.2	Chair (second left sitting) of Liverpool Orange Lodge circa 1930s with family (Courtesy of author)	73
Fig. 4.3	Women's pilgrimage, 1926 (Courtesy of the Women's Library, LSE)	76
Fig. 5.1	BUF Women's Corp, 1939 (Courtesy Mary Evans Library/Marx Memorial Library)	101
Figs. 5.2 and 5.3	Pearl Bickerstaffe in about 1937 and with Rodney, 1949 (Courtesy of Pat Bickerstaffe)	108
Fig. 6.1	Women of the Amazon Defence Corps, from the *Liverpool Daily Post*, 24 July 1940 p4 (Courtesy of Mirrorpix)	134
Fig. 6.2	Women recruits from the Caribbean (Courtesy of the National Army Museum, London)	137
Fig. 6.3	Princess Anne unveiling the memorial to Noor Inayat Khan at Gordon Square in Bloomsbury, London on 12 November 2012 (Courtesy of Shrabani Basu)	139
Fig. 7.1	Chaos at the Housewives League Conference (Courtesy of Mary Evans picture library)	156
Fig. 9.1	Advert from *Coventry Evening Telegraph*, 6 April 1971 (Courtesy of author)	200

Fig. 9.2	Front cover of *Socialist Woman* 1973 created by a feminist collective (Courtesy of author)	201
Fig. 9.3	Anti-abortion rally marching down Digbeth, Birmingham 20 June 1971, *Birmingham Post* (Courtesy of Mirror/Reach Licensing)	208
Fig. 9.4	*The Dolly Mixtures* in their Carmen Miranda costumes (Courtesy of Margaret Fleck)	216
Fig. 9.5	Five surviving members of *The Dolly Mixtures*—Hilda Joyce, Sylvia Nichols, Doris Ashcroft, Margaret Fleck and Betty Dickenson with Tom Kelly (sitting R) (Courtesy of Leah Strug)	217
Fig. 10.1	Advert for Centre (Courtesy of Women's Library, Glasgow)	230
Fig. 10.2	Decorating the fence at Greenham Common (Courtesy of author)	240
Fig. 10.3	Embracing the Base at Greenham Common (Courtesy of author)	241

CHAPTER 1

Introduction: Themes and Debates

In 1906, the Anglo-Indian social reformer Olive Malvery published *The Soul Market*, a book about the lives of women at the sharp end of exploitation: factory and shop workers, waitresses, barmaids, costermongers and seamstresses. In her chapter about dressmakers, she wrote of a 'large and fashionable establishment with a ground floor show-room and basement workrooms—horrible little stuffy places, with inadequate ventilation and bad light' where thirty young women were employed. 'Day after day, in this miserable little workroom, half-starved and ailing girls were kept working at high pressure on wages which ranged from four shillings to thirty shillings a week. They had no time to live, but existed from day to day as the slaves of society.'[1] Employers were breaking the law, but few inspectors came to check, and when they did, the factory falsified the pay and conditions. *The Soul Market* was the first book to rouse 'the public to shame and sympathy' and certainly helped inspire the campaigns against such injustices. As Olive Malvery pointed out, 'the creation of a public sentiment must precede any reform'.[2]

Throughout the century, activists like Olive Malvery campaigned for better pay, reasonable working hours and acceptable conditions for women workers. *Women and Activism in 20th Century Britain: Making a Difference across the Political Spectrum* identifies and celebrates many of the women who campaigned for women's employment rights but it points out that even when activists agreed about the need to improve women's working conditions, they would often disagree about how to achieve it. An early contentious issue concerned protective legislation: one group of activists favoured laws which prevented women from working in occupations considered unhealthy or dangerous; others fought for a woman's right to choose.

Over and beyond campaigns around work, the diversity of women's engagement is breathtaking. Of course, there are different definitions of what is meant by activism.[3] In this book, I have taken activism to mean action to bring about

© The Author(s), under exclusive license to Springer Nature Switzerland AG 2022
P. Bartley, *Women's Activism in Twentieth-Century Britain*, Gender and History, https://doi.org/10.1007/978-3-030-92721-9_1

changes or improvements in the way things are done, and here I am writing about women who participated in a wide range of activities from local activism to campaigns which had national and sometimes international resonance.

The reasons why women took action were as various as the campaigns themselves. Some women sought to redress a personal, local, national or international injustice, some took action in response to a death or injury of a loved one, some were motivated by religious zeal and some had an ambition to create a newer, better world in Britain and beyond. Some just wanted to stop the reform clock and return to an idealised version of a lost past. Since not every individual, not every group, not every organisation, not every campaign, not every fight or issue can be included in a short book, I have tried instead to provide a sense of the multidimensional nature and political diversity of women's activism in twentieth-century Britain.

Women's Activism, then, is an introduction to the variety of women's engagement, not a comprehensive survey. Much has been omitted. For example, I have focused on secular organisations and campaigns rather than those attached to religious groups. An altogether more dedicated volume would be needed to do justice to those women across the belief spectrum: many of them from the Catholic, Anglican, Jewish, Muslim, Sikh, Hindu and other faiths who have challenged traditional norms within their various respective religions. There is also no special focus in this book on women activists in political parties. Labour had a number of separate women's groups: for example, the Women's Labour League from 1906 to 1918; the Standing Joint Committee of Industrial Women's Organisations from 1916 to 1953; and the National Joint Committee of Working Women's Organisations from 1953 to 1993.[4] Similarly, the Conservatives had the Primrose League, the Central Women's Advisory Committee, the Conservative Women's Organisation and the Women's Unionist and Tariff Reform Association.[5] The Liberal Party had the Women's Liberal Federation. Similarly, women set up a range of women's organisations like the Women's Social and Political Union, the National Union of Societies for Equal Citizenship, the National Union of Townswomen's Guilds, the Mothers' League and the National Federation of Women's Institutes. This is not the place to recount the history of these groups, and they will only be discussed where they become involved in particular issues. Where discussions on such matters do arise in the text, I have used footnotes to enable readers intrigued by a particular issue to explore further. I would recommend *Women's History Review* and *Women's History Today, the Journal of the Women's History Today Network* for up-to-date research on these areas of women's history.

This book examines how activist demands changed during the twentieth century. The Britain of 1900 was a very different place from the Britain of a hundred years later, and some of the concerns of activists at the beginning of the century were quite different from those at its end. Moreover, two world wars and the vicissitudes of the 1930s Depression changed the very nature of activism during these periods. These sceptred islands too have four discrete nations: women from England, Ireland, Scotland and Wales often had different issues to resolve at different times. Nevertheless, history shows continuity as well as change, and a number of themes and concerns are seen to develop through the century—birth control, sexuality, equal opportunities, employment rights and parliamentary rights are just a few which broadened their scope and gathered momentum as the century progressed. To take one example: at the beginning of the century, women did not have the vote, neither were they allowed to be MPs, a perceived injustice that was partially remedied after the First World War. This success led to other sets of demands like the need for equal franchise and the need to have more women in Parliament. In 1928, equal franchise was achieved but women had to wait until the end of the century to be better represented in the House of Commons. In 1997, after a campaign led by Clare Short MP, 101 Labour women were elected to Parliament. When power was devolved to the Scottish Parliament and Welsh Assembly, the Labour government introduced proportional representation, a system which enables more women to be elected than under a first-past-the-post one.

However, *Women and Activism* does not focus upon women parliamentarians, except when they take up extra-parliamentary campaigns and try to change the law. Nevertheless, activism is an important part of parliamentary democracy, pushing sometimes-reluctant politicians to enact progressive reforms, or indeed stop them from happening. In some cases, MPs became encouraged to advance a number of causes largely because activists gained widespread public support for their campaigns. The dynamic relationship between activists—local or otherwise—and politicians is one which is explored in this book. Chapter 8, for example, features Hull fishwives who campaigned for better safety on trawler ships and persuaded the government to enact their proposals. Other more famous campaigns by women—votes for women, abortion rights, equal pay and police reform—also played an important part in persuading Parliament to change the law.

Activists were always aware of the need to change public attitudes, to raise awareness and to shift people's perceptions if they were to achieve their aims. This was particularly evident in issues around sexual politics. The campaign to stop the *Sun* from publishing photographs of bare-breasted women on page three of the paper was one such action. So too was Mary Whitehouse's campaign, examined in Chaps. 9 and 10, to clean up theatre and television. Perhaps one of the most successful was the campaign for lesbian and gay rights. At the beginning of the century, homosexuality was considered abnormal, seen as an aberration which offended against the country's moral values. In the late 1980s, despite the government's attempt to criminalise 'the promotion of homosexuality', attitudes began to change as lesbians and gays challenged such prejudices. By the end of the century, lesbians and gays were confident enough to 'come out' to an increasingly sympathetic public.

The book is neither a hagiographical nor a Whig version of women's history. Here are no picture-perfect women advancing their position throughout the twentieth century. On the contrary, the book shows that progress was not just uneven and irregular but could also be regressive and reactionary. The point that women are not a homogenous group, all fighting for the same rights on the same ticket, is emphasised. Women, of course, are both united and divided by their age, class, disability, ethnicity, gender, gender identity, nationality, political persuasion, religious affiliation and so on. *Women and Activism* shows how Black and Asian women might well experience different gender oppressions from that of white women. In 1970 a number of white women interrupted a Miss World contest, protesting that it objectified women. A young woman from the Caribbean island of Grenada won. For the white protestors, the beauty contest degraded women; for Black women it affirmed that Black is beautiful in a society that was racist and whose Eurocentric view of what constituted goodlooks demeaned Black women. Consequently, romantic ideals of sisterhood, of women reaching out across class, race and politics to form an ideological circle of righteousness are shown to be a chimeric fantasy, driven more by concepts of patriarchy than by women's lived experiences. Such an idealistic view of women was a cornerstone of radical feminist theory in the 1970s and 1980s—a view that had some merits in that it promoted a belief that women, collectively, could change the world, or at least bring about changes to their immediate environments.

Women and Activism explores why even feminist activists were not a uniform group—they often held differing views on how the position of women could and should be improved. At the beginning of the century, there were fractures within the suffrage movement about how to achieve equal franchise; during the interwar period, feminists diverged over equal rights and welfare feminism; in the 1970s and 1980s, tensions developed between socialist and radical feminists and between Black and white feminists. For example, in the 1980s Black activists challenged the feminism of white activists. Moreover, Black women were being written out of history: while women's campaign against pit closures is well known, the role of Black women activists who collected money and food for the striking miners and their families is barely acknowledged in the historical records.

Discussions in the book show that the notion of a left-right divide can be unhelpful when discussing women's activism. Left-wing women did not always advance progressive politics; right-wing women did not always adopt reactionary positions. In the early part of the twentieth century, for instance, a number of socialist women were strongly opposed to birth control, whereas conservative women (albeit sometimes for eugenic reasons) actively supported the idea of women having access to contraception. Later in the century, reproductive rights became a cornerstone of feminist politics—access to birth control was one of the first demands of Women's Liberation. But even this issue was complicated by activists who questioned the widespread use of Depo-Provera as a contraceptive for women. The challenge was made because Depo-Provera was issued more or less exclusively to Black and Asian women who experienced the unpleasant side effects of the drug.

Nevertheless, the book pays attention to women who, from different social classes, ethnic backgrounds, religious beliefs and political views, did unite on a number of issues. Campaigns associated with women's suffrage, anti-Fascism, trafficking in women, pornography, lesbian and gay rights all feature women from different political, religious and social backgrounds fighting together to remedy perceived affronts. Chapter 5, for example, shows how in the 1930s the left-wing firebrand Ellen Wilkinson and the right-wing Scottish Unionist the Duchess of Atholl overcame their political differences to work together to fight the common enemy of fascism.

The methods used by women activists were diverse and often ingenious. The suffragettes broke the law in imaginative and creative ways and, in doing so, shattered one traditionally held view of womanhood as fundamentally passive, demure and law-abiding. When women were granted a partial vote, unlawful activism diminished significantly as many women returned to more customary methods of protest. Nevertheless a small minority of female activists were not content with letter writing, leafleting and political lobbying and continued to use suffragette methods. In 1929, two communist women chained themselves to balcony railings in protest at the government's handling of the financial crisis. When stewards tried to stop one of the women from shouting out, she bit his hand.[6] In the 1980s, lesbians abseiled into the House of Commons in protest against proposed laws on homosexuality.

Many women have been forgotten—or indeed have never been heard of outside of their local area—because, as Sheila Rowbotham points out, 'they were not at the centre of power, nor were they engaged in heroic acts or glitzed with glamour'.[7] In 1972, a group of eight women sought to raise money to buy a dartboard for men who were in the local hospital being treated for cancer. They called themselves *The Dolly Mixtures*: they sang, danced and told jokes in working-men's clubs across the north east of England. *The Dolly Mixtures* sought to make a difference to the world in which they lived—just as thousands of other women, in various towns and villages, did in thousands of different ways. *Women and Activism* shows how women were involved in local actions, sometimes in response to a tragedy, sometimes against a local injustice, sometimes to bring about improvements in their neighbourhood. Their actions did not make the national press, nor did they have national ramifications, yet for the women and those concerned their campaigns made a difference to many lives. Such women were not full-time or seasoned campaigners, nor did they always take a great interest in national affairs. Yet they gave freely of their time and energy to remedy injustices or improve the places in which they lived. These women are unsung heroines—only rarely do they receive any historical attention. *Women and Activism* rescues some of these women from historical obscurity and helps reframe what is meant by women's activism. 'No one is too small to make a difference', as Greta Thurnberg's title usefully reminds us.[8]

Historiography

In Alan Bennett's play, *The History Boys*, an 'A' level teacher, one Mrs Lintott, tells her boy pupils, 'History is a commentary on the various and continuing incapabilities of men. What is History? It is women following behind with a bucket. ... Can you imagine how depressing it is to teach five centuries of masculine ineptitude?' Bennett's play was first published in 1983, by which time History—with a capital H—had moved on, a little bit. In the 1970s, women's history had reappeared as a significant force.[9] It was definitely a political force, emerging from the Women's Liberation Movement, and sharpened by new directions in social history, by the flourishing of History Workshop and by that excoriating radical manifesto by Sally Alexander and Anna Davin.[10] It began with left-wing leanings: feminist historians wrote about working-class women whose lives had been ignored. One of the first books on women's history, Sheila Rowbotham's *Hidden from History* was written by a socialist feminist activist, and this sparked off a significant growth in women's history.[11] In 1991, the Women's History Network was founded by feminist historians to promote women's history. By the twenty-first century, women's history was (almost) mainstream: in 2021, nine books on women's history were submitted to the Women's History Network book prize, a prize awarded only to first-time authors.[12]

Both as historians and as women, we were fully aware of the ways in which history can help form a sense of self, can create a personal identity and can confirm or deny feelings of self-worth. As feminists, we felt that the fact that women's manifest absence from the story of the past somehow explained and justified our insignificance and inequality in the present. As feminist historians, we believed that by taking control over the past, we would help create and control both the present and the future. History and historical research thus became a form of activism as we sought to reconfigure History by unravelling the well-knit narrative of men's ideas and activities and replacing it with a different story. The following authors, all historical activists in one form or another, are among many who have redefined the past, reshaped the present and the created paradigms for a different future.

Women and Activism draws on an impressive historiography which has largely been created since the 1970s. Histories of the women's movement are plentiful: Olive Banks' *Becoming a Feminist: The Social Origins of 'First Wave' Feminism*,[13] Brian Harrison's *Prudent Revolutionaries: Portraits of British Feminists between the Wars*,[14] Harold Smith's (ed) *British Feminism in the Twentieth Century*,[15] Barbara Caine's *English Feminism 1780–1980*,[16] Martin Pugh's *Women and the Women's Movement in Britain 1914–1999*,[17] Joni Lovenduski and Vicky Randall's *Contemporary Feminist Politics: Women and Power in Britain*,[18] Sue Morgan's (ed) *The Feminist Reader*[19] and Margaret Jolly's *Sisterhood and After*.[20] A number of books have been written by feminists who bring a personal dynamic and perspective to their writing: Sheila Rowbotham's *The Past is Before Us*,[21] Anna Coote and Beatrix Campbell's

Sweet Freedom: The Struggle for Women's Liberation[22] and Amanda Sebestyen's *'68,'78,'88: From Women's Liberation to Feminism*.[23] Significantly, a number of these authors were activists, campaigning for equal rights for women and writing about it too. I, too, am a 'participant observer', having taken a small part in Women's Liberation, abortion campaigns, women's refuges and Greenham Common. I am still trying to rescue women from historical obscurity.

It is important to note that some activists were critical of women's liberation. A number of Black women viewed it as a white movement which did not take into account white privilege and sometimes verged on being racist. It was felt that the predominantly middle-class and white women of the Women's Liberation Movement (WLM) did not understand how race and class intersect with gender to oppress women. Black women activists insisted that 'black women experience a sexism that is racialised and a racism which is gendered'.[24] In so doing, Black and Asian women brought a fresh perspective to British feminism and to activism. Beverly Bryan, Stella Dadzie and Suzanne Scafe's *Heart of the Race*,[25] is a powerful evocation of the lives of Black women activists.[26] Rozina Visram's *Ayahs, Lascars and Princes*[27] was one of the first histories to document the lives of the Indian community. Amrit Wilson's *Finding a Voice: Asian Women in Britain*[28] and Julia Sudbury's *Other Kinds of Dreams: Black Women's Organisation and the Politics of Transformation*[29] both offer new theoretical approaches and additional material to the story of women's activism. In their challenge to white feminism, Black activists overturned traditional conceptual notions of class and patriarchy and introduced the world to 'intersectional' politics, a framework which identifies multiple factors of advantage and disadvantage, and stresses the point that these 'intersect' at various times. More recently, *Black Lives Matter* has established the need to rewrite History not just to retrieve the stories of BAME individuals but also to question the very nature of the British past. *Women's Activism* features Black and Asian activists—from Olive Malvery at the beginning of the twentieth century, to Claudia Jones in mid-century, to Jayaben Desai in the 1970s and Doreen Lawrence in the latter part of the twentieth century—to illustrate the diversity of their activism. Of course, there is more that unites women than divides them: poverty, inequality, legal injustice, sexual violence, pay and working conditions among them. Natalie Tomlinson's *Race, Ethnicity and the Women's Movement in England, 1968–1993*,[30] challenges the view that white and Black activists were in conflict by exploring mixed-race collectives and organisations such as Women Against Imperialism and Women Against Racism and Fascism.

In an exciting new piece of research, June Hannam and Karen Hunt make the case for politics to be widened and deepened to include 'local political cultures and histories of women's neighbourhood activism'.[31] The authors argue that those who examined women's political activism too narrowly focused on a biographical approach, studied various organisations or else concentrated on parliamentary politics.[32] They argue that a new approach is needed, one that looks at the interrelationships between women's formal and informal political activity.[33] As they point out, it is in the local that the majority of women meet politics. *Women's Activism* contributes to this narrative by examining a variety of activist endeavours at a local level and pointing to new ways of interpreting women's participation in direct action.

A number of studies have examined grassroots activity and mass movements like the abortion campaigns and peace protests. David Marsh and Joanna Chambers's *Abortion Politics*,[34] Barbara Brookes' *Abortion in England 1900–1967*,[35] Ellie Lee's *Abortion Law and Politics Today*,[36] Olivia Dee's *The Anti-Abortion Campaign in England, 1966–1989*[37] and Clare Debenham's *Birth Control and the Rights of Women: Post-Suffrage Feminism in the Early Twentieth Century*[38] all focus on both the right to abortion and the campaigns against it. Dorothy Thompson's *Over Our Dead Bodies, Women Against the Bomb*,[39] James Hinton's *Protests and Visions, Peace Politics in 20th Century Britain*[40] and Jill Liddington's *The Long Road to Greenham, Feminism and Anti-Militarism in Britain since 1820*[41] all examine women's participation in peace movements.

Other studies have a broader scope, such as Adam Lent's *British Social Movements Since 1945, Sex, Colour, Peace and Power*,[42] or have focused on a particular period such as Jonathan Moss' *Women, Workplace Protest and Political Identity in England, 1968–85*.[43] Helen Lewis' *Difficult Women*[44] is a well-written, accessible, thoughtful critique of a number of important campaigns and the best introduction to the subject. Krista Cowman's excellent *Women in British Politics, c1689–1979*[45] examines some areas of women's politics and is a useful complement to *Women and Activism* even though it begins long before the twentieth century and finishes in 1979.

There are numerous political biographies of women politicians: from Nancy Astor to Ellen Wilkinson, from Jenny Lee through to Margaret Thatcher. There are also histories of women politicians more generally, including Pamela Brookes' *Women at Westminster*,[46] Melville Currell's *Political Woman*,[47] Elizabeth Vallance's *Women in the House*,[48] Melanie Phillips' *The Divided House*[49] (1980), Rachel Reeves' *Women at Westminster*[50] and Paula Bartley's *Labour Women in Power*[51] (2019). *Women's Activism* has more of a bottoms-up approach by showing how activists encouraged sympathetic MPs either to enact change or to prevent it from happening.

Women were active in party politics, beyond Parliament. There are a number of excellent monographs of women in the Labour Party, including Christine Collette's *The Newer Eve: Women, Feminists and the Labour Party*,[52] Pamela Graves' *Labour Women, 1918–1939*,[53] June Hannam and Karen Hunt's *Socialist Women* and Nan Sloane's *The Women in the Room*.[54] Conservative women have fared less well in the history of women's activism, both because historians of the Conservative Party tended to focus on famous male figures and because early feminist historians who were mostly on the left were reluctant to research the political opposition.

There is a stereotype of a typical Conservative woman who is the preserver of law and order, part of a 'blue rinse brigade' of 'hangers and floggers' and one of 'hell's grannies'.[55] Indeed, Conservative women have been characterised as 'a pack of savage matrons in mink baying for blood and flogging and capital punishment'.[56] Moreover, 'Conservative women are either presented in an ancillary role of discreet sandwich making and envelope-filling activities or as honorary men and bullying men at that'.[57] These caricatures are manifestly shallow: many Tory women have played a significant role in furthering female equality. Indeed, Conservative women were involved in various women's campaigns such as votes for women, greater protection for prostitutes, women's nationality rights, women's rights during wartime and equal pay. A number of Conservative MPs—like Nancy Astor and Irene Ward—were committed feminists who would, at times, oppose their own party's policies if they considered them detrimental to women. More recently, there is a growing awareness of the Conservative women's contribution to politics. Beatrix Campbell's *Iron Ladies: Why do Women Vote Tory?*,[58] Joni Lovenduski and Pippa Norris' *Women in Politics*,[59] G. E. Maguire's *Conservative Women*[60] and Clarisse Berthezène and Julie Gottlieb's path-breaking *Re-Thinking Right-Wing Women, Gender and the Conservative Party, 1880s to the present*[61] offer fresh insights into this corner of the political arena. As Berthezène and Gottlieb point out, the Conservative Party dominated electoral politics in the twentieth century, was 'successful at organising women and engaging them at the grass roots',[62] thus making it imperative to examine Conservative women's history and 'to challenge the focus, agenda and paradigms of both orthodox political history and gender studies'.[63] *Women and Activism* will add to the story of Conservative women by focusing on their activism and arguing that it was not always 'conservative'.

Not all activists shared a liberal agenda. The twentieth century is littered with women who tried—and failed—to halt progress or who promoted a non-democratic non-parliamentary way of governing. Martin Durham's *Women and Fascism*[64] challenges the accepted belief that fascism was simply a misogynistic male movement by showing how women played a significant part in various Fascist groups in Europe and in Britain. Later, Julie Gottlieb's meticulously researched and theoretically groundbreaking *Feminine Fascism*[65] illustrates how British women such as Rotha Lintorn-Orman in the 1920s and those in Oswald Mosley's British Union of Fascists in the 1930s propagated 'an antidemocratic, male centrist and racist creed', yet at the same time affirmed female agency.[66] Fascism was defeated but its ideology permeated other groups and organisations, and women joined these too.

Women and Activism draws on this historiography, but for the most part it uses original research to provide a powerful impression of the actions taken by diverse groups of women who set out to make a difference to their locality, their country and sometimes the world. Chapters are arranged chronologically, but within each chapter, topics and themes are identified and examined separately. Taken together, the chapters show how women's activism comes to embody a stimulating story of progress and reversals, of commitment and uncertainty, of competing rights and of challenging wrongs. The story of women's activism is not tidy or well ordered. It is messy and unorthodox. And full of surprises.

NOTES

1. Olive Malvery, *The Soul Market*, Hutchinson, 1907, p. 180.
2. Ibid., p. 185.
3. See Vicky Randall, *Women in Politics*, Macmillan, 1987; Catherine Lee and Anne Logan, 'Women's agency, activism and organisation', *Women's History Review*, Vol 28 Issue 6, 2019.
4. See Christine Collette, *The Newer Eve, Women, Feminists and the Labour Party*, Palgrave Macmillan, 2009.
5. G. E. Maguire, *Conservative Women, A History of Women and the Conservative Party, 1874–1997*, Palgrave, 1998.
6. *Aberdeen Press and Journal*, 4 October 1929, p. 7.
7. Sheila Rowbotham, *Dreamers of a New Day*, Verso, 2011, p. 240.
8. Greta Thurnberg, *No One Is Too Small to Make a Difference*, Penguin, 2019.
9. There were notable women historians of women before the women's liberation movement took off: for example, in the 1920s and 1930s, Alice Clark's *Working Life of women in the seventeenth century*, Ray Strachey's *The Cause*, Sylvia Pankhurst's *The Suffragette Movement*, Ivy Pinchbeck's *Women Workers and the Industrial Revolution* and Barbara Drake's *Women in Trade Unions*; in the 1950s and 1960s, Olive Banks' *Feminism and Family Planning in Victorian England*, Pamela Brookes' *Women at Westminster* and Constance Rover's *Women's Suffrage and Party Politics in Britain, 1866–1914*.
10. Sally Alexander and Anna Davin, 'Feminist History', *History Workshop*, Spring 1976.
11. Pluto, 1975.
12. See womenshistorynetwork.org for information about the organisation and the prize.
13. University of Georgia Press, 1986.
14. OUP, 1987.
15. University of Massachusetts Press, 1990.
16. OUP, 1997.
17. Macmillan, 2000.
18. OUP, 1993.
19. Routledge, 2006.
20. Oxford Oral History Series, 2019.
21. Thorsons, 1989.
22. Wiley-Blackwell, 1982.
23. Prism Press, 1988.
24. Julia Sudbury, *Other Kinds of Dreams: Black Women's Organisation and the Politics of Transformation*, Routledge, 1998.
25. Verso books, 2018, first published 1985.
26. Beverly Bryan, Stalla Dadzie and Suzanne Scafe, *Heart of the Race, Black Women's Lives in Britain,* Virago 1985.
27. Pluto, 1986. Later, Rozina Visram's *Asians in Britain, 400 years of History* (Pluto, 2002) continued the story.
28. Virago, 1978.
29. Routledge, 1998.
30. Palgrave, 2016.

31. Karen Hunt and June Hannam, 'Towards an Archaeology of Interwar Women's Politics: The local and the Everyday' in Julie V Gottlieb and Richard Toye (editors), *The Aftermath of Suffrage*, Palgrave Macmillan, 2013, p. 124.
32. Karen Hunt and June Hannam, 'Towards an Archaeology of Interwar Women's Politics: The Local and the Everyday' in Julie V Gottlieb and Richard Toye (editors), *The Aftermath of Suffrage*, Palgrave Macmillan, 2013.
33. Ibid.
34. Junction Books, 1981.
35. Routledge, 2012.
36. Palgrave Macmillan, 1998.
37. Routledge, 2019.
38. Tauris, 2014.
39. Virago, 1983.
40. Radius, 1989.
41. Virago, 1989.
42. Palgrave, 2001.
43. MUP, 2019.
44. Vintage, 2019.
45. Macmillan, 2010.
46. Peter Davies, 1967.
47. Rowman and Littlefield, 1974.
48. Athlone Press, 1979
49. Sidgwick and Jackson, 1980.
50. I. B. Tauris, 2019.
51. Palgrave Macmillan, 2019.
52. Palgrave Macmillan, 2009.
53. CUP, 1994.
54. I. B. Tauris, 2018.
55. Julie Gottlieb and Beatrix Campbell, 'The Iron Ladies revisited', *Women's History Review*, Volume 28, Issue 2, 2019.
56. *Daily Telegraph*, quoted in Sam Blaxland, 'Women in the organisation of the Conservative Party in Wales, 1945–1979, *Women's History Review*, Volume 28, No 2, 2019, pp. 236–256.
57. Clarisse Berthezéne and Julie Gottlieb, 'Considering conservative women in the gendering of modern British politics', *Women's History Review*, Volume 28, Issue 2, 2019.
58. Virago, 1987.
59. OUP, 1996.
60. Palgrave, 1998.
61. MUP, 2017.
62. Clarisse Berthezène and Julie Gottlieb, *Re-Thinking Right-Wing Women, Gender and the Conservative Party, 1880s to the present*, MUP, 2017, p. 1.
63. Ibid., p. 2.
64. Routledge, 2006.
65. Bloomsbury, 2000.
66. Julie V Gottlieb, *Feminine Fascism: Women in Britain's Fascist Movement, 1923–1945*, Bloomsbury, 2000.

CHAPTER 2

A New Age: 1900–1914

It was 1900. Queen Victoria was on the throne, the Conservatives were in office and the British were fighting the Boers in South Africa. Life across the United Kingdom was emphatically hierarchical: the rich man was in his castle, the poor man was at his gate, women remained at home and white men ruled most of the world. Into this seemingly calm and ordered life burst a political whirlwind, a whirlwind created by women who protested at being subjugated and treated so unequally. Not all women shared the same political perspective, neither did they always agree on tactics, policies or programmes of action but they all shared a similar purpose: to make a difference to people's lives.

Life was tough for most women. Lady Mary Hamilton, daughter of the Duke of Hamilton, would soon be the richest woman in the United Kingdom with an income of over £100,000 a year,[1] but at the lower end, working-class women were expected to live on less than 12s (60p) a week, a mere £33 a year. At the start of the century only 29% of women were in paid employment and only 10% of these were married. According to the 1901 census, the most numerous women workers were servants, factory workers and laundresses, jobs which were characterised by low pay and low self-esteem. At the bottom of the heap were women who worked at home often in squalid, dilapidated and crowded houses and who suffered unduly low rates of pay and excessive hours of work—they were called 'sweated workers'. One member of the House of Lords stated that there was 'no depth of human misery so profound as that of the lot of the victims of sweated industries. It is a life of ceaseless, grinding, monotonous toil, commencing from the tenderest childhood and lasting to the grave, and that in squalid dens and evil surroundings, with never the slightest taste of the joy of life'.[2] A woman homeworker who carded hooks and eyes was lucky to earn 10s (50p) a week for an 18-hour day: the average wage for working-class men was £1.70.

© The Author(s), under exclusive license to Springer Nature Switzerland AG 2022
P. Bartley, *Women's Activism in Twentieth-Century Britain*, Gender and History, https://doi.org/10.1007/978-3-030-92721-9_2

Fighting for Workers' Rights

A number of women, often encouraged by sympathetic men, were outraged at the way members of their sex were treated (Fig. 2.1). They decided to investigate and report on these injustices in order to raise public awareness and then to lead campaigns to improve the lives of women who struggled to make a living. In 1904, Olive Malvery, the Anglo-Indian campaigning journalist, wrote about the lives of the most vulnerable women in the London job market, the flower-makers, the dressmakers, the matchbox-makers and others. The most wretched, ill-paid and unhealthy trade of all was fur pulling. These women lived in dismal houses with the windows closed tight because 'the slightest draught makes their work almost impossible. It drives the fine hair and fluff into their eyes, nostrils and lungs'.[3] In her book *The Soul Market*, Malvery spoke of fur-pullers' houses reeking 'with the sickly smell of decaying skins which was so nauseating that when I got into the room where the pulling was done I could not breathe … the overpowering stench arising from the skins, that were heaped everywhere, made me almost sick. Skins were piled onto the table on which also stood some crockery… in the corner was a miserable

Fig. 2.1 Olive Christian Malvery, 1904 (Courtesy of Rebecca Odell and the British Library)

bed—on which was also piled a heap of skins—and in the midst of all this filthy horror a little baby lay fast asleep'.[4] Women in this trade earned an average weekly rate of 50p.[5]

Meanwhile, the Scottish trade unionist Mary Macarthur, who was also aware of the predicament of the homeworker and of the importance of publicity, persuaded Henry Brailsford, editor of the *Daily News*, a radical paper founded by Charles Dickens and now owned by George Cadbury, to expose the plight of sweated workers.[6] On 2 May 1906, Henry Brailsford, Mary Macarthur, Margaret MacDonald[7] together with the Fabian Society and other organisations set up a Sweated Industries Exhibition at the Queen's Hall in London to win sympathy for the working conditions experienced by these women. It was opened by Princess Beatrice, the youngest daughter of the late Queen Victoria and her daughter Princess Ena.[8] Between 40 and 50 homeworkers from across Britain were brought in to show the monotonous and ill-paid drudgery of their lives. Baby bonnet- and bootmakers, bristle pickers, nail-makers, cardboard box-makers, button carders, cigarette case-makers, chain-makers, doll-makers, paper flower-makers, matchbox makers, sack menders, vamp beaders (those who sewed beads on shoes), pom-pom-makers and fur-pullers gave demonstrations of their work, and visitors listened to lectures from leading activists like the former shopworker and trade unionist Margaret Bondfield[9] and middle-class radical Gertrude Tuckwell about the evils of sweated labour.[10] It was reported that two fashionably dressed aristocratic ladies broke down and left the exhibition in tears at the conditions experienced by the women,[11] while for others it became 'a fashionable social function' where rich women spent their time between lunch and afternoon tea enjoying a bit of poverty porn.[12] Nearly 30,000 people visited during its six-week run. Similar exhibitions were held all over England, Wales and Scotland, all of which generated sympathy for the most exploited of women workers.[13]

The publicity generated by Malvery, Macarthur and the Sweated Exhibitions led to such widespread condemnation that an atmosphere for change was generated. There was a three-pronged attack on the use of sweated labour: one from the trade unions, one from campaigning organisations and one from the government. In the same year as the Exhibition, Mary Macarthur, concerned that the low wages of working-class women were linked to women's lack of organisation, set up the National Federation of Women Workers (NFWW) to campaign for better pay and improved working conditions.[14] About 80,000 women joined the hundreds of branches being formed across the United Kingdom. The NFWW attracted 'garment makers, cardboard box and paper bag makers, tea, jam and sweet packers, ammunition workers, net makers, laundry workers and cleaners, textile workers and chain makers', all industries which were characterised by low pay, poor conditions and all-too-often intermittent work.[15]

In 1906, Mary Macarthur also helped found the National Anti-Sweating League, an all-party pressure group which campaigned to change the law. Paying workers decent wages was considered more essential, more helpful and to the point than paying entry fees to awareness-raising exhibitions. Fortunately, Macarthur set up the NFWW, the Sweated Exhibition and the Anti-Sweating League at a propitious time. The Liberal Party had just won a landslide victory and was set on social reform. In 1907, it appointed a Select Committee on Homework to which many of the leading women activists—Margaret Bondfield, Mary Macarthur and Gertrude Tuckwell—gave evidence.[16] The result of the Select Committee's recommendations was the passing of the first Trade Boards Act (1909) which targeted four, largely female, trades: ready-made tailoring; cardboard box-making; chain-making and lace-making. Trade Boards fixed rates of hourly rates of pay: 3¼d (0.01p) per hour in tailoring 2½d in chain-making, 3d in box-making and 2¾d in lace-making. In 1913, four other largely female trades, shirt making, confectionery, hollowware and tin box-making, were brought under the acts; by 1921, the acts covered 35 trades.[17] As a result of these activists and a sympathetic government, certain groups of working-class women were guaranteed a minimum wage. Homeworkers like the fur-pullers were not covered by the acts.

Nothing to Lose But Their Chains[18]

In the summer of 1910, the first Trades Boards Act was put to the test by a group of women chain-makers in Cradley Heath, West Midlands, the centre of the chain-making industry. Here women made chains in sheds at the back of their house, often with their young children put in the corner of the shed out of the way and their babies lying in 'wooden boxes under the anvils screaming as they were showered with sparks'.[19] For the women, it was hot, sweaty demanding work and grossly underpaid but it meant that women could stay at home and involve their older children in making the chains. These chain-making women looked forward to almost a doubling of their wages when the Trades Board set their hourly rate at 2½d—11s3d (56p) for a 54-hour week. It was not to be: many of the employers refused to pay this new rate and expected the women to cave in through hunger. Fortunately for the chain-makers the newly formed NFWW stepped in and a strike was called. Over 1000 women stopped work. Julia Varley, the local NFWW organiser and former suffragette, adopted the methods of the suffrage movement and produced eye-catching leaflets to publicise the plight of the chain-maker. On 24 August, a 'tumultuous demonstration of defiance' took place in Cradley Health when women chain-makers marched through the streets at night, headed by a band lit by paraffin flares.[20] The ten-week strike was won by the women, largely because of the efforts of Mary Macarthur and Julia Varley in gaining widespread publicity both nationally and internationally and raising £4000 in donations towards the strike. All sections of the community gave money: some like those of 6d came from a 'poor working woman' whereas others came from affluent women like the Countess Beauchamp who donated £100. Mary Macarthur commented that she 'was glad the women had risen at last, and had cast their chains from them in more senses than one.'[21] The average wage of the chain-maker increased from 5s (25p) to 11s (55p) a week; £1500 was left over from the strike fund which was used to build a Worker's Institute on the site where the meetings had taken place.[22] The Institute building is now in the Black Country Museum, Dudley.[23]

The NFWW organised a number of other strikes to gain a minimum wage for other sweated workers. During the summer months of 1911, a variety of women workers—jam and pickle makers, sweet factory workers, ragpickers, bottle washers and tin box-makers—went on strike. It was a very hot summer with temperatures in London reaching 98°F/36.5°C: about 2000 babies and toddlers died in August through drinking bad unrefrigerated milk. Adults sweated in their crowded unsanitary houses and went without sleep to work in the factories where the temperature was even more unbearable.[24] On one of the hottest days, women who worked in a sweet factory in Bermondsey went on strike: they were followed by women in other workshops and factories. Mary Macarthur and her NFWW colleagues went down to the area, set up their headquarters and began to organise the strikers. By September, they had negotiated rate increases for the women who worked in 18 out of the 21 trades. [25]

The NFWW emerged at a time of great industrial, social and political unrest: troubles in Ireland, an intransigent House of Lords, the suffrage movement and increased strike action all caused problems for the Liberal Government elected in 1906. It has been suggested that much of the industrial conflict that characterised this period was created by women. One of the biggest disturbances occurred at the American-owned Singer sewing machine factory in Glasgow which employed half of the city's female workforce. It was precipitated by the action of 12 women cabinet polishers who had walked out of the factory in protest at a proposed increase in working hours and a reduction in wages. They were followed by 2000 other women and later by the men. Eventually, over 10,000 workers of both sexes went on strike. In response, Singer closed the factory, threatened to move it elsewhere and warned striking workers that they would be blacklisted. Three weeks later, the strike collapsed, and in an unparalleled example of victimisation Singer sacked 400 workers, including those who were thought to be too intransigent and all the known strike leaders. One of them, Jane Rae, went on to become a suffragette, local councillor and a JP, where she imposed the toughest penalties on men guilty of domestic abuse.

On the Shop Floor[26]

Another key organisation for women, the Women's Industrial Council,[27] helped by collecting information about the poor wages and conditions of women workers. At one time, it employed Margaret Bondfield to work as an undercover agent under the pseudonym Grace Dare to gather information about shop workers. This was another job characterised by low pay, long hours and poor conditions, and in Bondfield's report, gathered over two years, she told of how shop assistants were locked into a circle of poverty and deprivation. They suffered petty tyrannical regimes: fined for giving the wrong change, breaking goods, chatting with colleagues, sitting down, coming late to work, making a noise, being cheeky to a superior, using bad language, bringing matches or newspapers to the premises, letting a customer leave without a purchase and even addressing a customer as Miss instead of Mrs. One firm had 176 rules, including one which covered 'any mistake not before mentioned'.[28]

Shop assistants who worked in large department stores were expected to 'live-in' with the cost of accommodation and food deducted from their meagre wage. The living-in system not only robbed the assistant of independence but was humiliating and degrading as assistants had to obey petty house rules even after the shop was closed: to go to bed at a time dictated by the employer, to extinguish candlelights at 11 pm, not to stay out overnight without permission and so on. In many cases, 20 or more women assistants slept two in a bed 'in a single room of the barest and most barrack-like kind'.[29] Food was generally monotonous and unappetising, and 'the nourishment is not sufficient for a growing youth or girl doing a long day's work'.[30] All too often, 'a girl found on going down to breakfast in the morning that the menu was "doorsteps and scrape". ... Sometimes the food was inedible so "high" that we cannot touch it'.[31] Not surprisingly, shop assistants spent their meagre wage on food to supplement their diet.[32]

Margaret Bondfield's exposure of shop working conditions and the pressure of women's groups provided the radical Liberal MP Charles Dilke with the information and impetus he needed to help change the law: the various Shop Acts 1904, 1906 and 1911 gave a half-day's holiday to shop workers, a maximum working week of 60 hours and abolition of both the living-in system and the humiliating practice of fines and deductions.

Fighting for Families

In 1908, the Fabian Women's Group was founded to lobby Labour MPs.[33] The group only numbered around 200, yet its contribution to British politics was greater than its numbers suggest. Women were not entitled to the parliamentary vote, nor were they able to be MPs but they were able to vote in local elections and for various government-run bodies. The Fabian Group campaigned for women to get elected onto Poor Law and School Boards and to serve as local councillors: Emmeline Pankhurst was among the first women to be elected Poor Law Guardian. The Fabians also publicised the extent of female poverty and campaigned to help end it. One of its first initiatives was to commission an inquiry into the lives of working-class women. In 1913, it published its first piece of research, Fabian member Maud Pember Reeves' *Round About a Pound a Week*, which recorded the daily budgets and daily lives of working families in Lambeth, London, and showed how unfair life in Britain was for some of its people.

In 1912, the Women's Co-operative Guild (WCG) employed Margaret Bondfield to research maternity care. Her conclusions encouraged the general secretary of the WCG Margaret Llewelyn Davies to ask women to write in about their experiences. This led to the publication of *Maternity: Letters from Working Women*, a heart-rending volume of letters outlining the experiences of working women. 'The life stories', Bondfield recalled in later years, 'of 400 women were given in their own words ... Of these 400 women, 26 were childless, and 26 did not give definite figures; the remaining 348 had 1,396 live children, 83 still births and 218 miscarriages. In an extreme case we find a woman married at 19, having 11 children and 2 miscarriages in 20 years'.[34] The mortality rates were shocking and so too was the health of those who survived: 'miserable draggle-tailed anaemic children with defective teeth, defective eyesight'. Margaret Bondfield railed against the high level of infant mortality among the working class, which stood at 67.67 per thousand. 'Did it occur', she cried, 'to the mother weeping over her babe that it might have been a singer, a poet or a great statesman? Dead, because of conditions which were alterable; dead, because of insanitary dwellings and other causes. Had it ever occurred to them it was communal murder, it was the slaughter of the innocents'.[35] In Bondfield's view, the issues of pregnancy, birth and after-care were some of the most serious problems that Britain faced. In 1911, the Liberal government was persuaded by these arguments and passed a Health Insurance Act, which provided the wives of insured men and insured unmarried mothers with a maternity benefit of 30s and a benefit of 7s6d a week while the mother was off work. It was the first public recognition of a 'national responsibility for motherhood'.[36]

SUFFRAGE CAMPAIGNS

At the time, only men were allowed to vote—a male-only Parliament made the laws which women had to obey. A number of women activists wanted the right to participate in the political process with an aim to improve the working conditions and the health of the downtrodden females depicted above. Women's suffrage organisations were formed in the nineteenth century, and by the beginning of the twentieth century, the movement appeared to be united and strong. The National Union of Women's Suffrage Societies (NUWSS) founded in 1897 was growing under its president, Millicent Fawcett: by 1914, the NUWSS had 52,000 members across Britain and published its own paper *The Common Cause*. Other groups were formed, representing other groups of women and different ways of organising. In 1903, the Lancashire and Cheshire Women Textile and Other Workers' Representation Committee (LCWT) was founded by the university-educated Esther Roper and the aristocratic Eva Gore-Booth specifically for working-class women. The two encouraged working-class women to participate at a senior level: several textile workers and trade unionists took leading roles in the society.[37]

In 1903, frustrated at the slow pace of the existing women's suffrage movement, Emmeline Pankhurst and her daughters Sylvia, Christabel and Adela founded the Women's Social and Political Union (WSPU) at their home in Manchester. Soon the organisation adopted a confrontational style of politics and became notorious for its militant and violent actions. Many of their stunts were extraordinarily inventive: in 1909, two suffragettes posted themselves to the prime minister by visiting the East Strand Post Office and asking the staff to stamp and address them to 10 Downing Street. In 1911, suffragettes boycotted the ten-yearly census by skating all night, eating at a vegetarian restaurant, staying in groups at various houses and hiding in a cupboard in the House of Commons. Many, like Queen Victoria's god-daughter Duleep Singh, refused to pay their taxes. Suffragettes later turned to violence. In the early months of 1913, women placed gunpowder containers laced with nails in the Cabinet Minister Lloyd George's house at Walton Heath, Surrey. They also set fire to several other country houses, damaged a church in Hampstead Garden Suburb, burned down grandstands at two Scottish racecourses, wrecked railway stations and tried to blow up Dudley Castle and St Pauls' Cathedral. They destroyed Ballikinian Castle in Stirlingshire. Telephone and telegraph wires were cut, and letters in post-boxes were ruined by acid or ink being placed in them. Hundreds of orchids in Kew Gardens were destroyed, several golf courses were trashed, windows were broken and paintings held in galleries were vandalised. Windsor Castle was closed to the public.[38] By 1914, the WSPU was notorious for its militant actions: in the seven months prior to the war, there were 107 arson attacks by suffragettes.

These illegal activities led to trial and imprisonment: between 1906 and 1914, over 1000 suffragettes were put in gaol. Many of them went on hunger strike in prison: the first was Scottish suffragette Marion Wallace Dunlop, who had been found guilty of printing a suffragette slogan on the walls of Parliament. Her hunger strike inspired others to do the same. However, the government, concerned that suffragettes might die, began to force-feed them. In one of her imprisonments, Kitty Marion was force-fed through the nose three times a day for five weeks and five days, no fewer than 232 times. She wrote, 'I clenched my teeth … and suddenly I felt something penetrate my right nostril which seemed to cause my head to burst and my eyes to bulge. Choking and wretching as the tube was forced down to the stomach and the liquid was poured in, most of which was vomited back when the tube was withdrawn.'[39] During her time in prison, she lost 2stone 8lb.

The result of hunger striking and forcible feeding took a toll on health. The first Scottish suffragette to be force-fed, Ethel Moorhead, was only released from prison when she became seriously ill with double pneumonia brought upon by being force-fed 25 times. Many women had their health irreparably damaged, and died at a younger age than would normally have been expected. This treatment was authorised by the Liberal government, which prided itself on its commitment to human rights—a few years earlier, these same male MPs had protested vociferously against the treatment of prisoners in the Boer Wars.

In 1913, the Liberal government, fearful of bad publicity if a suffragette was to die in prison, passed the Prisoners (Temporary Discharge for Ill Health) Act, which released hunger strikers from prison 'on licence' if their health was in danger. Once a suffragette had regained her health, she was rearrested and imprisoned again. It was quickly dubbed the Cat and Mouse Act because of a cat's habit of playing with its prey, allowing it to escape then clawing it back again. Emmeline Pankhurst was the first person to 'benefit' from this new law: in 1913 alone, she was arrested, released and rearrested at least six times, each time getting weaker and weaker.

Suffragettes put themselves in danger in other ways. Many were brutally attacked and sexually assaulted on demonstrations and other public events. The most infamous and well-reported assault took place on Black Friday, 18 November 1910, when approximately 300 suffragettes marched to the House of Commons to protest against the failure of a suffrage Bill. The police, instructed not to arrest the suffragettes, forced the women back, kicked them, twisted their breasts, punched them and thrust knees between their legs. Other incidents are less well known but appallingly common. For example, when a small group of suffragettes heckled Lloyd George in a small village in Wales, they were subjected to the most dreadful brutality. The first woman to interrupt was dragged away by the crowd and beaten with sticks 'on the head, in the face and on other parts of her body'.[40] When four other women tried to intervene, they received even worse treatment. 'One woman was stripped to the waist, and one man pulled a bunch of her hair out and boastfully waved it to the view of those around him. A second of these four women was heavily thrown to the ground', and then lifted and thrown into a ditch where the crowd threw missiles at her. The remaining two were knocked about until they became unconscious and had their skirts ripped, cut up and distributed among the crowd as souvenirs.[41] Such women were willing to give up their lives, not just their modesty, for the vote.

Nonetheless, it is important to remember that the suffrage movement was wider than the NUWSS and the WSPU, which have dominated the historiography of the suffrage movement. There were many other societies besides these two which campaigned for women's suffrage. Professional women founded their own suffrage societies: the Artists' Suffrage Franchise League,[42] the Actresses' Franchise League,[43] the Women Writers Suffrage League[44] and the London Graduates' Union for Women's Suffrage[45] were among them. Similarly different religious denominations set up suffrage groups: the Catholic Women's Suffrage Society,[46] the Church League for Women's Suffrage,[47] the Friends' League for Women's Suffrage[48] and the Jewish League for Woman Suffrage[49] represented women from particular religious backgrounds. Women even set up suffrage organisations which reflected their political affiliations, such as the Conservative and Unionist Women's Franchise Association.[50] And there were breakaway groups from the WSPU like the Women's Freedom League (WFL) and the East London Federation of Suffragettes (EFLS). From this list, it seems as if most women were able to join a suffrage group which represented their profession, religion or political affiliation. The membership of these groups may have overlapped with the two national bodies with some members joining the WSPU and some joining the NUWSS. By 1914, there were approximately 56 different societies with a combined membership of 300,000.

Not every country in the United Kingdom wanted to be led by either of the main suffrage organisations. The NUWSS and the WSPU had active branches all over England, Scotland and Wales but Irish groups chose to be independent. Indeed, there were several Irish organisations: one of the most influential was the Irish Women's Franchise League formed because Irish women had no desire to be led by Englishwomen.

Opposition to Votes for Women

Some women disagreed with votes for women and campaigned against it. In 1908, Mary August Ward, a best-selling novelist of the period became founding president of the Women's National Anti-Suffrage League (ASL). She was joined on the Committee by the well-known explorer Gertrude Bell and feminist social reformer Violent Markham. In 1910, the Scottish branches reorganised to form the Scottish National Anti-Suffrage League under the leadership of Violet Graham, the Duchess of Montrose. By July that year, there were 104 branches of the Anti-Suffrage League with approximately 16,000 members across the United Kingdom. The ASL gathered over 400,000 signatures on an anti-suffrage petition and published its own paper, the *Anti-Suffrage Review*. Members of ASL believed that women were not biologically capable of appreciating the complexities of war, diplomacy, finance, commerce and high politics. Opposition to the vote was also mixed up with eugenic concerns about the future of the race, and a belief that women's place was in the home as guardians of racial purity. Women's primary duty, it was believed, was to produce healthy babies to contribute to the national stock.[51] Suffragists were accused of contributing to this decline, argues Martine Faraut, by rocking the foundations of the family, lowering the birth rate and accelerating the degeneracy of the British race.[52] In 1912, at a mass rally in the Albert Hall, Violent Markham argued that women's citizenship was as great as men's but 'unlike our Suffragist friends, we do not fly in the face of hard facts and natural law' because the roles of men and women were biologically different.[53]

Not all feminists favoured *women's* suffrage. Margaret Bondfield, Margaret MacDonald and a number of other socialist women preferred to campaign for full adult suffrage rather than what was a limited vote for women. Only men who owned property or paid local tax—58% of the adult male population—had the vote; thus, the suffrage campaign for votes for women on the same terms as men would exclude most working-class women. Not surprisingly, these feminists were opposed to 'the idea of a limited franchise on a property basis, because it seemed … that it was tipping the scales against the workers by strengthening the political power of the propertied classes'.[54] Moreover, they feared that a limited franchise would be detrimental to the campaigns for socialism since it would consolidate the class composition of the electorate.

In December 1907, Bondfield engaged in a public debate with Teresa Billington-Greig, a leading suffragette and founder of the Women's Freedom League. Bondfield put forward the case for universal adult suffrage; Billington-Greig spoke in favour of a limited female suffrage. Bondfield's talk was class focused: she believed in sex equality but she wanted sex equality for her class. She wished those women campaigning for votes for women 'good luck ... and may they get it! But don't let them come and tell me that they are working for my class'.[55] She reminded her audience that women like the suffragist leader Millicent Fawcett and Lady Frances Balfour supported a limited suffrage because it was an effective barrier to the 'dangerous demand for Adult Suffrage'.[56] Bondfield claimed that democracy would 'stand with folded hands while the privileged classes dig deeper trenches round their fortifications ... The question of the vote is a political question, and the real antagonisms are not those of sex but of class'.[57] Bondfield feared that a limited Bill admitting some women would confirm the existing property basis for the franchise. She was only too aware that neither men nor women shop assistants, the people she represented, had the vote because the living-in system meant they did not qualify as a ratepayer or householder. Shop workers, she told her audience, were known to be 'a vote-less class, the men as well the women—political non-entities'.[58] And if women gained the vote on the same terms as men, both male and female shop workers would remain disenfranchised. Bondfield wanted to 'sweep away the existing franchise and substitute one man one vote, one woman one vote, on a short residential qualification'.[59] Many agreed with Bondfield. There were a number of adult suffrage societies: the Adult Suffrage Society; the National Council for Adult Suffrage; and the People's Suffrage Federation which had as its motto, 'One Man One Vote; One Woman One Vote'.

The majority of women were probably more apathetic than antagonistic towards votes for women. Membership of the suffrage movement may have been large but the majority of women did not belong to any suffrage group. Nor did they belong to an anti-suffrage organisation. Nonetheless, despite schisms and irreconcilable differences, the women's suffrage movement became a powerful political force within Victorian and Edwardian Britain. By 1914, largely because of its intensive campaigning, it had forced women's suffrage on to the agenda of all the political parties and had made votes for women one of the foremost issues facing the governing Liberal Party.

PROTECTIVE LEGISLATION

Women activists also disagreed over sex-based protective legislation, that is, laws which aimed to safeguard women workers from long hours and poor working conditions. On the one hand, social reformers like Margaret MacDonald and trade unionists like Margaret Bondfield wanted Parliament to shield women from gross exploitation by making it illegal for them to take up certain jobs. On the other hand, suffragists and suffragettes like Eva Gore-Booth and Annie Kenney wanted women to choose their own fate, not be dictated to by a male government. The Liberal government, more influenced by trade unionists than suffragists, heeded the advice of Bondfield and others and sought to protect the lives of barmaids and pitbrow workers by banning them from working.

Last Orders

At the beginning of the twentieth century, there were 100,000 pubs in England and Wales alone. The bar area across the United Kingdom was usually men-only. It was fairly basic with wooden floors often covered with sawdust to absorb the spitting and beer-spilling, bare benches and stools and a minimum of home comforts. There was allegedly a lot of drunkenness and bad behaviour. Young unmarried women seldom entered in case they were thought to be prostitutes coming in to pick up customers. Indeed, in many pubs women were barred because of this association—some pubs kept this ban in place until the 1980s. Drink became a moral and political issue: Margaret MacDonald claimed that barmaids were associated with 'vulgarity, assault, murder and suicide' and were used as 'decoys to increase the sale of drink ... they had to be enticing'.[60] The British Women's Temperance Association (BWTA), encouraged by a government report on the lives of barmaids and the fact that Glasgow refused to renew the pub licences of those who employed barmaids, campaigned to ban women from working in pubs.[61] They held meetings, wrote leaflets, pressurised magistrates to refuse licences to pubs which employed women and organised petitions. In 1907, the Liberal government, persuaded by these arguments, proposed to ban women from working as barmaids.

Other women disagreed. Those mostly concerned—the 100,000 or so barmaids—did not 'intend to submit to their removal in a passive spirit'.[62] A women-only meeting was convened at Holborn Town Hall, packed full with 'every class of female worker behind the bar, from the landlady to the youngest of barmaids'.[63] Although men were excluded, a number of them barged in with the intention of making fun, whistling songs such as 'Beer, beer, glorious beer' and trying to intimidate the women. The women were not cowed and forged ahead with their campaign. On 29 November 1907, the suffragists Eva Gore Booth,[64] Esther Roper,[65] Sarah Dickinson and nine barmaids went to London to meet the Liberal Home Secretary Herbert Gladstone to persuade him that the proposed legislation would bring 'great distress, want and poverty' to the women concerned. Gladstone assured them that the government would give 'fair consideration' to their request.[66] In February 1908, the Liberal government put forward a Licensing Bill to regulate pub licenses in Britain by controlling opening hours, restricting the number of licenses and effectively banning the employment of women. One of its clauses proposed that licensing justices could refuse licenses to public houses employing women. The all-male

Parliament believed that the lure of an attractive barmaid encouraged men to linger too long over their pints.

In March, Eva Gore Booth and Esther Roper set up the Barmaids Political Defence League to defend the right of 100,000 women to work in public houses.[67] It issued a manifesto protesting against the Bill and sent it to every MP asking them to oppose the offending clause.[68] Over the coming months, the issue of the barmaids came to dominate Manchester's political life, largely because of the Defence League and an unexpected parliamentary election. In April 1908, Prime Minister Henry Campbell-Bannerman resigned and was replaced by Henry Asquith, who in turn promoted Winston Churchill (then a Liberal MP) to president of the Board of Trade. At the time, newly appointed Cabinet Ministers were expected to resign their seats and stand for re-election. Churchill was expected to win: he had beaten the Conservative candidate William Joynson-Hicks by a huge majority in the last election. The two protagonists differed over the treatment of barmaids. Churchill was in favour of prohibiting women from working in bars, thinking them seedy, sleazy places; Joynson-Hicks was in favour of allowing women to continue to work as barmaids.

The leaders of the Barmaids Defence League conducted an ostentatious and outrageously extravagant campaign to oust Churchill. Constance Gore-Booth, the future Irish Nationalist who was set to be the first-ever woman to be elected to Parliament, drove her sister Eva and Esther Roper in a vintage carriage pulled by four white horses throughout the city of Manchester. It was a dramatic spectacle: three young and attractive women driving a fine-looking carriage, parking it in Stevenson Square, delivering speeches, distributing leaflets and telling their audience not to vote for Churchill. Every house in the constituency was sent a flyer asking voters to support the barmaids. To everyone's surprise, Churchill lost the election.

The League kept up the pressure. On 14 May, the League held a well-attended meeting at Holborn Town Hall, London, and persuaded a number of influential MPs—Wilfred Ashley, Lord Cecil—to speak on the right of barmaids to work. In their view, it was an 'arbitrary and tyrannical' attempt to close a trade which employed such large numbers of women.[69] On 13 June 1908, the League organised an outdoor meeting in Trafalgar Square which attracted over 2000 listeners. Constance Gore-Booth delivered a passionate speech at the bottom of Nelson's column, declaring 'we are told the bar is a bad place for women, but the Thames Embankment at night is far worse'.[70]

On 2 November 1908, the Licensing Bill was debated by 355 men in the House of Commons. As a result of pressure from women activists, the Liberal government withdrew the clauses banning women from public houses. Not everyone agreed. Some thought it essential that women 'be protected from the snares, temptations and dangers of the public house' because it was 'impossible to have healthy and vigorous motherhood as long as there were barmaids'.[71] The Labour Party leader, Ramsay Macdonald argued that pub work and prostitution were inextricably linked because no one 'could touch pitch without being defiled'. Barmaids were employed because 'their employment increased the consumption of drink, because where women were employed there was a great deal of dalliance at the bar. ... The atmosphere was abominable, and the conversation that went on was disgusting and disgraceful. .... Women were taken on simply as decoys to bring men into the bar, simply to increase the sale of drink'.[72] He was 'exceedingly sorry' that the government had yielded to pressure.[73] F. E. Smith believed that it was 'profoundly ill-judged to come forward in the alleged cause of morality in a House in which the female vote was not represented .... Women were denied a voice in the decision'.[74] Women were unrepresented in the House but the campaign led by Booth and Roper was an unqualified success.

Pitbrow Women

A few years later, another set of women—the pitbrow workers—had their livelihoods threatened. On 2 August 1911, a House of Commons Select Committee debating the Coal Mines Bill suggested that 'no girl or woman ... shall be permitted to be employed' to sort coal on the pitbrow. Pitbrow women worked on the top of the mine, sorting coal on conveyor belts, loading wagons and hauling heavy tubs brought up from the coalface. They worked in dusty, damp and unhygienic conditions, pushing and pulling heavy tubs and lifting large lumps of coal, all of which was allegedly beyond their strength. There was a related anxiety because pitbrow women worked in the outdoors, unprotected from the frosty winter and hot sweltering summers. One miner stated that he had 'seen these women and young girls, married women and widowed women pulling and tugging wagons on the pit banks, twisting themselves almost to death in an atmosphere so thick with coal dust that they could scarcely breathe'.[75]

Once again, the amendment to curtail women's employment appeared to be a humane gesture on the part of enlightened men within the Select Committee: all of those who voted for women to be barred from working had impeccable political credentials and were motivated by the inhumane conditions on the pit brow.[76] They believed that the work was too arduous for women and wholly unfitted for the 'weaker sex'. However, this humanitarian gesture must be placed within the context of the gender assumptions of the period. Underpinning much of the argument about protective legislation was a belief that mining women were unfeminine and unsexed creatures who belonged to an antediluvian past. Pitbrow work was considered to be unsuitable for women because it robbed them of their femininity. Much was made of the atmosphere of the pit heads which were covered in muck and coal dust which made it hard, dirty and repulsive work. Some members of the Select Committee believed that pitbrow work was not a proper place for women as 'the proper place for a miner's daughter is at home ...to assist the mother in the home; to be educated and trained for their future life as a wife and mother'.[77] It was believed that pitbrow women became masculinised by their occupation. Moreover, miners feared that women unfairly competed for jobs which were the preserve of vulnerable ex-miners—pitbrow work was the refuge of men who were too old or injured to work underground.

Pitbrow women did not agree with the proposed reforms because it meant the loss of approximately 6000 female jobs and consequently women's economic independence.[78] All the major suffrage organisations: the Lancashire and Cheshire Women's Textile and Other Workers Representation Committee (LCWT); the Women's Social and Political Union (WSPU); the Women's Freedom League (WFL) and the National Union of Women's Suffrage Societies (NUWSS) joined to support working-class women in their struggle. Both the pitbrow women and the suffragettes disagreed with the left-wing male alliance and called for Parliament to reject the amendment to the Coal Mines Bill.

Esther Roper, one of the leaders of the LCWT, argued that it was an 'absolute insult that men should sit in that House voting themselves salaries of £400 a year in order that they might then have leisure to vote away the wages of thousands of women'.[79] Between August and December 1911, the LCWT held meetings which attracted audiences of over 1000, introduced the pitbrow women to key Liberal MPs and wrote articles in their support. The NUWSS and the WFL believed that it was a male conspiracy to stop women's right to work. One of their key figures, Maude Royden, complained that 'men alone have the power to decide ... what work women shall be allowed to do'.[80] The WSPU sent Annie Kenney, an inveterate campaigner, former cotton factory worker and charismatic speaker, to Wigan to help pitbrow women organise their opposition to the proposed legislation. Throughout the campaign, the WSPU's paper *Votes for Women* carried double-page feature articles about the plight of the pitbrow women and placed their campaigning expertise at the disposal of the workers by organising deputations and meetings.

Both the suffragists and the suffragettes had long experience of organising meetings, deputations and demonstrations, writing leaflets, newspapers and pamphlets, skills at a premium in any political campaign, and skills that were put to great effect in helping the pitbrow women. Together they challenged the masculine political establishment which they believed was conspiring to return women to life-at-home. They won: pitbrow women continued working for another 60 years.

Sexual Politics

For some suffrage activists, the vote was as much about sexual politics as it was about improving women's working conditions. Once again, there were differences. In 1911, Dora Marsden and Mary Gawthorpe founded *The Freewoman*, publishing articles which supported tolerance for homosexuality and advocated free love. So too did Jane Hume Clapperton, a Scottish WSPU and WFL member, who was in favour of birth control and the right of women to sexual pleasure.[81] Others like Millicent Fawcett and Christabel Pankhurst thought otherwise and wanted the vote to clean up public life and to ensure that men and women adhered to the same moral principles of celibacy before marriage and faithfulness within it. Emmeline Pankhurst confidently assumed that votes for women were necessary to eliminate the sexual double standard, whereby it was acceptable for men, but not women, to engage in premarital sex. When Emmeline Pankhurst had been a Poor Law Guardian, she was distressed by the number of single mothers who were in the workhouse because men refused to marry them or pay them maintenance. Throughout her life, she constantly made references to the abhorrent selfishness of male sexual activity. Her daughter, Christabel, went further and insisted that venereal disease would be eliminated once women had the vote (she claimed that 75% of men were infected with gonorrhoea and 25% with syphilis). In her pamphlet *The Great Scourge*, she argued that female inequality was the fundamental cause of venereal disease. Once women were better educated and gained quality jobs, she argued, they would not be dependent on men for money. They would then be able to say a firm 'No' to men who wanted sex with them outside marriage, thus reducing the risk of venereal disease. Christabel Pankhurst promoted a twofold political programme of chastity for men and votes for women. Indeed, she fervently believed that once women were enfranchised, laws could be passed to transform male sexual behaviour, arguing that 'apart from the deplorable moral effect of the fact that women are voteless, there is this to be noticed—that the law of the land, as made and administered by men, protects and encourages the immorality of men, and the sex exploitation of women'.[82] This extract from her pamphlet, which might read a little strangely to modern eyes, needs to be placed within historical context. People in Edwardian Britain were anxious about the increase of venereal disease and its far-reaching effects not only on the health of the individual but on that of the nation.

The vote was also seen as a device that could be used to curb unfair legislation against prostitutes and ultimately to end prostitution. Suffragists believed that women became prostitutes because they did not earn enough to support themselves. Armed with the vote, women could press for higher wages and better jobs thus eliminating the need to earn money from prostitution. Christabel Pankhurst went further and argued that prostitution was based on male vice, which could only be eradicated once women had the vote.

A number of women were concerned about international prostitution called the 'white slave trade'. In 1902, largely due to the efforts of British women in the National Vigilance Association, a conference of influential delegates from 16 countries ratified an International Convention for the Suppression of the White Slave Traffic. This agreed to the appointment of specially trained officials at railway stations and seaports to keep an eye out for vulnerable girls; to keep a surveillance over employment agencies which found work for women; and to question known prostitutes of foreign origin as to how they were recruited. Scotland Yard set up a White Slave Traffic Branch and employed Eilladh Macdougall to set up a home in Lambeth for victims of white slavery.[83] Groups like the Salvation Army, Church Army, Jewish Association for the Protection of Girls and Women, the Society for the Rescue of Young Women and Children, the National Union of Women Workers (NUWW) and the National Vigilance Association led deputations to the Home Office to express their concern about the white slave trade, demanding the law be changed.[84] In 1912, Olive Malvery published another best-selling book, *The White Slave Market*, which argued that there was a widespread enslavement of girls internationally and that British authorities should act to prevent it. Malvery wanted 'the excessive sentences passed on the women window-smashers make us hope that men who injure and wrong women will now be severely dealt with also. ... To break a window is not comparable to selling an innocent girl into slavery. ... From time to time in this country a few men are arrested, convicted and punished ... but the punishment inflicted is far too trivial'.[85] She demanded that MPs take up the issue, change the law to revoke the 'reasonable cause to believe' that a young girl was over 16, make it easier for police to arrest men on suspicion of being pimps who once convicted should be imprisoned, whipped with a dozen lashes and sentenced to hard labour. In December 1912, the government was persuaded by this motley combination of feminists and social purists to pass a new Criminal Law Amendment Act, known as the White Slave Act. It enacted Malvery's recommendations, revoked the 'reasonable cause to believe' clause, allowed police to arrest suspected pimps and procurers without a warrant, increased the fines for brothel owners and authorised prison authorities to whip the men who were sentenced.

The 'Irish question'

Other suffragists took a different journey. Constance Gore-Booth, married to a Polish count and now Countess Markievicz, had begun her political career calling for votes for women but refocused her efforts to campaign for Irish nationalism. She, along with many others, condemned Britain's rule over Ireland. Countess Markievicz joined Sinn Fein, Inghinidhe na hÉireann (Daughters of Ireland), and wrote regularly for the women's nationalist journal *Bean na hÉireann* (Women of Ireland).

Other women activists wanted Britain to remain united and for Ireland to remain within the United Kingdom. The Women's Unionist and Tariff Reform Association (WUTRA) supported the Ulster Unionists in their fight against Home Rule, collecting over £12,000 and the promise of hospitality for over 5000 refugees in the event of a civil war. In the early months of 1914, the WUTRA promoted their campaign 'Help the Ulster Women and Children' in towns and cities across Britain.

Undoubtedly the Irish question dominated politics in the early twentieth century.[86] In April 1912, Asquith presented his Home Rule Bill to Parliament. Unfortunately, he faced the stubborn resistance of the Ulster Unionists backed up by the Conservative Party, which used its majority in the House of Lords to reject the Bill. In 1914, the Home Rule Bill was eventually passed, only to be suspended because of the outbreak of war.

The WUTRA not only helped the Ulster Campaign but also played a significant role in framing the debate about consumption and citizenship, helped advance women's position in the Conservative Party and 'played a pivotal role' in developing a consensual form of politics, particularly what became known as 'Baldwinite Conservativism'.[87] It was formed after the Conservatives lost the 1906 election in a Liberal landslide victory and was led by Mary Maxse, the daughter of Joseph Chamberlain. The WUTRA's main interest was tariff reform, that is, abolish free trade, impose government taxes on imports and transform the British Empire into a single trading block. In contrast, the WUTRA regarded free trade with Europe as a threat to prosperity and believed that Germany and other countries would dump their manufactured goods in Britain, and undercut our home industries. With its local study circles and amateur dramatic societies, WUTRA focused on educating women about tariff reform arguing that it was a housewife's issue and that they should not 'draw aside their skirts, lest they become soiled and focus all their energies on their own domestic circles' but become engaged with the debate.[88] By stating that 'politics was a duty for the respectable woman in her role as housewife',[89] WUTRA's leader hoped to play an important role in 'advancing women's position' in the Conservative Party by trying to promote the party's record of progressivism and identifying with working class women's cultural lives.[90] Not surprisingly, WUTRA vehemently opposed socialism, claiming (falsely) that children would be taken from their mothers 'to be nourished in the cold bosom of the state' and threatening that it would undermine all British values.[91] The organisation was concentrated in southern England and the West Midlands, where there was a significant middle class, and never really took hold in the northern manufacturing towns, because imposing taxes on products like raw cotton would affect trade and lead to a decline in living standards.[92]

In April 1914, Marie Jane Howe wrote an article in *The Conservative and Unionist Women's Franchise Review*. In her piece, she argued that women were incapable of organisation because 'no two women can ever be friends—women are cats'.[93] Yet this chapter has shown the opposite to be true. Women collaborated, sometimes across the class and political divide, to fight against the inequality, injustice and exploitation from which so many of them suffered. Of course, women were not a homogenous group, and there were disagreements over politics, over policy and over practice but there was very little of the spiteful behaviour that Howe suggests. Women's political activism seemed robust. Moreover, the belief in Britain as the champion of domestic stability had been severely undermined by the women's movement. There were achievements too—some improvements in pay and working conditions; women had kept their right to work in certain trades; and the campaign for the vote was gathering strength. The twentieth century seemed to augur well for activists.

Notes

1. *Daily Gazette*, 1 January 1900, p. 4.
2. Lord Ampthill, HL Debates, 26 October 1908, vol 194, cc 1558–64.
3. Olive Christian Malvery, *The Soul Market*, Hutchinson, 1907, p. 187. See https://www.olivemalvery.com for a superb overview of her life by Rebecca Odell.

4. Olive Christian Malvery, *The Soul Market*, Hutchinson, 1907, p. 187.
5. Malvery was also concerned about the 'poor and homeless' women whose only crime was 'abject poverty. An article 'Nobody's Women' painted the awful plight faced by such women. She used the profits from her writing to establish housing for homeless women—Night Shelters—and invited 1000 working girls from the East End to her wedding.
6. Mary Macarthur (1880–1921) was born in Glasgow to owners of a drapery business. She moved to London and worked in the Women's Trade Union League; in 1906, she founded the National Union of Women Workers; in 1907, she founded the *Woman Worker*, a monthly journal. She was an honorary secretary of the People's Suffrage Federation, which campaigned for adult suffrage. In 1911, she married William Anderson. In 1918, Mary stood as Labour candidate for Stourbridge but was defeated. She died, aged 40, from cancer. See Cathy Hunt's biography, *Righting the Wrong, Mary Macarthur 1880–1921*, West Midlands History, 2019.
7. Activist, socialist, feminist, Fabian member and wife of the future Labour Prime Minister Ramsay MacDonald.
8. *Aberdeen Journal*, 3 May 1906, p. 6.
9. See Paula Bartley, *Labour Women in Power*, Palgrave Macmillan, 2019 for a biography of Bondfield.
10. Richard Mudie-Smith, *Sweated Industries, being a handbook of the 'Daily News' Exhibition, May 1906*, Bradbury, Agnew and co, 1906.
11. *Hull Daily Mail*, 11 June 1906, p. 4.
12. Cathy Hunt, *Righting the Wrong, Mary Macarthur 1880–1921, The Working Woman's Champion*, West Midlands History, 2019, p. 83.
13. See Shelley Pennington and Belinda Westover, *A Hidden Workforce, Homeworkers in England, 1850–1985*, Macmillan Education, 1989.
14. Cathy Hunt, *Righting the Wrong, Mary Macarthur 1880–1921, The Working Woman's Champion*, West Midlands History, 2019.
15. Ibid., p. 60.
16. Nan Sloane, *The Women in the Room, Labour's Forgotten History*, I. B. Tauris, 2018. ILEA exhibition on Home-workers, 1980 by Carol Adams, Paula Bartley and Cathy Loxton.
17. In 1945, Trade Boards were replaced by wages councils.
18. I am grateful to Jan Anslow, whose grandmother was a chain-maker in Cradley Heath, for help in this section. See Sheila Blackburn, 'Employers and Social Policy: Black Country Chain-Masters, The Minimum Wage Campaign and the Cradley Heath Strike of 1910, *Midland History*, 12:1, 1987 for an academic survey and Tony Barnsley, *Breaking Their Chains*, Bookmarks, 2011 for an account of Mary Macarthur's role in the campaign.
19. Nan Sloane, *The Women in the Room, Labour's Forgotten History*, I. B. Tauris, 2018, p. 166.
20. *The Daily News*, 25 August 1910, p. 5.
21. *The County Express*, 3 September 1910, p. 3.
22. Later in the century, it was due for demolition. However, a £1.1 million Heritage Lottery Fund allowed it to be taken down brick by brick and moved to the Black Country Museum, where it is now located.
23. See Tony Barnsley, *Breaking Their Chains*, Bookmarks, 2011.

24. Nan Sloane, *The Women in the Room, Labour's Forgotten History*, I. B. Tauris, 2018, p. 179.
25. Ibid., p. 180.
26. See Paula Bartley, *Labour Women in Power* for a fuller discussion of this.
27. The WIC was founded in 1894 by Clementina Black to research the conditions experienced by low-paid workers in order to help in legislative reforms.
28. Quoted in Pamela Cox and Annabel Hobley, *Shopgirls*, Arrow Books, 2014, p. 37.
29. *London Daily News*, 11 April 1901, p. 6.
30. Ibid.
31. Letter to Margaret Bondfield quoted in Margaret Bondfield, *Socialism for Shop Assistants*, the Clarion Press, 1909, p. 4.
32. *Preston Herald*, 18 August 1906, p. 13.
33. The Fabian Society was founded in 1884. It attracted a number of Beatrice Webb, Emmeline Pankhurst, Margaret Bondfield, Ellen Wilkinson, Annie Besant and other intellectuals. It became known as the intellectual wing of the Labour Party.
34. Margaret Bondfield, 'Women and the Factory System, Conditions—Past and Present', *Labour*, July 1934, p. 255
35. *Burnley Express*, 5 August 1908, p. 3.
36. Margaret Bondfield, *A Life's Work*, 1948, p. 129.
37. See Jill Liddington's path-breaking *One Hand Tied Behind Us: The Rise of the Women's Suffrage Movement*, Virago Press, 1978. More has been written on women's suffrage than any other women's campaign. The best book to start with is Diane Atkinson's *Rise Up Women! The Remarkable Lives of the Suffragettes*, Bloomsbury, 2018. Others include Paula Bartley's *Votes for Women 1860–1928*, Hodder and Stoughton's 1998 and *Emmeline Pankhurst*, Routledge, 2002; Julia Bush's *Women Against the Vote: Female Anti-Suffragism in Britain*, OUP, 2007; Krista Cowman's *Mrs Brown is a Man and a Brother*, Liverpool University Press, 2004; Elizabeth Crawford's *The Women's Suffrage Movement; a Reference Guide*, Routledge, 1999; Claire Eustance, Joan Ryan and Laura Ugolini's *Suffrage Reader: Charting Directions in Suffrage History*, Bloomsbury, 2000; Brian Harrison's *Separate Spheres: The Opposition to Women's Suffrage in Great Britain*, Croom Helm, 1978; Sandra Stanley Holton's *Feminism and Democracy: Women's Suffrage and Reform Politics, 1900–1918*, CUP, 1986; Maroula Joannou and June Purvis, *The Women's Suffrage Movement: New Feminist Perspectives*, MUP, 1998; Angela V. John and Claire Eustance's *The Men's Share: Masculinities, Male Support and Women's Suffrage, 1890–1920*, Routledge, 1997; Hilda Kean's *Deeds Not Words: The Lives of Suffragette Teacher*s, Pluto, 1990; Leah Leneman's *'A Guid Cause': The Women's Suffrage Movement in Scotland*, Aberdeen University Press, 1991; Rosemary Owens Cullen's *Smashing Times: A History of the Irish Women's Suffrage Movement, 1889–1970*, Gill and Macmillan,'s2005; Martin Pugh, *The March of the Women: A Revisionist Analysis of the Campaign for Women's Suffrage, 1866–1914*, OUP, 2000; June Purvis and Sandra Stanley Holton's *Votes for Women*, Routledge, 2000; June Purvis' *Emmeline Pankhurst*, Routledge, 2002; Constance Rover's *Women's Suffrage and Party Politics in Britain, 1866–1914*, Routledge and Kegan Paul, 1967; Sarah-Beth Watkins' *Ireland's Suffragettes: The Women Who Fought for the Vote*, the History Press, 2014.

38. 'A Year's Record,' *The Suffragette*, 26 December 1913, p. 258,
39. Kitty Marion, quoted in Diane Atkinson's *Rise Up, Women!*, Bloomsbury, 2018, p. 175.
40. *Daily Mirror*, 23 September 1913, p. 4.
41. Ibid.
42. Founded in 1907 by women artists to help with the first suffrage demonstration held that year. The Artists' Suffrage League designed banners, leaflets, cartoons, postcards and posters for the NUWSS but it remained a separate organisation. Many were members of the Women's Guild of Arts, established in 1907. See Zoe Thomas, *Women Art Workers and the Arts and Crafts Movement*, MUP, 2020, for an overview of this group.
43. Founded in 1903 at the Criterion restaurant in London. It was open to anyone involved in the theatre and worked for votes for women by staging plays. The League helped both the WSPU and the NUWSS and neither supported nor condemned militancy. Two of its leading member s belonged to the WSPU.
44. Founded in 1908 to obtain the vote for women on the same terms as men and to use methods 'proper to writers—the use of the pen'. It was set up by WSPU members.
45. Founded in 1909 and linked to the NUWSS. Membership was open to male and female graduates of the University of London. One of its vice presidents was Elizabeth Garrett Anderson, who was, until 1911, a members of the WSPU.
46. Founded in 1911 to bring together Catholic men and women to campaign for the vote. It was non-party and was committed to using peaceful methods.
47. Founded in 1909 to bring together members of the Church of England in order to campaign for the vote. It believed in the power of prayer to gain the vote, and on the first Sunday of every month special prayers were said in support of women's suffrage. It used peaceful protest but would not declare itself opposed to militancy.
48. Founded around 1911 by members of the Society of Friends who were known as Quakers.
49. Founded in 1912 to unite Jewish suffragists of all shades of opinion. It believed in peaceful methods but synagogue services were occasionally interrupted by its members.
50. Founded in 1908 to work for votes for women on the same terms as men. It opposed full universal suffrage. It refused to work for MPs opposed to votes for women
51. It later amalgamated with the Men's League for Opposing Women's Suffrage. See Martine Faraut, 'Women resisting the vote: a case of anti-feminism?', *Women's History Review*, September 2007.
52. Martine Faraut, 'Women resisting the vote: a case of anti-feminism?', *Women's History Review*, September 2007, p. 612.
53. Bush, Julia, 'British Women's Anti-Suffragism and the Forward Policy, 1908–1914', *Women's History Review*, Vol 11, Number 3, 2002.
54. Margaret Bondfield, *A Life's Work*, Hutchinson, 1948, p. 82.
55. Margaret Bondfield and Teresa Billington-Greig, Sex Equality versus Adult Suffrage, Verbatim Report of Debate, December 3rd 1907, p. 15.
56. Ibid.
57. Quoted in Agnes Mary Hamilton, *Margaret Bondfield*, Leonard Parsons, 1984, p. 84?

58. Margaret Bondfield and Teresa Billington-Greig, *Sex Equality versus Adult Suffrage*, Verbatim Report of Debate, 3 December 1907, p. 15.
59. Margaret Bondfield, *Shop Workers and the Vote*, People's Suffrage Federation, 1911, p. 9.
60. Margaret MacDonald quoted in Gifford, Lewis *Eva Gore Booth and Esther Roper*, Pandora Press, 1988.
61. This ruling was overturned by the secretary of state for Scotland. See *The Barmaid Question*, https://white-ribbon.org.uk for an overview of this campaign.
62. *The Globe*, 15 March 1907, p. 3.
63. Ibid.
64. Eva Gore Booth (1870–1926) was the daughter of an Irish baronet and his wife and sister to Constance Markiewitz, the first woman to be elected to the British Parliament. She was involved in campaigns on behalf of pitbrow women, flower sellers and barmaids. She co-founded the Lancashire and Cheshire Women Textile and Other Workers' Representation Committee, a suffragist organisation.
65. Esther Roper (1868–1938) was the daughter of a Church Missionary Society parents. In 1891, she was awarded a degree from Owens College, Manchester, one of the first women to achieve this. Between 1894 and 1905, Roper was secretary of the Manchester National Society for Women's Suffrage; in 1903, she co-founded the Lancashire and Cheshire Women Textile and Other Workers' Representation Committee with Eva Gore Booth. In 1913, she moved to London and became involved in the Women's Peace Crusade.
66. *Manchester Courier and Lancashire General Advertiser*, 29 November, 1907, p. 7.
67. David Beckingham, 'Banning the barmaid: times, space and alcohol licensing in 1900s Glasgow', *Social and Cultural Geography*, accessed on-line December 2019; Sonja Tiernan, 'Eva Gore-Booth champion of the barmaids', *Irish Independent News*, 1 July 2012.
68. *Evening Telegraph*, Dundee, 16 March 1908, p. 2.
69. *Manchester Courier and Lancashire General Advertiser*, 15 May 1908, p. 7.
70. Gifford Lewis, *Eva Gore Booth and Esther Roper*, Pandora Press, 1988.
71. Dr Rutherford, MP for Middlesex, Hansard, 2 November 1908, vol 195 cc 796–907.
72. Hansard, 2 November 1908, vol 195 cc 796–907.
73. Ibid.
74. F. E. Smith, Hansard, 2 November 1908, vol 195 cc 796–907.
75. Mr Smillie, Miners' Federation Annual Conference Report, October 1911, p. 33.
76. The men who voted for the amendment consisted of six Labour MPs, eight Liberals and one Conservative. At least five of the Labour MPs were former miners. The Conservative MP was a progressive who was active on the Slave Trade Commission. Those who voted against belonged to the established right wing.
77. Paula Bartley, 'Suffragettes, class and pit-brow women', *History Review*, December 1999, p. 80.
78. Ibid.
79. Esther Roper, *Wigan Examiner*, 5 October 1911.
80. Maude Royden, *Votes and Wages*, NUSWW, October 1911.

81. See Tanya Cheadle, *Sexual Progressives, Reimagining Intimacy in Scotland, 1880–1914*, MUP, 2020.
82. Christabel Pankhurst, 'The Great Scourge and How to Fight It', S. Jeffreys, *The Sexuality Debates*, Routledge and Kegan Paul, 1987, p. 318.
83. Louise Jackson, 'The Regulation of Violence in Interwar Britain', in Shani D'Cruze's *Everyday Violence in Britain*, 1850–1950, Pearson, 2000.
84. *The Times*, 9 February 1904, p. 2.
85. Olive Malvery, *The White Slave Trade*, Hutchinson, 1912.
86. The Act of Union of 1800 abolished Ireland as a separate kingdom and joined her with Great Britain to form the United Kingdom. The Irish Parliament disappeared, and Ireland was represented at Westminster. The Union between the countries was denounced as a fraud, producing subordination not equality.
87. See David Thackeray, 'Home and Politics: Women and Conservative Activism in Early Twentieth-Century Britain', *Journal of British Studies*, Vol 49, No 4, 2010, for the history of WUTRA.
88. Ibid.
89. Ibid.
90. Ibid.
91. Ibid.
92. See Diane Urquhart "Open the eyes of England": female unionism and conservatism, 1886–1914', in Clarisse Berthezène and Julie Gottlieb, *Re-Thinking Right-Wing Women, Gender and the Conservative Party, 1880s to the present*, MUP, 2017, for an overview of this.
93. *The Conservative and Unionist Women's Franchise Review*, 1 April 1914, p. 377.

CHAPTER 3

The Home Front: 1914–1918

On 4 August 1914, when Britain declared war on Germany, Emmeline Pankhurst was in France recovering from her tenth hunger strike. Once home, this intuitive politician suspended all suffragette activities, insisting that the war was a battle between the enlightened democracy of Britain and the autocratic militarism of Germany. She argued that there was no point in continuing to fight for the vote when there might be no country to vote in. Her Manichean vision of the world was shared by her daughter, Christabel, who pleaded for Britain to aid the 'feminine' France against 'over-masculine' Germany. Ironically, one of their greatest principles, that of the unity of women, disappeared in a puff of jingoistic nationalism when they redirected their militant intransigence to the war effort.[1] The leader of the National Union of Women's Suffrage Societies (NUWSS) Millicent Fawcett was more circumspect, though she recognised that patriotic action might strengthen women's claim for the vote. It was, she proclaimed, a 'time for resolute effort and self-sacrifice' to 'prove ourselves worthy of citizenship'.[2] Other suffrage organisations such as the Conservative and Unionist Women's Franchise Association and the Church League for Women's Suffrage also ceased their activities and worked to support the war effort. In marked contrast, Sylvia Pankhurst's East London Federation of Suffragettes (ELFS) and Charlotte Despard's Women's Freedom League (WFL) rejected what they saw as unthinking patriotism, criticised the war as an imperialist venture and continued with their suffrage activities.

SUFFRAGE ACTIVISTS AND THE WAR EFFORT

Most suffragists, whether they accepted or opposed the war, involved themselves in some type of war work, redirecting their organisations to serve a new civic purpose. It was merely a change in political direction for women suffrage activists as they began fighting for the country, instead of fighting for the vote. These women saw war work as reinforcing their claim to citizenship and of conferring respectability on the suffrage cause. This way they were demonstrating that they were responsible, mature, and more than capable of taking part in the democracy that they had worked hard to defend.[3] Christabel Pankhurst argued that women's help in the war would 'make the difference between defeat and victory' and urged the government to mobilise women for war service.[4] The scale and speed by which Emmeline Pankhurst threw herself into a vigorous campaign in which the defeat of Germany took precedence over everything else were astonishing. She placed the Women's Social and Political Union (WSPU) and its funds at the disposal of the government and called for both military and industrial conscription. In June 1915, the government took her advice and announced that it would include women in the National Register.

On 3 June 1915, Emmeline Pankhurst chaired the first of her weekly War Service Meetings at the London Pavilion. She approached the gathering as a suffrage call to arms and urged 'the Government to establish universal obligatory national war service for men and women'[5] and to set up a national organisation to recruit women as a reserve army of labour to replace the men needed at the front.[6] 'We are faced', Pankhurst proclaimed, 'by the danger of losing our freedom as a nation. The question is literally one of life and death. ... We must do more to maintain British honour and prestige; we must do more to save the liberties which the enemy would destroy. We must do more to save this country and the Empire. In short, we must win'.[7]

On 17 July 1915, through heavy drizzle and gusty winds, Emmeline Pankhurst led a Great Procession of Women, known as the Right to Serve March. It had 125 delegations, 90 bands and around 20,000 demonstrators waving the flags of the Allied Powers. The leaders of the procession sat in a car decked out in red, white and green flowers; a girl in a tattered dress carried a torn flag personifying Belgium. Others wore national costume: French women wore red caps of Liberty, Serbian women wore peasant costumes, each British section carried Union Jack flags. Banners included 'Shells made by a wife may save her husband's life', 'Women believe in duty as well as rights' and 'We demand the right to serve'.[8] The overall colour scheme was red, white and blue. In the same year, the suffragettes renamed their paper *Britannia*, changed the name of the WSPU to the Women's Party and set up a National Register of women workers: by the autumn, over 110,000 women had registered. This change of direction by the most famous suffragettes gave rise to the white feather movement where young women gave out the 'white feather of cowardice' to men of service age not in uniform.

Not to be outdone, in the first week of the war the London NUWSS opened the Women's Service Bureau. Soon it was helping Belgian refugees and organising War Relief Committees, Red Cross Units, Hospital Stores and Canteens. Mary Lowndes (former vice chair of the Artists' Suffrage League and activist in the Women's Guild of Arts) helped them set up a Welding school in Notting Hill which turned out a steady supply of skilled women workers for the aircraft factories (Fig. 3.1). It trained women in basic engineering, glass blowing and

3 THE HOME FRONT: 1914–1918   39

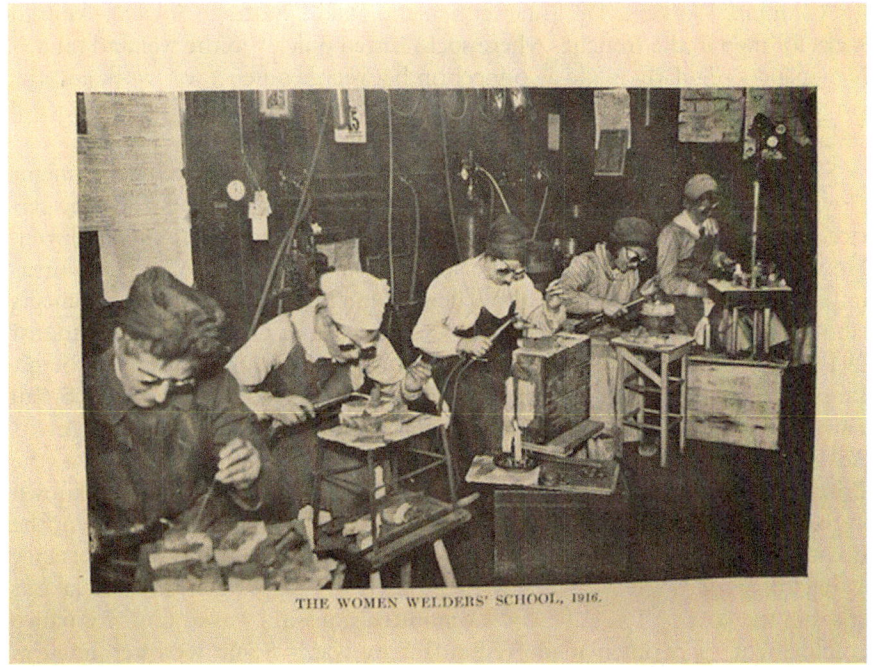

Fig. 3.1 The Women Welders' School, from Ray Strachey *Women's Suffrage and Women's Service*, published by London and National Society for Women's Service, 1927 (Courtesy of author)

acetylene welding, beginning on a 'very small scale, with only one blowpipe; now between twenty and thirty pupils can be trained at the same time.'[9] Other training schools were also opened by the London NUWSS. These provided the first 200 female bus conductors and trained mechanics, recruited taxi drivers and prepared women for the more skilled aspects of munition work. By the end of the war, the suffragist-led Women's Service Bureau had become one of the most influential organisations, involved in a range of women's work.[10]

The Manchester Society for Women's Suffrage (MSWS) agreed to stop its suffrage campaign to help 'sufferers from the economic and industrial dislocation caused by the war'.[11] The MSWS was keen to keep on its suffrage staff and found jobs for its paid workers organising voluntary help for the relief of distress caused by war.[12] Ellen Wilkinson, a future Cabinet Minister, was one of them. When the two staple trades of the region, cotton and knitting, collapsed at the outbreak of war, she commandeered a large room, borrowed machines and tables, appealed in the press for materials and second-hand clothing and opened a sewing room. Soon the workshop employed 150 women.[13]

Scottish suffrage societies offered their services to the war effort. The Dundee and Edinburgh Woman Suffrage Society lent its organisation and offices; the Glasgow and West of Scotland Edinburgh organised an Exchange for Voluntary Workers. The Innerleithen and Falkirk Suffrage Societies knitted socks for men in the trenches where socks rotted quickly in the wet and mud.[14] Newspapers regularly made a connection between women's war work and the vote, often arguing that 'women had clearly demonstrated their patriotism and suitability for British citizenship'.[15]

Shortly after war broke out, there was a dramatic increase in female unemployment as traditionally female work such as dressmaking and domestic service crumpled. By September 1914, 44.4% of women were unemployed. However, one woman's misfortune was another woman's political opportunity. Queen Mary, concerned about female unemployment, invited women's labour organisations to help her relieve some of the distress. On 19 August 1914, the Queen's Employment Advisory Committee on Women's Employment was formed: leading Labour women—Mary MacArthur, Susan Lawrence, Marion Phillips and Margaret Bondfield—agreed to act on its Advisory Committee. It was the first all-woman committee to be backed by the British government. These ladies, one newspaper eulogised, were 'well-known in the industrial world, and can be trusted to work from within and present the situation in its true light. They have all held and hold positions of importance as regards women's work and have been used to grappling with acute labour crises in the past'.[16] The Advisory Committee's mission was to find alternative employment for women made redundant by war.[17] Some were retrained as poultry farmers (working a 60-hour week for 3d an hour, nowhere near enough to live on); others took up bootmaking and other low-paid jobs.[18] In addition, Queen Mary's Workshops were set up for women from the textile trades and the 'distressed sections of the community'. Queen Mary's charitable enterprise laid down 'ideal' terms of employment such as a maximum 40-hour week and a wage of up to 50p a week. Bondfield became involved in 'a great fight …on behalf of the women employed in the Queen's workrooms. They are asking for a rise of a half-penny an hour. At present the rate of pay is 3d an hour, with a maximum of 10s (50p) a week. Everyone will admit this was only a bare subsistence rate before the rise in prices; now it is starvation pure and simple'.[19] The wage offered was less than the Trade Boards' rates which led to Sylvia Pankhurst calling them 'Queen Mary's Sweatshops'. Bitter and justified as such taunts were, Sylvia Pankhurst turned her former suffrage campaign into charity work by setting up a toy factory, a baby clinic, nursery and two subsidised restaurants. Pankhurst's efforts to ameliorate the poor conditions of working-class women was amongst many philanthropic attempts by middle-class women to rescue their working-class sisters. The Red Cross, the Prince of Wales' fund, the Soldiers and Sailors Dependants Fund were among those which proliferated during the war. Each of these gave middle-class women a new and respectable way to contribute to the war effort and to redirect their activism.

The war was political: women were told that they worked not just for an employer but for their country. Government posters urged women to 'Do Your Bit, Replace a Man for the Front', making women's work a civic responsibility as well as an economic necessity. By January 1915, two million men from a male labour force of 10.6 million had joined the armed forces, and after January 1916 when conscription was introduced, labour shortages were acute. In March 1915, the Board of Trade made it compulsory for every woman to register at the Labour Exchange, an action which was criticised by Margaret Bondfield because it 'threatened to flood the labour market with volunteers willing to take employment on any terms'.[20] For working-class women, war offered an alternative to the grossly exploitative job of domestic service or sweated labour. Women went into engineering, agriculture, transport and government offices. They replaced men as bus drivers, window cleaners, chimney sweeps, coal deliverers, electricians and firefighters—all jobs previously considered inappropriate for women. The number of female bus conductors rose from half a dozen to about 2500.

Emmeline Pankhurst worked with her old adversary Lloyd George, now minister of munitions, to help meet the prodigious demand for military weapons. Munitions showed the biggest increase in female labour: in 1914, the Woolwich Arsenal employed 125 women; by 1917, the number had increased to over 25,000. Arsenal factories, desperate to increase production, recruited women to make ammunition, guns and high explosives. Women filled shells, made bullets, assembled detonators and 'devil's porridge, in other words cordite, all hazardous work. In the Woolwich Arsenal about 37% of women suffered from stomach pain, nausea and constipation as a result of TNT poisoning. Other symptoms included skin rashes, giddiness, drowsiness, swelling of hands and feet and yellow skin, which earned the young women the sobriquet "Canary Girls". In 1916, the first deaths from toxic jaundice were reported. Eventually, responding to pressure from the National Federation of Women Workers reduced the amount of time women worked with TNT.[21] Munition workers feared explosions more than poisoning, and safety measures were introduced to avoid accidents: each woman had to hand over all her personal belongings including matches, cigarettes, wedding rings and other jewellery before entering the shell filling section. Women wore protective clothes without any metal zips, garters rather than suspender belts, and caps to tie up long hair because Kirby grips were banned. Punishment for women breaking these rules was harsh: Elizabeth Halliwell from Bolton was given six weeks hard labour for carrying matches. Despite these precautions, accidents were common. The most horrendous occurred at the factory in Silverton where an unspecified number of women were killed in an explosion. Londoners saw the sky light up bright red for miles around the city yet; for reasons of national security, the accident was not reported in the press.[22]

Fighting for Workers' Rights

Women's participation in the war effort increased their participation in trade unions. In 1914, women's trade union membership stood at 437,000, but by the end of the war it had increased to 1,209,000, a much faster growth even than their numbers in the workforce. However, the wages paid to most women, from munition workers to chimney sweeps, was far lower than those paid to men. Margaret Bondfield, Mary Macarthur, Ellen Wilkinson and other women trade unionists were committed to protect these new women workers from being underpaid and from working in poor conditions. In order to safeguard them and the men they replaced, Bondfield suggested five basic protections: that all women registering for war service join a union; that women receive equal pay for equal work; that no woman be employed on less than a living wage; that women be given suitable training; that after the war men should get their jobs back.

The First World War turned equal pay into a major issue. The majority of women, from cotton factory weavers through to civil servants received less pay than their male colleagues. At the time, employers insisted that women be paid less than men: firstly, because women usually quit their jobs when they got married and so were not worth training; secondly, because men were physically stronger; and thirdly, because men had greater family responsibilities. Consequently, when women replaced men who were called up to fight, employers tried to pay them less. Ellen Wilkinson, former suffragist and now trade union organiser, insisted that 'the rate for the job, not the sex of the worker', should be the only criterion for pay.[23] By later 1916, Wilkinson had negotiated male rates of pay for women in 57 different co-operative societies across the United Kingdom.

It was tough fighting for workers' rights in wartime, particularly when the government claimed that war made it necessary to erode all manner of civil liberties. Four days after war was declared, the government passed the Defence of the Realm Act (DORA), an act which was amended six times during the war to control the lives of civilians. It was even used to 'ban bonfires, whistling in the street and flying kites'.[24] In 1915, a Munitions of War Act reinforced DORA by forbidding strikes and making it a criminal offence for workers to leave their job without permission. Nonetheless, protests and strikes still occurred. In 1917, Gertrude Hardman, a 31-year-old widowed munition worker, was arrested and charged under DORA for speaking out about the unhealthy conditions in her local factory.[25] In November 1915, a strike was only narrowly averted at the Scottish Parkhead and Paisley munition factory by Mary McArthur and the NFWW, which persuaded the government to force the factory owner to increase women's wages. On 9 September 1916, Ellen Wilkinson was caught up in an industrial action in Plymouth when the co-operative society refused to increase the pay of its female workforce. Over 1000 workers downed tools, closed their tills and shut up shop. Nancy Astor and her MP husband Waldorf Astor met Ellen Wilkinson in an attempt to resolve the conflict. Eleven weeks later, the strikers returned to work, with little resolved. In September 1917, 400 women at Dumfries' munition factory went on strike for an adjustment in hours of work, improvements in the arrangements for night working and the dismissal of the middle-class female supervisor.[26] Between late October 1917 and early 1918, an acrimonious and long strike took place at the East Hope Street munition work at Clydeside when the owner refused to award a negotiated pay increase, accused the women of not working hard enough and sacked four of them. Immediately, 55 women came out in sympathy, and within a week 284 out of the 370 women struck in support. Following threats by unions to bring the whole of the Clyde out, and after a meeting of several thousand on Glasgow Green on 25 November, there were questions in the House of Commons. The owner relented, reinstated the women and agreed to pay the increase.[27] At times, strike action by women turned violent. In 1918, a tram strike by female conductors in Liverpool turned particularly nasty when women strikers pulled conductors still working out of their cars, threw mud at the drivers, smashed the windows of the trams and cut the trolley ropes.[28]

Margaret Bondfield 'protested against the tyrannical way in which the Munitions Act was being worked and instanced cases where the liberty and civil rights of the working people were being filched'.[29] In a speech to the 1916 Labour Party Conference, Bondfield demanded a 'drastic revision of the Munitions Act with a view to preventing the pretext of war being used for the greater coercion and subjection of Labour; to that end the Conference demands the restoration of individual right of contract'.[30] She saw that the excuse of war was being 'used for many reactionary purpose for the curtailment of the freedom of speech and writing, for the growth of child labour, for the rendering null and void of labour protective laws, for the spreading of industrial compulsion'.[31] As a result of Bondfield and the work of the NFWW, a basic wage for munition workers was secured, even though equal pay was a long way off. In 1919, with the war safely over, the Munitions Act was repealed. Meanwhile, in February 1916 a group of Labour women set up the Standing Joint Committee of Industrial women's Organisations (SJC). Women's trade unions, the Women's Labour League, the Women's Co-operative Guild and the Railway Women's Guild all affiliated. In 1917, two SJC women—Marion Phillips and Beatrice Webb—were appointed to Lloyd George's Reconstruction Committee to help draw up plans for the post-war period.[32]

THE WOMEN'S EMERGENCY CORPS AND ITS OFFSHOOTS

Some former suffrage activists turned to new forms of engagement: war action. Two days after the declaration of war, Evelina Haverfield, a former suffragette,[33] her colleague, the actress Decima Moore, and several members of the WSPU set up the Women's Emergency Corps (WEC). They claimed that 'women of all classes' joined the WEC, including those who drove carts to Covent Garden[34] but in reality, as Diane Atkinson has shown, it 'bustled with suffragettes, fashionable actresses, a couple of duchesses and a marchioness, and a handful of lady novelists' as well as a number of countesses and ladies.[35] It saw women's war work as the 'female equivalent of fighting for one's nation'.[36] One of its posters copied Lord Kitchener's appeal saying, '*Women! Your country needs you. Today the country needs every woman no less than it needs every man .... We call to the women of the country to come and help us. Come*

Quickly![37] The WEC had a two-fold aim: to find a 'suitable outlet for the many offers of help from women of all classes and to provide jobs for those thrown out of work by war' and to help release men to enlist in the armed forces.[38]

During the first two weeks the WEC dealt with over 10,000 women looking for jobs. Women were placed into groups: as doctors, dispensers, trained nurses, interpreters, chauffeurs, cyclists, motor cyclists, messengers, cooks, gardeners, tram conductors or ticket collectors.[39] A number of departments were set up: a toy-making factory, a knitting unit, an interpreting division, a nursing branch and a motorcycle messenger service. In its first half-yearly report, the WEC reported that it had engaged 3600 volunteers, found jobs for 460 women, distributed two tons of clothing, served up 28,378 meals in their kitchens and dealt with 3700 Belgian refugees.[40] Early in February 1915, on behalf of the WEC Norah Hackett took a canteen to French troops fighting on the Front and each day provided them with hot soup, coffee, chocolate, biscuits, bread and cheese. The women also distributed cigarettes, matches, handkerchief, soap, biscuits and chocolates to the men about to go to the trenches.[41]

Belgian Refugees

At the beginning of the war, more than 200,000 Belgian refugees displaced by the German invasion of their country fled to Britain. The WEC was the first organisation to meet the refugees and 'help people arriving in misery and hopelessness',[42] sometimes in a state of destitution. These refugees, with their children, their hand-luggage, 'their bundles and a few possessions hastily gathered together, a saucepan sticking out here, or a doll emerging there', asked for international sympathy.[43] Dora Black, a former suffragette who later married Bertrand Russell, spoke of how 'pathetic it was to see them, bent and worn old peasant women, who had hoped to end their days in peace by their children's fireside; weary mothers with enormous families of strapping children with big blue eyes and wild wisps of yellow hair'.[44] Dora Black was 20-year old, skilled at languages and keen to be an interpreter for the WEC. Interpreters like Black, some of whom spoke several languages, were sent to the various London railway stations to meet the refugees, advise them about hotels, offer homes and drive them to their destinations. In its first few months, the WEC provided 600 interpreters, collected surplus food from the London markets to distribute to Belgian refugees, found accommodation for 2000 and provided 1675 with clothes.[45]

Women's desire to lend a hand was considerable. Flora Louise Shaw, Lady Lugard and Edith Balfour Lyttelton (an executive member of the National Union of Women Workers and member of the Central Committee for Women's Employment) set up the War Refugees Committee (WRC) to coordinate relief efforts. They were overwhelmed with offers of practical help and support: cheques, clothing and food flooded in. A number of organisations such as the Women's Tariff Reform League and the Ladies' Automobile Club as well as religious organisations—Catholic, Protestant, Jewish and Nonconformist—all offered to help in any way they could.[46] Between December 1914 and February 1915, the Folkestone branches of the Salvation Army, the Quakers and the Catholics provided beds for nearly 9000 refugees and served nearly 71,000 meals.[47] Besides clothes and shoes, refugees were provided with 'combs, brushes, soap, hairpins, bootlaces, braces, needles, cotton, thimbles and knitting needles'.[48]

Women's Volunteer Reserve

The WEC helped set up the Women's Volunteer Reserve (WVR), whose members thought of themselves as women soldiers.[49] Its members bought their own khaki uniform and learned to parade and drill. They were taught first aid by one of the first women doctors, instructed in morse signalling and given the military rank of either private or officer.[50] Once qualified, WVR women ran canteens for soldiers, transported the wounded, administered first aid to returning soldiers and drove vans to various docks and factories.[51] Dolly Shepherd remembers driving a van full of gold ingots to the docks.[52]

As Diane Atkinson points out, two of the most famous women, Elsie Knocker and Mairi Gooden-Chisholm, worked on the front line.[53] At first, the two were hired as dispatch riders for the WEC and spent their first months delivering messages on their motorbikes. They both wore trousers, leather boots and overcoats and became known as 'Valkyries in knicker-bockers'. They joined the Flying Ambulance Corps, a Corps set up by Dr Hector Munro, who advertised for first-class nurses who were able to ride and drive 'with nerves of iron'.[54] The two women fitted the vital requirements and went on to help wounded Belgian soldiers in a field hospital near Dunkirk. Soon the two women realised that more men could be saved if they were treated as near to the front line as possible since many died from shock in the ambulances taking them to hospital. They left the Flying Corps and installed their own dressing station in a cellar in a partly destroyed house in Pervyse, just 100 yards from the trenches, sometimes carrying the wounded from No Man's Land on their shoulders to their make-shift hospital. Elsie Knocker, who could speak German, sent notes over to the enemy when they wanted to retrieve bodies. The Germans allowed them to do so and told them to wear woollen hats rather than steel helmets to avoid being shot.[55] Here they spent the next three years nursing the wounded: Elsie gave them urgent treatment, and Mairi drove them to the nearest hospital. The two shared some of the same discomforts as soldiers, sleeping in their clothes, rarely able to wash, with their underclothes sticking to their bodies and scraping 'the lice off with a blunt edge of a knife'.[56] On two occasions, they got caught up in bayonet charges, and found themselves 'clearing up the mess' of soldiers who had been stabbed by Germans. The German soldiers used bayonets with sawed edges, making the wounds even more gruesome.[57]

Mairi Chisholm, still in her late teens, drove the wounded to hospital 15 miles away, which 'was a real strain—no lights, shell-shocked pavie roads mud-covered, often under fire, men and guns coming up to relieve the trenches, total darkness, yells to mind one's self and get out of the way, meaning a sickening slide off the pavie into deep mud—screams from the stretchers behind one … two or three of these journeys by night and one's eyes were on stalks, bloodshot and strained'.[58] The two looked after men and boys with mangled bodies, shattered jaws, arms and legs smashed to pieces or else missing and brains hanging out. The two women won numerous medals for bravery and for saving the lives of thousands of soldiers. They were called the 'Angels of Pervyse'.

There were a number of other groups formed by former suffragists and suffragettes. At 10:00 am, Thursday 15 September 1914, a Women's Hospital Corps left Victoria Station for Paris. The Corps, as with many of the other relief organisations, was founded by former suffragists. Dr Louisa Garrett Anderson and Dr Flora Murray headed a team which included 20 doctors, nurses and orderlies. Their base was the Claridge Hotel in the Champs Elysées, Paris, which had been fitted up as a hospital.[59] The unit had first-rate equipment, including an X-ray machine in what was originally the hotel's hairdressing salon and an operating theatre which was formerly the ladies' cloakroom.[60] Later, the two women set up a hospital in Wimereaux, and afterwards opened a large military hospital in London. Newspapers praised the fact that they had abandoned their suffrage activities and were devoting 'their remarkable energies and undoubted powers of organisation to various forms of charitable and relief work'.[61]

May 'Toupie' Lowther, a former suffragette, skilled fencer and body-guard for Emmeline Pankhurst, was another individual who wanted to be of use in the war. In 1916, she secured permission to take a unit to the front line, obtained 22 cars from friends and relatives and led a group of more than 25 women drivers to the war zone. For four months, they carried over 10,000 wounded to the hospitals. But they wanted to do more. Eventually, they went as a unit to the Front wearing the same cap and helmet as French soldiers and receiving the same 'indemnité de combat' of five sous and a tobacco ration. 'It was a wonderful time', said 'Toupie' Lowther, 'we were often 350 yards from the German line awaiting the wounded, under camouflage. … We served under many different generals …. Always working with the most advanced dressing stations'.[62] Her unit was awarded the Croix de Guerre by the French government.

In August 1914, Dr Elsie Inglis, a former member of the Edinburgh National Union of Women's Suffrage Societies and founder of the Scottish Federation of Women's Suffrage Societies, set up the Scottish Women's Hospitals (SWH), an all-female voluntary unit which employed women as doctors, nurses, orderlies, cooks, administrators and ambulance drivers.[63] Inglis and her team relied on former suffrage activists with their expertise in fundraising to help raise money for the SWH. Sarah Pedersen points out that former branches of the Scottish suffrage societies raised 'funds to support a named bed for a year, with suffrage societies in towns as diverse as Motherwell, Lerwick and Hawick' providing beds named after their town (Fig. 3.2).[64]

Fig. 3.2 Women ambulance drivers, from *The Great War*, 19 April 1919 (Courtesy of author)

The SWH attracted over 1500 women to work in the 14 field hospitals they set up in seven different occupied countries. Undaunted by their close proximity to the firing lines and the threat of aerial bombardment, the women of the SWH set up their camps, prepared X-ray theatres and dressing rooms and began to treat severely wounded and battle-weary soldiers. The first unit opened in northern France with 600 beds, a fully equipped laboratory and a casualty station. In its four years of operation, it treated 10,861 patients.

Later, Elsie Inglis relocated to Serbia where she was joined by Evelina Haverfield. Conditions were harsh: food was in short supply, medicine was often unavailable, qualified medics thin on the ground and typhus was raging. Vera 'Jack' Holmes, the former chauffeur of Emmeline Pankhurst and very close friend of Haverfield, came out to work in the transport unit. Both Inglis and Haverfield were taken prisoner and repatriated to Britain. Undeterred, the two went to southern Russia, where they helped equip and staff a hospital, again employing a female-only staff. One of them, Yvonne Fitzroy, wrote that 'it is no light job undressing and washing a badly wounded six-foot-odd

Russian who cannot understand what you want of him ... so many come in dying or unconscious or delirious ... these poor broken creatures are brought here in springless cards to find a straw mattress to lie on, to have to suffer tortures, the horror of gangrene or tetanus'.[65] The unit remained there before being forced to retreat when the harshness of the weather, the conditions of their vehicles and the outbreak of the Russian revolution made their lives impossible.[66] Haverfield returned to Britain and spent the remainder of the war campaigning for Serbia.

One female couple ran a mobile radiography unit. Nina Hollings (sister of the suffragette composer Ethel Smythe) and Lady Helena Gleichen (great-niece of Queen Victoria) both trained as radiographers with Marie Curie and set off in December 1915 to work on the Italian front. Lady Helena persuaded her family to donate money for a mobile radiography unit and a purpose-built car. The two women were close—Lady Helena thought their friendship equalled that of the Ladies of Llangollen—and needed to be. It was a dangerous and demanding job driving between 11 different field hospitals and even more dressing stations, dodging bombs and bullets to help surgeons locate the pieces of metal embedded in the bodies of wounded soldiers. They were the only women ever to be in charge of an X-ray unit, taking over 17,000 X-rays. Helena said that the 'bustle and noise, the groaning, the cries for "Mamma Mia", the smell of disinfectants and the smell of blood' made the place a 'nightmare'.[67]

In November 1916, the two were summoned by General Lombardo to attend an event at the Gorizia Opera House. When they arrived, all the seats had been removed, and the 'floor of the house was packed with soldiers standing shoulder to shoulder. ... Tier after tier, the boxes were decorated by wreaths of different coloured roses' which had been picked by the soldiers the night before.[68] As the women were escorted to their box, 'all the men turned towards us, standing at attention, and the officers ... rose to their feet and saluted.'[69] A bugle sounded and the General spoke, saying that he was there to 'do honour' to those who had served Italy. 'Soldiers here present', he said, 'we greet these two English women whom we look upon, not as two of our most gallant officers, but as beloved members of our families, and we offer them, and ask them always to wear the medal we have had struck for all the officers who took part in the Victory of Gorizia'.[70] Both Nina and Helena were later awarded the medal for Military Valour by Victor Emmanuel, the King of Italy. Lady Helena was also awarded the OBE; in 2017, Nina Hollings' medals were sold at auction for £5500.[71]

The women who worked in war zones faced similar dangers as men in the armed forces. Some were wounded, gassed or taken prisoner. Many did not survive. On 5 August 1915, Edith Cavell, director of a nurses' training school and clinic in Brussels which was now part of German-occupied Belgium, was arrested for smuggling allied prisoners to safety. Her school and clinic headed an underground network, hiding approximately 200 British, French and Belgian soldiers by disguising them as patients, providing them with false passports and helping them escape into allied territory. On 7 August, Cavell was arrested, kept in solitary confinement, interrogated and forced to confess. On 12 October 2015, she was shot at dawn by a firing squad.[72] It was called 'judicial murder'. The two men who had betrayed her were both killed—one by a bullet in the forehead, the other by a dagger thrust in the chest—by those who resisted the German occupation.[73]

OTHER WOMEN'S ORGANISATIONS

Middle-class and upper-class women joined the many quasi military organisations set up to support the war effort, allowing them to demonstrate their patriotism and develop a range of political, administrative and organisational skills. In 1917, Lady Londonderry formed the Land Army, many of whose recruits came from middle-class or upper-class backgrounds, to raise food production after Germany's campaign of submarine warfare disrupted food imports. Selection boards turned down girls they believed lacked the high moral fibre needed for farm life and told their recruits to expect chivalry and respect from men. On the farm, women were expected to work in jobs such as ploughing, planting, harvesting and tending the cows and other animals, while the farmers were busy trying to enlarge the acreage of land under cultivation and increase food production (Fig. 3.3).

Fig. 3.3 Women in the Land Army, spraying fruit trees, from *The Great War*, 19 April 1919 (Courtesy of author)

In 1916, the Women's Auxiliary Army Corps (WAACS) was formed to free men to go to the front. The WAACS provided cooks, clerical workers and drivers for the army, freeing up 12,000 men for the trenches. Over 57,000 women served with it; 9000 of them worked in France. In 1917, the Women's Royal Naval Service (WRENS) was set up to employ women as cooks, postwomen, waitresses in the officers' mess, telegraphists and in intelligence. In 1918, the Women's Royal Air Force (WRAFS) employed women as drivers, typists, telephonists and storekeepers but some did train as welders and carpenters to work on the aeroplanes. These women were called penguins: birds who could not fly (Fig. 3.4).

Other uniformed services which were set up by women for women included the Voluntary Aid Attachments (VAD). These women nursed soldiers both at home and at the front—the former suffragette Princess Duleep Singh nursed Indian soldiers wounded on the Western Front. The VAD was joined by the Women's Volunteer Reserve (WVR), where women were taught the basics of gardening, carpentry, telegraphy, camp cooking, camp sanitation, signalling and nursing.

In 1915, the Women's Institute was formed to revive village life, 'which in the past has been regarded as intolerably dull, providing little or no opportunity for social intercourse and the interchange of ideas'.[74] It was also hoped that rural women could help with the wartime food shortage. Accordingly, the WI encouraged women to grow and preserve food for war-torn Britain. Women were given lectures on bee-keeping, poultry-keeping, soft toy-making, bread making, potato cookery, fruit bottling, drying and preserving vegetables, rabbit keeping, cheesemaking, pig keeping, how to make the most of fuel saving and how to save labour. In Maggie Andrews' *The Acceptable Face of Feminism, the Women's Institute as a Social Movement*,[75] the Women's Institute is seen to be very much more than just jam and Jerusalem. Many of the leading figures in the early days supported women's suffrage and wanted to empower these rural working-class women who endured some of the worst social conditions and most limited opportunities. The WI insisted that it was a non-party political and non-sectarian organisation, yet it educated its members in political issues and encouraged activism by its members. At the newly formed Reading branch, women listened to lectures on 'Women as Empire Builders' and 'Current Events'.[76] By 1918, around 760 WIs had been established with 50,000 members. It was to prove to be 'one of the most significant legacies of the First World War'.[77]

Sexual Politics

During the war, there was an increasing fear that venereal disease (VD) was on the rise. In 1915, the government, concerned about the health of British troops, passed the Defence of the Realm Act (DORA) 13a, which detained and prosecuted any woman with VD who solicited or had sexual intercourse with a member of the armed forces. In effect, it was a rerun of the notorious

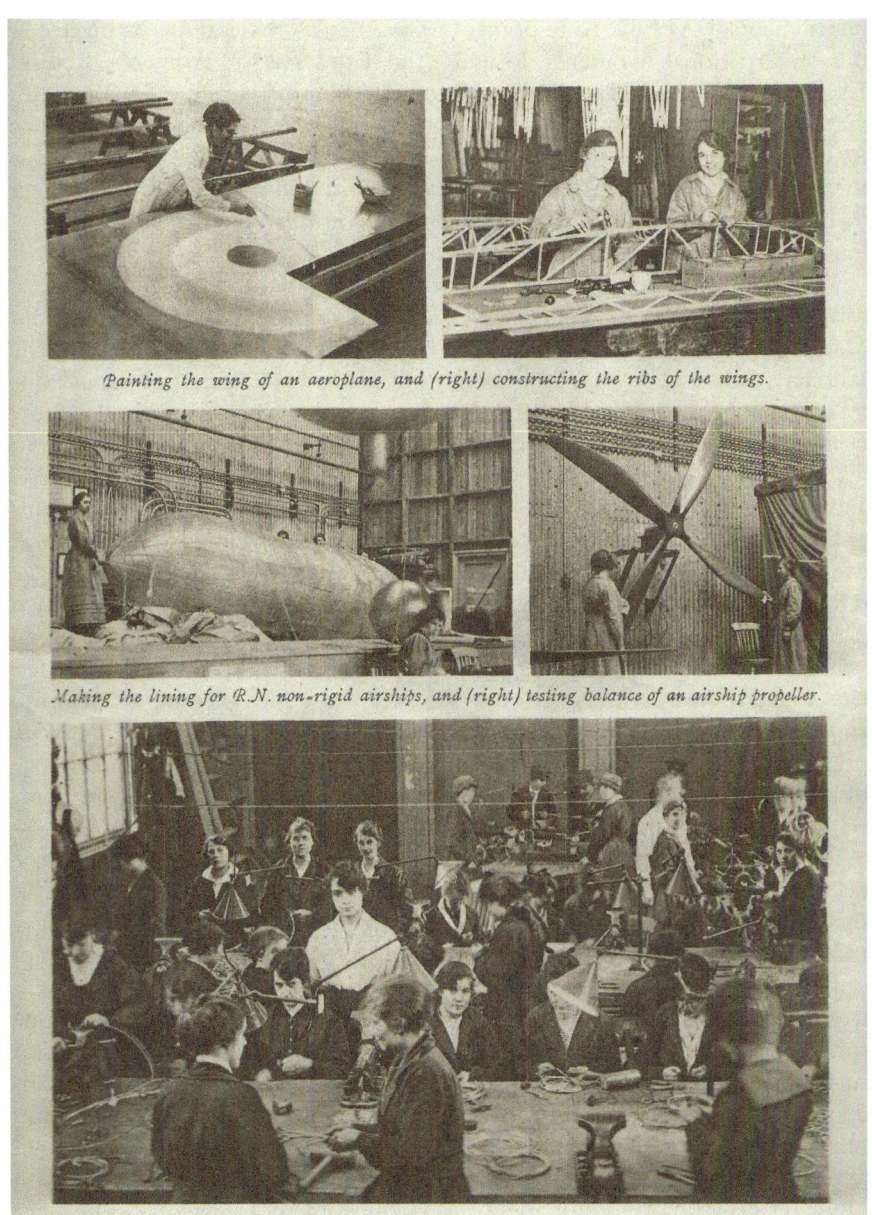

Fig. 3.4 WRAFS from *The Great War*, 19 April 1919 (Courtesy of author)

Contagious Diseases Acts. In 1915, the Association for Moral and Social Hygiene (AMSH) was formed to campaign against Regulation 13a and the current solicitation laws. This labelled women who were charged with soliciting as common prostitutes and subjected them to special laws and punishments.[78] As Julia Laite points out, women's organisations as diverse as the 'International Women's League, the Conservative Women's Reform Union, the Women's Liberal Federation, the Church League for Women's Suffrage, the Salvation Army, the National British Women's Temperance Association and the Young Women's Christian Association' protested against these iniquitous laws.[79] Maud Royden, a feminist and campaigner for women to become priests, argued that 'denying to prostitutes the ordinary rights of human beings ... is fundamentally vicious'.[80]

Women tried other tactics to help women in sexual danger. Nina Boyle, a former member of the WFL who had been imprisoned three times, and Margaret Damer Dawson, an anti-vivisectionist campaigner, set up the Women's Police Service (WPS).[81] Many of their early recruits were former suffragettes. It may seem odd that women who had often broken the law now wanted to be part of law enforcement but recruits insisted they wanted to 'challenge male control of the law'.[82] It had long been an ambition of feminists and social purity activists, argues Philippa Levine, to set up a separate women's police force to deal with the specific problems faced by women and children.[83] More specifically, they feared that men were trying to recruit Belgian female refugees as prostitutes when they arrived at the railway stations. Policewomen patrolled streets and parks, and even burst into homes if they suspected immoral behaviour. These women police, fully uniformed in dark blue with hard felt hats, helped patrol certain districts to 'protect' (i.e. control) young women and children and to maintain 'decent' standards of behaviour. In 1916, the WPS organised a nightly patrol of Battersea Park, believing that the mere presence of a woman in uniform had a restraining influence on 'unruly girls' and prevented them from engaging in sexual acts.

The National Union of Women Workers (NUWW), concerned about the decline in moral standards of young working-class girls now earning money of their own, also set up their own women's patrols to police the streets to ensure that young women behaved themselves and to 'protect girls in the vicinity of camps and barracks' from the sexual advances of soldiers.[84] By early 1915, there were 900 patrols checking 'the streets, parks, pubs, and even houses in large towns, in areas where it was feared that women might seduce young soldiers or succumb to men's advances'.[85] In Ireland, the women worked in religious tandem: a Protestant and a Catholic worked in unison to avoid accusations of bias.[86]

Soon there were conflicts over policing methods. Nina Boyle disagreed with Margaret Dawson over enforcing a curfew on women of allegedly 'loose character' near an army base at Grantham. Boyle also opposed a curfew on 'women of a certain class' between 7 pm and 8 am in Cardiff. In the end, the disagreements became unresolvable, and the two parted company. Dawson replaced Boyle as her deputy with Mary Allen, another suffragette who had served three prison terms, undergone hunger strikes and suffered forcible feeding. Dawson and Allen expanded the organisation by policing factories and munition works, acting as timekeepers, searching the workers for matches, metal objects and stolen goods and acting to deter potential strikes. They were accused of overstepping their authority by forcibly entering private houses, demanding to inspect bedrooms and tyrannising women whose husbands were absent. Nina Boyle saw them as trying to oppress rather than help, and she condemned their activities.[87] In 1916, she left Britain and went to Macedonia and Serbia to help in relief work.

During the war, the 'illegitimacy' rate jumped from 4% to 6% of all births. In 1918, the National Council for the Unmarried Mother and her Child (NCUMC) was formed with a threefold aim: to make sure that fathers acknowledged and supported their children; to help single mothers to keep their children; and to make sure that such children were not discriminated against.[88] The NCUMC pointed to the heavy mortality rate among babies born to unmarried mothers; they, along with the War Babies and Mothers' League, tried to remove the stigma of 'bastardy' from such children and named them 'war babies' instead of 'bastards' or 'illegitimate', which were words current at the time. Helped by their campaigns, infant welfare came to dominate. In 1918, the Maternity and Child Welfare Act required local authorities to look after maternity and child welfare and gave them powers to award grants for 'home-helps, lying-in homes, food for expectant and nursing mothers and children, creches and day nurseries, convalescent homes and hospital treatment for children up to five years'.[89] Emmeline Pankhurst, encouraged by the government, led a campaign to adopt girl babies born to single mothers whose partners were in the armed forces. She established her own orphanage, the Adoption Home for Female Children, and placed former suffragettes Annie and Jessie Kenny in charge of it. Mrs Pankhurst herself adopted three of the girl babies, and her daughter Christabel adopted one.

Other suffragists fought against official attempts to curtail the behaviour of wives of men serving in the armed forces.[90] The government paid a separation allowance to the wives of soldiers and sailors, an amount that depended on the rank of the serviceman, whether he was a soldier or a sailor and whether he had children. Wives of sailors of the lowest rank received 60p a week; wives of soldiers received 75p, not really enough to live on, especially when they had to wait five or six weeks to receive the pay. Even so, the government believed that wives squandered their allowances on drink which led to unseemly behaviour. The Home Office told local police officers that 'the allowances granted to the wives and dependents are now on a more liberal scale than hitherto and the result has been to put in the hands of many of them larger sums than they have previously enjoyed ... and may be led to careless spending of money and excessive drinking'.[91] In October 1914, an Army Council Memorandum on the 'Cessation of Separation Allowances and Allotments to the Unworthy' asked police to list the names of wives and daughters who were in receipt of separation allowances and ensure they were fit enough to receive them.[92] Consequently, if a woman was suspected of drinking too much or being too friendly with other men, she was investigated, charged, and, if found guilty, had her separation allowance stopped. Some pubs even banned soldiers' wives.

Sylvia Pankhurst argued that the separation allowance should not be liable to forfeiture, or threat of it. On 18 January 1915, she, along with former suffragist Charlotte Despard, formed the League of Rights for Soldiers' and the Sailors' Wives and Female Relatives to secure separation allowances and pensions and to agitate for an improvement in the conditions for dependents of men in the forces. On 23 January 1915, Sylvia Pankhurst led a demonstration to Trafalgar Square, followed by a deputation to the Home Office and a later one to the War Office to demand that the Army orders be withdrawn, that separation allowances should be a right and not dependent on government charity and that the allowances be increased to a living wage.[93]

The League held weekly meetings, campaigned widely for improvements and acted on behalf of women who had lost their allowances. The League, insisted Sylvia Pankhurst, would act as a lawyer to secure justice for those who had had their allowances stopped.[94] The cases Sylvia Pankhurst dealt with were shocking: one soldier had returned from the front wounded and paralysed in both arms, unable to feed himself and suffering from acute pain. He had been discharged as unfit for further military service and his pay had stopped along with his wife's Separation Allowance. Sylvia Pankhurst wrote to the War Office, and a pension was arranged.[95]

THE RENT STRIKES

War encouraged self-sacrifice but it also encouraged greed. As more and more women moved to the cities to work in the munition factories, it caused a shortage of homes to rent and rising prices from property owners who greedily took advantage of this. Tenants refused to pay the increases and went on rent strike. One of the most effective actions was led by the Glaswegian former suffragettes Helen Crawfurd and Agnes Dollan, who insisted that the government stop landlords—whom they called the enemy at home—from raising their rents. In May 1915, the women took their own action by refusing to pay any increase. A Woman's Housing Association was formed which eventually recruited 15,000 members. It organised an elaborate system of pickets who stood on duty outside each threatened house. When the pickets gave the signal that bailiffs were approaching a particular house, all the women in the neighbourhood came to defend it.[96] Each time a bailiff came to evict a tenant, women took collective action and threw flour, fish and other missiles at them. The Bailiff would leave. On 7 October 1915, a demonstration of 800 mostly 'respectably dressed women, some carrying infants and others leading young children by the hand' marched from the various quarters of the city where rent strikes were in progress to George Square, Glasgow, to demand a rent reduction.[97] For Mary Barbour, a carpet printer, it was her first taste of political activism. Soon she was organising tenants' committees to resist eviction—these became known as 'Mrs Barbour's Army'. Clyde munition workers in three of the large shipbuilding yards gave support by sending an ultimatum to the government threatening action unless a Rent Act was passed.[98] In November, 10,000 workers downed tools and marched to the Glasgow Small Debt Court to protest against the situation of 18 munition workers who were on trial for not paying their rent. The court case was dropped. It was seen as a great victory, a tribute to the power of the organised workers. The rent strike spread: tenants in Birmingham, Dundee, Northampton, Bermondsey, Tooting, Canning Town, Swansea and Dulwich also went on rent strike, actions which encouraged the government to introduce the Rent Restriction Act by which rents were pegged at a pre-war level.[99] Mary Barbour went on to become one of Glasgow's first women councillors, the first woman Baillie and one of the first magistrates, spending the rest of her life fighting to improve the lives of working-class women in her district. Folk singer A. Hulett wrote a song 'Mary Barbour's Army' to commemorate her political activity.[100]

Peace Movements

Not all suffragettes and suffragists supported the war. The NUWSS was bitterly divided: some like Millicent Fawcett wholeheartedly supported the war effort; others were ambivalent; and still others were unwilling to countenance war in any shape or form. Eventually, these disagreements led to an acrimonious break-up of the NUWSS—all the national executive, apart from Millicent Fawcett and the Treasurer, resigned and in September 1915 formed the British section of the Women's International League for Peace and Freedom. The suffragettes also split into three groups: the Suffragettes of the WSPU, the Independent WSPU and the United Suffragists, all of which continued to hold suffrage meetings during the war. The Women's Freedom League and The East London Federation of Suffragettes opposed the war completely.

For some, the war was judged to be an imperialist war fought over territorial rights. Great Britain, which had colonised large parts of the world, was challenged by Germany who wanted its own 'place in the sun'. War, it was argued, meant millions of workers killing each other in the interests of their bosses. These were brave statements as a wave of nationalism was sweeping the country, men flocked to enlist and jingoism was rife.

The war was a moral shock to the trade unionist Margaret Bondfield, coming 'suddenly, unexpectedly, as a surprise'.[101] In Bondfield's view, the war was unjustifiable, a 'negation of Christianity'.[102] Most women, she believed, hated war or any other 'method of destroying human life; they are interested in the preservation and nurture of human life, not its destruction'.[103] She had taken a pacifist position during the Boer Wars, and was 'still more of a pacifist at this date'.[104] In her view, one of the great scandals of the war was 'the attitude of mind which regarded human life as the cheapest thing to expend. ... "To militarise" the worker meant to turn him into unskilled cannon fodder'.[105]

In April 1915, a total of 1136 women from 12 different countries travelled to the Hague to a conference of the International Women's Suffrage Alliance to discuss how to end the war. One hundred and eighty British women tried to attend the conference, only to be thwarted by the British government, which refused to issue passports: only three managed to get there, Chrystal Macmillan, Kathleen Courtney and Emmeline Pethick-Lawrence. Women from the Netherlands, Germany, Sweden, Norway, Austria, Denmark, Hungary, Italy, Belgium, Canada and America—some representing countries at war with each other—attended and set up the Women's International League for Permanent Peace.[106]

Undeterred, women travelled to Berne Switzerland later that month for a secret international conference of Socialist and Labour women organised by the revolutionary, Clara Zetkin.[107] Secrecy was essential because of the Hague experience. Four British delegates joined 24 other women representing Germany, France, Russia, Poland, Holland, Switzerland and Italy.[108] Delegates called for a speedy end to the war, urged that no humiliating conditions be imposed on defeated nations and upheld the rights of nationalities to self-determination.[109] The British delegates also proposed that 'the menace of the armament interests and their huge international organisation' be curtailed.[110] It was a courageous decision to make their pacifism public since most people in Britain were swept away by xenophobic fervour.

Back in Britain, the women set up a national branch of the organisation—the Women's International League—and by 1916, it had recruited 2458 members, published a number of anti-war pamphlets and leaflets and had held numerous meetings. On 23 July 1916, the Scottish activist and former suffragette, Helen Crawfurd, organised an anti-war demonstration in Glasgow which attracted thousands of women. The Women's Peace Crusade, as it was known, spread across Britain. Throughout the next year, outdoor meetings were held in a number of towns and cities across the United Kingdom, badges representing the Angel of Peace were sold and banners saying 'Spades not Guns', 'No More War' and 'I want my Daddy' were carried by children.[111] The leaders were mainly former suffragists or suffragettes such as Charlotte Despard, Emmeline Pethick Lawrence or else political activists and trade unionists like Maud Royden and Margaret Bondfield.

These pacifists met with great hostility: newspapers rarely advertised their meetings; police banned their demonstrations, and sometimes supporters of the war used violence against the women who dared to protest against it.[112] Women pacifists were called traitors, spied upon, harassed and sometimes imprisoned. When Margaret Bondfield spoke at a woman's peace demonstration in Lancashire, Bondfield 'could scarcely be heard owing to the opposition, the jeering, and the singing of patriotic songs. Some sods were thrown, and the meeting had to close'.[113] Successive Defence of the Realm Act (DORA) rulings made anti-war campaigners liable to imprisonment. The peace activist Alice Wheeldon was imprisoned for ten years for allegedly wanting to kill Lloyd George and helping conscientious objectors hide from the military authorities.[114] As Jill Liddington points out, the Women's Peace Crusade, despite only attracting a minority of women, was the 'first truly popular campaign linking feminism and anti-militarism'.[115]

Some Irish feminists took it further and fought against the British. During the war, Constance Markiewicz supported armed rebellion against the British government and took part in the 1916 Easter Rising as second in command of a battalion of the Irish Citizen's Army. Her troops faced a week of intense fighting before surrendering. Markievicz was sentenced to death, but because she was a woman, it was commuted to life imprisonment. Markiewicz, in a Cat and Mouse chase, spent the next few years in and out of prison. She was released in June 1917 after a general amnesty, only to be rearrested for her involvement in another plot and imprisoned again.

Conclusion

Undoubtedly, the war upset the votes for women campaign, and many suffrage campaigners redirected their energy to wartime direct action. Nonetheless, the campaign for the vote did not disappear: the NUWSS and the WFL continued to hold suffrage meetings throughout the war. The Stirling Catholic Women's Suffrage Society wrote to their local MPs urging support for women's suffrage; others advocated votes for all over the age of 21.[116]

War made everyone political. In this respect, the somewhat artificial distinction between women activists and nonactivists disappeared as in a kind of herd conformity everyone in the country was recruited to active service. Not all women agreed with the country's militarisation and protested against what was seen as an imperialistic venture.

The war upset electoral politics too. Thousands of sailors and soldiers were disenfranchised because they did not meet the residency requirements needed. The government, realising the potential political upset if members of the armed forces were not able to vote, decided on a complete review of the electoral process. The Speaker's Conference was set up to examine parliamentary reform. It recommended votes for women but limited the franchise to certain groups. On February 1918, the Representation of the People Act became law awarding the vote to all men over 21 and to women over 30 who were on the local government register or married to men who were. Over one-third of women remained disenfranchised until 1928: mostly young, single and working-class women, live-in domestic servants and women over the age of 30 who lived with their parents or in furnished rooms. But a new era was about to begin, and freshly confident women turned their attention to remedying other injustices.

Notes

1. Paula Bartley, *Emmeline Pankhurst*, Routledge, 2002; *Votes for Women*, Hodder and Stoughton (third edition) 2007 and June Purvis, *Emmeline Pankhurst*, Routledge, 2002.
2. Ray Strachey, *Women's Suffrage and Women's Service*, London and National Society for Women's Service, 1927.

3. Krista Cowman, *'Mrs Brown is a Man and a Brother'*, *Women in Merseyside's Political Organisations, 1890–1920*, Liverpool University Press, 2004.
4. *Daily Mail*, 1 July 1915, p. 4.
5. *The Suffragette*, 11 June 1915, p. 137.
6. Ibid., 2 July 1915, p. 184.
7. *Daily Mail*, 7 July 1915, p. 3.
8. Ibid., 6 July 1915, p. 3.
9. *Jus-Suffragii*, 1 October 1916, quoted in Angela K Smith, *Suffrage Discourse in Britain during the First World War*, Ashgate, 2005.
10. Angela K Smith, *Suffrage Discourse in Britain during the First World War*, Ashgate, 2005.
11. *The Common Cause*, 14 August 1914, p. 391.
12. MSWS Executive Report, 6 October 1914.
13. *The Common Cause*, 20 November 1914, p. 554.
14. Sarah Pedersen, *The Scottish Suffragettes and the Press*, Palgrave Macmillan, 2017, p. 159.
15. Ibid., p. 160.
16. *Burnley News*, 22 August 1914, p. 5.
17. *Manchester Courier and Lancashire General Advertiser*, 20 August 1914, p. 4.
18. *The Common Cause*, 19 March 1915.
19. *Daily Herald*, 13 February 1915, p. 1.
20. Margaret Bondfield, *A Life's Work*, Hutchinson, 1948, p. 144.
21. Gertjan de Groot and Marlou Shcrover, *Women Workers and Technological Change in Europe in the nineteenth and twentieth centuries*, Taylor and Francis, 1995.
22. See Deborah Thom, *Nice Girls and Rude Girls, Women Workers in World War 1*, I. B. Tauris, 2000, for an overview of women's experiences in war.
23. *AUCE Journal*, September 1917.
24. UK Parliament, accessed 9 January 2021.
25. 'The Trials and Tribulations of the Lancaster and Morecambe Munitionettes', *Documenting Dissent*, accessed 7 January 2021.
26. See Myra Baillie, *The Women of Red Clydeside: Women Munitions Workers in the West of Scotland During the First World War*, D.Phil, McMaster University, 2002.
27. Ibid.
28. *The Times*, 10 July 1918, p. 3.
29. *Dundee Courier*, 6 December 1915, p. 5.
30. Margaret Bondfield, Labour Party Conference, Bristol, 1916.
31. *Daily Express*, 28 January 1916, p. 6.
32. See Christine Collette, *The Newer Eve, Women, Feminists and the Labour Party*, Palgrave, 2009, for a discussion of the SJC.
33. She had been found guilty of 'disarray' three times and had been imprisoned.
34. *The Times*, 11 August 1914, p. 3.
35. Diane Atkinson, *Elsie and Mari Go to War*, Preface, 2009, p. 3. The Duchess of Sunderland and the Marchioness of Londonderry were two such women.
36. Lucy Noakes, 'Women's Military Service in the First World War', *Women, War And Society, 1914–1918*, Imperial War Museum, internet accessed 17 January 2020.
37. Ibid.

38. Women's Emergency Corps, Half Yearly Report, August 1914 to 31 January 1915; *The Gentlewoman*, 29 August 1914.
39. Ibid.
40. *Sheffield Daily Telegraph*, 26 March 1915.
41. *Common Cause*, 19 March 1915.
42. WEC Annual Report, August 1914–January 1915.
43. *Votes for Women*, October 9th 1914, p. 13.
44. Michael Page, *Dora Black: A volunteer with the Women's Emergency Corp*, Surrey Heritage, 27 June 2007.
45. *Common Cause*, 12 March 1915.
46. Lucy Noakes, 'Women's Military Service in the First World War', *Women, War And Society, 1914–1918*, Imperial War Museum, internet accessed 17 January 2020.
47. Ibid.
48. Lady Lugard, 'The Work of the War Refugee Committee', *Journal of the Royal Society of Arts*, March 1915.
49. Lucy Noakes, 'Women's Military Service in the First World War', *Women, War And Society, 1914–1918*, Imperial War Museum, accessed 17 January 2020.
50. Interview with Dolly Shepherd, WEC member, Imperial War Museum.
51. Lucy Noakes, 'Women's Military Service in the First World War', *Women, War And Society, 1914–1918*, Imperial War Museum, internet accessed 17 January 2020.
52. Interview with Dolly Shepherd, WEC member, Imperial War Museum.
53. See Diane Atkinson, *Elsie and Mari Go To War*, Preface, 2009.
54. *The Vote*, 4 September 1914, p. 306.
55. Diane Atkinson, *Elsie and Mari Go to War*, Preface, 2009.
56. Elsie Knocker quoted in Gill Thomas, *Life on All Fronts, Women in the First World War*, Cambridge University Press, 1989, p. 34.
57. Interview with Mairi Chisholm, Imperial War Museum.
58. Mairi Chisholm, quoted in 'Scottish Women's Hospital Unit', *Spartacus Educational*, internet accessed 16 January 2020.
59. *Clifton Society*, 17 September 1914, p. 9.
60. *Common Cause*, 12 May 1916, p. 3.
61. *The Globe*, 23 October 1914, p. 3.
62. *The Lancashire Daily Post*, 5 August 1919, p. 8.
63. Angela K Smith, *Suffrage Discourse in Britain during the First World War*, Ashgate, 2005.
64. Sarah Pedersen, *The Scottish Suffragettes and the Press*, Palgrave Macmillan, 2017, p. 163.
65. Quoted in Angela K Smith, *Suffrage Discourse in Britain during the First World War*, Ashgate, 2005, p. 85.
66. After the war, Evelina Haverfield and her partner Vera Holme built a children's health centre in Bajina Basta. Elsie Inglis was awarded the Order of the White Eagle, the highest military medal awarded in Serbia at the time and the first woman to receive the award. She is also commemorated on the £50 Scottish bank note.
67. Helena Gleichen quoted in Kathryn Atwood, *Women Heroes of World War 1: 16 Remarkable Resisters, Soldiers, Spies and Medics*, Chicago Review Press, 2014.
68. Dix Noonon Web Auction catalogue, July 2017.

69. Ibid.
70. Ibid.
71. Ibid., July 2017.
72. After the war, her body was exhumed and brought back to Britain. She was reburied in Norwich Cathedral.
73. See National Archives, Records of the Security Service, KV2 822, for a file on Edith Cavell.
74. *The Mercury*, 28 November 1919, p. 4.
75. Lawrence and Wishart, 2015, 2nd edition.
76. *The Reading Observer*, 7 October 1916.
77. Maggie Andrews, *The Acceptable Face of Feminism*, Lawrence and Wishart, 2015 (2nd edition), p. 42.
78. Julia Laite, *Common Prostitutes and Ordinary Citizens, Commercial Sex in London, 1885–1960*, Palgrave Macmillan, 2012, p. 123.
79. Ibid.
80. Ibid.
81. See Louise Jackson, *Women Police, Gender, Welfare and Surveillance in the Twentieth Century*, MUP, 2006, for an in-depth survey of women's involvement in policing work.
82. Marc Brodie, 'Boyle, Constance Antonina', *DNB*, 2004.
83. Philippa Levine '"Walking the Streets in a Way No Decent Woman Should": Women Police in World War 1', *The Journal of Modern History*, Vol 66, March 1994, pp. 34–78.
84. *The Vote*, 3 October 1919, p. 348.
85. Gail Braybon and Penny Summerfield, *Out of the Cage, Women's Experiences in Two World Wars*, Pandora, 1987, p. 109.
86. Philippa Levine '"Walking the Streets in a Way No Decent Woman Should": Women Police in World War 1', *The Journal of Modern History*, Vol 66, March 1994, p. 45.
87. *The Leeds Mercury*, 26 July 1917, p. 7.
88. Pat Thane, 'Unmarried Motherhood in Twentieth-Century England', *Women's History Review*, vol 20 No 1 2011.
89. Martin Pugh, *Women and the Women's Movement in Britain*, Palgrave Macmillan, 2000, p. 18. See Pat Thane and Tanya Evans, *Sinners? Scroungers? Saints? Unmarried Motherhood in Twentieth Century England*, OUP, 2012, which details the rise of 'illegitimate' births and its impact on society.
90. Laura Mayall, 'Suffrage and Political Activity', *Women, War and Society, 1914–1918*, Imperial War Museum, internet accessed 17 January 2020.
91. Home Office Report, quoted in *The Woman's Dreadnought*, 12 December 1914.
92. Gail Braybon and Penny Summerfield, *Out of the Cage, Women's Experiences in Two World Wars*, Pandora, 1987.
93. See Janis Lomas 'Soldiering On: War Widows in First World War Britain' in Maggie Andrews and Janis Lomas, *The Home Front in Britain, Images, Myths and Forgotten Experiences since 1914*, Palgrave Macmillan, 2014.
94. *Woman's Dreadnought*, 10 April 1915.
95. Ibid., 11 September 1915, p. 315.
96. *The Labour Leader*, 28 October 1915, p. 9.
97. *The Edinburgh Evening News*, 7 October 1915, p. 5.
98. *The Labour Leader*, 18 November 1915, p. 8.

99. *The Woman's Dreadnought*, 16 October 1915, p. 344.

> In the tenements o' Glesga in the year one nine one five
> It was one lang bloody struggle tae keep ourselves alive
> We were cootin oot the coppers tae buy wor scraps o food
> When the landlords pit the rent up just because they could, A 'the factories were hummin'
> there was overtime galore
> But the wages they were driven doon tae subsidise the war
> Out came Mrs Barbour fae her wee bit single end
> She said I'll organise the lassies if I cannae raise the men
>
> Mrs Barbour made a poster saying 'we'll no pay higher rent
> Then chapped on every door of every Govan tenement
> She said 'pit this in the windae an' when ye hea me bang the drum
> We'll run oot and chase the factor a' the way tae kingdom come'. (A Hulett, *Mary Barbour's Army*)

100. Margaret Bondfield, *A Life's Work*, Hutchinson, 1948, p. 137.
101. MB Notebook, undated, Archives and Special Collections Library, Vassar College Libraries, Box 12, Folder 16.
102. Margaret Bondfield, *A Life's Work*, Hutchinson, 1948, p. 137.
103. Ibid., p. 138.
104. Ibid., p. 152.
105. Jill Liddington, *The Long Road to Greenham, Feminism and Anti-Militarism in Britain since 1820*, Virago, 1989.
106. Clara Zetkin (1857–1933) was born into a Protestant German family. She was a socialist feminist, one of the leading figures of the far-left, a co-founder of the Independent Social Democratic Party of Germany and later a member of the German Communist Party. She was forced to leave Germany when Hitler came to power, and went to the USSR.
107. Margaret Bondfield, Marion Phillips, Mary Longman and Ada Salter.
108. *The Scotsman*, 6 April 1915, p. 8.
109. Ibid., 10 April 1915, p. 3.
110. Gill Thomas, *Life on All Fronts, Women in the First World War Women in the First World War*, CUP, 1989.
111. Ibid.
112. *Evening Despatch*, 13 August 1917, p. 7.
113. Jill Liddington, *The Long Road to Greenham, Feminism and Anti-Militarism in Britain since 1820*, Virago, 1989.
114. Ibid., p. 129.
115. Sarah Pedersen, *The Scottish Suffragettes and the Press*, Palgrave Macmillan, 2017.

CHAPTER 4

The Not-So-Roaring Twenties: 1918–1929

No sooner had the First World War ended than countries were hit by a deadly global pandemic which infected about a third of the world's population, killing between 20 and 50 million worldwide and approximately 250,000 in the United Kingdom. Called the Spanish flu, it was like the virus that swept the world in 2020; only this time it took the lives of young adults rather than the elderly. Nonetheless, the Liberal prime minister, Lloyd George, optimistically promised to create a land fit for heroes.

For young women like Rose Smith, such promises rang hollow. On 9 October 1919, this 20-year-old laundry worker was caught in the flame of a boiler fire and burned around the face and arm. The injury was not considered serious, and she continued at work. Soon septic poisoning set in, and she died a week later. Her employer denied culpability, insisting that Rose had no right to be near the boiler and even accused her of trespassing. Eventually, after an intervention by her trade union, Rose's employer paid £125 to her family.[1]

Trade Union Activism

Even without the inbuilt dangers, laundry work was hot, backbreaking and exhausting. The air was thick with steam, the floors swilling with water: laundry workers' feet were generally wet. Compounding these unhealthy and hazardous conditions, the pay was not sufficient to live on. Now a trade union activist, Ellen Wilkinson decided there was distinct room for improvement. In 1917, she fought hard to set up a Laundry Board to fix minimum rates of pay and maximum hours of work. In November 1920, the Board negotiated an age-related pay scale: 12s a week for those under 13, rising to 30s for those over 18 years of age, and a 48-hour week for all.[2] Employers disobeyed or tried to circumvent the law, prompting women to take action. In June 1924, 300 workers at Edinburgh's Co-operative Society went on strike to reduce their working hours from the illegal 60-hour week imposed by their employers.³ The strike was 'satisfactorily settled' when their hours were reduced to the legal limit of 48 hours.⁴

Faced with low pay and poor working conditions, women joined unions to fight for their rights. In 1919, for the first time ever, women bedmakers in the all-male Cambridge colleges—at Trinity, John's, Corpus Christi, Jesus, Magdalene—joined a union set up by the National Federation of Women Workers (NFWW) to ask for better pay, shorter hours and improved working conditions. They hoped that the 'heads of the colleges will deal promptly and adequately' with their demands and asked that undergraduates 'will be resolute in insisting that the women upon whom their comfort depends shall not be underpaid or overworked'.⁵ There is no evidence that Cambridge bedmakers went on strike to achieve their goal, even though strikes were common across the private sector. Julie Arnot claims that 'more days were lost through strike action in 1919 than were lost during the period of the "Labour Unrest" of 1910–1914 and the greatest ever number of strikes were recorded in 1920'.⁶

In early 1920, women in the catering trade, who were paid subsistence wages for working long, unsociable hours, went on strike in Glasgow for better pay and union recognition. Wages were not only meagre—under 10s a week— but waitresses were fined for a range of misdemeanours: 1s for breaking a plate, 9p for breaking a cup, 6p for a saucer, 2s for a wine glass and 3d for being late.⁷ In May, women fish-curers at Grimsby went on strike, some demonstrated angrily outside their workplace, some smashed windows of the British Fish Curing Company where non-unionised staff remained at work.⁸ In August, Blackpool hotels and restaurants closed their doors to holidaymakers when a strike by waiters and waitresses left them without staff. The women were the most militant. One newspaper commented, 'Never call them the gentle sex again. They struck terror wherever they went. At one time, some raided the few remaining public bars which were still open, broke into the kitchen at the Manchester Hotel breaking glasses and smashing tables'.⁹ The Catering Trades Union negotiated better pay and conditions and the women returned to work.

One of the most publicised strikes took place in May 1920, when 400 employees at John Lewis' department store went on a 'fresh-air strike' in protest at not being allowed to leave the premises during working hours. Moreover, shop assistants still experienced low wages and inadequate working conditions despite the pre-war campaigns of women like Margaret Bondfield. Young women employed at large prestigious stores still lived in, were forced to obey petty rules, and paid £25 a year or less and no matter how 'hard and unjust the treatment … they were absolutely powerless to defend themselves'.¹⁰ As more and more assistants joined the Shop Assistants' Union, they became strong enough to take action to improve their pay and humiliating working conditions. The strike at John Lewis was almost unanimous, only 60 workers remained in the store and the business nearly collapsed. The female strikers gained support from across the class and political spectrum. The National Union of Railwaymen boycotted the firm and instructed its members not to deliver or collect goods from John Lewis. Nancy Astor wrote expressing sympathy because she had 'always felt very strongly on this subject, and I believe the struggle for better conditions is a great cause'.[11] Over £1000 was collected in support of the strikers. Queen Mary gave a large donation. Mr John Lewis, the owner, was unyielding, refused to negotiate and declined to meet MPs or trade union representatives. Unsympathetic to his core, Mr Lewis threatened the strikers and told the 200 women who lived-in to quit their accommodation, thus leaving them homeless—local residents were entreated to offer temporary accommodation.[12] Led by Hilda Canham, the strike lasted nearly six weeks before a settlement was negotiated. Shop assistants were given the right to leave the premises on their ¾-hour break, and live-in conditions improved. In 1929, Mr Lewis' son Spedan Lewis, who had replaced his father as head of the organisation, initiated a partnership scheme giving staff a share in the profits and a role in decision-making.

In 1921, the British economy collapsed, and unions fought hard against reductions in pay and deteriorating working conditions. In May 1922, 2000 women boot and shoe workers in Leicester went on strike in protest at pay cuts.[13] Newspaper reported that the streets were 'gay with girls, ranging in age from 16 to 35, who walk arm-in-arm shop gazing and making the most of their temporary holiday. Each wears a tiny brass shoe brooch, a sign of her union'.[14] The union ordered the women back to work, only to be 'greeted with ironical cheers and laughter'.[15] Eventually, the firms agreed not to impose the pay cut.

On Monday 3 May 1926, strike action reached its peak when the TUC called a general strike in support of the coal miners who had had their wages reduced. Millions of women and men stopped work. Labour women activists organised flying squads of speakers supporting the strike. In stark contrast, a number of suffrage activists were in the opposite camp, driving cars and motorcycles to transport women to work and thus undermine the miners' action.[16] Just before the strike, the former WSPU leader Flora Drummond organised a demonstration and a meeting at the Royal Albert Hall, a meeting which was marshalled by members of the British Fascist party. She beseeched women to continue working in any future strike.[17] Five years earlier, Flora Drummond had helped set up the Women's Guild of Empire, a 'patriotic', non-party league which adopted the slogan of 'Peace, Unity and Concord'. Drummond saw the Guild as a way to entice working-class women away from the Labour Party and its allegedly damaging influence. To this end, she wrote an article for the *Sunday Express* urging women to persuade their husbands to keep working; otherwise wives would stop doing the cleaning and the cooking. The women's police force recruited 1000 women to help break the strike action.

After nine days, the TUC called off the strike and everyone, apart from the miners, returned to work. The miners, demanding 'not a penny off the pay, not a minute off the day', remained on strike for a further six months. By now, the Conservatives were in office.[18] The minister of health, Neville Chamberlain, vowed that striking miners would receive 'not one scrap of assistance' and reduced outdoor relief to below unemployment benefit. Immediately, Labour women activists set up the Women's Committee for the Relief of Miners' Wives and Children to raise money for miners' families most in need. There were pitiable accounts of children who were too hungry to walk to school, of others whose boots were in pawn and who had to go barefoot to the soup kitchens, of babies whose features bore the mark of coming death from malnutrition and of emaciated women who went without food so that their children could eat. Ellen Wilkinson became chair of the Committee and joined with Labour colleagues Margaret Bondfield, Susan Lawrence and Marion Phillips and others in fundraising and collecting food to feed the families of miners. It came to be known as the 'industrial Red Cross'.

A number of feminists across the political spectrum were sympathetic: Conservative MP Nancy Astor remarked that she would be a 'red-hot communist' if she had to endure the working conditions of miners; the Christian, pacifist and suffragist activist Maude Royden spoke of the need for both government and employers to recognise that the miners were part of the 'brotherhood of man'. Many women took part in fundraising activities: the actress Sybil Thorndike spoke alongside five miners' wives at a large London hall; the Liberal MP Margaret Wintringham appealed in *The Times* for donations to help the women and children; Nancy Astor broadcast on the radio to raise money; and the Save the Children Fund raised a special fund to provide food and milk for nursing and expectant mothers and children under school age. Not all women sympathisers were famous figures. The wife of a striking Welsh miner, Beatrice Green, set to work fundraising for the Women's Committee. She organised soup kitchens to feed 1600 people every day in her home town of Abertillery, helped provide food and blankets for pregnant women and organised the temporary fostering of children.[19] By the end of May, the Women's Committee was raising over £2000 a day nationally; by January 1927, when the Fund closed, it had raised £313,844 (the equivalent in 2021 of £19 million).[20] The success of the committee and other appeals led to unfortunate and unforeseen results—the money, food and clothing collected was deducted from the women's state benefits.[21] In December, six months after the General Strike ended, the hungry miners were forced to return to work on the owners' terms.

Parliamentary Activism

In her book, *Unshackled: The Story of How We Won the Vote*, Christabel Pankhurst commented, 'the World War was over. The Peace was signed. The women's war was over. The vote was won. A new chapter was opening.'[22] The WSPU was dissolved. In November 1918, more than 8.5 million women over the age of 30 were given the vote; at the same time, Parliament gave women over 21 the right to stand for Parliament. It appeared illogical: women without the vote could still be elected as MPs. The 24-year-old Jennie Lee, for example, was elected to Parliament before she was old enough to cast her ballot. However, as Mari Takayanagi points out, men had long been able to stand for Parliament before they could vote. Nonetheless, for many former suffrage activists, these inequities provided new crusading challenges: to help women become MPs and to redress suffrage inequalities.

Activists campaigned for women to be elected to Parliament, regardless of their political affiliation. In December 1918, the first election where women were eligible to stand, 17 women out of a total of 1623 candidates put themselves forward.[23] Despite the strenuous campaigning of women's groups, only one woman was successful. Christabel Pankhurst, with a well-funded, Coalition supported campaign and widespread and sympathetic press coverage, lost the election in Smethwick to a Labour male candidate.[24] So too did a number of other well-known activists, including Emmeline Pethwick-Lawrence, Charlotte Despard and Mary Macarthur. And in a cruel twist of irony, the only woman who was elected—Constance Markiewicz—did not take her seat in the House of Commons. Constance Markiewicz, former suffrage activist and sister of Eva Gore-Booth, was a convicted prisoner who had been jailed for treason and sentenced to death for killing a police officer and wounding a British soldier during the 1916 Irish Easter Rising.[25] While Markiewicz was in Holloway prison, she stood for election as a Sinn Féin candidate which was committed to establish an independent republic. Sinn Féin won 73 out of 101 seats in Ireland, refused to sit in the House of Commons and established its own parliament in Dublin. This was the beginning of nationalist movements across the Empire that led to its eventual demise.

The first woman to take her seat in Parliament won her seat in a by-election. On 15 November 1919, the American-born Nancy Astor—now Viscountess Astor—was elected to Parliament for a Plymouth constituency. 'The joy', wrote *The Woman's Leader*, 'that the first woman had been elected to Parliament was tempered, for many of us, by disappointment that she should be represented by someone entirely outside our own world; someone ... as an extraordinarily brilliant and witty society hostess than as a serious or experienced politician'.[26] They had hoped that someone more seriously inclined like Mary Macarthur, Emmeline Pethick-Lawrence, Charlotte Despard or the charismatic Christabel Pankhurst would be the first woman to be elected. However, Nancy Astor defied expectations. Shortly after she took her seat, Astor wrote to the Women's Freedom League (WFL), saying that 'since I am the first woman to take her seat in the House of Commons, I feel that I have a special opportunity of helping Women's Societies'.[27] In her letter, she stated that she was anxious to know the WFL's opinions, and asked them to send her their literature and to keep her informed of future activity. Astor was determined to do her best to be useful to women and insisted that 'the fact of having a woman in Parliament ought to be of considerable advantage to women's movements' because she could ask questions and afford 'an easier channel for making representations to Government'. Astor also wrote to the *Common Cause* declaring that she felt it a 'great responsibility to be the first woman to sit in Parliament and that she would need all the help she could get'. She hoped that 'we women shall be able to stand up for what we believe in without regard for party politics'.[28] She was true to her word, employing the former suffragist Ray Strachey as her political secretary to advise her on women's issues. Newspapers reported that Astor had brains, wit, great wealth and rank along with a fervid desire to help the lowly.[29] She said she was 'longing for socialism' but that she wanted the 'Socialism of Christ, not the Socialism of the Independent Labour Party'.[30]

In Spring 1921, Nancy Astor invited representatives from all the leading women's organisations to her grand house in St James' Square to meet sympathetic male MPs. Here she set up a Consultative Committee whereby women and MPs could meet informally once a month and chat about political issues. It became a political soirée, of the kind that used to be organised by nineteenth-century society hostesses, rather than a crusading group, largely because Nancy Astor had a 'strong feeling about the value of personal contact between members of Parliament and women'.[31] Labour women's organisations did not participate.

Feminist activists had initially viewed Astor's election sceptically, yet by 1923 they were praising her untiring readiness to promote women's interests, even though they were fully aware that Nancy Astor's parliamentary style was idiosyncratic—she was infamous for interrupting MPs and making audible, often acerbic, remarks while Members were speaking. Her enemies called her 'Lady Dis-Astor'. Activists liked her because she broke party barriers and befriended the women MPs who arrived later. In 1921, Astor was joined by the Liberal Margaret Wintringham, a former NUWSS activist, and in 1923 the Conservative and former actress Mabel Hilton Philipson, both of whom had won their seats in a by-election. In the 1923 General election, eight women were elected, a success attributed to the National Union of Societies for Equal Citizenship's (NUSEC) campaigning efforts (Fig. 4.1).[32]

Three of them, Arabella Susan Lawrence, Dorothy Jewson and Margaret Bondfield, were the first Labour women MPs, all activists with a long history of fighting for workers' and women's rights. One was a Conservative, Kathleen, Duchess of Atholl, president of the Perthshire Women's Unionist Association and organiser of district nursing; one was a Liberal, Vera, Lady Terrington. At the next general election in October 1924, all three Labour women lost their seats as did the two Liberals. Only one Labour woman, the former suffragist and trade union organiser Ellen Wilkinson, was elected. In 1926, Susan Lawrence and Margaret Bondfield returned to Parliament, both winning seats at a bye-election, as did the Conservative Gwendolen Guinness and the president of the Women's National Liberal Federation, Hilda Runciman. In 1929, 14 women were elected, 9 of them new to Parliament, all of them activists in one form or another before they became MPs.[33] All, regardless of political affiliation, were welcomed by Nancy Astor, who regularly hosted events for them.

What is striking about these early women MPs is the way that they worked with activists and each other to further women's rights. Undeniably, this whole decade is unique in the remarkable and impressive sense that women activists and parliamentarians worked closely together over common concerns. It could not have happened before because there were no women MPs and would not

Fig. 4.1 Seven of the eight women: Dorothy Jewson, Susan Lawrence, Vera Terrington, Margaret Bondfield (L-R standing) Margaret Wintringham, Nancy Astor, Mabel Hilton Philipson (L-R sitting) (Courtesy of Christine Hankinson, Leeds Postcards)

happen so frequently in the future because party loyalty started to claim priority over female solidarity. In these years, women's organisations made great efforts to encourage the few female MPs to back their causes in Parliament: for instance, Eva Hubback acted as NUSEC's parliamentary secretary, quickly becoming an effective lobbyist. Women from across the political spectrum—the Conservative Nancy Astor and the Duchess of Atholl, Labour's Ellen Wilkinson, the Liberal MP Margaret Wintringham and the Independent Eleanor Rathbone worked together on a number of women's issues. Not all women felt the same need to collaborate: Margaret Bondfield replied, 'Emphatically No', when asked whether she would cooperate with Nancy Astor.

Political Parties and Activism

Critically, two-thirds of women were now voters, and political parties began to look at these newly enfranchised women with sharpened interest. The Conservative Party quickly altered its structure to accommodate women. The Women's Unionist and Tariff Reform Association was disbanded and replaced by the Central Women's Advisory Committee, a new Conservative Party women's organisation under the leadership of Tory activist and wife of a party whip,

Caroline Bridgeman. She set about forming women's Conservative branches across the country.[34] In 1921, it held its first conference in 1921 and in 1928 affiliated to the Conservative Party. Under Bridgeman's guidance, the Conservative Party made it mandatory for at least one woman from each constituency to be chosen as a delegate to national conference, thus assuring a large number—36% in 1927—of women at Conservative Party conferences. Consequently, the look of a Conservative Party conference with rows full of women contrasted sharply with the masculine ones of Labour with its rows of male trade unionists. In addition, the male chair of the Conservative Party increased the number of women on the National Executive by about a third, made Lady Iveagh vice chair of the National Union and Margorie Maxse deputy principal agent of the party. By 1928, there were nearly a million women members, far more than the other political parties combined. In the lead-up to the 1929 election, Conservative women were out in force, campaigning across the country with their Conservative message. Reports from the constituencies showed that 'the battalions of Mr Baldwin's feminine supporters' were becoming bigger and bigger.[35] In one constituency, over 103,000 envelopes were addressed by voluntary women helpers.[36] These women directly appealed to the female voter. Mrs Amery, wife of the secretary of state for the dominions, maintained that Conservative women wanted 'no more wars, and no more general strikes. We want peace and goodwill between all classes at home and between the nations'.[37] They worked hard in support of their male MPs. Mrs Lucy Baldwin, wife of the prime minister, was particularly energetic, founding the Unionist Women's Institute to attract working-class women to Conservatism. In the period of just a few days, she attended an Early Closing Association lunch in the city, opened a bazaar at Tunbridge Wells, received guests at a London ball organised by the Women Unionists of Wales, laid a foundation stone at Hampstead Health Institute, broadcast on behalf of the National Birthday Fund for Maternity Services and attended the opening of the 'Lucy Baldwin Maternity Hospital'. Her motto was, 'Let us do all the good we can, to all the folk we can, in all the ways we can.'[38] Conservatives tried hard to recruit the new woman voter: one prospective candidate for South East St Pancras wrote a letter to each new female voter congratulating her on the appearance of her name in the new register as a result of his Conservative Government's Equal Franchise Act.[39]

Labour appointed nine regional officers to set up women's sections, and within a few years practically every local branch of the Labour Party had a women's society. Labour women also increased their influence in their party through the Women's Labour League (WLL), which was headed by a politically skilled chief woman officer, Dr Marion Phillips. Four WLL members were elected to the party's National Executive, the governing body of the Labour Party—all of whom were well-established figures in the Labour movement: Ethel Snowden, Ethel Bentham, Mary Macarthur and Susan Lawrence.[40] Undoubtedly, these women helped shape Labour's commitment to social policies such as widows' pensions and maternity payments, and they tried (unsuccessfully) to make their voices heard over birth control and family allowances. In 1927, there were around 300,000 members of the women's section.[41]

In addition, after the war almost 250,000 women joined a left-wing group, usually the Women's Co-operative Guild, the Independent Labour Party, the Communist Party or the Labour Party. Many joined more than one organisation. These women generally came from the 'respectable' section of the working-class who were angry at the poverty which surrounded them. One spoke of watching a family being 'thrown out into the street, furniture and clothes taken away, left only what they wore'; another spoke of seeing children dressed in rags and walking barefoot; another of families without hot water or a lavatory; yet another of a naked woman laying starving on a mattress.[42] They wanted to change this disgraceful situation and improve the lives of the poorest and most vulnerable.

Membership of the Women's National Liberal Federation (WNLF) dropped after the war to just over 95,000, reflecting the decline of the party itself. As Martin Pugh points out, 'many Liberal women felt somewhat alienated from party politics as a result of pre-war controversies ... and preferred to work within the independent, non-party women's organisations.'[43] Indeed, when the WNLF put forward a programme which included many of the demands of feminist activists such as divorce law reform, women police, equal guardianship and equal pay, none was included in any Liberal election manifesto.

An ultra-nationalist group was newly formed. On 6 May 1923, Miss Rotha Beryl Lintorn-Orman founded the British Fascisti, as an extra-parliamentary para-military movement. Within a few months, she had (allegedly) enrolled over a quarter million members, all of whom were prepared to fight the Red communist scourge which she believed was strangling Britain.[44] The British Fascisti set up Children's Clubs: at one meeting in Belfast, over 80 children were introduced to fascist ideas. At the time, it was seen as little more than 'Conservatism with knobs on' as it encouraged its members to vote Conservative, supported the Orange cause in Ireland and advocated an unblinking, unthinking nationalism.[45] Miss Lintorn-Orman loved militia uniforms and officialdom: women members wore all-black uniforms. Linton-Orman had been active in the First World War, first as Women's Ambulance Service and later with the Scottish Women's Hospital Group, receiving the Croix de Charité for her work.

In December 1926, the band of the British Legion welcomed a large audience at the Drill Hall, Folkestone, who had come to listen to Miss Rotha Lintorn-Orman. In her speech, she claimed that her party was not a political party but a patriotic party which stood for three things: the king, the British Empire and Christianity. She urged women not to buy German and foreign goods, to oppose the Communist and Labour Party which taught 'the most disgusting and revolting blasphemy'[46] and to remove 'aliens' from the British Isles. The meeting ended with the singing of the national anthem. Fortunately, neither she nor her newly named British Fascists Limited were taken seriously, and it virtually collapsed during the 1926 General Strike when its members defected to another strike-breaking organisation.

Others set up nationalist groups to oppose or support imperialism. In 1914, Cumann na mBan (the Women's Council), a woman's group dedicated to fighting for an independent Ireland, had been formed in Dublin and soon spread across the island and to areas in Britain with a significant Catholic population. The Anglo-Irish War (1919–1921) presented women activists with new challenges both on the island of Ireland and in Britain. One branch in Belfast distributed newspapers, raised funds, visited prisoners, transported weapons and found safe houses for Irish Republican Army (IRA) men in hiding. Some like Mary and Elizabeth McClean used their home to shelter fugitives and to distribute weapons like the two cases of semi-automatic pistols sent from America;[47] others like May Laverty and Mary Donnelly helped plant bombs and other explosive devices. Mary Hackett was dismissed when 50 rounds of ammunition and bombs were found at her workplace.[48] In Britain, as Mo Moulton points out, two disparate yet intersecting groups of women—working-class women from the Irish diaspora and middle-class former suffragists—fought against the harsh treatment wrought upon the Irish people by British troops.[49] In England, Cumann na mBan women provided 'crucial safe houses for those on the run and space to store arms and carry on other illegal activities ... it also raised funds and transported guns to Ireland' and helped the IRA in various acts of sabotage.[50] One of its members, Cis Sheehan, 'took many clandestine trips, transporting arms, ammunition and sums of money raised in America to Dublin'.[51] In 1922, Ireland was divided into the independent Irish Free State and the six counties of Ulster which remained under British rule. The consequences were worryingly foreseeable.

At the other end of the political spectrum, female lodges of the Orange Order, a Conservative Protestant group which wanted to remain part of Britain, grew exponentially. The Ulster Women's Unionist Council (UWUC), founded before the war, became the largest women's political organisation in Northern Ireland. It was notoriously anti-Catholic: Catholics, and even women who married Catholics, were not allowed to join. The UWUC mostly engaged in hosting fundraising events and helping in election campaigns, but they also stood for election themselves and took part in anti-Catholic riots, its members willing to throw bottles and stones at their opponents.[52] In 1921, Julia McMordie became the first Ulster Unionist MP to be elected to Stormont, the Northern Ireland Parliament.[53] Branches were formed in Scotland and England too. Glasgow's Orange-women focused on getting sympathisers elected to Education authorities because they feared that the Roman Catholic Church might exert undue influence on state schools. Their language—'Rome on the Rates' and the 'Papist Menace'—reflects a strong anti-Catholic persuasion as does their policy to 'secure the return of good, sound Protestants' in the elections.[54] Demonstrations were common: on 12 July 1927, 10,000 marches turned out in Liverpool for the annual procession. Despite the pouring rain, the women of Liverpool Orange Lodge (LOL), dressed in white with an orange sash like those in Fig. 4.2, marched with their men through the streets of the city, accompanied by bands of brass, fife and concertinas. Many dressed

Fig. 4.2 Chair (second left sitting) of Liverpool Orange Lodge circa 1930s with family (Courtesy of author)

up as Queen Mary, the wife of King William of Orange. Hundreds of 'little children, girls, and young women were clad in the flimsiest of white apparel'. It was, one paper commented, like a suffrage procession.[55]

Local Political Activism

Women activists played a significant role in local government too, as councillors, Poor Law Guardians, magistrates and on Boards of Education. In the 1920s, approximately 500 women from the Co-operative Guild, Labour and Independent Labour Party (ILP) became either councillors or magistrates. In 1925, 20 women were elected to the London County Council, and some of them, like Susan Lawrence and Ruth Dalton, were well-known Labour activists. It is clear that these Labour women 'improved the quality of life for untold members of their class who were always on the verge of being overwhelmed by the problems associated with urban poverty'.[56] These newly elected local councillors and Poor Law Guardians often made a huge difference to the lives of individuals. Councils had important responsibilities such as housing, education, public health, maternity and child welfare. Hannah Mitchell, a local Labour councillor, focused on the health and well-being of women and children. One achievement was to build a washhouse where 'housewives could hire a deep tub, have plenty of hot water, hot-air dryers and ironing tables to do their laundry'.[57] Mitchell's example is one of many: public swimming baths, hospitals, baby clinics, playgrounds, public lavatories and libraries were built after pressure from women councillors. Pamela Graves argues that Labour women's focus on 'baby clinics, school medical inspection, free milk and meals, more nursery and secondary schools' improved the lives of so many working-class women, achievements that 'have had scant recognition'.[58] Jessie Stephen, a Poor Law Guardian in Bermondsey, eased the punitive conditions in the workhouses by getting rid of the psychologically damaging 'rituals of deference which obliged old people to stand up when a guardian entered the room' as well as the practice of separating unmarried mothers from the rest of women and lecturing them on their so-called sinful lives. She also stopped the practice of inmates eating their meals on uncomfortable benches and replaced them with tables and chairs.[59] These—usually Labour—councillors and Guardians 'improved the quality of life for untold numbers of their class who were always on the verge of being overwhelmed by the problems associated with urban poverty', a branch of political activity that is all too often ignored, and rarely celebrated.[60] Residents in Tottenham would have been grateful to Mrs Kitchener, who won a battle to put bathrooms into local council homes. These women fought against unsympathetic colleagues, a 'strong undercurrent of anti-feminism' and a Conservative government which wanted to keep rates down. In 1921, five women Poor Law Guardians, one of whom was Susan Lawrence, were sent to prison for refusing to lower local authority payments to the destitute.

Activism and Women's Organisations

It used to be argued that when women achieved a limited franchise feminism lost its vital spark. This opinion is now widely discredited—in fact, a 2014 issue of *Women's History Review* was devoted to examining how feminist activism continued, and how policies and practices were adjusted to historically changing circumstances.[61] As Breitenbach and Wright point out, women's organisations in Glasgow and Edinburgh 'demonstrated an enthusiastic engagement' with a variety of issues from women's political representation, to lobbying local governments and developing a range of services targeted at women.[62]

At the time, newspapers predicted that newly enfranchised women would play an important part in shaping the political destiny of the country.[63] The *Daily Mail* urged its women readers to take an interest in the government of the country and to 'make themselves worthy of the name of citizen'.[64] Readers were beseeched to join women's organisations to help solve the numerous post-war problems like housing and infant welfare. After the war, there were at least 130 women's organisations, ranging from women's sections in the established political parties through to organisations like the Women's Institutes (WI) which held firmly to a non-party political stance.[65] The main women's organisations include NUSEC, the Six Point Group,[66] the National Council of Women (NCW) and the London and National Society for Women's Service (previously the London Society for Women's Suffrage Societies) all of which fought for women's rights. There were also several pressure groups: the Married Women's Association, the National Union of Women Teachers, the National Association of Women Civil Servants, the Open-Door Council, the Housewives League which focused on particular issues.[67] Religious groups like the Roman Catholic St Joan's Social and Political Alliance and the Union of Jewish Women and the largest working-class women's organisation, the Women's Co-operative Guild, flourished. All these groups, at different times, worked—at times—together to advance women's rights and in Ireland for independence. In many ways, the post-war women's movement, with its various groups, different crusades and diverse beliefs, was in effect the heir of Victorian feminism, a feminism that had been sidelined because of the fight for the vote.

In 1919, the Women's International League was renamed the Women's International League for Peace and Freedom (WILPF). It enjoyed a membership of over 4000, grouped into 51 local branches. Twenty-five British women—including Charlotte Despard, Ethel Snowden and Ellen Wilkinson—travelled to Zurich for the first post-war meeting of the WILPF. The delegates from the occupied countries were 'scarred and shrivelled by hunger and privation', largely because of a food blockade by the victorious powers. One woman was 'tortured by daily news of her daughter dying of tuberculosis in a sanatorium ... The sanatoria and hospitals had no linen, and babies were born into newspapers, and dressings had to be washed again and again'.[68] In 1919, harrowing images of starving emaciated children and women prompted the WILPF to set up a Save the Children Fund, an organisation that to this day works to reduce child poverty. In 1921, the Fund provided daily meals to 300,000 Russian children who would have starved without its intervention.[69]

The WILPF conference coincided with the publication of the terms of the Treaty of Versailles. Immediately, the conference, with its non-recriminatory stance and its welcoming of all participants regardless of their country of origin, sent a strongly worded criticism of the savage terms imposed on Germany to the Allied Forces gathered at Versailles. The seeds, they argued, of future war were sown by its terms. Their critique was ignored (Fig. 4.3).

In May 1926—the time of the General Strike—a woman's Peace Pilgrimage set out from Carlisle, Cardiff, the Midlands and Lands End, holding meetings in towns and village before meeting up in London. The demonstrators wanted the British government to sign a League of Nations' clause to accept compulsory arbitration when countries were at odds with each other. The pilgrimage was supported by a variety of women's groups: NUSEC, NCW, British Women's Temperance Association, Women's Cooperative Guild, and the National Union of Women Teachers. When the West Country pilgrims marched past a well-known girls' school near Bristol, they saw its garden wall hung with supportive banners and girls from the school shouting support.[70] The women had learned the importance of spectacle from the suffrage movement. The 10,000 strong demonstration that converged on Hyde Park on 19 June made a 'very effective display as they streamed down Piccadilly, with the bright blue of their banners and little fluttering flags ... one section carried small banners

Fig. 4.3 Women's pilgrimage, 1926 (Courtesy of the Women's Library, LSE)

representing all the countries in the League of Nations ... then came a woman riding a white horse and wearing a long blue mantle'.[71] The March ended on 19 June in a mass demonstration in Hyde Park where 10,000 marchers gathered to hear speakers like Emmeline Pethick-Lawrence, Margaret Bondfield, Millicent Fawcett, Margaret Wintringham and Ellen Wilkinson.

Progress and Setbacks

Between 1918 and 1929, there were 21 pieces of legislation which affected women, mostly brought in by a Conservative government.[72] Certainly, politicians appeared more willing to support women's rights both because women were now part of the electorate and because women MPs and women's groups put pressure on them to do so. The reforms listed below were largely achieved because women MPs and activists—many from NUSEC—worked closely together with a few sympathetic men to help change the law. Here they had some notable successes (see below) though not all their campaigns were successful.

> **Acts 1918–1929**
> 1919: *Sex Disqualification (Removal) Act*
>   1920: *The Married Women's Property Act (Scotland)*
>   1922: *Criminal Law Amendment Act; Married Women's Maintenance Act; Infanticide Act*
>   1923: *Matrimonial Causes Act; Bastardy Act*
>   1925: *Guardianship of Infants Act; Widows, Orphans and Old Age Contributory Pensions Act;*
>   Nancy Astor's Bill to reform prostitution laws failed.
>   1928: *Representation of the People Act*
>   1929: *Age of Marriage Act*

Until 1919, the legal system, like that of Parliament, was totally male. Women activists—from suffragists to social purists—expressed concern that 'girls and women were badly served by an all-male legal profession, judiciary, magistracy, police service and penal establishment'.[73] Margaret Nevinson, NUWSS activist and author, commented that legally women were under the jurisdiction of men who 'take them, handle them, try them, sentence them, imprison them (without one woman present, not even in the jury), even hang them by the neck until they are dead'.[74] The Sex Disqualification (Removal) Act changed this by establishing that women could be appointed to any 'public function, civil or judicial office, post or profession'.[75] But permission did not mean acceptance. As Anne Logan argues, although the door was open, 'action was needed to force it wide' and women had to fight hard to be part of the legal profession, either as paid barristers or lawyers or as unpaid magistrates and jurors.[76] Women's organisations like the Six Point Group, the WFL, NUSEC, the National Council of Woman's Public Service and the Magistrates' Committee campaigned and pressurised the various departments to register women as JPs or magistrates. A number of distinguished activists became the first magistrates: Margaret Wynne Nevinson, Lady Denman, Gertude Tuckwell, Beatrice Webb, Margaret Lloyd George, Margaret Wintringham, Mavis Tate are just some of the more famous examples. These newly appointed magistrates, along with their newly appointed solicitor and barrister colleagues, helped activists promote real change, particularly in family law and laws which affected women.

The Law and Sexual Politics

In December 1920, an Edinburgh youth, Hermand Davidson, was sent to prison for six months for 'behaving indecently; towards two girls aged five and six'.[77] It was a clear case of child sexual abuse. However, if a man claimed that he believed the girl was over 16, the sexual age of consent, or if he claimed that the girl had agreed to being abused, then he was declared innocent. Women's organisations objected to this let-out clause and campaigned to change the law to protect young girls from their sexual predators. Under the leadership of a former suffragette Alison Neilans, the Association for Moral and Social Hygiene (AMSH) led a broad coalition of women's groups including the WFL, the NCW and NUSEC to change the law to raise the age of consent, abolish the 'reasonable belief' clause and extend the time limit for prosecution. The 1921 bill failed because a number of male MPs introduced a wrecking amendment on lesbianism—labelled as 'gross indecency between females'—by attempting to criminalise it.[78] The amendment delayed the bill, and it ran out of parliamentary time.

Nancy Astor, who had been on the Select Committee which examined this issue, continued to lobby hard to change the law. In 1922, a new Criminal Law Amendment Act (CLA Act), this time sponsored by the government, withdrew the 'reasonable cause' to believe and removed the defence that a girl under the age of 16 had consented to abuse. Consequently, when Henry Murphy was found guilty of indecently assaulting an 11-year-old and a 13-year-old girl between late 1922 and early 1923, respectively, he was given three years penal servitude.[79] No longer could men claim that they had a 'reasonable cause to believe' that the young girls abused were over 16 or had consented to their indecent assault. The CLA Act was seen by the *Common Cause* as a real victory, 'representing the happy issue of a struggle extending over ten years' and not least to the 'presence and influence of women Members at Westminster'.[80]

Critically, these new laws needed to be enforced. Many of the women's organisations like the NCW, the Six Point Group and NUSEC campaigned for an increase in women police officers to ensure the law was well administered. In 1919, the first women police officers, most of whom had been in the Voluntary Women Patrols of the First World War, joined the Metropolitan Police. Their leader, Commander Mary Allen, spoke forcibly of the need for women to patrol public parks to safeguard children who 'were in terrible danger of assault from the men who haunted those places for no other purpose. She pointed out that Battersea Park was an especially dangerous spot, and gave instances of shocking assaults on quite young children, one a baby three months old'.[81] The Devon Standing Committee sought women police officers because 'during the past four years there had been quite 80 cases of assault, more or less serious, of girls whose lives had been very likely ruined'.[82] In December 1925, backed by Nancy Astor, Mrs Philipson and a number of cross-party male MPs, Ellen Wilkinson introduced her first-ever bill: to make women police compulsory in boroughs and cities. On Monday 7 December, the day before the bill was introduced, the home secretary—Joynson Hicks—received a deputation organised by NUSEC and led by Eleanor Rathbone. It consisted of representatives of 27 organisations and representatives from all the political parties in support of Wilkinson's proposals.[83] The bill was not opposed by the government; the home secretary voiced his approval, and it was passed without division. Not all forces welcomed women: the chief constable of Manchester disapproved of women police. In 1921, only four uniformed women police officers were employed in Manchester, a statistic that did not improve until the 1930s.

There was an inconsistency about the age of sexual consent: the age was set at 16 yet boys were still able to marry at 14 and girls at 12, an irregularity which women campaigned to redress. *The Woman's Leader* argued that Britain was 'among the most backward countries with regard to this question' and that the 'low age of marriage is used as a cloak for luring away quite young girls by an offer of marriage'.[84] At its Annual Conference, NUSEC proposed that the age of marriage should be at least as high as the age of consent and set to work to pressurise the government to raise the age of marriage. The government responded to their campaign, set up a Select Committee of the House of Lords and took evidence from NUSEC, the Mothers' Union and St Joan's Social and Political Union. In 1929, the Age of Marriage Act raised the age of marriage to 16, sending out a clear message that marriage was meant to be a union between two consenting adults.[85]

In 1920, the National Council for the Unmarried Mother and her Child (NCUMC) persuaded Neville Chamberlain to introduce a private member's bill to change the 'Bastardy' laws. At the time, unmarried mothers without supportive friends or family were forced to go to the workhouse to give birth; and the only way women could obtain a paternity order was through the Courts. The Poor Law Guardian, suffrage activist and writer Margaret Wynne Nevinson was among the many feminists who criticised the current laws as unjust.[86] When the government took up the issue and published its recommendations, the response from women's groups was disparaging. The WFL wrote to MPs criticising the proposals penalising mothers if they refused to provide the fathers' name, or which made the children of unmarried parents wards of Court.[87] The WFL also 'strongly' objected to the use of 'bastard' and urged that the word 'bastard' and 'bastardy' be deleted from the legal vocabulary. In addition, the WFL recommended that impecunious and friendless single mothers should be accommodated in local authority Maternity Hospitals rather than in workhouses. The bill was passed, went to a Select Committee and was altered in the light of the suggestions made by women's organisations such as the NCUMC. For instance, the government doubled the weekly amount that fathers were expected to pay. When the bill, now renamed the Children of Unmarried Parents Bill, went to the Lords, it was introduced by Nancy Astor's husband. It became law in 1923. In 1926, prompted by the campaigns of the NCUMC, the law allowed children to be 'legitimised' by the subsequent marriage of the parents.[88]

Another legal iniquity concerned the death penalty for women found guilty of killing their newborn infants. In the 17 years up to March 1921, 60 women were condemned to death, one of whom was executed.[89] In 1921, a 21-year-old woman from Leicester, Edith Mary Roberts, was tried, convicted and sentenced to death for killing her newborn baby.[90] Shortly after her conviction, the NCW, the Women's Co-operative Guild, NUSEC and other women's groups wrote to Nancy Astor to raise the case in Parliament. Three women activists and magistrates—the Labour woman's officer Marion Phillips, the trade unionist Gertrude Tuckwell and Margaret Lloyd George—met with a few Home Office mandarins to commute the sentence. On 6 June 1922, Edith Roberts was quietly released on licence. On 20 July 1922, urged on by women's organisations and drafted by Labour Women, an Infanticide Act (previously named the Child Murder Trial Bill before women objected to its name) received Royal Assent. This act allowed women to be convicted of infanticide, rather than murder if it could be proved that the defendant was suffering from 'mental disturbance' due to puerperal insanity after childbirth. The first trial after the act had passed took place at Lincoln Assizes, where a 19-year-old domestic servant was accused of strangling her newborn daughter. In sentencing the accused to four months imprisonment, the judge 'said he was most thankful that under the new Act, which was a most wise and humane piece of legislation, it was not necessary to put the girl on trial for murder'.[91] The WFL was pleased that these 'desperate girl-mothers' were no longer condemned to death.[92]

Once married, women were trapped because the law made it difficult for wives to leave or divorce their husbands, injustices that women's organisations pressurised Parliament to remedy. In 1922, Margaret Wintringham seconded a Separation and Maintenance Orders Bill, which allowed women to apply for an order of separation and claim maintenance before leaving her husband, her children and her home. The Catholic Women's Suffrage Society, along with a range of other women's organisations, gave her support. A year later, the Matrimonial Causes Act, a bill drafted by NUSEC's legal advisors like Helena Normanton, and backed by Nancy Astor and Margaret Wintringham, brought England and Wales in line with Scotland by ending the sexual double standard of divorce law.[93] Previously, a man could sue for divorce simply on the basis of his wife's adultery, whereas a woman had to prove aggravating factors such as rape, incest, sodomy, cruelty or desertion if she wanted to divorce her husband. This meant, feminists argued, that whereas infidelity was condemned in a wife, it was condoned in a husband. The bill, which was a private member's bill, was passed by an overwhelming majority. Women living in Scotland did not have to remedy such injustices as there had been gender equality in Scottish divorce law for centuries.[94]

In addition, women activists wanted to reform the guardianship law with regard to small children.[95] At the time, fathers were the legal guardians of legitimate children and mothers the legal guardians of 'illegitimate' ones. The NUSEC lobbied MPs and encouraged women to write to their MPs to change the law so that mothers could enjoy the same rights and responsibilities as fathers. One MP complained that 'suffragettes without a job' pestered him constantly.[96] However, most women were now voters and needed to be accommodated, a fact recognised by the solicitor general, who stated that 'as women voters were exercising great pressure', the matter should be examined.[97] In 1924, the Liberal MP Margaret Wintringham introduced a NUSEC-drafted Private Members' Bill, which was supported by all the other women MPs, irrespective of party affiliation. In 1925, the government substituted it with their own bill which watered down the NUSEC proposals by establishing equal parenting rights only after a court case. It took until 1973 for mothers to be granted full equality.

Not all Bills promoted by women's organisations and put forward by women MPs were successful. Each year about 300 women were arrested for soliciting; men were never charged because prostitution itself was not a crime.[98] The female president, chair and secretary of the Association for Moral and Social Hygiene complained about the sexual double standard and campaigned to change the law.[99] They were supported by other women's groups such as the Catholic St Joan's Social and Political Alliance, which wanted the law to be repealed and substituted by one applicable 'to all persons who annoy or molest others in the streets or public places'.[100] It was considered wrong that women were prosecuted for selling their bodies, whereas men who bought their services went free. On 22 June 1926, Nancy Astor introduced a private members Public Places (Order) Bill, which advocated equal treatment of the sexes in prostitution laws and the elimination of the term 'common' prostitute from the legal code. Her bill failed, and equal treatment of the sexes in prostitution had to wait until the Policing and Crime Act 2009.

Differences Between Activists

Post-war feminists, like the pre-war suffragettes and suffragists, were not always united and often held different ideas about how to achieve a just world for women. On the one hand, some activists thought women were different from men and wanted women's traditional role as housewife and mother to be recognised and honoured; on the other hand, others believed that women were equivalent to men and wanted a straightforward equality with the opposite sex. Three of the biggest controversies which divided activists related to family allowances, protective legislation and to birth control. All too often, these disagreements had a class dimension, as middle-class and working-class feminists held different views about how to improve the lives of women.

Family Allowances

In 1919, Eleanor Rathbone replaced Millicent Fawcett as president of NUSEC. Rathbone wanted to focus on welfare for mothers and family allowances payable to women; others in the organisation favoured equal rights. Some have argued that this distinction was between the 'Old Feminists' like Millicent Fawcett, who favoured equality with men, and the 'New Feminists' like Rathbone, who emphasised the differences between the sexes and wanted women's familial role to be recognised. However, the differences between the two were not as sharp as some historians, keen to tidy up the past, suggest. Nonetheless, some differences were irreconcilable: in 1927, NUSEC formally separated into the National Council for Equal Citizenship and the Townswomen's Guilds because of these different objectives, though both groups continued to cooperate.

Eleanor Rathbone led the campaign for married women to be given a family allowance by the state if they cared for their children at home. In this way, it was argued, women's unpaid work in the home was rewarded and married women given some measure of financial independence. Rathbone, all too conscious of the poverty of working-class families in her home town of Liverpool, believed family allowances would help ward off child poverty by giving women a measure of financial control. Not everyone agreed. Feminists like Millicent Fawcett opposed family allowances because they consolidated women's role in the home rather than emancipate them from it; Labour veterans like Marion Phillips opposed family allowances fearing they would 'increase the irresponsibility of fatherhood';[101] and trade unionists were worried that family allowances would depress male earnings and undermine their battle for the 'family wage' whereby working men were paid more because they were responsible for the welfare of their families.

Protective Legislation

Protective—or what some termed 'restrictive'—legislation remained a controversial question for feminists, just as it had been before the war. In many ways, the controversy highlighted class differences within the women's movement: for the most part, working-class women, trade unionists and Labour Party women favoured protective legislation, whereas middle-class feminists had no wish to support restrictive measures which threatened to keep women out of jobs. A number of middle-class feminists believed that men in the male-dominated Labour Party wanted women out of the job market because they feared women would take their jobs. In contrast, Labour feminists like Ellen Wilkinson believed that women who worked long hours in dangerous factories and workshops needed all the protection they could get. In 1923, Labour's SJC suggested a maximum 48-hour week, the abolition of night work and of work in dangerous trades. This proposal formed the basis of Labour's 1924 Factory Bill, a bll to which NUSEC objected, sending letters of protest to MPs.[102] The bill failed. Mary Bell Richards, National Union of Boot and Shoe Operatives, complained that middle-class feminists had no idea 'what it was like to sit continuously for five hours with your eyes glued to the needle of a power machine'.[103] In March 1926, in one of the most eloquent speeches of that session, Wilkinson introduced the second reading of her Private Members' Bill to the House of Commons. It was a Factory Bill designed to give a 38-hour week for women and young people, safer machinery, better health, lighting, ventilation and sanitation. The Factory Bill was praised on all sides—and then defeated by the Conservative government.

There were consequences for the women's movement too. Pamela Graves argues that the struggle over protective legislation 'left a political division between feminism and socialism' by reinforcing the view that feminism was a middle-class movement 'hostile to the interests of the working-class'.[104] Certainly, the belief that women are not a homogenous group united by a common sexuality but are as divided as men in terms of class and political beliefs was reinforced. Both sides lost out. As a direct consequence, the majority of Labour women stopped collaborating with feminist organisations like NUSEC on other issues such as equal franchise. The feminist movement had lost a major ally. In turn, 'as feminism became unacceptable as word or creed', Labour Party women stopped putting forward woman-centred policies. Nonetheless, politics is never as tidy as Graves suggests. Labour women continued to work with women's organisations and across the political divide on women's equality, keeping both feminism and socialism alive.

Birth Control

Women disagreed over birth control too, though not rigidly along class lines. Birth control, as Clare Debenham points out, 'was important in providing self-determination for women in the way that the rubber sheath, which could easily be purchased in chemists, provided self-determination for men'.[105] At the time, it was illegal for state-run health clinics to give advice on this subject: indeed health visitors, nurses and doctors lost their jobs for doing so or, as famously happened to Rose Witcrop and Guy Aldred, were arrested, put on trial and found guilty under the Obscene Publications Act for publishing pamphlets which gave advice on contraception. In 1918, Marie Stopes published a guide to contraception, and in 1921 she opened the first of her (privately run) birth control clinics in Holloway, London, followed by others across the country. In 1926, the Women's Welfare and Advisory Clinic opened in Glasgow.[106] Feminists and women's groups like the Labour Party Women's Sections, the Women's Co-operative Guild, NUSEC and the Workers' Birth Control Group campaigned for birth control information to be provided by the state. Eleanor Rathbone used the NUSEC's journal *The Woman's Leader* to promote birth control for married women. In a leading article, the paper asked, 'Is birth control a feminist reform?' with the underlying argument that it was. Eleanor Rathbone was particularly fearless about promoting birth control, a brave characteristic of a single woman who might face all sorts of sexual innuendoes and accusations of personal immorality. The NCW passed resolutions in favour of birth control and the president of the WI gave her support.

Labour feminists, who included Dora Russell and Labour MPs like Dorothy Jewson, Susan Lawrence and Margaret Bondfield, founded the Workers' Birth Control Group to 'bring within the reach of working people the best and most scientific information on Birth Control' and to bring pressure on Parliament to recognise birth control as a Public Health issue.[107] They had a tough job, fighting not only public opinion but the Catholic Church and the Labour Party as well. In July 1924, the Labour Party Women's Conference passed a resolution—only six voted against—urging the party to campaign to allow GPs to give birth control advice to married couples. In the debate, Dora Russell insisted that it was four times more dangerous for women to bear children than for men to work as coal miners, then considered the most dangerous occupation of all.

Despite the overwhelming support of the Women's Conference, both Marion Phillips, 'who assumed the role of policing agent for the male party leaders',[108] and the Labour Party executive rejected the proposal for the distribution of birth control information, claiming that it was an 'essentially individual and domestic matter on which it would be highly inappropriate for any political Party to dogmatise'.[109] Unlike pay, working conditions and hours of labour, the control of one's body was seen as an individual—not a class—matter. Labour's reluctance to promote birth control was complicated. Birth control was associated with the eugenic movement with its beliefs in racial purity. A number of eugenicists correlated intelligence with social class and urged that the working class should stop producing too many children because they diluted the national stock: such ideas were anathema to the Labour Party. In addition, Labour feared losing votes if they supported birth control, particularly since a 'good many Labour MPs had been returned on Irish Catholic votes'.[110]

Fed up with Labour Party intransigence and the eugenist birth control movement, Dora Russell and a group of 200 women formed the Workers' Birth Control Group with the sole aim of making birth control available to working-class women. It was, as Graves points out, 'an outstanding example of an effective single issue lobbying organisation', providing speakers, writing letters, holding public meetings and pestering MPs.[111] Despite Russell's endeavours, women were denied the right to discuss birth control at Labour's annual conferences. Labour women were effectively being silenced. Eventually, in July 1930 Arthur Greenwood, Minister for Health in the recently elected Labour government, quietly presented a Memorandum to the Cabinet which permitted local authorities, if they wished, to provide birth control clinics and information to married mothers about birth control 'where further pregnancy would be detrimental to health'. It was a step forward in women's control over their own bodies.

The Equal Franchise Campaign

Women may have won a limited franchise, but it was not an equal one. Several groups—NUSEC, the WFL and the Six Point Group—along with sympathetic MPs like Nancy Astor and Ellen Wilkinson led the campaign to extend the franchise to women over the age of 21 and to single women. From 1918 to 1928, they were 'a thorn in the side' of successive governments.[112] According to Joanna Alberti, 'some of the pre-war atmosphere of the suffrage movement was recreated in the years from 1926 to 1928'.[113] On 3 July 1926, in the first suffrage demonstration since before the war, a mass meeting of around 3500 women representing over 40 societies converged on Hyde Park. At the head of the procession, young women carried a gold banner bearing the words 'Votes for the Women Left Out', followed by a mass of moving colour: scarlet and gold, blue, green, yellow, white and purple 'blazed in the sunshine as banner, streamer and standard swayed with the swing of the marching women'.[114] Contingents of professional women including teachers, doctors, journalists, accountants, shop assistants, solicitors, architects and income tax experts; 13 branches of the women's section of the Labour Party; and women who belonged to the National Federation of General and Municipal Workers, all carrying their colourful banners marched along, united in sisterhood.[115] Veterans of the 'Old Gang' of women's suffrage campaigners such as Emmeline Pankhurst, the 82-year-old Charlotte Despard and Millicent Fawcett joined them.[116] There was an actresses' contingent dressed in green and pink and carrying banners of former heroines like Ellen Terry and a Processional Cross of the League of the Church Militant. Representatives from all three political parties: the Conservative Mrs Hilton Philipson, Labour's Ellen Wilkinson and the former Liberal MP Margaret Wintringham marched behind a 'Big Ben' banner in black on a red ground, party politics forgotten in a common cause. Nancy Astor, who had played a significant part, was absent, engaged in 'other parts of the earth' promoting women's rights.[117] The marchers were accompanied by several bands, including Scots and Irish pipers. There were 15 platforms with over 60 women speakers.[118]

As a result of this successful march, the Equal Political Rights Campaign Committee was set up by the Six Point Group, which together with NUSEC held even more meetings and demonstrations to further the cause for equal votes for women. Women activists kept up the pressure. Led by Lady Margaret Rhondda, they kept up a campaign of letter writing and deputations. Women MPs helped by asking questions in the Commons as to when women would gain equal suffrage. The Duchess of Atholl, who had previously been wary of women's suffrage, gave them support. Each year, at least one private members' bill was introduced by MPs from across the party spectrum; each year, it failed for one reason or another.[119]

On 29 March 1928, the home secretary Mr Joynson Hicks presented a government bill giving votes to women on the same terms as men. The Conservative Prime Minister Stanley Baldwin had succumbed to pressure from a variety of women's organisations, especially Conservative ones. A leading figure in the Conservative Women's Advisory Committee threatened that 'great discontent will ensue' unless there was action on equal franchise.[120] Baldwin had also given a pledge to Dame Caroline Bridgman, the chair of the Women's Unionist Organisation that he would back an extension of women's suffrage. Nonetheless, the government's eventual public commitment was a surprise: Nancy Astor outmanoeuvred Joynson Hicks in a parliamentary debate and forced him to concede that votes for women would be introduced that session.[121] The motion was passed by 387 votes to 10 on a day when 218 MPs, one of whom was

Winston Churchill who opposed women's suffrage, were absent. On 2 July 1928, the Equal Franchise Bill received Royal Assent: the WFL held a victory celebration for 250 guests at a London hotel. Both Joynson-Hicks and Stanley Baldwin sent messages of congratulations to the women's groups.

CONCLUSION

In some histories of the period, the 1920s are depicted as 'roaring', as a time of untold freedoms and liberated women. For privileged women with their cropped hair, lipstick mouths and short dresses who smoked freely, drank the night away in clubs, cocktail bars and jazz clubs, and enjoyed their hedonistic lifestyle, it was certainly 'roaring'. Such descriptions of the period, however, are deficient, and the 'Roaring Twenties' was a misnomer for most women. In contrast to 'flapper' girls, the life of large numbers of working-class women was drab and distinctly burdensome. For many women in Britain, the decade was a time for political action rather than a time of dancing the Charleston across a parquet floor. Equally significantly, the 1920s were unique in that activists from across the political spectrum worked closely together on some issues to advance women's rights.

Undoubtedly, women's activism was successful on a number of fronts. With the establishment of electoral democracy, Britain could now claim she had a representative government. With their newly acquired voting power, feminists were optimistic that they could improve the lives of their sisters by working collectively. Certainly, female politicians and activists in the 1920s buried political differences to work together—as women—on several issues, many of which came to fruition. Consequently, it is tempting to represent the 1920s as a golden age in which women submerged their differences to fight for the common female good. Of course, this misses the point that women activists came from diverse backgrounds, with differing convictions and agendas. Women activists never accomplished complete consensus: there were too many class, religious and political differences to overcome. In future, because of changing historical circumstances, even this imperfect congruity was challenged and found deficient. Unquestionably, after 1929 British politics became less pluralistic and more and more divided along party lines with predictable consequences for female activism.

NOTES

1. Ellen Wilkinson, *The AUCE Journal*, February 1920.
2. *Aberdeen Daily Journal*, 10 November 1920, p. 4.
3. Julie Arnot, *Women workers and Trade Union participation in Scotland, 1919–1939*, DPhil, 1999.
4. *Edinburgh Evening News*, 21 June 1924, p. 10.
5. *Woman Worker*, April 1919, p. 5.

6. Julie Arnot, *Women workers and Trade Union participation in Scotland, 1919–1939*, DPhil, 1999.
7. Ibid.
8. *Daily Mail*, 20 May 1920, p. 2.
9. *Daily Independent*, 17 August 1920, p. 5.
10. *The Woman's Leader*, 7May 1920, p. 311.
11. *Western Morning News*, 18 May 1920, p. 2.
12. *The Manchester Guardian*, 27 April 1920. See Pathé News *The Oxford Street Shop Strike 1920*.
13. *Western Daily Press*, 17 May 1922, p. 8.
14. *The Shields Daily News*, 18 May 1922, p. 1.
15. *Nottingham Journal*, 19 May 1922, p. 2.
16. *The Woman's Leader*, 28 May 1926, p. 138.
17. See Steven Woodbridge, Kingston University website, posted 15 August 2020.
18. Liberals: 1918–1922; Conservatives: 1922–1923; 1924–1929; Labour (minority): 1924; 1929.
19. Sue Bruley, *Beatrice Green and the unsung heroines behind 1926s Lockout*, Walesonline, accessed January 2021.
20. *Nottingham Evening Post*, 31 May 1926, p. 1.
21. Sheila Lewenhak, *Women and Trade Unions*, Ernest Benn, 1977.
22. Hutchinson, 1959, p. 295.
23. Only four of them were Labour: Mrs Emmeline Pethick Lawrence (Manchester Rusholme), Mrs Charlotte Despard, (Battersea North), Mrs H M Mackenzie and Mrs Mary McArthur (Stourbridge).
24. See Nicoletta F Gullace, 'Christabel Pankhurst and the Smethwick election: right-wing feminism, the Great War and the ideology of consumption', *Women's History Review*, Volume 23, Issue 3, 2014.
25. The sentence was commuted to life in prison on account of her sex.
26. *The Woman's Leader*, 14 December 1923, p. 368.
27. *The Vote*, 19 December 1919, p. 439.
28. *The Common Cause*, 9 December 1919, p. 4.
29. *The Weekly Telegraph*, 27 December 1919, p. 4.
30. Nancy Astor, quoted in *Western Times*, 7 November 1919, p. 12.
31. Edith Lyttelton, *The Observer*, 17 April 1921, p. 8.
32. NUSEC was formerly the NUWSS. It redirected its campaign for women suffrage to help women use the vote effectively.
33. Nine were Labour (Susan Lawrence, Margaret Bondfield, Ellen Wilkinson, Jennie Lee, Dr Ethel Bentham, Mrs Mary Agnes Hamilton, Lady Cynthia Mosley, Dr Marion Phillips, and Edith Picton-Turbervill), three were Conservative (Nancy Astor, Duchess of Atholl, Countess of Iveagh), one Liberal (Megan Lloyd George) and one Independent (Eleanor Rathbone).
34. See G. E. Maguire, *Conservative Women, A History of Women and the Conservative Party, 1874–1997*, Palgrave Macmillan 1998 and David Thackeray 'At the heart of the party? The women's Conservative organisation in the age of partial suffrage, 1914–28' in Clarisse Berthezène and Julie Gottlieb, *Re-Thinking Right-Wing Women, Gender and the Conservative Party, 1880s to the present*, MUP, 2017, for a longer analysis.
35. *Devon and Exeter Gazette*, 23 April 1929, p. 3.
36. Ibid., 21 May 1929, p. 5.

37. Ibid., 16 April 1929, p. 3.
38. Ibid., 18 March 1929, p. 2.
39. Ibid., 11 March 1929, p. 3.
40. Martin Pugh, *Women and the Women's Movement in Britain*, Macmillan, 2000.
41. Thanks to the anonymous reviewer of this book for this information.
42. Pamela Graves, *Labour Women*, CUP, 1994, p. 46.
43. Martin Pugh, *Liberals and Women*, website of the Liberal Democrat History Group.
44. Julie V. Gottlieb, *Feminine Fascism: Women in Britain's Fascist Movement*, I. B. Tauris, 2003.
45. Julie V. Gottlieb, Rotha Beryl Lintorn-Orman, *DNB*, 2008.
46. *Folkestone Express, Sandgate, Shorncliffe and Hythe Advertiser*, 13 December 1926, p. 7.
47. Sean O'Coínn, *The Forgotten Volunteers*, Belfast Cultural and Local History Group, 2020.
48. Margaret Ward, *The Women of Belfast, Cumann Na mBan Easter Week and After*, internet source.
49. Mo Moulton, '"You Have Votes and Power": Women's Political Engagement with the Irish Question in Britain, 1919–23', *Journal of British Studies*, January 2013.
50. Ibid., p. 199.
51. Ibid., p. 201.
52. *Guardian*, 17 May 1920, p. 7.
53. *In the Name of the Sisterhood*, Exhibition at the Museum of Orange Heritage. Thanks to Coleen Lodge for sending me images of the panels of this exhibition. It was due to open in 2020 but was unable to do so because of the pandemic.
54. D. A. J. MacPherson, 'The Emergence of Women's Orange Lodges in Scotland: gender, ethnicity and women's activism, 1909–1940', *Women's History Review*, Vol 22, Issue 1, 2013, p. 53. See Deborah Butcher, *Ladies of the Lodge: A history of Scottish Orangewomen, c.1909–2013*, PhD, London Metropolitan University, 2014.
55. *The Liverpool Echo*, 12 July 1927, p. 9.
56. Pamela M Graves, *Labour Women, Women in British Working-Class Politics 1918–1939*, CUP, 1994, p. 180.
57. Ibid., p. 172.
58. Ibid., p. 178.
59. Pamela M Graves, *Labour Women, Women in British Working-Class Politics 1918–1939*, CUP, 1994.
60. Ibid., p. 180.
61. See *Women's History Review*, Vol 23, Issue 3, 2014, for a discussion of the range of women's activity during the interwar period.
62. See Esther Breitenbach and Valerie Wright, 'Women as Active Citizens: Glasgow and Edinburgh, c1918–1939, *Women's History Review*, Vol 23, Issue 3, 2014, p. 413.
63. *The Pall Mall and Globe*, 9 March 1921, p. 11.
64. *Daily Mail*, 1 January 1920, p. 9.
65. In 1918, the Women's Institute (WI) held its first Annual General Meeting. By 1925, the Women's Institute, under the leadership of Lady Lucy Denman, had

grown to 4000 Institutes with a membership of over 25,000. Like the WSPU, it was an all-women organisation. Many women saw the WI as an extension of their suffrage work: former suffrage activists—Elizabeth Robins, Grace Hadow and Helena Auerbach former treasurer of the NUWW—were leading members. Moreover, members of the WI took part in many of the feminist campaigns of this period such as equal pay, the right of married women to work, equal guardianship and widows' pensions. Lady Denman chaired the Birth Control Council.

66. On 17 February 1921, Lady Rhondda set up the Six Point Group (SPG) and exhorted newly enfranchised women to take up the banner of the suffragists and suffragettes and continue the fight for women's rights. The SPG saw itself as a sequel to the WSPU and certainly attracted a number of former suffragettes as well as politicians like Nancy Astor. Lady Rhondda also founded *Time and Tide*, a weekly feminist journal, produced by an all-woman team, which gave work to a number of left-wing interwar writers and activists such as Elizabeth Robins, Winifred Holtby, Vera Brittain, Ellen Wilkinson and Rebecca West. In 1922, Lady Rhondda, who had inherited the title from her father, campaigned to sit in the House of Lords, where men of her rank were automatically appointed. She was unsuccessful, and it took until 1963 before women hereditary peers could take their seats in the Lords. See A. V. John, *Turning the Tide, the Life of Lady Rhondda*, Parthian, 2013.

67. Caitriona Beaumont quoted in Helen McCarthy, 'Parties, Voluntary Associations, and Democratic Politics in Interwar Britain', *The Historical Journal*, Vol 50, No 4, 2007. See also Caitriona Beaumont, *Housewives and Citizens. Domesticity and the Women's Movement in England, 1928–64*, MUP, 2013.

68. Jill Liddington, *The Long Road to Greenham*, Virago, 1989, p. 137.

69. See savethechildren.org.uk.

70. *The Manchester Guardian*, 15 June 1926, p. 5.

71. *The Manchester Guardian*, 21 June 1926, p. 10. See Pathé News, *Law Not War*, for a newsreel of the demonstration and shots of Margaret Bondfield and Ellen Wilkinson speaking.

72. See Pat Thane, 'What Difference did the Vote Make?' in Amanda Vickery et al., *Women, Privilege and Power, British Politics, 1750 to the Present*, Stanford University Press, 2011, for a discussion of the reforms and the reform campaigns.

73. Anne Logan, 'In Search of Equal Citizenship: The campaign for women magistrates in England and Wales, 1910–1939', *Women's History Review*, Vol 16, Issue 4, 2017, p. 501. See also Anne Logan, *Feminism and Criminal Justice. A Historical Perspective*, Palgrave, 2008.

74. Cheryl Law, *Suffrage and Power, The Women's Movement, 1918–1928*, I. B. Tauris, 1997.

75. Anne Logan, 'In Search of Equal Citizenship: The campaign for women magistrates in England and Wales, 1910–1939', *Women's History Review*, Vol 16, Issue 4, 2017, p. 501.

76. Ibid., p. 501.

77. *Aberdeen Press and Journal*, December 29th 1920, p. 3.

78. See Caroline Derry 'Lesbianism and Feminist Legislation in 1921: the Age of Consent and "Gross Indecency between Women"', *History Workshop Journal*, Vol 86, Autumn 2018, for an incisive examination of this.
79. *The Scotsman*, 6 July 1923, p. 6.
80. *Common Cause*, 18 August 1922, p. 2.
81. *Hastings and St Leonards Observer*, 21 October 1922, p. 5.
82. *The Western Times*, 25 February 1927, p. 2.
83. The organisations included NUSEC, Association of Headmistresses, Association for Moral and Social Hygiene, British Commonwealth League, British Federation of University Women, Federation of Working Girls' Clubs, Girls' Friendly Society, League of the Church Militant, London Society for Women's Service, National Free Church Women's Council, Liverpool Women's Police Patrols Committee, Matron's Council for Great Britain and Ireland, Six Point Group, Standing Joint Committee of Industrial Organisation, St Joan's Social and Political Alliance, Union of Jewish Women, Women's Auxiliary Service, Women's Freedom League, Women's Guild of Empire, Women's International League, Women's National Liberal Federation, Women Sanitary Inspectors' and Health Visitors' Association, Women's Unionist Association, Kensington Vigilance Society, Kensington and Paddington SEC, Reading SEC and City of London SEC.
84. *The Woman's Leader*, 10 June 1927, p. 143.
85. In Scotland, people could marry without parental consent; in the rest of the UK, parents had to give consent up to the age of 21.
86. *The Vote*, 26 March 1920, p. 548.
87. Sir F. Banbury, quoting a letter from the WFL, HC debate, May 1920, vol 128, cc2395–2453.
88. Pat Thane, 'Unmarried Motherhood in Twentieth Century England', Women's History Review, Vol 20, Issue 1, 2011.
89. *The Woman's Leader*, 13 January 1922, p. 577.
90. Daniel J. R. Grey, 'Women's Policy Networks and the Infanticide Act 1922', *Twentieth Century British History*, Vol 21, No 4, 2010.
91. *The Vote*, 23 November 1922, p. 348.
92. Ibid., p. 412.
93. See Judith Bourne, *Helena Normanton and the Opening of the Bar to Women*, Waterside Press, 2016.
94. I am grateful to the anonymous reviewer for this information.
95. Mari Takayanagi, *Parliament and Women c1900–1945*, PhD, King's College London, p. 81.
96. Ibid.
97. Ibid.
98. Martin Pugh, *Women and the Women's Movement in Britain*, 2000.
99. *The Woman's Leader*, 22 January 1926, p. 416.
100. *The International Women's Suffrage News*, May 1927, p. 102.
101. Pamela M Graves, *Labour Women, Women in British Working-Class Politics 1918–1939*, CUP, 1994, p. 99.
102. Ibid., p. 141.
103. Ibid., p. 145.
104. Ibid., p. 149.

105. Quoted in Clare Debenham, *"Grassroots feminism" a study of the campaign of the Society for the Provision of Birth Control Clinics, 1924–1938*, PhD, University of Manchester, p. 183.
106. See Esther Breitenbach and Valerie Wright, 'Women as Active Citizens: Glasgow and Edinburgh, c1918–1939, *Women's History Review*, Vol 23 Issue 3 2014.
107. Workers' Birth Control Group leaflet, 1927.
108. Pamela M Graves, *Labour Women, Women in British Working-Class Politics 1918–1939*, CUP, 1994, p. 86.
109. Labour Party Conference, 1925.
110. Quoted in Clare Debenham, *"Grassroots feminism" a study of the campaign of the Society for the Provision of Birth Control Clinics, 1924–1938*, PhD, University of Manchester, p. 183.
111. Pamela M Graves, *Labour Women, Women in British Working-Class Politics 1918–1939*, CUP, 1994, p. 90.
112. Mari Takayanagi, *Parliament and Women c1900–1945*, PhD, King's College London, 2012, p. 104.
113. Ibid., p. 122.
114. *The Courier and Advertiser*, 5 July 1926, p. 4.
115. *The Woman's Leader*, 9 July 1926, p. 219.
116. *Lincolnshire Echo*, 3 July 1926, p. 5.
117. Ibid., 5 July 5h 1926, p. 4.
118. The platforms represented a wide range of organisations such as the Actresses Franchise League, the Anglican League of the Church Militant, Women's Election Committee, Youth, NUSEC, London Society for Women's Service, WFL, British Commonwealth League, St Joan's Social and Political Alliance, National Women's Liberal Federation, Six Point Group, National Council of Women, Federation of Women Civil Servants and the Women's International League, Actresses' Franchise League, National Union of Women Teachers, Labour and Trade Unions, League of the Church Militant (*The Woman's Leader*, 2 July 1926, p. 201).
119. In 1919, a bill was presented by Labour MP, Benjamin Spoor; in 1920, two bills by Labour MP Thomas Grundy and by Conservative Sir Park Goff; in 1921, by Labour MP Walter Smith; in 1922, by Labour MP Walter Smith and by Independent Conservative, Lord Robert Cecil; in 1923, by Liberal MP Isaac Foot; in 1924, by Labour MP William M Adamson and by Constitutionalist MP Hugh Edwards; in 1925, by Labour William Whiteley; in 1926, by Liberal MP William Wedgwood Benn; in 1927, by Labour MP Haden Guest; in 1928, by Conservative MP Joynson-Hicks as a government bill. Taken from Mari Takayanagi, *Parliament and Women c1900–1945*, PhD, King's College London, 2012.
120. Mari Takayanagi, *Parliament and Women c1900–1945*, PhD, King's College London, 2012, p. 125.
121. See Mari Takayanagi, '"Does the right hon. Gentlemen mean equal votes at 21?", Conservative women and equal franchise, 1919–1928', *Women's History Review*, Vol 28, Issue 2, 2019.

CHAPTER 5

The Hungry Thirties: 1930–1939

Now an equal franchise had been won, what next? What might political activists do now? What aspects of inequality and injustice might women focus on? What new campaigns might they initiate? What issues would dominate on the road to egalitarianism? Would the new female electorate change the nature of politics?

Certainly, many hoped that the addition of so many women voters would generate women MPs. There was an expectation in the 1930s that women MPs would represent their sex, not just their constituents or their party.[1] History, of course, is not a straight line of progress with women taking incremental steps towards equality—unexpected events can cause the most concrete of plans, the most imaginative of strategies or the most idealistic of philosophies to collapse. In the 1930s, women activists were tested by two major political crises: firstly, the Wall Street Crash, and, secondly, the rise of fascism, both of which threatened women's fight for equality.

One of the first tests involved a woman who had broken through the political glass ceiling: Margaret Bondfield. Ramsay MacDonald, prime minister of a new minority Labour government, had appointed her Minister of Labour, the first ever female cabinet minister. All the women's organisations 'heartily rejoiced' at Bondfield's appointment.[2] Leading women across the political spectrum—Emmeline Pethick Lawrence, Margaret Llewelyn Davis, Nancy Astor, the Duchess of Atholl, Mrs Corbett-Ashby and the Marchioness of Londonderry—wrote personal letters of congratulation. The National Union of Societies for Equal Citizenship (NUSEC) hosted a lunch to celebrate the success of the new minister and the recently elected female MPs. Eleven of the 14 women MPs attended, along with a number of distinguished activists: Margaret Bondfield sat next to the Liberal Millicent Fawcett, who sat next to the Conservative Nancy Astor, party politics put to one side in the euphoria of celebrating the progress of the women's movement.

The Wall Street Crash

Soon after her appointment, Margaret Bondfield was confronted by the cataclysmic economic fall-out from the Wall Street Crash. When she took office, the Unemployment Fund had a deficit of nearly £37 million, and was to increase further. By the end of 1930, the economy was in free fall, and as unemployment figures ineluctably climbed, Margaret Bondfield asked Parliament to increase the borrowing limit.[3] Again and again, Parliament pumped more money into the Fund until it reached £150 million.

Margaret Bondfield was pressurised to cut expenditure. She reluctantly acquiesced and excluded short-time, part-time and seasonal employees and all married women from unemployment benefits. It was a tough decision: Bondfield was a feminist, and had spent all her life fighting for the rights of working-class women.[4] There were protests. Three Labour women, Jennie Lee, Cynthia Mosley and Ellen Wilkinson, worked with the Independent MP Eleanor Rathbone and the Conservative Nancy Astor to oppose the policy. Outside Parliament, Rebecca West and Emmeline Pethick-Lawrence voiced their objections too. Their cries remained unheeded. The bill was carried by 221 to 20 votes: and a large tranche of married women were removed from the unemployment register.

Other reductions in expenditure were discussed and led to the break-up of the Labour government. Ramsay MacDonald resigned as Labour leader and became prime minister in a Conservative-dominated coalition government. All the Labour women—Ellen Wilkinson, Margaret Bondfield, Susan Lawrence, Leah Manning and Jennie Lee—and most of the men, refused to join it. When Parliament met after the summer recess, the newly formed National Government cut the pay of all those paid by the state and cut benefits by 10%. At the same time, the government imposed one of the most heart-breaking policies of the decade—the Household Means Test. All family income, including the meagre wage of teenage children and all savings, had to be declared. Even free school milk was calculated in assessing benefits.

In 1931, after a devastating electoral defeat for Labour, the Conservative Irene Ward replaced Margaret Bondfield as MP for Wallsend. Her Tyneside constituency was—like Northern Ireland, industrial Scotland, South Wales and parts of Lancashire—an area reliant on older industries like shipbuilding and mining, and one of the worst hit by the Depression. In her election speech, Ward pledged never to forget 'her obligation to maintain the trust of those constituents who were not natural Conservative voters', insisting that she was not a 'die-hard' Conservative but a progressive one.[5] Irene Ward abstained from the vote on the Means Test despite a three-line Whip. In her opinion, her Wallsend constituents faced 'extreme distress and hardship' because there was little work and the Means Test would be a final degradation for them.

For many, the Means Test led to an increasing identification with class rather than gender politics.[6] Labour women condemned the test: former MP Susan Lawrence insisted that it brought 'great hardship upon the families of the unemployed' and criticised the way in which long term unemployed workers were 'deprived of participation in medical treatment under the National Health Insurance'.[7] Statistics in the 1930s showed a clear correlation between life expectancy, infant and maternal mortality and poverty. In 1933, Labour Party women published a report arguing that the high level of maternal mortality in areas of great unemployment was due to poor nutrition and women's tendency to feed their husbands and children rather than themselves. Local branches of NUSEC tried to help: women in Bolton set up a soup kitchen for the unemployed in their district.[8]

Women protested against the Means Test: in 1934, when benefits were cut further, Welsh women stormed the dole office in Merthyr. Some had tried to march from Rhondda to Cardiff in order to confront the Prince of Wales, who was visiting the city. The demonstrators broke through three police cordons but were eventually stopped at Pontypridd.[9] Two Labour MPs, Barbara Ayrton-Gould and Ellen Wilkinson, urged their party to lead the Hunger Marches, which were being organised to publicise the plight of the unemployed. In 1932, the communist-dominated National Unemployed Workers' Movement (NUWM) organised a 'Great National Hunger March against the Means Test', which attracted around 3000 people from around Britain, particularly from the depressed areas like Wales, Scotland and the North of England where unemployment was highest. One of the organisers of the NUWM, a Mrs M. Brown, led a group of 50 women marchers from Burnley to London. Mrs Harriet Paisley, a 62-year-old woman with 17 children joined the march, as did a young woman of 16. Each woman carried a knapsack which contained a drinking cup, spare underclothes, stockings and, in some cases, an extra pair of shoes.[10] They were treated well in Northampton, were given hot meals 'the first they had in three days', enjoyed a bath at the former workhouse and received 'numerous gifts from sympathisers, including articles of clothing, stockings, socks and shoes'. Local unemployed shoemakers repaired their shoes. Each marcher was given a pack of ham sandwiches when they left.[11] At times, the weather was dreadful: when they arrived at Bletchley, they were wet through and had to dry their clothes in front of a fire at the Co-operative Hall. The women relied on local authorities and town councils to help them with food and lodging. Not all areas were willing to do so. At Burton on Trent, the Trades Council refused help but the mayor, Miss Mary Goodger, took pity on them and paid for them to have breakfast at a local café.[12] Moreover, these marchers met with a great deal of police brutality—brutality which led directly to the foundation of the National Council for Civil Liberties.

In 1934, another Hunger March of around 2000 unemployed from 17 regions in Britain—from Glasgow to Plymouth, from Cardiff to Norwich—marched to meet in London's Hyde Park. About 75 Scottish women, some wearing clogs and all carrying shoulder packs and tin utensils, walked to London: they stopped at the Keir Hardie Hall in Derby, were given a hot meal at Swadlincote, fed by the Miners' Welfare at Tamworth, accommodated at the Poor Law Institutions in Nuneaton and Coventry and stayed in a public hall at

Finchley, London.[13] When the women lodged at Nuneaton workhouse, they complained about the number of black beetles in the room—the casual wards had been closed for 12 months, and because the workhouse manager arranged for the room to be heated, it had 'aroused the beetles from their hibernation'.[14] When the marchers reached London, they delivered a petition to the House of Commons and a letter to Ramsay Macdonald's daughter Ishbel from women 'who have marched from Scotland, Durham, Lancashire, Yorkshire, South Wales etc', asking for an 'hour of her time' to tell her about the conditions of unemployed women.[15] She was unavailable to meet them since she did 'not feel that an interview with an army of marchers' would help.[16] One female Conservative MP was even more unsympathetic: the Conservative Duchess of Atholl asked the Home Secretary to take steps to prevent hunger marchers holding mass meetings and thus gaining undue sympathy.[17]

In 1936, Labour MP Ellen Wilkinson publicised the plight of her own constituency, whose unemployment rate stood at 67.8%, by organising the Jarrow Crusade. In her moving account of the march, with that evocative title *The Town that was Murdered*, Ellen made this particular hunger march a symbol of the 1930s.[18] Meanwhile, NUSEC organised a deputation to the minister of health to 'press for an increase in the rates of unemployment benefit to women'.[19]

Other women went on rent strike. In Stepney, then a poor working-class area of London, women led a number of rent strikes under the aegis of the Stepney Tenants' Defence League. Henry Srebrnik notes that women 'chaired most of the tenants' committees ... organised opposition to eviction attempts, were in the forefront of demonstrations and even picketed shoppers in the West End of London'.[20] One all-women's committee turned their block of flats into a 'fortress', put barbed wire around the building and guarded each entrance. Even the milkman had to secure a permit before delivering the milk. When 84 police officers arrived to reclaim the buildings, tenants armed themselves with sticks, shovels and saucepans and a brutal fight occurred. Rabbis, priests, vicars, the mayor of Stepney and around 15,000 others demonstrated against the police brutality, the incident was raised in the House of Commons, and eventually the owners of the property agreed to fairer rents for their tenants.

WOMEN'S ORGANISATIONS AND THEIR CAMPAIGNS

As a result of the Depression, the 1930s used to be thought a time when the women's movement in Britain virtually disappeared, a view which was later challenged by feminist historians. Some of the larger women's groups, namely the Mothers' Union, the Young Women's Christian Association, the Catholic Women's League, continued to flourish. The Mothers' Union, with over a half a million members, was according to Catriona Beaumont 'one of the most conservative women's organisations' in interwar Britain, campaigning against easier divorce and attempts to legalise abortion.[21] The YWCA and the CWL shared the beliefs of the Mothers' Union and campaigned against divorce, birth control and abortion. Nonetheless, as Beaumont points out, these groups were willing to join some feminist campaigns like those for family allowances and better health care for women.[22]

A number of secular groups like the Women's Institute and the National Council of Women (NCW) as well as recognisably feminist women's groups such as the Women's Freedom League (WFL), the Six Point Group, the London and National Society for Women's Service and the Women's Co-operative Guild continued to press for women's rights.[23] Both the Townswomen's Guilds and the National Council for Equal Citizenship had a suffragist past and used the suffragist colours of red, white and green.[24] Three of the major campaigns of these activists concerned abortion law reform, equal pay and reform of the Nationality Laws. Here, women across the political spectrum collaborated to campaign for justice and found sympathetic women MPs from all parties ready to help them get the law changed.[25]

Reforming the Abortion Laws

Many of the bigger women's organisations such as the Women's Co-operative Guild, the NCW, the London and National Society for Women's Service and the National Council for Equal Citizenship favoured reforming what they considered to be heinous and punitive abortion laws. For these women, abortion rights became part of a new vision of women's entitlements.[26] There was much to correct. The 1861 Offences Against the Person Act decreed that women could be 'kept in penal servitude for life' for self-inducing or for helping others to attempt an abortion. This was slightly amended by the 1929 Infant Life Preservation Act which allowed abortion for the 'preservation of the life of the mother'.

In 1931, as Lesley Hall points out, a sexual taboo was broken by *Time and Tide*, the paper of the Six Point Group, when it published letters about abortion. Stella Browne, a leading birth control campaigner, called for a reform in the abortion law because 'suicides, hideous injuries, blood poisoning, permanent invalidism, madness and … secret blackmail' had resulted from women being denied an abortion.[27] Class discrimination prevailed. Wealthy women could pay for a relatively safe abortion from sympathetic doctors who used antiseptics and were well versed in the use of 'curettage', a surgical procedure which was performed under anaesthetic and involved scraping the inside of the womb to remove the foetus. Less fortunate women were forced to self-induce by taking medicine that allegedly cured 'menstrual blockages'—one of the cheapest was lead-based and highly poisonous and led to blindness. Some used a soap and water douche; others used crochet hooks and knitting needles. Thousands sought help from backstreet abortionists. Each of these methods regularly led to death from haemorrhages and/or peritonitis. Yet despite the risks involved, abortion was seen by working-class women as a cheap way of family limitation.[28] An enquiry by the Ministry of Health in 1932 and 1937 showed that abortions were a significant cause of maternal mortality. In the late

1930s, a survey undertaken by the Joint Council of Midwifery reported on the hardships faced by women who had sometimes as many as 12 children to feed on a very low income, who lived in overcrowded homes with no access to running water and who lived with 'cruel and violent' husbands who insisted on 'having their way' regardless of the consequences.[29] More tragically, in enduring abortions, these women paid a heavy price, often with their life.

In 1936, in a West End café, a group of feminists founded the Abortion Law Reform Society: Cecily Hamilton, Mavis Tate, Stella Brown and Dora Russell were among its leading members.[30] Birth control and abortion was closely linked. Many feminists like Stella Browne believed abortion, like contraception, was about a woman's inalienable right to control her own body. As Lesley Hall points out, Marie Stopes and others would occasionally—and only very privately—suggest 'the evacuation of the uterus' and recommend a doctor who could perform it.[31] One of the women who helped at Stopes' birth control centre later confessed, 'we all knew one or two people who could do planned abortions. It was highly illegal and probably all the committee helped people. … We all did. The amount of prison sentences that I could have accumulated!'[32] Two of the Mitford sisters, Diana and Jessica, confessed to having abortions: right-wing Diana, pregnant by Oswald Mosley, had her foetus removed in a Harley Street nursing home, and left-wing Jessica in an East End slum.

The government was urged to change the law. On 11 February 1936, the Conservative Minister of Health, Sir Kingsley Wood, received a deputation from the National Council of Women (NCW) and a cross-section of women MPs. The vice president of the NCW, Lady Ruth Balfour, submitted a resolution which had been passed unanimously at her annual conference. The resolution urged the government to 'appoint a representative committee to inquire into the incidence of abortion', to how the law dealt with criminal abortion and attempted abortion, and to 'consider what measures, if any, are advisable to improve the existing position'.[33] Nothing came of this deputation, nor the many others which followed.

Women tried other tactics. On 14 June 1938, a distinguished gynaecologist and obstetric surgeon, Aleck Bourne, terminated the pregnancy of a 14-year-old girl who had been gang-raped by a group of soldiers. Bourne had been persuaded to do so by Joan Malleson and other members of the Abortion Law Reform Society who wanted to use the girl's abortion as a test case to challenge the law. After the abortion had been concluded, Bourne sent the medical documents to the attorney general, was duly arrested, put on trial at the Old Bailey, and charged with 'unlawfully using an instrument with intent to procure a miscarriage'. He faced a life sentence. Also liable to be charged was the teenager who had had the abortion, her father, Dr Joan Malleson, who had sent her to Dr Bourne, and Dr Peter Wingate, resident obstetric officer at St Mary's Hospital where the operation took place. The attorney general prosecuted Bourne, a reflection of just how serious the legal judgement surrounding the case was thought to be. However, after 40 minutes, the jury unanimously pronounced Bourne 'Not Guilty', and a legal precedent was set: that abortions were not unlawful if performed in good faith and with the object of 'preserving the life of the mother', either physically and mentally.[34] Many hoped that this trial would lead to a change in the law. It did not, though a legal precedent had been set: doctors who performed abortions on vulnerable women would no longer be prosecuted. In 1939, an Interdepartmental Committee on Abortion recommended no change in the abortion laws on the grounds it would destroy the 'religious and ethical teaching and ... fundamental principles on which society is based' and would provide 'an added temptation to loose and immoral conduct. There would ... almost inevitably be a tendency for promiscuous sexual intercourse to be more common'.[35] It would take a future group of feminists to campaign for further abortion law reform. And even this small legal right to abortion did not apply in Northern Ireland: abortion was only permitted for the 'purpose of preserving the life of the mother'. Those found guilty of procuring an abortion for other reasons were punished by penal servitude for life.

Campaigning Against the Nationality Laws

In 1929, supported by Nancy Astor and the newly re-elected Labour women MPs, Ellen Wilkinson had tried to introduce an Aliens Bill to amend the nationality laws.[36] As the law stood, a foreign woman automatically acquired British nationality on marrying a British subject whereas a British woman lost hers when she married a foreigner, then called an 'alien'. Once again female MPs from both sides acted as parliamentary representatives for the various women's groups such as the NCW. The bill would afford women the right to retain their British nationality on marriage to 'an alien' and took away the right of 'alien' women to gain British nationality on marriage. The loss of nationality had serious repercussions: women were not allowed to vote or stand for election in either municipal or parliamentary elections. For NUSEC and other women's organisations like the London and National Society for Equal Service, this was a denial of citizenship, a denial that suffragists had worked so hard to redress. When this bill failed, most women MPs and the women's organisations continued to press for change, holding numerous meetings, conferences and deputations to the Home Office. On 31 July 1930, a memorial bearing the signatures of 222 MPs from all parties was presented to the Labour prime minister asking him to help pass the Nationality of Married Women Bill, which was to be introduced by Captain Cazalet, husband of the Conservative MP Thelma Cazalet. In 1931, 40 women's organisations sent a deputation to the Home Secretary, J. R. Clynes, who agreed that the government should 'restore to a British-born woman the political and other privileges' that she lost on marriage.[37] Unfortunately, against the advice of the Home Secretary, the Labour Cabinet rejected the bill. In 1933, the National Government put forward the British Nationality and Status of Aliens Bill, which allowed women to remain a British subject on marriage but took away her citizenship. This fell far short of what the women activists wanted, and some reverted to pre-war suffragette tactics: one activist threw herself on to the foreign secretary's car bonnet, refused to leave and was arrested.[38] All the women MPs, apart from Florence Horsbrugh, voted against the bill, party politics forgotten in a moment of female solidarity. The bill passed but women continued to press for change: in July 1935, Mavis Tate presented a petition to the Commons, signed by representatives of over a hundred women's organisations, asking for equal nationality rights.[39] In 1948, the British Nationality Act finally stated that a woman's marriage to an 'alien' would not affect her nationality or her civil rights: it had taken 34 years to redress that inequality.[40]

Campaigning for Equal Pay

Many feminists felt that now they had won equal franchise, they 'must put double energy into working for equal pay'.[41] A campaign, sponsored by 25 women's organisations, was launched to demand equal pay for civil servants. The various women's groups focused on equal pay in the civil service for two main reasons. Firstly, the service employed both men and women in the same type of jobs making the conventional argument that women and men did distinctive work and therefore should be paid differently unsustainable. Secondly, feminists believed that once female civil servants gained equal pay, it opened the way for teachers and other public service workers.[42]

Many of these organisations had significant numbers of women who had been trained in the suffrage days and knew how to coordinate a crusade. On 17 March 1936, the campaign culminated in a meeting at Caxton Hall, which attracted such a huge crowd that an overflow meeting had to be held nearby. The meeting passed a resolution to be brought forward in the House of Commons calling on the government to establish one salary scale which would apply to all civil servants, male or female. They also canvassed sympathetic MPs. On April Fool's Day 1936, Ellen Wilkinson introduced a private member's motion to the House of Commons to 'place women in the Civil Service on the same scales of pay as apply to men'. Ellen Wilkinson's proposal was surprisingly carried by 156 to 148, and the government defeated. The Duchess of Atholl was the only female MP to speak against it. A 'typically vigorous' appeal came from Nancy Astor, who urged her male colleagues to 'disregard the Whips and assert their independence'.[43] However, the Conservative prime minister, Stanley Baldwin, refused to accept the outcome, called for a second vote and asked that it be treated as a vote of confidence. In the next division, the government imposed a Three Line Whip, castigated Tory MPs, who were 'notoriously lax in their attendance' and won the vote, though only as a 'result of considerably diminished prestige'.[44] Female civil servants were forced to wait until 1956 to receive equal pay.

Fascism and the Fights Against It

The Great Depression shook up—and often destroyed—parliamentary democracy. A number of countries responded to the economic turmoil by turning to extremes. Tragically, many of the democracies of Europe collapsed as Italy, Germany and Spain became fascist. The 1930s was also the 'Fascist decade' in Britain.[45] In 1931, Oswald Mosley founded his New Party, which later became the British Union of Fascists (BUF), an anti-semitic and xenophobic group. His wife Cynthia resigned from the Labour Party and reluctantly joined her husband's BUF—she was 'profoundly working-class at heart' and 'had wanted to 'put a notice in *The Times* to the effect that she dissociates herself' from her husband's fascist tendencies.[46] Mosley's organisation grew steadily, rising dramatically from 20,000 to 50,000, helped by the *Daily Mail*, which published sympathetic articles extolling its twisted ideals. In May 1933, Cynthia Mosley died from peritonitis. By the time she died, she had moved away from her husband's fascism and his closeness to Lord Rothermere, the *Mail*'s proprietor.[47] In 1936, Oswald Mosley married his lover Diana Mitford, who was more sympathetic to fascism (Fig. 5.1).

Fig. 5.1 BUF Women's Corp, 1939 (Courtesy Mary Evans Library/Marx Memorial Library)

The BUF set up a Woman's Section, and women soon comprised around 25% of the membership. Women members wore a grey skirt, a black blouse, a black beret and a party badge; no make-up or trousers were allowed. The adoption of a mixture of anti-semitism, nationalism, economic self-sufficiency and a pledge to improve the lives of those less well-off in Britain appealed to a number of women as did 'the familiar fascist themes of patriotism'.[48] In 1932, for instance, 17-year-old 'Jane' joined the BUF. She was 'deeply patriotic' and also appalled by the 'state of deprivation in large sections of society'.[49] Similarly 'Lorna', aged 18, stated that she 'wanted something new and dynamic, not just the old part of politics. I suppose I was a bit of a socialist, because obviously you wanted better conditions when you saw these back-to-back houses'.[50] Women found Mosley's ideas attractive: here was a man who promised drastic action to improve the lives of people. The BUF was anti-war, a stance which attracted both those with pacifist ideals and those with pro-German sympathies who feared another conflict with Britain's previous adversary. In addition, the BUF's adherence to strict standards of morality attracted some women, particularly those who had been active in the social purity movements.

A number of former suffragettes—Mary Richardson. Norah Elam, Mercedes Barrington and the pioneer of women police, Mary Allen—joined the BUF. The BUF's mixture of feminism and patriotism, along with the glamour of a uniform and military discipline, was a heady mix for these former activists. In 1934, Mary Richardson, the former suffragette who had defaced the Rokeby Venus, became the women's organiser of the British Union of Fascists.[51] As Hilda Kean points out, Richardson saw fascism as a continuation of her suffrage work. 'I was first attracted to the Blackshirts', said Richardson, 'because I saw in them the courage, the action, the loyalty, the gift of service, and the ability to serve which I had known in the suffrage movement'.[52] The BUF used women like Richardson, who was a great speaker and a role model, to recruit other women. However, most former suffrage activists were appalled by the fascists and their racist ideology.

The most famous of all fascist women were the aristocratic Mitford sisters, Diana and Unity. These were two of the daughters of Baron Redesdale and his wife Sydney, cousins of Clementine Churchill, and sisters of the communist activist Jessica and the socialite Deborah, future Duchess of Devonshire. Diana led the way, leaving her first husband for the widowed Oswald Mosley, whom she secretly married at the home of Joseph Goebbels with Adolf Hitler as guest of honour. Unity became a member of the BUF and relished wearing the black shirt uniform and making the fascist salute. In 1934, the two sisters visited Germany as part of the BUF delegation to the Nuremberg rally where Unity began her hero worship of Adolf Hitler. On a later visit, Unity engineered a meeting with Hitler and soon became part of his entourage, making gross anti-semitic speeches and revelling in the Nazi attention. Unity was feted by Hitler, given a private box at the 1936 Berlin Olympics and awarded an engraved gold swastika badge for her fascist sympathies. In June 1940, Diana was arrested and imprisoned without trial for three years under Defence Regulation 18B. After the war, Diana and Oswald Mosley moved to France and became close friends with the Duke and Duchess of Windsor who lived nearby.

Women in the BUF took an active role in the organisation 'from secretarial and administrative work, to selling newspapers on the street, or acting as stewards at BUF meetings'.[53] They wore their black fascist uniform, sold *Action*, trained in combat methods and wrote propaganda material targeted at women. Some became important local and area organisers: Yolande Mott, who had joined the BUF at eighteen, was not just women's organiser for the whole of Merseyside but helped organise the men too. For some, there was an 'atmosphere of personal freedom, and the excitement of youth'—somewhat like the suffragette experience. 'Pauline' spoke of there being an 'excellent dance' every Saturday in Kings Road, London, and of helping to bust a drugs ring in the area. Women also belonged to the 'tough squad', trained to deal with violence at the demonstrations and meetings. One had a 'pretty tough fight with a communist at the Manchester Free Trade Hall. Fortunately, she wore black underwear so managed to come out of it with dignity even when her shirt was ripped'.[54]

One of the most ferocious battles took place on 7 June 1934 at a rally held in Olympia when fascists attacked hecklers with ferocious brutality, regardless of whether they were men or women. One woman had her face scratched and her hair torn by female fascists before being beaten and evicted by nine Blackshirts.[55] All the political parties and most of the press denounced this fascist brutality. In contrast, Mary Richardson compared the violence to 'Black Friday', a day when suffragettes were physically attacked and sexually assaulted; in this incident, she claimed Blackshirts were the victims of violence.[56]

The Fight Against Fascism

Unlike elsewhere in Europe, parliamentary government held its ground and fascism did not put down deep roots in Britain. Nonetheless, many were worried that in Italy, Germany and Spain, dictatorship usurped democracy. As Gottlieb points out, the rise of fascism 'revitalised the women's movement in staunch opposition to the male supremacy, misogyny and terror characteristic of fascist regimes and movements'.[57] Here women were willing to cross political lines, especially when the rise of fascism threatened the very existence of democracy.

Certainly, there was significant opposition in Britain to fascism. Between 4 and 7 August 1933, a World Congress of Women was held in Paris where approximately 1500 women from all parts of the world gathered together at a conference to proclaim their hatred of war and fascism. The opening speech was delivered by Edith Haden Guest, who urged women of all countries to fight against the dangers of fascism and war. A new organisation was formed: the Women's World Committee Against War and Fascism (WWC). The British Section brought together women as disparate as Sylvia Pankhurst, Charlotte Despard, Vera Brittain, the Countess of Warwick, Sybil Thorndike, Ellen

Wilkinson, Vera Brittain, Storm Jameson and Maud Royden.[58] The Six Point Group affiliated; the Labour Party denounced it as a communist front and banned members from belonging to it.

Italy

In 1922, Italy became the first European country to turn Fascist when Benito Mussolini and his National Fascist Party took power in Italy, imposed a totalitarian state, crushed any opposition, became progressively anti-semitic and increasingly imperialistic. Schools and universities were forced to conform to Fascist doctrine or were silenced, the press was obsequious or was shut down, parliament was destroyed, strikes forbidden and brute force took the place of democratic discussion and persuasion. Wearing black shirts, the fascists beat up and killed their opponents or else degraded them by forcing them to drink castor oil, with humiliating outcomes. Sylvia Pankhurst, along with her Italian partner Silvio Corio, led the campaign against Italian Fascism, particularly when it resuscitated its old Roman past by invading and colonising Abyssinia (Ethiopia), a country that was ruled by the Regent Ras Tafari, who later became Emperor Haile Selassie. Ethiopia was the only independent country in Africa, the only country to have resisted European invasion, thus 'a beacon in the anti-colonial struggle'.[59] The British government and three leading newspapers backed Mussolini. The League of Nations, which had been set up to stop imperialist aggression, refused to interfere. In stark contrast, Sylvia Pankhurst used all her political skills to gain publicity: writing to newspapers and confronting politicians and leading figures to warn them of the dangers of Italian aggression. She predicted that a Second World War was inevitable if the democratic powers ignored the situation. Hitler, she predicted, would take note of the international disinclination to intervene and would follow Mussolini's example by annexing his own desired territories. Some of the British public agreed—a Peace Ballot in 1934 showed that ten million favoured economic sanctions and six million supported military intervention to help the beleaguered invaded country. The war ended in May 1936 with an Italian victory and the proclamation of the king of Italy as the emperor of Abyssinia. As Italian troops marched into Addis Ababa, Sylvia Pankhurst published her first edition of New *Times and Ethiopia News*, which she edited for the next 20 years.[60]

Germany

On 30 January 1933, Adolf Hitler became chancellor of Germany, and a new terrifying social order emerged which shook the very foundations of world order. Totalitarian terror escalated as his Nationalsozialistische Deutsche Arbeiterpartei (National Socialist German Workers' Party—the Nazis) tightened its grip, persecuted and murdered the opposition, gay and disabled people, Jewish people and the Roma.

In May 1933, the left-wing firebrand Ellen Wilkinson and the right-wing Flora Drummond shared a platform at a meeting organised by the Six Point Group on the plight of Germany.[61] The meeting agreed to write to the German Embassy protesting 'against the definite attack that is being made by the National Socialist Government of Germany on the woman's right to earn her living and her right to serve the community on public bodies'.[62] The Six Point Group, with its influential female vice presidents—Viscountess Rhondda, Lady Violet Bonham Carter and Winifred Holtby—became a 'storm centre for feminist anti-fascist thought and campaigns'.[63]

In October that year, the Women's World Committee ran a campaign to secure the release of women political prisoners in German concentration camps, sending a deputation of ten women to plead for the release of women held in prison without trial. One of the organisers, Alice Campbell, told several newspapers about Frau Worth, a woman who had hanged herself while being held in a concentration camp as hostage for her husband who had fled the country. Women, like Worth, were 'treated with extreme brutality, solely on account of politics, race or pacifist beliefs of their husbands and fathers'.[64] As a result of delegations from various countries, a number of these women were released, though there were normally just three distinct phases in the response of officials, 'first they were extremely polite, then they became evasive and finally forcible and savage'.[65] Eleanor Rathbone, now independent MP for the Combined English Universities, immediately understood the threat of Fascism and Nazism. From 1938, she led the Parliamentary Committee on Refugees, constantly pleading for the right of Germans fleeing Nazism to enter Britain. She asked people not to travel to Germany, at the time a popular destination for British tourists. Indeed, when I was looking through family albums with my late half-Jewish mother-in-law, I came across a photograph of her standing very near an officer dressed in an SS uniform. She was on a school trip and, like many tourists, remained oblivious to what was happening.

In May 1934, Mavis Tate, Conservative MP, flew to Germany to secure the release of Frau Seeger, the wife of a former Social Democrat member of the Reichstag, who had been imprisoned with her 21-month-old baby in a concentration camp at Dessau. Frau Seeger was the only woman in the camp, taken there solely because of her husband's politics. He had been imprisoned in another camp, had escaped and written a book denouncing the Nazis. Tate had a number of secret meetings with the Nazi authorities and persuaded them to allow her to go to Dessau, pick up Frau Seeger and return to Britain in a German aircraft.[66]

Meanwhile, the Duchess of Atholl, who was fluent in German, read *Mein Kampf* to understand the 'nature and intentions of the German regime' from the original source. She concluded that 'Germany is the only serious danger to peace in Europe'.[67] As Stuart Ball points out, the Duchess discovered that the English version had left out the more threatening, aggressive sections that might prove unattractive to British readers. The Duchess translated the omitted parts and passed them to Winston Churchill.

In contrast, there were a number of 'high-society hostesses who ran pro-Nazi salons' such as Lady Cunard, Dame Maggie Greville, Nancy Astor and Lady Londonderry. They wanted to encourage a more positive relationship between Britain and Germany and formed the 'nucleus of a pro-German lobby' trying to make Nazism respectable.[68] Astor invited the leading Nazi von Ribbentrop to her London house just after the Nazi occupation of the Rhineland, where they played musical chairs, and she whispered to her other guests to let the Germans win.[69] Others like Lady Snowden, wife of the former Labour Chancellor, visited Germany and commented favourably on the Nazi regime. These 'Guilty Women' as Gottlieb points out were Nazi sympathisers and apologists, willing to ignore the increasingly anti-semitic and dictatorial direction of Germany. One of the most influential society hostesses was Edith, Lady Londonderry, a supporter of women's suffrage, founder of the women's Land Army, former member of the Women's Volunteer Reserve, founding member of the Townswomen's Guilds and president of the Conservative Women's Advisory Committee. She was married to one of the richest men in Britain, and used this power to host glittering parties at Londonderry House, where she fostered Anglo-German friendship. She wrote regularly to both Hitler and Goebbels claiming that she was trying to encourage pro-German sympathy among MPs and in the press, though in a grossly anti-semitic sentence warned them that the newspapers were 'largely controlled by Jews'.[70] In 1934, when von Ribbentrop visited London, Lady Londonderry was all too eager to entertain him, holding a weekend party in his honour when he became ambassador.[71] Ribbentrop was known in those circles as 'Londonderry Herr'.[72]

Fearing for their lives, many Jewish people and those who opposed the Nazis fled Germany. By the end of 1938, the NCW was concerned about the welfare of refugees, especially children. In December 1938, 602 unaccompanied children (part of the kinder transport) had arrived in Harwich: the NCW helped expedite their entry permits and found homes for some of the children.[73] In 1939, the Conservative government restricted the entry of (mostly Jewish) refugees, including children, fleeing from Nazi persecution: each refugee had to be sponsored and a financial guarantee given that they would not be a drain on the exchequer. The NCW sent a strong letter to the national press opposing this new legislation but to little effect. Despite government reluctance, women like former WSPU activist Hilda Clark, Bertha Bracey and Eleanor Rathbone helped rescue nearly 10,000 Jewish children from Germany and Nazi-occupied territories.[74]

Spain

On 24 August 1937, Elizabeth Pearl Bickerstaffe celebrated her 17th birthday. Shortly before her birthday, she began a Spanish Civil War Scrapbook, a collection of newspapers cuttings about the Spanish Civil War. Just over a year earlier, the Spanish army, led by General Franco, had rebelled against the newly elected left-wing government because it disapproved of the new government's land reforms, its restoration of Catalan autonomy, its banning of the Fascist Party and the transfer of right-wing military leaders to posts outside Spain. These Spanish army officers had plotted against the democratically elected Republican parties, and in July 1936, civil war broke out between the Fascist rebels and the legitimate government. About 500,000 people died as a result of this brutal conflict. The British government refused to intervene. The horror that was felt by Elizabeth Bickerstaffe over the coup d'etat was shared by others. Campaigns across Britain were begun to help the Spanish Republic, campaigns which were 'to become the most widespread and representative movement since the mid-nineteenth century ... and the most outstanding example of international solidarity in British history'.[75] Young Elizabeth experienced 'that same visceral engagements with events in Spain and with the pain, mingled with defiance and diminishing hope, that accompanied the slow and agonising defeat of Spain's elected government'.[76]

Elizabeth Pearl Bickerstaffe, an ordinary young woman from Doncaster, had been 'radicalised by poverty and the social injustices of the inter-war years'.[77] Her father was a 'strong union man', a member of the Labour Party and chair of the South Yorkshire National Unemployed Workers' Movement. Miss Bickerstaffe too joined the Labour Party and became a staunch trade unionist, passing onto her son Rodney Bickerstaffe 'the values of solidarity and supporting the underdog, values that she learnt from and were reinforced by the war in Spain. ... She was outraged by injustice at work and in the wider community, in Britain or anywhere else in the world'.[78] She inspired her son Rodney to dedicate his life to fighting for workers' rights: he became a leading trade unionist, helped to create UNISON and persuaded the 1997 Labour government to introduce the minimum wage. Rodney Bickerstaffe was a founder member of the International Brigade Memorial Trust, saying it was 'vital that future generations learn the lessons of what happened in Spain' (Figs. 5.2 and 5.3).

The outbreak of the Spanish Civil War and its ensuing horrors led to voluntary efforts to help those afflicted: the Spanish Women's Committee for Help to Spain, Labour women's Spanish Relief Committee, the Women's Committee Against War and Fascism and women-led organisations such as the Basque Children's Committee were among the various organisations which were formed to help. Many of the leading figures in the Aid movement were women. Women MPs from across the party benches—the independent Eleanor Rathbone, Labour's Ellen Wilkinson, the Liberal Megan Lloyd George, Conservative's Duchess of Atholl, Thelma Cazalet and Irene Ward—and activists outside Parliament—Leah Manning, Audrey Russell, Janet Vaughan, Isabel Brown, Violet Bonham-Carter—all worked together to coordinate humanitarian efforts for Spain and to ameliorate the dire conditions resulting from the Spanish Civil War. Their efforts yielded results. In 1936, the National Joint Committee for Spanish Relief (NJC) was set up after an all-party parliamentary visit to Madrid reported on the dreadful conditions there. The Duchess of Atholl became chair and Eleanor Rathbone vice chair of the new deliberately non-sectarian organisation. The aim of the NJC was to coordinate efforts to

Pearl Bickerstaffe in about 1937.   *Pearl and Rodney in 1949.*

Figs. 5.2 and 5.3 Pearl Bickerstaffe in about 1937 and with Rodney, 1949 (Courtesy of Pat Bickerstaffe)

'relieve the suffering of children, of civilians, helpless in face of the terrors of modern war, of the sick and wounded'.[79] On many issues—from women's suffrage which she had initially opposed—the Duchess was on the right wing of the Conservative Party. However, she became a fierce anti-fascist, publishing a searing condemnation of Franco in *Searchlight on Spain*.[80]

The provision of humanitarian aid was perhaps the most crucial service to the Spanish government. The Standing Joint Committee of Industrial Women's Organisations (SJC) set up the Spanish Relief Committee initially to 'provide knitted garments of every description' for mostly homeless women and children, fleeing from 'barbarous air attacks'.[81] Knitting circles were established in Southampton, Gateshead, Bradford, Newcastle, Glasgow, Shrewsbury, Gloucester, Cheltenham, Liverpool and South Wales. By April 1937, the collective had knitted 9075 garments, bought a further 10,942 from the Co-op and received 1607 as a gift from the Tailors' and Garment Workers' Union, who also donated 156 blankets and 71 rolls of cloth.[82] The Scottish branch of the Spanish Women's Committee took over a disused factory to make clothes.[83] Female undergraduates from Girton and Newnham colleges sold hot sausages and bread rolls in Cambridge as a way of collecting money for Spanish people. Individuals and organisations responded generously: in 1937, the popular novelist and travel writer Ethel Mannin donated her life savings of £1000 to help buy a food ship to go to Spain to feed those trapped in Bilbao. Women across Britain—from the Co-op women who sold milk tokens on behalf of the Spanish women and children to those involved in Labour's *Milk for Spain* Campaign—donated time and energy to help the Spanish legitimate government. Groups such as the Kent hop-pickers, the Inland Revenue Staff Federation and the Scottish Wholesale Society donated money. Each month, Dorothy Cadbury organised 24 cases of a mixture of milk and cocoa powder, each case provided drinks for 100 children.[84] In Sheffield, one restaurant manageress led a campaign to collect tinned and packet food to ship to Spain. A van with a loudspeaker playing Paul Robeson's song 'Sometime I feel like a motherless child', a song he recorded for the Basque Children's Fund, toured the streets. When enough food had been collected, it was taken by barge to Hull, where it was shipped to Spain.[85] Other women organised day schools to educate women into the perils of fascism, went on demonstrations against the BUF and 'spearheaded and supported consumer and travel boycotts, organised bazaars, sent "snowball" letters to urge women to refuse to buy goods' coming from the fascist countries.[86]

At 6:40 am, Friday 21 May 1937, the *SS Habana*, built to carry 800 passengers, left Bilbao with 3840 children, 200 female teachers and assistants and 10 priests on board. It had been requisitioned by the Basque Children's Committee to bring refugee children to safety in Britain. Leah Manning, now joint secretary of the Committee Against War and Fascism, and former suffragette Edith Pye flew over to help bring the children to Britain. Once on the ship, the children were packed in like sardines—on the bulkheads, in the state rooms, in the corridors and even in the swimming pool. Leah Manning 'slipped and slithered from one pool of diarrhoea and vomit to another' as distressed children became seasick.[87]

On Saturday evening, the ship arrived at Southampton harbour. The children were met by a welcome committee which included Katherine, Duchess of Atholl. In May 1937, the Duchess of Atholl and Eleanor Rathbone, respectively chair and vice chair, had set up the Basque Children's Committee to organise the evacuation and the care of these Basque children. The Duchess of Atholl thought it a credit 'to the true humanity latent in everybody, a humanity which ultimately outweighs political and religious differences' that the child refugees were in Britain through the concerted efforts of people with widely differing political views.[88] She had had an enormous challenge to persuade the very reluctant Stanley Baldwin and the Conservative government to accept any refugees at all; finally, the government relented and allowed a single boatload of refugee children as long as they could be supported by charitable funds. Atholl's recently formed Children's Committee had to guarantee 10 shillings a week for each child rescued. The government refused to give financial support to help the refugees: the children were helped solely by the generosity of their British hosts.

When the children disembarked, they were taken to a 'city of canvas'—500 bell tents and several enormous marquees—where they were housed.[89] The feeding of the 4000—the provision of 4000 oranges, several tons of onions, 500 gallons of milk a day, 4000 portions of chocolate and copious amounts of bread and butter—was challenging for the organisers. Each day, hungry frightened children, many of whom had a 'disconcerting tendency' to hoard bread under their clothes, were fed and comforted. Arrangements were made to evacuate the children to homes across the United Kingdom.[90]

The Duchess of Atholl and the Committee were responsible for managing and financing the 40 or so homes later set up to house and look after the child refugees. The Sunderland Committee asked people to donate 7s a week to their home or for the Townswomen's Guild and the Women's Institutes to club together to foster one or more children. Eighty-four people, they argued, who paid one penny a week could support one child; in return, the individual or group would receive a photograph of their foster child and from time-to-time news, letters and drawings.[91] Ellen Wilkinson persuaded her Union, NUDAW, to raise a voluntary levy for a period of three months to help finance it. Many branches of NUSEC offered help: the Ashton-under-Lyme branch of NUSEC raised £100, a number of local branches offered to finance refugee children, and many members joined local Refugee Committees.[92]

In September 1937, 24 laughing children from the Basque area of Northern Spain 'leaned out of carriage windows and waved excitedly' as their train pulled into Dundee train station.[93] The 14 girls and 10 boys aged between 7 and 15 were placed under the care of a former missionary, Miss M. Wilson at Mall Park, Montrose Home, a large country house which had been donated by the president of the Free Breakfast Mission. Miss Wilson had lived in Spain for ten years and spoke fluent Spanish, an obvious advantage in looking after children who knew little or no English. She was one of many unknown and unrecognised heroines who had responded to an appeal from the Duchess of Atholl to help take care of the refugee children.

In April 1937, Eleanor Rathbone, the Duchess of Atholl, Dame Rachel Crowdy and Ellen Wilkinson visited Spain on behalf of the National Joint Committee for Spanish Relief. In Barcelona, they were welcomed by the Republican government keen to gather as much support from England as it could. They visited Valencia and met the Republican leader Dolores Ibarruri, known as La Pasionaria. In Madrid, 'shells from rebel six inch guns, smashing in the street outside, tearing through the roof of a theatre blew mangled bodies of women and children' through the doorway of the hotel where the women were having lunch. Their car was standing nearby. Before they could drive away, the body of one of the victims had to be wiped off it. For the women, it was a gruesome reminder of the reality of war. These experiences made an impact on all four women, and they all returned with a new commitment to organise relief schemes and to convince the British government that Franco and his army were being assisted by German and Italian forces.

Shortly after their return from Spain, Guernica—the cultural capital of the Basque population—was 'wantonly and ruthlessly' bombed by the German air force.[94] Leah Manning, who was visiting nearby, heard the sounds of bombers overhead: 'helpless to do anything we watched from the hills. Until nearly eight in the evening, incendiary bombs and high explosives rained down every twenty minutes. The town was open and defenceless; it was crowded with market day visitors and as people fled from the destruction they were dive-bombed and machined-gunned from the air.'[95] Two-thirds of the population were killed or wounded. The world was shocked by this massive murder of civilians, commemorated by Picasso in his painting, *Guernica*. On Thursday 8 May, identifying with the fate of the Republicans and frustrated by Parliament's reluctance to do anything to help, Ellen Wilkinson broke down and sobbed during a debate on Spain in the House of Commons. The Labour Party denounced the bombing as an 'outrage upon humanity, as a violation of the principles of civilisation, and a manifestation of the merciless and inhuman spirit' of the Nazis and fascists.[96]

At the beginning of August 1936, Eleanor Rathbone, Megan Lloyd George, Leah Manning and Maude Royden had formed the Spanish Medical Aid Committee (SMA). In a report from Spain, Manning spoke of little children 'with stick-like limbs, abnormally swollen abdomens, vacant eyes and pallid complexions,' all due to undernourishment. Many of the refugees were sleeping without blankets on bare boards; the great majority had no change of clothing; the children had no shoes.[97] She pleaded for milk, flour, beans, sugar, cocoa, cod liver oil and malt, clothes, blankets and shoes. Raising funds for Spain, she claimed, was easy: it was quite common to raise £1000 at one meeting alone 'besides plates full of rings, bracelets, brooches, watches, jewelry of all kinds'.[98] NUSEC was supportive: the Bolton branch raised £200 for Spanish Medical Aid, 'providing a number of surgical beds as well as a quantity of bandages, clothing etc.'; the Liverpool branch lent its office for free; and the Ashton branch worked with other societies to fundraise.[99]

On 23 August 1936, the SMA sent out the first mobile field hospital consisting of four surgeons, eight technical assistants, six trained nurses, two quartermaster staff and one mechanic to look after the wounded in Spain.[100] Others followed: 126 male and female volunteers: doctors, nurses, orderlies, ambulance drivers, stretcher-bearers, pharmacists, radiologists, masseuse, all volunteers abandoned their careers to help in Spain.[101] Nurses worked under excruciatingly bad conditions: dirty sheets could not be washed because there was no soap; patients lay in bed naked because there were no pyjamas. Penelope Phelps, a nurse who had travelled with one of the first units, spoke of being short of anaesthetics and having to treat people who had been shot or injured from hand grenades without painkillers or antiseptics. She maintained that Spain was red with blood, not with politics. Blood was 'splashed over the streets and the gutters often run with it. Often my finger nails were blocked up with clotted blood, and my arms up to the elbows in it'.[102] On one occasion, a surgical team arrived to find there were no operating instruments and had to use kitchen equipment to amputate a man's leg.

Two British women—Ann Organ, a nurse, and Mavis King, a radiologist—saved hundreds of lives with a travelling operating theatre and a portable X-ray machine which had been sent from Britain. Another British nurse, Lillian Urmston, spent 22 months nursing on the Teruel front in Spain fixing up first-aid posts in farmhouses, tents, huts and even village churches. In September 1937, she worked on the ground floor of an old house—the second floor had been bombed and could not be used. They cleaned the first-aid station with cold water and toilet soap and used dried straw fastened around twigs as a mop and broom. These women had responded to the call for help from the Republican legitimate government: nursing was a political act. In January 1939, two nurses who had recently returned from Spain after two and a half years—26-year-old Angela Guest[103] and 23-year-old Eileen Palmer—distributed leaflets at the entrance to Downing Street. The two had gone to Spain as part of the International Brigade: Angela's brother died in the fighting. The leaflets they distributed made their political stand obvious. 'Chamberlain', they stated, 'is guilty of blood that has flown in Spain for two and a half years, because the legal Spanish Government has been deprived of the right to buy arms to defend itself against itself against foreign invaders. We British nurses who have served in Spain demand that Spain be given the right to defend herself. Send arms to Spain!' The two accused Neville Chamberlain of responsibility for the deaths of men, women and children in Spain because of his non-intervention policy. They walked up to No 10 and threw red paint hidden in two thermos flasks at the door, paint that was symbolic of the blood spilt in Spain. They were charged with 'insulting behaviour' and with damaging property: the charge of insulting behaviour was withdrawn but they were bound over for six months and ordered to pay 5s in damage.[104] In March 1939, the Spanish Civil War ended with a victory for Franco, the man who had led an armed insurrection against a democratically elected government. He remained in power until 1975.

Appeasement and the Road to War

As the 1930s progressed, Germany began to rearm and make increasingly aggressive territorial demands, including taking over Austria and Czechoslovakia. Some women called for action against the Nazis; others sought to placate Hitler by conceding territory to Germany in an attempt to avoid war. The women—and indeed men—who favoured accommodating Adolf Hitler and his band of thugs did so for a number of reasons: because the Nazis were seen as a bulwark against Communism; because the Treaty of Versailles was viewed as an injustice to a conquered nation; and because the nation held too many memories of the destruction and unnecessary deaths of the First Word War and had no wish to fight another. Two key organisations—Women's International League for Peace and Freedom (WILPF) and the Women's Co-operative Guild

(WCG)—remained committed to pacifism. Both were involved in the 1934 Peace Ballot, a ballot initiated by the League of Nations Union, which called for sanctions on aggressor nations.[105] A number of famous individuals—the writer Vera Brittain, the religious activist Maud Royden, the actress Sybil Thorndike, the former editor of the suffragist paper *The Common Cause* Helena Swanwick—remained absolute pacifists. In 1937, Virginia Woolf published *Three Guineas*, part of which was a critique of the relationship between war and masculinity and the ways in which women could prevent war.

The Munich Agreement

In 1937, Neville Chamberlain replaced Stanley Baldwin as Conservative prime minister and almost immediately began negotiating with Hitler. The Munich Agreement, an agreement signed by Chamberlain and Hitler giving the latter permission to annex the Sudetenland in Czechoslovakia where many ethnic Germans lived, was the culmination of the Conservative government's appeasement strategy. Chamberlain returned, waving his piece of paper, and promising to secure 'Peace in our time'. Britain breathed a sigh of relief; Czechoslovakia was dismembered. Violet Bonham-Carter tried to persuade Harold Nicolson to 'go all out and oppose the Government'. He refused.[106]

In October 1938, when the agreement was debated in the House of Commons over several days, a few women took part in the debate. Some of the women MPs condemned not just Chamberlain's betrayal of Czechoslovakia but the whole appeasement policy of the Conservative government towards fascism because it had 'landed us nearer and nearer to war'.[107] Eleanor Rathbone asked whether the government intended to make 'any further grant to the Czech government in compensation for the fortifications which they have abandoned at the request of His Majesty's Government?'; whether any arrangements had been made for the release of Czechs imprisoned or interned in Germany; and 'about the number of refugees' who had fled into the interior of Czechoslovakia to escape the advance of the Germans?'[108] The next day Rathbone focused on asking whether the government would guarantee the new frontiers of Czechoslovakia and whether the government was considering steps to prevent aggressive action by the Poles, Hungarians and Slovenes towards Czechoslovakia. When the government prevaricated, she asked it again, again and again. She never received an answer. Six months later, the Germans took over the rest of Czechoslovakia.

In contrast, Florence Horsbrugh was vehemently in favour of Chamberlain's Agreement, claiming that 'we women Members of Parliament have received many messages from associations of women, from married and single women all over the world, the enormous majority of whom are thanking God that a way of averting the disaster of war has been found'.[109] When the House divided on the motion that 'this House approves the policy of His Majesty's Government by which war was averted in the recent crisis and supports their efforts to secure a lasting peace', the House divided on party lines. Only 30 Tory MPs out of 386 declined to support the motion. All the Conservative women present in the House voted in favour; the Labour women, Eleanor Rathbone and Megan Lloyd-George all voted against.

Katherine Steward-Murray, the Duchess of Atholl, Conservative MP for Kinross and West Perthshire, who thought that Chamberlain's Munich Agreement was a 'shameful surrender',[110] was in America at the time of the vote trying to raise money for the Spanish Republican cause. Her views on appeasement were well known. Atholl telegrammed Churchill saying she would support any protest as the surrender of the Sudetenland was too dangerous.[111] This act of rebellion against Conservative Party policy, and her passionate crusade in favour of the Spanish Republic, led to the Whip being withdrawn and de-selection by her constituency. The by-election which followed was seen as a vote of confidence in Neville Chamberlain and his German foreign policy: the Duchess, now standing as an Independent candidate, was uncompromisingly against appeasement. She told her electorate that 'Munich has brought us no sign of the appeasement for which our Government had hoped. On the contrary, both Herr Hitler's speeches and the officially-controlled German Press have become increasingly aggressive. And there has been a persecution of the Jews in Germany of unparalleled brutality'.[112] Lady Rhondda ran a fundraising campaign through her journal *Time and Tide*, and Eleanor Rathbone travelled to Scotland to give support her campaign. Unfortunately, the Duchess' ideas were anathema to most of her constituents, who saw a vote for the Duchess as a vote for war. Her campaign was further undermined when 70 Conservative MPs, including Nancy Astor and Florence Horsbrugh, appealed to the electors not to vote for the Duchess. Florence Horsbrugh went to Dundee to campaign against her former colleague.[113] One female voter from Crieff told Mass Observation that she was 'voting for Mr Chamberlain, he saved (us from) war. You know I've always voted for the duchess, but you can't do better than what Mr Chamberlain did—an old man, he went to Germany, why they might have killed him'.[114] The Duchess of Atholl was defeated and never returned to Parliament. She blamed her defeat on 'the vote of the women'.[115]

The Conservative Women's Association (CWA), the 'largest, most active political organisation in interwar Britain',[116] favoured appeasement. Audiences at meetings expressed their delight at Chamberlain and his policy of conciliation. It was the hero worship of a matinee idol, of a knightly saviour who redeemed the world without a fight. It was, as Gottlieb observes, 'nothing less than star power, and messianic star power at that'.[117] At a meeting in Epsom, Conservative women enthusiastically renewed their confidence in their prime minister, arguing that by his 'patience and forbearance, by his vision and courage, he has saved the world from war'.[118] Each year Chamberlain spoke at the CWA's annual conference, and each year was thanked for his efforts to keep the peace between Britain and the rest of Europe. All over Britain, 'women Conservatives showed their consistent and unquestioning support for appeasement, their meetings becoming thanksgiving celebrations for the Prime Minister'.[119] The average Conservative woman, Gottlieb estimates, was more insular than other political women, showed little interest in foreign affairs and even less interest in helping victims of fascism. As one might expect, 'the sociable and non-confrontational forums in which Conservative women met and oiled the party machinery did not lend themselves to the politics of dissent'.[120] Instinctively, women in the CWA were the very embodiment of appeasement. The Ladies Grand Council of the Primrose League maintained that millions of women owed Chamberlain an immeasurable debt for his handling of the international situation.[121] Mrs Chamberlain believed that 'one of the most moving things, and one that has touched my husband deeply, has been the message of confidence which have been sent to him from the women of the country'.[122] Nancy Astor used her wealth, connections and weekend parties at her Cliveden family home to influence foreign policy, as did a number of Conservative society hostesses. Indeed, Conservative women were not noted for their knowledge of international affairs and mostly focused on getting Conservatives into Parliament, on local issues and in championing the British Empire rather than fighting for women's rights. Conservative women much preferred their Whist Drives, their social evenings, their sales of work and their annual trips to Morecambe and other seaside places to participating in political events.

Former suffragettes and feminists like Christabel Pankhurst, Cecily Hamilton, Dame Ethel Smyth, Maud Royden and Helena Swanwick congratulated Chamberlain for preserving the peace. The children's writer Enid Blyton was eulogistic, even writing verse in support of Chamberlain, ending with 'The Moment came and with it came the Man'.[123] Lady Londonderry was overjoyed when the Munich Agreement was signed.

Women were encouraged by the pro-Nazi *Daily Mail* and the *Daily Express* to create a world peace movement.[124] This led to a relationship between the BUF and the Peace Pledge Union, a situation that at first strikes one as odd. Pacifism, of course, takes many forms, from an absolute pacifism through to one that is contextual. And in the 1930s, some of those who wanted to prevent war tended to be from the far right, concerned that their beloved Britain would be at war with their treasured fascist Germany. The British Union of Fascists naturally supported appeasement: they had no wish to fight their brothers and sisters-in arms in Germany. Unity Mitford even went on a peace mission to Germany, insisting that the 'Powers could have tried harder for peace'.[125]

The female electorate agreed with the appeasement strategy: the 1935 General Election was regarded as the 'women's election' because candidates stressed their peace-loving credentials in an attempt to gain the female vote. Similarly, in the by-elections which followed, candidates targeted the female vote by arguing in favour of appeasement. Those who did usually won.

In the early part of the 1930s, left-wing women political activists also continued their 'war on war', until the rise of Nazism made their position untenable and they changed to a woman's war on Fascism.[126] In particular, as Sheila Rowbotham argues, women's peace organisations 'were caught in a difficult dilemma' by the threat of Fascism.[127] This solidified during the Italian invasion of Abyssinia, the illegal General Franco rebellion that led to the Spanish Civil

War and the Nazi re-militarisation of the Rhineland. Feminists like Ellen Wilkinson, Dora Russell, Eleanor Rathbone and Edith Summerskill believed that Fascism was too great a threat to ignore and supported rearmament. Violet Bonham-Carter, daughter of the former Liberal Prime Minister Asquith, condemned the Munich Agreement. 'We meet', she said, 'in a very dark hour'. The government had 'broken a great and honourable tradition of English foreign policy ... The keystone of that policy has been the refusal to truckle to the strong at the expense of the weak ... When the Prime Minister signed the Munich agreement he renounced all claims to moral leadership'.[128] Eleanor Rathbone argued that appeasement was a 'clever plan of selling your friends in order to buy off your enemies—which has the danger that a time comes when you have no friends left, and then you find you need them, and then it is too late to buy them back'.[129]

On 17 March 1939, the National Council for Equal Citizenship hosted a lunch celebration commemorating the 21st anniversary of equal women's suffrage at the Criterion, Piccadilly, a restaurant often used by the suffragettes for formal occasions. Many of the great and good were present: Edith Picton-Turbervill, Viscountess Snowden, Maude Royden, Emmeline Pethick-Lawrence, Eleanor Rathbone and Margaret Corbett Ashby. Nancy Astor sent a message of congratulation. Eleanor Rathbone gave a speech which was broadcast on BBC radio. In her presidential address, Edith Picton-Turbervill said that the 'freedom of women rested upon the same principles as did democracy; if democracy perished, women would lose their hardly-won freedom. We cannot ignore the alarming trend of world politics, which, among other evils, is fundamentally inimical to all the principles for which we stand'.[130] The Council agreed that the government should be asked to 'relax the present stringent conditions of entry of refugees into Britain' and provide money to help.[131] Two days before, Nazi troops had invaded Bohemia and Moravia, areas of Czechoslovakia, outside the Sudetenland. A few months later, Britain declared war on Germany: when war broke out, Unity Mitford shot herself in the head.

NOTES

1. In 1931, all the Labour women lost their seats, yet the number of women who gained seats was the highest ever: 15 women were elected: 13 Conservatives, 1 Liberal, Megan Lloyd George, and 1 Independent, Eleanor Rathbone. In 1935, nine women were returned to Parliament: six Conservatives, namely Nancy Astor, Duchess of Atholl, Thelma Cazalet-Keir, Florence Horsbrugh, Mavis Tate, Irene Ward; one Liberal, Megan Lloyd-George; one Independent, Eleanor Rathbone; and one Labour, Ellen Wilkinson. By 1939, three other Labour women had joined Wilkinson, winning their seats in by-elections: Mrs J L Adamson, Mrs A Hardie and Edith Summerskill.
2. *The Vote*, June 14th 1929, p188.
3. Margaret Bondfield, Hansard, 1 December 1930, vol 245, cc1827-952.
4. See Paula Bartley, *Labour Women in Power*, Palgrave Macmillan, 2019, for more detail.

5. Helen Langley, 'Ward, Irene Mary Bewick, Baroness Ward of North Tyneside', *DNB*, 2004.
6. Sheila Rowbotham, *A Century of Women*, Viking, 1997.
7. Susan Lawrence, Evening Sentinel, 4 March 1935, p6.
8. NUSEC Annual Report, 1935–36.
9. Sheila Rowbotham, *A Century of Women*, Viking, 1997, p180.
10. *Sheffield Daily Telegraph*, 24 October 1932, p7.
11. *The Lancashire Daily Post*, 22 October 1932, p8.
12. *The Mercury*, 21 October 1932, p4.
13. *Derby Evening Telegraph*, 10 February 1934, p1.
14. *Birmingham Gazette*, 16 February 1934, p9.
15. *Evening Telegraph*, 27 February 1934, p7.
16. *The Manchester Guardian*, 1 March 1934, p4.
17. *The Western Daily Press*, 23 February 1934, p1.
18. See Paula Bartley, *Ellen Wilkinson*, Pluto Press, 2014.
19. NUSEC Annual Report, 1936–7, p8.
20. Henry Srebrnik, 'Class, ethnicity and gender intertwined: Jewish women and the East London Rent Strikes, 1935–1940', *Women's History Review*, Vol 4, Number 3, 1995, p286.
21. See Caitriona Beaumont, 'Citizens not feminists: the boundary negotiated between citizenship and feminism by mainstream women's organisations in England, 1938–1939', *Women's History Review*, Vol 9 Issue 2, 2000, p415 and Caitriona Beaumont, *Housewives and Citizens. Domesticity and the Women's Movement in England, 1928–64*, MUP, 2013.
22. Ibid.
23. The National Council of Women, formerly the National Union of Women Workers, had been founded in the nineteenth century. It was an umbrella organisation that campaigned for women's rights. See Daphne Glick, *The National Council of Women of Great Britain, The First One Hundred Years*, NCW, 1995.
24. The two organisations had formed from the National Union of Societies for Equal Citizenship, itself an organisation which had sprung from the National Union of Suffrage Societies.
25. The National Council of Women, formerly the National Union of Women Workers, had been founded in the nineteenth century. It was an umbrella organisation that campaigned for women's rights. See Daphne Glick, *The National Council of Women of Great Britain, The First One Hundred Years*, NCW, 1995.
26. Stephen Brookes, '"A New World for Women", Abortion Law Reform in Britain during the 1930s', *The American Historical Review*, April 2001, pp431–458.
27. Quoted in Lesley A Hall, *The Life and Times of Stella Browne*, I. B. Tauris, 2011, p178.
28. Stephen Brookes, '"A New World for Women", Abortion Law Reform in Britain during the 1930s', *The American Historical Review*, April 2001, pp431–458.
29. James Thomas and Susan A, Williams, 'Women and Abortion in 1930s Britain', *Social History of Medicine*, Vol 11, August 1998, pp283–309.

30. Lesley Hall, 'Articulating Abortion in Inter-War Britain', *Women's History Magazine*, Issue 70, Autumn, 2012.
31. Ibid.
32. Ibid.
33. *British Medical Journal*, Vol 1, February 1936, p378.
34. *The Scotsman*, 20 July 1938, p10.
35. Interdepartmental Committee on Abortion 1939, quoted in Stephen Brookes, '"A New World for Women", Abortion Law Reform in Britain during the 1930s', *The American Historical Review*, April 2001, p458.
36. Bondfield and Lawrence were both re-elected in by-elections in 1926.
37. M. Page Baldwin, 'Subject to Empire: Married Women and the British Nationality and Status of Aliens Act', *Journal of British Studies*, Vol 40, October 2001, p547.
38. Ibid., p549.
39. Pamela Brookes, *Women at Westminster*, Peter Davies, 1967.
40. See M. Page Baldwin, 'Subject to Empire: Married Women and the British Nationality and Status of Aliens Act', *Journal of British Studies*, Vol 40, October 2001, pp522–556.
41. *The Vote*, 9 August 1930, p253.
42. See Helen Glew, *Gender, Rhetoric and Regulation, Women's Work in the Civil Service and the London County Council 1900–1955*, MUP, 2016.
43. *The Scotsman*, 2 April 1936, p11.
44. *Daily Herald*, 2 April p11.
45. Stephen Cullen, 'Four Women for Mosley: Women in the British Union of Fascists, 1932–1940', *Oral History*, Spring 1996, pp49–59. See also Julie Gottlieb, *Feminine Fascism: Women in Britain's Fascist Movement*, I. B. Taurus, 2003.
46. Harold Nicolson, *Diaries and Letters 1930–39*, Collins, 1966, p98.
47. In 1935, the Archbishop of Canterbury opened the Lady Cynthia Mosley Day Nursery at Kennington, London, built in memory of the late aristocrat. It accommodated 45 children under the age of five.
48. Stephen Cullen, 'Four Women for Mosley: Women in the British Union of Fascists, 1932–1940', *Oral History*, Spring 1996, p52.
49. Ibid.
50. Ibid., p54.
51. See Hilda Kean, 'Suffrage Autobiography: A Study of Mary Richardson', in Claire Eustance et al., *A Suffrage Reader*, Leicester University Press, 2000.
52. Mary Richardson quoted in Hilda Kean, 'Suffrage Autobiography: A Study of Mary Richardson', in Claire Eustance et al., *A Suffrage Reader*, Leicester University Press, 2000.
53. Quoted in Stephen Cullen, 'Four Women for Mosley: Women in the British Union of Fascists, 1932–1940, *Oral History*, Spring 1996, p56.
54. Ibid.
55. *Daily Herald*, June 11th 1934, p9.
56. Hilda Kean, 'Suffrage Autobiography: A Study of Mary Richardson', in Claire Eustance et al., *A Suffrage Reader*, Leicester University Press, 2000.
57. Julie Gottlieb, 'Feminism and Anti-Fascism in Britain: Militancy Revived?' in D. Copsey and D. Renton, *British Fascism, the Labour Movement and the State*, Palgrave Macmillan, 2005.

58. Martin Durham, 'Gender and the British Union of Fascists', *Journal of Contemporary History*, July 1992.
59. Mary Davies, *Sylvia Pankhurst, A Life in Radical Politics*, Pluto Press, 1999, p110.
60. Richard Pankhurst, *Sylvia Pankhurst, Artist and Crusader*, Paddington Press, 1979.
61. Gottlieb, Julie V, *'Guilty Women', Foreign Policy and Appeasement in Inter-War Britain*, Palgrave Macmillan, 2015.
62. Ibid., p41.
63. Ibid.
64. *Yorkshire Post and Leeds Intelligencer*, 15 October 1934, p6.
65. *The Lancashire Daily Post*, 1 November 1934, p9.
66. *Leeds Mercury*, 25 May 1934, p1.
67. Stuart Ball, 'The Politics of Appeasement: the Fall of the Duchess of Atholl and the Kinross and West Perth by-election, December 1938', *The Scottish Historical Review*, Vol 69, April 1990, pp49–83.
68. Gottlieb, Julie V, *'Guilty Women', Foreign Policy and Appeasement in Inter-War Britain*, Palgrave Macmillan, 2015, p87.
69. Rachel Reeves, *Women of Westminster*, I. B. Tauris, 2019, p31.
70. Quoted in Gottlieb, Julie V, *'Guilty Women', Foreign Policy and Appeasement in Inter-War Britain*, Palgrave Macmillan, 2015, p85.
71. Ibid., p38.
72. Interview with Lady Mosley quoted in Rosemary Caldicott, *Lady Blackshirts*, Bristol Radical Pamphleteer, 2017, p28.
73. Daphne Glick, *The National Council of Women of Great Britain, The First One Hundred Years*, NCW, 1995.
74. See Rose Holmes, *A Moral Business: British Quaker work with Refugees from Fascism, 1933–39*, PhD, University of Sussex, 2013.
75. Quoted in *A Spanish Civil War Scrapbook, Elizabeth Pearl Bickerstaffe's newspaper cuttings of the wars in Spain and China from August 1937 to May 1939*, International Brigade Memorial Trust and Lawrence and Wishart, 2015, p5. Thanks to the late Rodney Bickerstaffe, who gave me this book, compiled in honour of his mother.
76. Ibid., p1.
77. Ibid., p7.
78. Ibid., p11.
79. National Joint Committee for Spanish Relief, February 1937, p5.
80. Penguin, 1938.
81. Spanish Relief Committee leaflet 1936, Archives of the Trades Union Congress, 292/946/1/20, University of Warwick.
82. Spanish Relief Committee Minutes, April 1937, Archives of the Trades Union Congress, 292/946/1/4 University of Warwick.
83. Jim Fryth, *The Signal was Spain*, Lawrence and Wishart, 1986.
84. Rose Holmes, *A Moral Business: British Quaker work with Refugees from Fascism, 1933–39*, PhD, University of Sussex, 2013, p18.
85. Jim Fryth, *The Signal Was Spain*, Lawrence and Wishart, 1986.
86. Julie V. Gottlieb, *'Guilty Women', Foreign Policy and Appeasement in Inter-War Britain*, Palgrave Macmillan, 2015, p50.
87. Leah Manning, *A Life for Education*, Garden City Press, 1970, p131.

88. *Berks and Oxon Advertiser*, 11 June 1937, p2.
89. National Joint Committee for Spanish Relief, Bulletin No 7, 1937.
90. Ibid.
91. *Sunderland Daily Echo*, 31 May 1937, p6.
92. NUSEC Annual Report, 1938–9.
93. *The Evening Telegraph*, 17 September 1937, p6.
94. *Whitstable Times and Tankerton Press*, 20 November 1937, p8.
95. Leah Manning, *A Life for Education*, Garden City Press, 1970, p126.
96. NEC Manifesto, 28 April 1937
97. Leah Manning, *Report to the National Joint Committee on the Refugee Problem in Catalunya*, 2 October 1937.
98. Leah Manning, *A Life for Education*, Garden City Press, 1970, p120.
99. NUSEC Annual Report, 1937–8, p9.
100. *Bath Chronicle and Weekly Gazette*, 29 August 1936, p25.
101. *Medical Aid for Spain: the work of the Spanish Medical Aid Committee*, 28 December 1937.
102. Ibid., p11.
103. Angela was the daughter of Labour MP Hayden Guest and sister of David Guest, who had died fighting for the International Brigade in the Spanish Civil War.
104. Unattributed newspaper cutting, 1 February 1939. In Elizabeth Pearl, Bickerstaffe, *A Spanish Civil War Scrapbook*, International Brigade Memorial Trust and Lawrence and Wishart, 2015, p176.
105. Jill Liddington, *The Long Road to Greenham, Feminism and Anti-Militarism in Britain since 1820*, Virago, 1989.
106. Harold Nicolson, *Diaries and Letters 1930–39*, Collins, 1966, p327.
107. Ellen Wilkinson, HC Deb, 6 October 1938, vol 339 cc499–562.
108. HC Deb, 5 October 1938, Vol 339 cc309–17.
109. Florence Horsbrugh, HC Deb, 6 October 1938, vol 339 cc499–562.
110. Stuart Ball, 'The Politics of Appeasement: the Fall of the Duchess of Atholl and the Kinross and West Perth By-election, December 1938', *The Scottish Historical Review*, Vol 69, April 1990, pp49–83.
111. Julie V. Gottlieb, *'Guilty Women', Foreign Policy and Appeasement in Inter-War Britain*, Palgrave Macmillan, 2015, p228
112. Ibid., p228.
113. Ibid.
114. Quoted in Stuart Ball, 'The Politics of Appeasement: the Fall of the Duchess of Atholl and the Kinross and West Perth By-election, December 1938', *The Scottish Historical Review*, Vol 69, April 1990, p83.
115. Julie V. Gottlieb, *'Guilty Women', Foreign Policy and Appeasement in Inter-War Britain*, Palgrave Macmillan, 2015, p228.
116. Ibid., p101.
117. Ibid., p169.
118. *The Surrey Advertiser and County Times*, 10 May 1939, p3.
119. Julie V. Gottlieb, *'Guilty Women', Foreign Policy and Appeasement in Inter-War Britain*, Palgrave Macmillan, 2015, p124.
120. Ibid., p129.
121. Ibid., p165.
122. Ibid., p116.

123. Ibid., p204.
124. Ibid.
125. Quoted in Stephen Cullen, 'Four Women for Mosley: Women in the British Union of Fascists, 1932–1940, *Oral History*, Spring 1996, p54.
126. Julie V Gottlieb, *'Guilty Women', Foreign Policy and Appeasement in Inter-War Britain*, Palgrave Macmillan, 2015, p38.
127. Sheila Rowbotham, *A Century of Women*, Viking, 1997, p178.
128. Violet Bonham-Carter quoted in Julie V Gottlieb, *'Guilty Women', Foreign Policy and Appeasement in Inter-War Britain*, Palgrave Macmillan, 2015, p247.
129. Eleanor Rathbone quoted in Julie V Gottlieb, *'Guilty Women', Foreign Policy and Appeasement in Inter-War Britain*, Palgrave Macmillan, 2015, p239.
130. *The Scotsman*, 17 March 1939, p12.
131. *Birmingham Gazette*, 18 March 1939, p5.

CHAPTER 6

The Second World War: 1939–1945

On 1 September 1939, German troops invaded Poland. Two days later, Britain declared war on Germany. Public buildings were sandbagged, gas masks were issued, children were evacuated, the labour force was mobilised, men and women were conscripted, rationing was introduced and aluminium saucepans and iron railings were donated to the war effort. One million coffins were ordered. It was a war that would last for nearly six years, involve 61 countries, three-quarters of the world's population and the loss of 50 million lives. Britain was set to change, and once more women would subsume their own needs to work for the common good.

Parliamentarians and Political Activists

During the war, not only did women's organisations and MPs worked together to redress inequality but party politics and different versions of feminism were ignored in a wave of solidarity. In January 1940, a conference was held on 'The Status and Future of Women War Workers', to which representatives from 21 women's organisations—from the National Council of Women (NCW), the Women's Institutes (WI), National Council for Equal Citizenship (NCEC)—attended. The meeting was chaired by a 'smiling and conciliatory' Margery Corbett-Ashby, former suffragist and president of the Women's Liberal Federation, and a candidate in the 1918 election.[1] Labour's Edith Picton-Turbervill sat on her left. Corbett-Ashby maintained that 'they could not have the enormous change-over from peace to war conditions without creating a tremendous social revolution'.[2] Conference concurred and passed resolutions on 'security, the cost of living, women in industry, personal injury compensation, evacuation, broadcasting and married women's nationality status'.[3]

At the outbreak of war, there were 682 male MPs and only 12 women: 6 Conservatives (Nancy Astor, Florence Horsbrugh, Thelma Cazalet-Keir,

Viscountess Frances Davidson, Mavis Tate and Irene Ward); 4 Labour (Ellen Wilkinson, Jennie Adamson, Agnes Hardie and Edith Summerskill); 1 Liberal (Megan Lloyd-George); and 1 Independent (Eleanor Rathbone).[4] They were later joined by two widows, Beatrice Rathbone and Viola, Lady Apsley, both of whom replaced husbands killed on active service. Beatrice Rathbone (Eleanor's niece by marriage) married again, changed her name to Mrs Wright and in 1943 became the first woman MP to have a baby while in office. The women MPs—apart from Horsbrugh and Wilkinson, who were appointed ministers—still shared one office. This 'very able' group of nine women, forced to socialise in the same room, worked together in pursuit of women's equality. It began to assume, Pugh argues, 'the character of a party's headquarters', and moreover that of a woman's party.[5]

Three MPs—Nancy Astor, Mavis Tate and Ellen Wilkinson—helped to topple Neville Chamberlain, a man they thought unsuited to leading the war. Ellen Wilkinson particularly abhorred Chamberlain's politics, had accused him of moving Britain towards fascism when he signed the Munich Agreement and when he had refused to help the Republican government during the Spanish Civil War.[6] If Mr Chamberlain 'has his way', she insisted, 'you will certainly get a Fascist state in this country. Mr Chamberlain has shown no desire whatever to fight against Fascism. The whole policy of the Chamberlain Government has been to give in to the Fascist States'.[7] When the war went badly, Wilkinson blamed Chamberlain for it.

On 9 March 1940, Wilkinson's article 'Will the Old Man Cling to Power' was published in *Tribune*. In it, she argued that Britain was weakened by Chamberlain's catastrophically bad leadership. Her article, along with others in a similar vein, unleashed a wave of criticism, and Chamberlain was pressed to resign. On 10 May, Winston Churchill became prime minister, and Labour agreed to join his newly formed National Government. Florence Horsbrugh and Ellen Wilkinson were appointed ministers, and both became key figures in civil defence. Horsbrugh, as Parliamentary Secretary to the Minister of Health, helped organise the evacuation of one and half million children and mothers from the major cities to safer places in the country. Later, she took charge of the casualty services, set up hostels for those bombed out of their homes, assumed responsibility for health and sanitation in the shelters and helped draft the post-war National Health Scheme. 'Puffing briskly at a cigarette held levelly between the lips', she described herself as a 'representative of all the maiden aunts in Britain'.[8] Ellen Wilkinson was first attached to the Ministry of Pensions before being moved to a new job as Parliamentary Secretary to the Home Secretary, Herbert Morrison. She was initially responsible for shelter provision, facing colossal challenges as the British civilian population came under attack. Later on, when shelter provision improved, Wilkinson reorganised the fire services.[9] Both women suffered personally when their respective houses were twice bombed.

Arguably, the creation of a National Government should have meant less pressure on women to obey party policy. For some, it was like the heady days of the 1920s when women MPs and activists shared similar goals. There were four key battles where women MPs and activists worked together: women's work in the war, equal compensation, equal pay for teachers and equal sexual standards.

In January 1940, Ernest Bevin introduced industrial conscription for women between 20 and 21 years of age; in December 1941, all single women and childless widows between the ages of 20 and 30 were conscripted; by 1943, nearly 90% of single and 80% of married women were active in supporting the war effort. Women joined the workforce in unprecedented numbers, taking on jobs previously done by men which in turn led to a renewed debate about fairness in the workplace. On 28 June 1940, at a meeting in Eleanor Rathbone's house, Edith Summerskill, Mavis Tate and former suffragist Pippa Strachey formed a Woman Power Committee (WPC) to lobby the government over a range of issues concerning women, particularly equal pay and working conditions. The WPC, which, apart from Edith Summerskill and Agnes Hardie, was dominated by Conservative women, met every two weeks throughout the war to discuss women's issues.

Labour women MPs, fearing that the largely upper-middle-class WPC might undermine the work of trade unions, much preferred working with the Standing Joint Committee of Working Women's Organisations (SJC). Indeed, Ellen Wilkinson wrote to the Minister of Labour Ernest Bevin asking him not to support the WPC; Bevin took her advice, and in March 1941 circumvented the WPC by establishing a separate Women's Consultative Committee to advise on the recruitment and organisation of women workers. It consisted mainly of trade unionists and professional women as well as representatives from the three parties, Irene Ward, Edith Summerskill and Megan Lloyd George.

Fighting for Equality at Work

The WPC lobbied for a parliamentary debate to discuss the question of industrial conscription for women and gathered support from across the House. In March 1941, Irene Ward introduced the 'woman power' debate, the first-ever debate to be completely directed by women MPs. It was a united all-party female front to put women 'more fairly and squarely on the map'.[10] As Ward pointed out, 'when I use the pronoun "we", I am referring not only to my women colleagues in the House but speaking for a vast body of public opinion outside.'[11] The WPC planned the debate carefully, each woman choosing a different subject and practising it in front of the Committee beforehand.[12] Ten of the 12 women MPs spoke: Jennie Adamson, Thelma Cazalet-Keir, Viscountess Davidson, Agnes Hardie, Florence Horsbrugh, Megan Lloyd George, Agnes Hardie, Edith Summerskill, Eleanor Rathbone and Irene Ward. Nancy Astor regretted that she could not be there; Ellen Wilkinson was a minister and could not take part. It was, as Irene Ward who introduced the debate stated, 'the first time … we have got the women Members of Parliament of all parties united in a common policy'.[13] The next woman to speak, Cazalet-Keir, commented that if there were 40 or 50 women MPs, the debate would have been unnecessary because problems would have been rectified earlier. She then asked for more women to be appointed to senior posts in government-funded organisations. Flattery was used: Cazalet-Keir praised Herbert Morrison as a 'keen feminist' because he had appointed Ellen Wilkinson as his junior minister.[14] Agnes Hardie spoke against conscription for women, arguing that girls in her Scottish constituency were forced to leave their homes to work in bombed areas, had to put up with inferior billets and were obliged to share beds with strangers; Viscountess Davidson asked for more women police and greater efficiency in allocating women to work; Jennie Anderson argued for better nursery provision; Eleanor Rathbone defined herself as 'a 100 percent feminist' and spoke up for the need for equal pay for equal work; Edith Summerskill discussed women's working conditions and the need for more nurseries for the children of working mothers, and Mavis Tate, also insisting she was a feminist, called for equal compensation for war injuries. Florence Horsbrugh replied for the government, saying that it had 'listened to various points raised', that the 'main object is to put the right persons into the right places' and denied that conscription would be adopted.[15]

At times, the parliamentary debate marked more of a clash between male and female MPs rather than between parties. When Mrs Tate was asked by a male MP whether women ever made mistakes, she caustically replied, 'I should be the last woman in the world to say that women never make mistakes, especially when I look round and see some of the men they have brought into the world'.[16] Churchill torpedoed the debate by saying that such matters should not be discussed so openly because of national security and must only be raised in secret sessions.

Fighting for Equal Compensation

On Saturday 20 September 1941, Muriel Smart, aged 19, made a painful journey from her home in Plumstead to Trafalgar Square. She had lost both eyes, injured her legs and fractured her jaw when the factory in which she worked was bombed. She told the *Daily Mirror* that she had come up to central London because she only received 24s 2d a week compensation, whereas a man with similar injuries received 34s 2d.[17] She joined what the *Mirror* claimed was 'the biggest women's campaign since the suffragettes'.[18] Hundreds of the women at Trafalgar Square volunteered to canvas the country, distribute leaflets and ask people to write to their MPs about the unfair 1939 War Injuries Act, an act whereby women's compensation for war-related injuries was set at 33% less than men's. It was a legal anomaly that women found unacceptable: a woman's leg was worth considerably less than a man's.

On 25 November 1942, Mavis Tate moved an amendment to the War Injuries Act, regretting that she had to do so 'because I think it deplorable that after three years of war anyone should have to ... urge upon the Government the necessity for meting out justice to injured civilian women'.[19] She argued that it was 'not a party issue. It is not an issue between the sexes. It is an issue that is confined to justice'.[20] Edith Summerskill, Megan Lloyd George and Irene Ward spoke in support of their colleague. Almost to a woman, the backbenchers voted for Tate's amendment; Jennie Adamson, Florence Horsbrugh and Ellen Wilkinson, all of whom held government posts, voted against; Nancy Astor was not present. When it came to a vote, the women were defeated by 229 votes to 95. However, the government, aware that a number of women's groups—the Six Point Group, the WFL, the WI—had campaigned in support, accepted the injustice of the 1939 Act and set up a Select Committee on which five women MPs served. On 7 April 1943, Parliament voted to accept its recommendations of equal compensation.

Fighting for Better Pay

Encouraged by their success, activists pushed harder. In 1941, Mavis Tate formed an Equal Pay Campaign Committee (EPCC) to which 100 women's organisations affiliated. Its first parliamentary challenge—to gain equal pay for teachers—nearly succeeded. On 28 March 1944, Thelma Cazalet-Keir introduced an amendment to R. A. Butler's Education Bill to award equal pay to women teachers. The amendment was passed. The following day Churchill angrily demanded a reversal of the vote, calling the women's claim 'an impertinence'; Ernest Bevin threatened to resign if the motion on equal pay was not revoked. The vote was repeated, the Whips exerted their authority and the amendment was overturned. This time only 2 women, Edith Summerskill and Agnes Hardie, voted for equal pay: all the other 12 women either abstained or voted against, party loyalty overriding feminist commitment. It was a major defeat for the women MPs and a harsh disappointment for Cazalet-Keir, who was forced to vote against her own amendment. A couple of crumbs were offered: the marriage bar in teaching was abolished and a Royal Commission was set up to examine equal pay.

Women workers supported the war, but not at any price. As had happened in the First World War, women's trade union membership increased dramatically, rising from 0.9 million at the start of the war to 1.6 million at the end of it.[21] Women, angry and frustrated that their war efforts were not reflected in their pay, went on strike. In September 1941, about 1000 women at a large engineering works in Leeds walked out, despite the pleas of the shop stewards to remain at work. Subsequently, 1000 men stopped work in sympathy. The women had been asked to stop working on Sunday and to increase their weekday hours without the advantage of extra Sunday pay. It would mean, the women claimed, an extra two hours work for less pay. At the time, women received 38s for a 47-hour-week.[22]

Strikes were illegal. In May 1942, 30 women who had gone on strike in a Midlands firm were prosecuted for 'unlawfully taking part in a strike'.[23] The prosecution insisted that 'it was a serious thing in time of war for a strike to take place' and particularly because these 30 women had affected the work of several hundred more. Fortunately, the prosecution did not ask for 'severe penalties' because the women had by then returned to work: the women were fined 11s and not imprisoned.

In January 1943, the male-only Associated Engineering Union (AEU), after years of not accepting women members, allowed them to join the union. In some ways, this decision was forced on the AEU, whose members feared that women might be used as cheap labour when they replaced men conscripted to the armed forces. With this in mind, the union campaigned to abolish the category of 'women's work', favouring one rate for all workers.[24] In September 1943, nearly 12,000 women employed at a North East engineering works threatened to strike unless they were paid the same rates as men; at a North West aircraft factory, women threatened strike action; at Vickers, Barrow-in-Furness women went on strike and refused to go back to work until they were fairly paid.[25] In November, at a Rolls-Royce aircraft engine factory near Glasgow, 16,000 women workers and their male colleagues went on strike over equal pay. They refused to go back to work despite pleas from the shop stewards, trade union officials and their MP to return to work.[26] In December, at another engineering factory in the West of Scotland which supplied equipment for other factories, a strike of 2000 women workers held up production of urgently required materials 'vital for essential war services'.[27] Only 12 women voted to return.

Ernest Bevin, who like many male trade unionists favoured a family wage rather than equal pay, responded by organising a national women's conference. Strikes continued. In January 1944, a four-week strike of 2000 women at a West of Scotland plant were joined by 1000 men workers who came out in solidarity.[28]

Fighting for Sexual Justice

There was a 'massive upsurge in venereal infections', during the war.[29] Edith Summerskill believed that there were more casualties from the sexually transmitted disease than in the 'Blitz'.[30] The government took action: it gave out condoms and publicised the dangers of unprotected sex. It also introduced a revised version of the Contagious Diseases Acts, the notorious acts of the nineteenth century which Josephine Butler had successfully campaigned to remove. The new Regulation 33B allowed authorities the right to compulsory examine people for venereal disease (VD) if two people named them as being responsible for transmitting it. The regulation was in force for both sexes though—as usual—it was targeted at women. Florence Horsbrugh as parliamentary secretary of the Ministry of Health was in charge of controlling the disease and supported the regulations. Even so, she believed that legal powers alone would not combat the 'very considerable' increase in the 'hidden plague' and that the public should be educated about the 'moral, social and physical factors' involved.[31] On 19 February 1943, Horsbrugh visited Coventry to launch a campaign to educate the public against its spread.[32]

In contrast, women's groups campaigned to abolish Regulation 33B. The NCW called for the Regulation to be annulled.[33] The Rugby Business and Professional Women's Club insisted that the Regulation was 'potentially dangerous, that it was unconstitutional and unfair, and could not be worked properly'.[34] Women MPs tried to repeal the Regulation. Dr Edith Summerskill described it as a 'miserable little measure'; Mrs Agnes Hardie argued that it would open the way to the 'blackmailer, the informer and the poison pen; and Nancy Astor insisted that compulsion would not work and that it was 'panic legislation, not war legislation'.[35] The women were defeated 245 votes to 31.

Women's Organisations and the War Effort

Civilian life became regimented: war was making everyone's life political. 'If this war', the *Daily Mail*, commented, 'has brought any benefit to the British people, it is the sense of individual duty to the State. ... the readiness of men and women of all ages and conditions to serve in any capacity; to take orders; submit to discipline; surrender their normal standards of life; do anything, in fact, which would contribute to victory'.[36] Members of the largest women's organisations, many of them former suffragists and political activists, once more refocused their energies and committed to the war effort.

In 1938, the Home Secretary, realising that war was imminent, had invited Stella Isaacs, Marchioness of Reading and charity activist, to set up a voluntary organisation of women. Dutifully, Isaacs formed the government-funded Women's Voluntary Services (WVS), which soon became the largest women's organisation, co-ordinating the work of the various women's groups along government guidelines.[37] It was 'affiliated to 59 other women's groups—feminist, religious, cultural and professional'.[38] At the time, there was no effective welfare system and the government relied on these female volunteers to keep the country functioning. The work of the WVS was wide-ranging. They helped with the evacuation of mothers and children, helped to set up nurseries, 'ran clothing exchanges; distributed goods from abroad; provided vegetable hampers for sailors; made camouflage nets; collected salvage for recycling'.[39] In its first year, the Teignmouth WVS made 263 garments—pyjamas, dressing gowns and men's shirts—as well as 227 bandages and 125 wallets.[40] They served cups of tea, cooked food, ran mobile laundries and set up temporary bathrooms for those whose homes had been bombed. It was a mammoth undertaking: in London alone, 2,250,000 were made homeless by the 1940–1941 Blitz.[41] The WVS was efficient. Its Mobile Emergency Feeding Units were quickly assembled: in November 1940, the WVS served 15,000 meals a day to those left hungry and homeless by the Coventry blitz, bringing 'normality from awful abnormality'.[42]

Before the war, the Women's Institute (WI) had taken a strong anti-war stand, but was now forced to change its position. Nonetheless, out of respect for the beliefs of its Quaker members, the National Executive Committee recommended that civil defence such as 'gas mask drill, fire-fighting etc should not be taken by the Women's Institutes as organisations'.[43] By the end of the war, the WI worked with 11 government departments.[44] One of the most unusual arrangements was with the Board of Trade. Here WI women reared rabbits, cured the pelts and made coats, hoods and caps lined with rabbit fur to send to the Russian front during their bitterly cold winters. In two and a half years, the WI made 2071 fur-lined garments.[45] They also knitted garments for the British armed forces, but refused to mend holes in socks arguing that men should learn to darn their own.

As long as there are 'Women's Institutes in England, England will not starve', reported one newspaper.[46] Certainly, during the war, the WI played a significant and much-needed role in the production of food, for Britain was an industrial country and had become used to importing 50% of its meat and most of its vegetables, fruit, cheese and sugar. In 1939, the government helped finance the WI's 'Produce Guild', set up to encourage women to grow more food. Soon it had various sections: bee-keeping, dairy production, chutney and pickle making and vegetable preserving.[47] In addition, the WI taught members how to keep chickens, rabbits and goats and supplied them with potato, onions and other seeds to grow more food. In the Breconshire Beacons, the WI planted 130 acres of potatoes on top of one of the mountains.[48] It was a success: by the end of the war, individuals grew or produced 10% of the nation's food.

When in 1940 there was an excess of fruit which was doomed to rot on the trees or else be thrown away, the WI persuaded the government to allocate sugar for jam-making so that fruit was not wasted. There were strict rules about what could be made, how it was made and to whom it was allocated. The work had to be done cooperatively and collectively, and whereas the making of jams, jellies, chutneys and fruit syrups were encouraged, the making of homemade wines and cider was forbidden. Moreover, the sale of WI produce was strictly controlled and only sold to hospitals and other institutions or to shops which used rationing. In one particular burst of collective endeavour, over 70 tons of jam was made by local WIs across the country.[49] By 1941, 4500 village halls had been registered as jam-making centres, along with farm kitchens, school kitchens, private houses and outbuildings.[50]

Yet, as ever, the WI was so much more than jam and Jerusalem. The organisation was mainly a rural one, and its members found themselves to be key players in the evacuation process. On 30 August 1939, two days before the declaration of war, the government began to evacuate primary schoolchildren from potential danger areas, along with teachers and mothers with children under the age of five.[51] It was known as Operation Pied Piper. Local authorities were awarded power to requisition homes and force inhabitants to house evacuees. The Home Office turned to the WI to help. As Andrews points out in *Women and Evacuation*, the migration of children and women continued in waves throughout the war, blurred the boundaries between what was public and what was private and was 'as varied as the number of people involved'.[52] Family life was politicised. Within three days of its operation, 826,950 children, 523,670 mothers, 12,705 pregnant women and over 103,000 teachers were evacuated from the densely populated cities to the countryside.[53] At times, it was muddled, confusing and disorderly. Children were packed into trains, sometimes without lavatories, and sometimes sent to areas not expecting them. At Charlbury, Oxfordshire, the locals were expecting 113 London school pupils and their teachers when three busloads of pregnant women turned up.[54]

Foster mothers were paid 10s 6d for the first child and 8s 6d for subsequent children, nowhere near enough to care for them. Moreover, as the WI paper *Home and Country* complained, the government assumed 'that the housewife need not be paid anything for the time, energy, labour and skill spent in cooking, washing, ironing, mending and "minding" and doing housework for three or four extra children'.[55] Dorothy Evans, a former suffragette who had been imprisoned several times, and was now an active member of the Six Point Group, insisted that foster mothers were performing a national service and should be paid for their work.

Former suffrage activists helped in the evacuation process. Emmeline Pethick-Lawrence donated money towards the cost of evacuating children, and many ex-suffragettes who had houses in the country offered to have mothers and children to stay. Mrs Corbett Ashby told a reporter that she was now 'looking after a houseful of evacuated women and children' at her country home in Sussex.[56] Most of the time, it was ordinary women who helped. In Formby, Mrs Amy Roberts fostered no fewer than 30 boy children during the war, adopting three of them when their parents were killed.[57] The evacuation scheme relied on foster mothers, teachers, social workers and most of all on volunteers from the WI or the WVS. The women in these organisations helped in numerous ways: with billeting, with transport, with organising welcome parties, with finding clothes, making mattress covers and by cleaning and furnishing houses ready for evacuee families. The WVS set up 2000 clothing depots to help provide for those evacuated or had been bombed out of their homes. They sorted, catalogued and mended the clothes before distributing them to local centres, a difficult task especially after clothes rationing was introduced. They set up communal feeding centres, women and children centres, and Mothers' and Babies' clubs. They organised nurseries and provided indoor games for children. They set up classes which taught a range of skills or helped the evacuated women keep fit.[58] In 1944, in the middle of a doodlebug raid, thousands of WVS women escorted young children onto London trains destined for the Midlands and the North.[59] These women, forced by events to be activists, 'filled the gaps in local and national government provision'.[60] Indeed, the government encouraged local authorities to hand over the responsibility for evacuees to the women's organisations.

Large numbers of city children, who were without warm clothes or strong shoes, and had never seen a field or a cow or sheep, were allocated to women across the country. Villagers were shocked by the behaviour and condition of some of the city slum children: some suffered from ringworm, impetigo or scabies, and some had tuberculosis. Others wet their beds and appeared completely uncivilised. The physical state of the young evacuees prompted the National Council for Social Services to set up a Women's Group on Problems arising from Evacuation (later called the Women's Group on Public Welfare), an umbrella group comprising of 20 voluntary organisations like the WI, the WVS, the National Council of Women (NCW) and Labour's Standing Joint Committee of Women's Industrial Organisations (SJC). Margaret Bondfield was appointed chair. In 1943, the Hygiene Committee of the Women's Group on Public Welfare produced its report on evacuation *Our Towns*.[61] The Committee interviewed 27 people involved in the evacuation process, all but 2 of whom were women. For the first time, one half of the population found out what the other half looked like, sounded like and smelt like. Not since Charles Booth's study of the urban poor in the nineteenth century had an attempt been made to chart the lives of the neediest. It made for stark reading. Allegations were made that city children were 'dirty and verminous, guilty of enuresis (bed-wetting) and soiling by both day and night, ill-clad and ill-shod, that some never had a change of underwear or any night clothes and had been used to sleep on the floor, that many suffered from scabies, impetigo and other skin diseases'.[62] A number of children were 'sewn up for the winter' in calico smeared with fat to keep out the cold and stop bronchial infections; young women wore no protective pads when they menstruated; some had been used to defecating on newspaper, then throwing it away. The survey claimed that the statements were so sweeping that it almost seemed that 'a stainless countryside had been called upon to bear with a universally degraded town population'.[63] It was a familiar trope: the tainted, immoral, unhealthy and dirty townies versus the idealised morally upright clean and healthy villagers.

However, the survey pointed out, the trope was not always true. In any case, it added, townswomen were often not to blame when it was. Many lived in rooms with no cooking facilities, no water inside the house and an outside lavatory that was shared with others. The women's group made a number of recommendations to remedy each of these 'town scourges', including 'manufacturing soluble sanitary towels at a low price … through slot machines in schools' and elsewhere.[64] More crucially, the group put forward a radical report, insisting that poverty should be attacked from many angles: by ensuring security of employment at decent levels of pay, by controlling the prices of basic commodities, by instituting allowances for families with children, by setting up a national medical service and by a 'fuller study and control of commercial exploitation'.[65] The slums which existed, it was argued, were a result of low wages and insecurity. Trade and industry 'must take their place as servants, not masters, of the community'.[66] This report, with its condemnation of the poverty and inequality of working-class 'townies', was used by groups to press for social change. Additionally, the evacuation of so many urban women and their children gave rural women a glimpse of what life was like in the cities for the poorer section of the working class and convinced WI members of the need to create a new kind of society after the war had ended.

Meanwhile, by January 1940 about a million children had returned home to the towns and cities, lulled into a false sense of security by what was dubbed the 'phoney war'. In a radio broadcast, Florence Horsbrugh as parliamentary secretary to the Ministry of Health urged parents not to do so since it would put young lives in danger and risk the lives of 'gallant people' who rescued them from burning buildings.[67] In Spring 1940, the war began in earnest and evacuation began once more. It ended in September 1944 when Florence Horsbrugh announced the official return of the first batch of evacuees to the North and West of England, to Wales and to Scotland areas now considered safe.[68]

Protecting the Country

In October 1939, Churchill called for a volunteer defence force to help protect Britain, should the country be invaded. It became known as the Home Guard. A War Office Memo declared that 'Under no circumstances should women be enrolled in the Home Guard ... it is undesirable for women to bear arms'.[69] Women proved to be more imaginative than the government. In March 1940, Lady Helena Gleichen—who had worked as a radiographer in Italy during the First World War—set up her own defence system at her estate near Much Markle, Herefordshire.[70] She called them the Much Markle Watchers. Now in her late 60s, she lived with her First World War radiologist friend Nina Hollings. It was reported that Lady Helena 'liked to walk around her estate wearing a pork pie hat and riding habit, puffing on a cigarette, with a dog snapping at her heels'.[71] Her 80-strong army, consisting of staff and tenants, went on duty each night wearing white armbands with 'Much Markle Watcher' stencilled on them. They were also required to listen to military advice—such as how to shoot straight—from their leader in the evenings. When Lady Helena's request to the army barracks at Ross-on-Wye for 80 rifles, ammunition and a 'couple of machine guns if you have any' was refused, she took all the antique weapons—Pikes, Halberds and Flintlock muskets—from the walls of her stately home to use against the Germans.[72] Each night the Watchers patrolled the surrounding countryside searching for invading Germans and enemy parachutists (Fig. 6.1).

In June 1940, a group of 'fifty indignant female patriots', impatient at not being allowed to join the Home Guard, formed the Amazon Defence Corps. Its founder, Venetia Foster, was the first woman to win the prestigious King's prize for shooting in a competition with 861 men and 4 women. She stated that her 'main object will be to train women in the use of rifles'.[73] 'It's easy', she said, 'once you know how. Women should know how to handle as many types of firearms as possible, so that in case of invasion they can take over a gun from a man'.[74] Some were trained by Foster at her home in Hillingdon. Besides shooting practice, women were shown how to throw hand grenades.[75] Foster later joined the Auxiliary Territorial Service, where she taught young men how to shoot.

In December 1941, Edith Summerskill took over the Amazon Defence Corps, now known as the Women's Home Defence (WHD). Soon Edith

Fig. 6.1 Women of the Amazon Defence Corps, from the *Liverpool Daily Post*, 24 July 1940 p4 (Courtesy of Mirrorpix)

Summerskill was nicknamed 'Flossie Bang Bang'. Unlike other groups, the WHD did not have a uniform but wore an enamel badge as identification. Recruits were given weapons training, often by Home Guard volunteers, and practised with their rifles on Home Guard shooting ranges. In London, women practised at a shooting range in a Tottenham Court Road amusement arcade where they had legal access to a Winchester repeating rifle. In Hull women practised at the East Hill open-air shooting range.[76] In December 1942, 20 women from North Wales trained as guerrillas and were taught how to throw hand grenades and shoot with a rifle and Sten gun. They were seen as 'the most enthusiastic soldiers … quick to pick up the constructional details of weapons and the grenade'.[77]

By 1942, there were 250 female units in Britain; by 1943, the WHD alone had 30,000 members. These groups were technically illegal: after the experience of Mosley's Black Shirts, private armies were strictly forbidden in Britain. However, the government did not prosecute, possibly recognising the importance of such women to the defence of the country, possibly because it did not perceive the women as a threat. Eventually, in April 1943 and only after much lobbying by Edith Summerskill, the government conceded and allowed women to join the Home Guard as Auxiliaries: 20-year-old Mary Warshauer became part of the uniformed and armed Air Ministry's Home Guard unit tasked to defend the Ministry.[78] When it was evident that the WHD was no longer needed, it disbanded, and in December 1944 became the Women's Rifle Association.

The Air Raid Protection (ARP) unit was an offshoot of the WVS, attracting over one million women volunteers for civil defence. They drove ambulances and fire engines, worked as dispatch riders and telephone operators, kept watch for incendiary bombs and put out fires. Not all women were suitable. Patricia Wilde, aged 40, was among one of the first to volunteer for civil defence and was appointed as a London County Council (LCC) ambulance driver. The LCC was unaware that she had had 20 convictions for drunkenness. One morning, when she reported for duty 'the worse for drink', she was instantly dismissed and put on a banned list to make sure that she would never work for the council again.[79] She was given two months hard labour for being drunk and disorderly.[80] After this incident, the LCC asked Scotland Yard to help them 'comb-out' the 8000 ambulance drivers who had been 'hastily recruited' since the war began. They introduced stricter vetting: recruits had to reveal their motoring record and undergo a driving test which included night driving, being able to change a wheel and start an engine without a self-starter.[81]

Being an ARP was dangerous work. As soon as an air-raid siren went off, everyone, apart from the ARP, was expected to take shelter. Now, the ARP warden sprang into action. She patrolled her area, perhaps putting out a fire, perhaps rescuing people trapped in the debris and taking them to a first-aid station, perhaps collecting body parts for identification. It was distressing work. One spoke of finding a female who was decapitated and disembowelled. Birmingham ARP women tried to harden themselves by using raw meat to practise cleaning and bandaging wounds.[82]

Women's Auxiliary Forces

There was no lack of women ready to serve their country. By 1945, almost a half a million women belonged to one of the auxiliary armed services, the women's services run by women to support the men who fought. Women joined the Women's Auxiliary Air Force (WAAF), the Women's Royal Naval Service (WRNS) the Auxiliary Territorial Service (ATS) for the army and the Air Transport Auxiliary (ATA). Combat duty was for men; thus, women only acted in a supportive capacity. Nevertheless, women's lives were regulated and regimented with constant drilling and marching. Like men, women were subjected to regular inspections by their female sergeants, and had to ensure their uniform was immaculate, their buttons polished, and their shoes shiny. Even their toothbrush was inspected. They usually lived in Nissan huts made of corrugated iron with a stove in the middle as the only heat source, packed together at night in small iron beds with straw mattresses and horse-hair pillows. For some, it was dangerous: over 600 were killed and 700 seriously wounded doing military work. Women could also volunteer for civilian organisations such as the Women's Land Army, one of the Civil Defence Units or the Women's Volunteer Services (WVS).[83] In all the services, women's work was regarded as less important than men's—they were treated as second-class citizens and inequality of pay was taken for granted. Moreover, women in uniform had to put up with sexual innuendos: the ATS were denigrated as 'officers' groundsheets', the Land Army slogan 'Back to the Land' became to 'Backs to the Land' and the WRNS was featured as being 'up with the lark and to bed with a Wren'.

Women in the ATS drove vehicles, did the typing and clerical work, as well as cooking, cleaning, laundry work, looking after the stores and waiting on the officers. Its first controller was Helen Gwynne-Vaughan, a well-connected woman whose cousin was the Undersecretary of State for War and whose good friend was the first marshal of the RAF. She was paid 28s 8d (£1.43) a day, two-thirds of a major general's pay; other officers were paid two-thirds of their equivalent rank. The structure of the ATS mirrored the class system in Britain: almost all the top officers were upper class, which provoked Ellen Wilkinson into asking the secretary of state for war if he was aware that 'no qualifications other than a title' was necessary to join it.[84] In 1944, her theory seemed confirmed when Princess Elizabeth joined the ATS, persuaded by Chief Honorary Control-Commander Princess Mary to do so. Winston Churchill's daughter Mary was junior commander of the Hyde Park battery.[85] In contrast, the non-ranked women were drawn across society: some like Susan Lustig were Jewish refugees from Nazi Germany, keen to defeat the vicious regime. These volunteers received a free uniform of a khaki jacket and skirt, had their travel costs paid and food—four-fifths of the men's ration—provided. However, recruits were expected to provide their own woollen cardigan, two sets of underclothes, two pairs of stockings, one pair of shoes, an overcoat or mackintosh, a toothbrush, comb, hairbrush, knife, fork, spoon, a boot brush, a polishing brush and two towels themselves.[86] Later on in the war, women in the ATS worked in the anti-aircraft batteries, directing search lights and radar to spot enemy aircraft, drove and serviced the trucks and motorcycles, and did sentry duty. Occasionally, they were required to fire guns at enemy aircraft, particularly in less occupied parts of the country.

It was rapidly becoming apparent that there was a shortage of women auxiliaries. Doreen Venn, an ATS senior commanding officer, sailed to the Caribbean to recruit auxiliaries to work for the British army in the United States, Canada and Britain. Nearly 1000 Jamaican women applied, and after interviewing 500 women, Venn selected 65 to work in Britain.[87] In October 1943, the first batch of ATS recruits, a group of 24 young Jamaican women arrived in Britain, determined to do their duty and help their 'mother country'.[88] Esther Armagon from Jamaica and Norma Best from British Honduras (Belize) were among the recruits who sailed on an American troop ship to New Orleans, took a train to New York and embarked on the Queen Mary to Britain. In New Orleans, they were horrified by the 'white' and 'coloured' waiting rooms and seeing black people sitting on the back of the buses. In Britain, the two became clerical officers.[89] Diana Williams left British Guyana to join the ATS and was given a job retreading tyres at a depot in the West Midlands.[90] Large numbers of Caribbean women worked in Royal Army Ordnance depots. At one, the brigadier in charge 'spoke warmly of their intelligence, educational standards and conscientious work. The soldierly smartness of these West Indian volunteers struck one immediately'.[91] Women were helped by their home country: Barbadians gave £700 from their 'Win the War' fund to provide a YWCA club and hostel for women in the services. A young Barbadian, Dorothy Fenty was present when the club was opened by Lady Davson, chair of the Ladies' Committee of War Services (West India Committee), who had lived in the Caribbean for several years (Fig. 6.2).[92]

In 1939, the WAAF was reformed and headed by former WVS volunteer Katherine Trefusis-Forbes. By 1943, 182,000 women were recruited. At first, WAAFs worked as drivers, cooks and administrators. In an anonymous place called 'WAAFville', a group of 200 women were trained as chefs by a 'rubicund and not very tall' Sergeant.[93] However, after the Battle of Britain in 1940, women took on jobs such as 'plotting aircraft and radar signals, interpreting reconnaissance photographs, debriefing RAF crew after raids' and acting as meteorological officers.[94] They were also set to work on barrage balloons, repairing the seams and making sure they were fit for the purpose of holding up the cables which were lethal to enemy aircraft. In 1941, when even more men were released to fight, they took complete charge of the 500 lb hydrogen-filled balloons, positioning them correctly when a bombing raid was

Fig. 6.2 Women recruits from the Caribbean (Courtesy of the National Army Museum, London)

threatened and taking them down when it finished.[95] Lilian Bader, a Liverpudlian of Barbadian and Irish heritage, trained as an instrument repairer, passed her exams with a first-class award and doubled her pay from 22s to 44s a fortnight. She was 'the only coloured woman in a sea of white faces' at her camp in York.[96] She had felt 'strongly about the political situation', was distressed when Italians invaded Abyssinia and treated black soldiers abominably and disturbed by Hitler's anti-semitism. Lilian Bader wanted to do what she could to defeat fascism.

As the shortage of men increased, WAAFS were trained as taxi and ferry pilots in the ATA either to fly personnel to and from the various air bases or deliver fighter planes like Spitfires, Hurricanes and Oxfords from the factories to the airbases. Armed with a parachute, a Sidcot suit, flying boots, gloves, helmet, goggles, maps and some sandwiches, the ATA pilot stepped into the open cockpit, maybe to battle with wind and rain or snow and hail or driving mist to deliver the new aeroplane to its future fighting pilot.[97] These women were fearless. Daphne Pearson was the first woman to be presented with an award, the Empire Gallantry Medal, for climbing on to a crashed aeroplane which was ablaze and heavily laden with bombs and freeing the unconscious pilot. One of the ATA pilots was the feminist icon and celebrity figure, Amy Johnson. In 1930, she flew solo, with no radio link, in an open cockpit and often across uncharted territory, from England to Australia, the first woman to do so. She had planned her route from Britain to Australia by charting the shortest way using a ruler on the map. Until then her longest solo flight had been from London to her home in Hull. In January 1941, she died in an aircrash in the Thames Estuary while piloting a fighter aircraft from Prestwick to RAF Kidlington near Oxford. Some say the accident happened because she ran out of fuel; others claim she was brought down by friendly fire after failing to give the correct signal code when challenged. Whatever the cause of Johnson's death, she was a role model for women around the world, demonstrating, as *The Woman Engineer* recalled, 'that women can plan daring feats, can pay close attention to detail, can superintend and carry out a prescribed programme, can overcome obstacles as they are encountered, can learn from misfortune, can face disappointment without loss of courage'.[98] The head of the ATA, Pauline Gower, spoke of Amy Johnson's physical courage as an aviator and her commitment to the unspectacular flying, well below her capability, that she was expected to do in the service.

Other WAAFS trained as spies. Princess Noor Inayat Khan, a Sufi Muslim of Indian descent, was one of the first group of women to train as a wireless operator at the WAAF where her talent was recognised by the Special Operations Executive (SOE). Winston Churchill had set up SOE to spy, sabotage, distribute propaganda and work with local resistance groups in German-occupied Europe. The princess was recruited as a special agent and trained in the 'use of explosives, hand grenades and small arms' as well as lessons on how to evade capture.[99] Her faith and family values made her abhor violence but Khan wanted to fight fascist injustices. She also wished that Indians might 'win high military distinction in this war. If one or two could do something … which was very brave … it would help to make a bridge between the English people and the Indians'.[100] In mid-June 1943, Khan was given the pseudonym Jeanne-Marie Regnier, flown to northern France and sent to Paris to work under the code name Madeleine. She was given four pills: one to induce sleep, one to keep her awake, one to induce stomach problems and one to end her life. She left the gun allocated to all SOE field officers behind in London as she did not wish to kill anyone, even the enemy. A radio operator's life expectancy was six weeks but the princess at first evaded capture. Eventually, four months after she had arrived in France, Khan was arrested, probably betrayed by a double agent. In November, she was taken to a prison camp in Pforzheim, Baden-Württemberg, where she was kept handcuffed in solitary confinement for ten months before being transferred to the Dachau concentration camp. On 13 September 1944, she was badly beaten up and then shot with three other SOE agents: Yolande Beekman, Madeline Damerment and Elaine Plewman. Princess Noor Inayat Khan was posthumously awarded the French *Croix de Guerre* and the British George Cross and a commemorative stamp was issued. In 2012, a memorial bust was unveiled by Princess Anne in Gordon Square, London. The photograph shows the historian Shrabani Basu and members of the FANY with her (Fig. 6.3).

Most SOE activists were recruited directly from the First Aid Nursing Yeomanry (FANY) whose members often merged their work as nurses with

Fig. 6.3 Princess Anne unveiling the memorial to Noor Inayat Khan at Gordon Square in Bloomsbury, London on 12 November 2012 (Courtesy of Shrabani Basu)

espionage. By 1945, over 3000 women from FANY served with the SOE as signallers, cryptographers, dispatch riders, forging false passports and other official documents for use in occupied Europe. They also became secret agents. Thirty-nine of the 50 women who were sent to France as SOE agents were members of FANY: 12 were murdered and 1 died while working. Other women worked in Finland, Italy, Poland, the Far East, East Africa and India.

In 1939, the Women's Royal Naval Service (WRNS) was reformed. The newly recruited women were issued with a navy blue uniform consisting of 'two skirts and two jackets ... two pairs of blackouts (knickers) of navy artificial silk down to the knee; two pairs of black lisle stockings; two pairs of shoes, a raincoat,' an overcoat, six stiff white collars, six shirts, a tie and a hat with HMS woven into the taffeta ribbon round the brim.[101] Like women in the other women's organisations, they first served as cooks, drivers, clerical workers and other work considered to be appropriate to women. As the war developed and more men went off to fight, women trained as welders, mechanics and electricians and were directed to maintain torpedoes, depth charges and gun circuits, to repair the electrics on minesweepers, and make new parts for submarines. They were taught Morse code and teleprinting and how to transmit using a radio. In 1941, they crewed on tugs and motor launches, though not on the big naval ships. They were known as the glamorous service: after the war, the British airline, BOAC bought their uniforms and hats for their stewardesses.

In June 1939, former suffragist and WI activist Lady Gertrude Denman re-created the Land Army, and volunteers flocked to join it. It was the only women's civilian service which was directly under government control, with 30 civil servants from the Ministry of Agriculture and Fisheries organising the Army from Lady Denham's home in Sussex.[102] By September, 17,000 had been recruited, and, by 1944, 80,000 women were working as 'Land Girls'. Even women teachers and students willing to give up part of their summer holidays were asked to join the Land Army for seasonal work like potato planting, hoeing, haymaking, harvesting and threshing.[103] Recruitment posters showed healthy young women dressed in fawn corduroy jodhpur-like trousers, matching Aertex shirts, a green jersey, woollen socks and stout shoes holding a pitchfork or cuddling a newly born lamb.[104] Prejudice was common at first: farmers and farmworkers objected because they thought women would not be strong enough and/or would undercut men's wages. In fact, women soon tackled all farm work—'they milked, mucked out, slaughtered, castrated, helped mate, reared, fed, dug, sheared, planted, thinned, picked, harvested, hedged, fenced, ditched, ploughed, drove, excavated, thatched, cleared land', sawed logs, delivered livestock and exterminated vermin such as rats.[105] Some joined the Timber Corps, felling trees to use as props in the coal mines. For this work, women were paid 28s a week (10s less than men) and, out of this, 14s was deducted for board and lodging. These women were needed to feed the nation, especially when the shipping channels were closed or too dangerous to use.

Protecting Refugees

In 1939, the government restricted the entry of refugees fleeing from Nazi persecution. Each refugee had to be sponsored by someone who would guarantee financial support. As a result, refugees fleeing from the atrocities of German-occupied Europe relied upon the generosity of individuals, groups and charities. The NCW strongly opposed government policy, wrote to the leading newspapers to complain about its heartlessness and convened an ad hoc committee to try to change it. In 1937, the NCW persuaded the Home Office to admit women as domestic servants, and around 20,000 female refugees came in. Edith Morley, a lecturer at Reading and the first woman to be awarded a professorship at a British university, was one of many who stepped in to help. In 1938, determined to help save Jewish refugees fleeing from a potential agonising death, she set up the Reading Refugee Committee. As Morley poignantly wrote, death took many forms 'in concentration camps, by starvation, by gas, burning by steam, burning in closed buildings, mass electrocution, mass shooting and by the "death trains" in which … men, women, and children were slowly poisoned by chlorine gas as they stood on chemically active chloride of lime which burned their feet to the bone'.[106] Morley also helped set up a special subcommittee of the British Federation of University Women, which specifically helped academic refugees escaping from persecution. Dr Erna Hollitscher, an Austrian-Jewish woman who had left Austria following the 1938 German annexation (Anschluss), was appointed secretary, in charge of looking after the largely female immigrants, raising funds and finding work and homes for them all. It was difficult: many of these former female academics were only allowed to work as domestic servants.[107]

Eleanor Rathbone is the woman most associated with helping refugees and soon became known as the 'MP for Refugees'.[108] By now, she was a powerful and influential backbencher, relentless in her pursuit of justice and with no political party to exercise control over her. By temperament and experience, she was well suited to lead the Parliamentary Committee on Refugees, which she set up and which gathered support from nearly 200 MPs across the political spectrum. In a carefully worded policy, the Parliamentary Committee aimed to 'influence the Government and public opinion in favour of a generous yet carefully safeguarded refugee policy'. By this time, as a result of the German occupation of the Sudetenland and later the whole of Czechoslovakia, large numbers of Czechs had fled their country for safety. Eleanor Rathbone believed that Britain had a moral responsibility to accept the Czechs and urged the government to issue more visas and make it easier for these people to come to Britain.[109]

When war was declared, visas were cancelled, and it became impossible for refugees from Germany and German-occupied countries to come to Britain. Eleanor Rathbone switched her focus to protecting the 80,000 refugees now living in the country, 55,000 of whom were Jewish. All refugees, regardless of ethnicity or religion, were considered 'enemy aliens' by the government and were interviewed by newly constituted Tribunals to decide whether they should be interned or not. Each Tribunal—and there were 120 in all—allocated the 73,400 refugees they examined into three groups: Class A were immediately interned as suspects; Class B kept their freedom but were restricted in their movements such as not being allowed to travel more than five miles from where they lived; Class C were exempt from restrictions.

In May 1940, all German and Italian men aged between 16 and 60 living in coastal towns—27,600 in all—were ordered to be interned. On 11 June, when Italy joined the war, all Italian men between 16 and 70 were arrested; on 21 June, all German and Austrian men were arrested too. These men were arrested—often at night—and held in prisons or other public buildings, then sent to internment camps. Women MPs differed in their response: the Conservative feminist MP Mavis Tate agreed with internment; Eleanor Rathbone did not. In an effort to publicise their plight, Rathbone asked 80 parliamentary questions on the treatment of internees including 'the importance of separating Nazi internees from non-Nazis; the shocking living conditions in many of the camps; the food shortages and lack of medical care'.[110] Some of the worst camps were closed down as a result of Rathbone's criticisms. Moreover, on 15 July 1940, the government reversed its decision on labelling all Germans, Italians and Austrians as 'enemy aliens' and released more than a quarter of them. By March 1942, over 20,000 internees had been released, each one of whom had had their case painstakingly reviewed.

On 17 December 1942, Foreign Secretary Anthony Eden informed the House of Commons that the Nazis were planning to murder all Jewish people, that the plan to do so was well under way and that the British government deplored it. He condemned 'in the strongest possible terms this bestial policy of cold-blooded extermination … such events can only strengthen the resolve of all freedom loving peoples to overthrow the barbarous Hitlerite tyranny'.[111] One MP asked for members to 'rise in their places and stand in silence … against disgusting barbarism'. In an unprecedented instance the House of Commons rose to stand in silence in memory of the Jewish dead.[112]

These words were little more than empty rhetoric. Shortly before, on 27 October 1942, Eleanor Rathbone had led a delegation consisting of the Archbishop of Canterbury, the Roman Catholic Archbishop of Westminster, other illustrious churchmen, members of refugee organisations and MPs and members of the House of Lords to Home Secretary Herbert Morrison to ask for 2000 visas for children living in Vichy France in danger of being murdered by the Nazis. Herbert Morrison declined, arguing that it might lead to a rise in anti-semitism in Britain.

In March 1943, Rathbone set up the National Committee for Rescue from Nazi Terror to raise awareness of Nazi atrocities and thereby put pressure on the government. She drafted a 12-point programme which included the need to revise Britain's visa programme and the creation of a new approach to helping Jewish refugees. On 19 May 1943, a parliamentary debate took place:

Eleanor Rathbone was the only woman to speak in support of a rescue operation. She had been unable to protect the 800 who died on the *Arandora Star*, a ship containing Category A 'aliens' en route from Liverpool to Canada, which was torpedoed by a German U-boat on 2 July 1940. She was equally unable to help save the six million European Jews who were murdered by one of the cruellest regimes on earth.

OPPOSITION TO THE WAR

Some women were against the war because they were fascists. Thirty-nine women, members of the now-banned British Union of Fascists (BUF), were imprisoned in Holloway, to be interned later on the Isle of Man.[113] In July 1940, Olive Evelyn Baker, a 39-year-old nurse from Bath and member of the BUF, was sentenced to five years penal servitude for publishing and distributing postcards advertising a German radio station.[114] Some BUF members were put on trial under the Official Secrets Act. Mrs Marie Louisa Augusta Ingram, the German-born wife of a Royal Air Force sergeant, was put on trial for 'conspiring to obtain information which might be useful to the enemy'.[115] She had allegedly asked a corporal in the Royal Tank Corps to supply her with blueprints of the tanks so that she could pass them on to Germany. At her trial, she denied the charge but stated that she admired Hitler and she had joined the BUF because she felt National Socialism 'which had done much for Germany could do the same for England'.[116] A photograph of Hitler and two swastika flags were found at her home. She was sentenced to ten years penal servitude.

Other members of the BUF were imprisoned under Defence Regulation 18B. which empowered the Home Secretary to detain any person who was thought to be a danger to public safety or defence, a law targeted at hardcore fascists. In 1940, a few weeks after the birth of her second son, Diana Mosley was arrested and interned in Holloway prison under these emergency regulations. Her husband, Oswald, was already in prison. The former suffragette Nora Dacre Fox was also interned in Holloway. Fox was released in 1942 and helped look after Unity Mitford, Diana's sister, after her suicide attempt.[117] The Mosleys were allowed to live together in prison, grew vegetables in a garden and ordered food to be delivered from outside prison. In 1943, the two were released and placed under house arrest until the end of the war.[118]

Other members of the BUF lived freely. Mary Allen, former suffragette and founder of the Women's Police Service and the Women's Auxiliary Service, was a member of the BUF, 'quite openly and proudly'.[119] She had spoken at meetings held by Mosley and advocated a negotiated peace with Hitler. In her book *The Lady in Blue*, she spoke of being entranced by Adolf Hitler, spellbound by his 'hypnotic gestures, his passionate, forceful voice and his visionary eyes'.[120] Her fascist views hit the headlines, and questions about her were raised in the

House of Commons as to the appropriateness of her membership of the Women's Auxiliary Service: the country was assured that she had 'not escaped the notice of the authorities'. Nonetheless, she was not arrested despite calls for her and other fascists to be 'withdrawn from circulation'.[121]

Other women were opposed to war because of their pacifism. Two famous writers, Vera Brittain and Ethel Mannin, spoke up against the war. Brittain consistently criticised the government for its saturation bombing of Germany, whereas Mannin refused to do war work. Nonetheless, pacifism was not as widespread as it had been in the First World War: of the 1714 applied to be registered as conscientious objectors, only 83 were unconditionally registered.[122] It was tough being a conscientious objector. Birmingham Council suspended its women conscientious objectors from working for the duration of the war.[123] During the war, 257 women were prosecuted for refusing to do war work and 214 were imprisoned.[124] The first woman, a 21-year-old domestic servant from Newcastle-upon-Tyne, Constance Bolan, was arrested for her pacifism, refused to pay the 40s fine and was imprisoned in Durham gaol for a month. Another committed pacifist, Kathleen Derbyshire, spent 14 days in Strangeways, Manchester, sewing mail bags and being verbally abused by the female prisoner officers, one of whom told her that 'our men are fighting for sluts like you. … If I had my way you'd certainly be hanging from the end of a rope'. All the prisoners were kept in their cells during an air raid, laying on their beds in the dark and listening to the bombs fall. It was, Derbyshire commented, 'sheer mental torture'.[125] Active pacifists were put under surveillance. For example, Mrs Phillis Annie Skinner was observed to be an 'ardent pacifist', and a 'strong-willed woman' who was an active member of the Peace Pledge Union.[126]

Conclusion

On 8 March 1945, women celebrated International Women's Day at meetings in 21 towns and cities across Britain.[127] From across the class, religious and political spectra, they found they shared principles in common as a result of their war experiences. Many agreed that they deserved a better world when the war was over. Most meetings adopted the International Women's Charter, which called for three interconnected rights: firstly, the right of mothers 'to bring children into a world free from the fear of want and war; the provision by every Government of decent health services and houses fit to live in'[128]; secondly, the right of women workers to enter all industries and professions, to receive equal pay for equal work and to enjoy the same opportunities as men for training and promotion; thirdly, the right of women as citizens to enjoy equal democratic status with men, that is, the opportunity to vote and serve on committees, juries and public bodies. In Gloucester, nearly 200 women representing 28 different women's organisations pledged to devote their efforts to building a 'lasting peace and a world in which happiness and security could be shared by all'.[129] In Preston, Lancashire women demanded the right to 'help in the shaping of peace'.[130] In Aberdeen, the Housewives Association called for 'the same opportunities as men, with equal pay for equal work' and criticised the fact that there were so few women in Parliament.[131] At the Albert Hall, London, several thousand listened to Megan Lloyd George's plea for women to be delegates at the forthcoming international conference in San Francisco.[132]

Women activists achieved one of their objectives before the end of the war. In April 1945, Florence Horsbrugh and Ellen Wilkinson accompanied Anthony Eden, Clement Attlee and other prominent figures to the San Francisco conference. Here, the task of the delegates was to create a world organisation to replace the now-defunct, and discredited, League of Nations. Horsbrugh presciently warned that 'microbes are no respecters of frontiers' and that the development of air transport made diseases of 'remote and backward lands a matter of practical concern to nations with most advanced social arrangements'.[133] During the conference, the war in Europe ended and the group returned to Britain. Women looked forward to a brighter future, a better world and a return to more familiar types of activism.

NOTES

1. *The Yorkshire Post and Leeds Mercury*, 27 January 1940, p6.
2. *The Scotsman*, 27 January 1940, p10.
3. Samantha Clements, *Feminism, citizenship and social activity: The role and importance of local women's organisations, Nottingham, 1938–1969*, PhD, University of Nottingham, 2008, p173.
4. *The Yorkshire Post and Leeds Mercury*, 27 January 1940, p6.
5. Martin Pugh, *Women and the Women's Movement in Britain*, Macmillan, 1992, p276.
6. AUCE Annual Delegate Meeting, 1938, p43.
7. AUCE Annual Delegate Meeting, 1939, p10.
8. Martin Pugh, 'Horsbrugh, Florence Gertrude', *DNB*, 2004.
9. See Paula Bartley, *Ellen Wilkinson*, Pluto, 2014.
10. *Sunderland Echo*, 15 March 1941, p1.
11. HC Debates, 20 March 1941, vol 370, pp315–400.
12. See Harold L. Smith, 'The Womanpower Problem in Britain during the Second World War', *The Historical Journal*, Vol 27 No 4, December 1984, pp925–945.
13. Irene Ward, HC Debates, 20 March 1941, vol 370, pp315–400.
14. Thelma Cazalet-Keir, HC Debates, 20 March 1941, vol 370, pp315–400.
15. HC Debates, 20 March 1941, vol 370, pp315–400. This debate is well worth reading, and is available on Historic Hansard at api.parliament.uk.
16. Mavis Tate, HC Debates, 20 March 1941, vol 370, pp315–400.
17. *Daily Mirror*, 22 September 1941, p4.
18. Ibid.
19. Mavis Tate, HC Debates, 25 November 1942, vol 385, pp735–827.
20. Ibid.

21. Ian Gazeley, 'Women's Pay in British Industry during the Second World War', *The Economic History Review*, Vol 61, No 3, August 2008, pp651–671.
22. *Leeds Mercury*, 27 September 1941, p5
23. *The Birmingham Mail*, 7 May 1942, p1.
24. Ian Gazeley, 'Women's Pay in British Industry during the Second World War', *The Economic History Review*, Vol 61, No 3, August 2008, pp651–671.
25. *Daily Mirror*, 22 September 1943, p8.
26. *Northern Daily Mail*, 4 November 1943, p8.
27. *The Sunday Post*, 19 December 1943, p3.
28. *Daily Record*, 11 January 1944, p3.
29. Lesley Hall, *Sex, Gender and Social Change in Britain Since 1880*, Macmillan, 2000, p133.
30. *Evening Express*, 15 December 1942, p8.
31. *The Coventry Evening Telegraph*, 20 February 1943, p4.
32. Ibid.
33. *The Birmingham Post*, 3 December 1942, p1.
34. *The Advertiser*, 22 June 1943, p1.
35. *The Courier and Advertiser*, 16 December 1942, p3.
36. *Daily Mail*, 3 July 1940, p2.
37. Martin Pugh, *Women and the Women's Movement in Britain*, Macmillan, 1992. See James Hinton, *Women, Social Leadership and the Second World War, Continuities of Class*, OUP, 2002, for a thorough study of the WVS.
38. Samantha Clements, *Feminism, citizenship and social activity: The role and importance of local women's organisations, Nottingham, 1938–1969*, PhD, University of Nottingham, 2008.
39. Sue Bruley, *Women in Britain since 1900*, Macmillan 1999, p106.
40. *The Western Times*, 20 December 1940, p4.
41. Maggie Andrews, *Women and Evacuation in the Second World War, Femininity, Domesticity and Motherhood*, Bloomsbury, 2019.
42. *The Staffordshire Advertiser*, 30 November 1940, p8.
43. Quoted in Anne Stamper, *Countrywomen in war time – Women's Institutes 1938–1945*, paper delivered to the Second International Conference on the History of Voluntary Action, Roehampton Institute, September 2003.
44. These included the Treasury, the Ministry of Food, the Board of Education, the Board of Trade, the Ministry of Agriculture, the Ministry of Health, the Ministry of Supply, the War Office, the Air Ministry, the Ministry of Information and the Home Office.
45. Anne Stamper, *Countrywomen in war time – Women's Institutes 1938–1945*, paper delivered to the Second International Conference on the History of Voluntary Action, Roehampton Institute, September 2003.
46. *Derby Evening Telegraph*, 13 March 1943, p3.
47. Maggie Andrews, *The Acceptable Face of Feminism*, Lawrence and Wishart, 2015.
48. Ibid.
49. Sue Bruley, *Women in Britain since 1900*, Macmillan 1999.
50. See Maggie Andrews, *The Acceptable Face of Feminism*, Lawrence and Wishart, 2015.
51. The largest number of children came from London, Manchester and Salford, Merseyside, Tyneside and Sunderland, Birmingham and the West Midlands,

Leeds and Bradford, Portsmouth and Southampton, Sheffield and the East Midlands and Teeside. Reception areas included Lancashire, Sussex, Yorkshire, Kent, Cheshire, Essex, Northants, Hertfordshire, Suffolk, Somerset and Surrey. (D. Ibberson, *Our Towns*, OUP, 1943)
52. Maggie Andrews, *Women and Evacuation in the Second World War, Femininity, Domesticity and Motherhood*, Bloomsbury, 2019, p19.
53. Ibid.
54. Juliet Gardiner *Wartime Britain 1939–1945*, Headline, 2004, p28.
55. Quoted in Maggie Andrews, *The Acceptable Face of Feminism*, Lawrence and Wishart, 2015, p166.
56. *The Scotsman*, 8 September 1939, p4.
57. *The Formby Times*, 12 May 1945, p1.
58. Maggie Andrews, *Women and Evacuation in the Second World War, Femininity, Domesticity and Motherhood*, Bloomsbury, 2019.
59. Ibid.
60. Ibid., p146.
61. D. Ibberson, *Our Towns*, OUP, 1943.
62. Ibid., p4.
63. Ibid.
64. D. Ibberson, *Our Towns*, OUP, 1943, p100. The provision of cheap sanitary towels or tampons still concerned feminists in the early twentieth century because such items were classed as 'non-essential, luxury goods' and had 5% VAT added on to their price. Campaigns to get rid of the tax on such items finally succeeded in 2020.
65. D. Ibberson, *Our Towns*, OUP, 1943, pxviii.
66. Ibid., pxix.
67. *Dumfries and Galloway Standard and Advertiser*, 25 October 1939, p5.
68. *The Evening Telegraph*, 26 September 1944, p4.
69. Home Office Circular quoted in Juliet Gardiner *Wartime Britain 1939–1945*, Headline, 2004, p247.
70. *Britannia and Eve*, 1 September 1943, p43.
71. Midge Gillies, *The Guardian*, 9 June 2006, p6.
72. David Carroll, *Dad's Army: The Home Guard 1940–1944*, The History Press, 2002.
73. *The Scotsman*, 4 July 1940, p1.
74. Venetia Foster, *Fulham Chronicle*, 12 December 1941, p2.
75. *The Lancashire Daily Post*, 22 July 1940, p1.
76. *Hull Daily Mail*, 9 November 1940, p5.
77. *Daily Mirror*, 14 December 1942, p5.
78. *The Conversation*, University of Warwick, accessed 11 May 2020.
79. *Daily Mail*, 5 January 1940, p7.
80. Ibid., p7.
81. *Daily Mail*, 3 January 1940, p7.
82. *Birmingham Gazette*, 23 May 1940, p6.
83. Annette Mayer, *Women in Britain, 1900–2000*, Hodder and Stoughton, 2002.
84. Carol Harris, *Women at War in Uniform, 1939–45*, Sutton Publishing, 2003, p25.
85. Ibid.
86. Ibid.

87. *Nottingham Journal*, 12 July 1943, p1.
88. *Manchester Evening News*, 15 October 1943, p3.
89. After the war, Esther trained as a nurse and became a matron; Norma trained as a teacher and became a head. Both settled in Britain.
90. Carol Harris, *Women at War in Uniform, 1939–45*, Sutton Publishing, 2003.
91. *Market Harborough Advertiser*, 23 June 1944, p22.
92. *The Surrey Advertiser and County Times*, 20 February 1943, p3.
93. *Daily Mail*, 1 April 1940, p4.
94. Juliet Gardiner *Wartime Britain 1939–1945*, Headline, 2004, p508.
95. Ibid.
96. See *Caribbean Women in World War 11*, Vimeo on demand. After the war, Lilian Bader studied at the University of London and became a lecturer at a local college.
97. Amy Johnson, 'A Day's Work in the ATA', *The Woman Engineer*, March 1941, p89.
98. *The Woman Engineer*, March 1941, p81.
99. Rozina Visram, *Ayahs, Lascars and Princes*, Pluto Press, 1986, p142.
100. Ibid. See also *Timewatch* 'The Princess Spy', BBC 2. Her SOE personnel is located at HS 9/836/5 at the National Archives.
101. Juliet Gardiner, *Wartime Britain 1939–1945*, Headline, 2004, p514.
102. Dorothy Sheridan, *Wartime Women, a Mass-Observation Anthology*, Phoenix Press, 1990.
103. *Daily Mail*, 4 April 1940, p7.
104. Juliet Gardiner, *Wartime Britain 1939–1945*, Headline, 2004.
105. Ibid., p526.
106. Edith Morley, *Before and After, Reminiscences of a Working Life*, Two Rivers Press, 2016, p164. Thanks to Libby Bennett for giving me this reference.
107. See Anne Summers, *Christian and Jewish Women in Britain, 1880–1940, Living with Difference*, Palgrave, 2017.
108. See Susan Cohen's *Eleanor Rathbone and the Refugees*, Vallentine Mitchell, 2010.
109. Dr Susan Cohen, *Eleanor Rathbone and the Refugees*, talk at the Royal Historical Society, January 2016.
110. Ibid.
111. Anthony Eden, HC Deb 17 December 1942, vol 385 cc2082–7.
112. Mr Cluse, HC Deb 17 December 1942, vol 385 cc2082–7.
113. *The Liverpool Echo*, 5 July 1941, p4.
114. *Daily Mail*, 6 July 1940, p5.
115. Ibid.
116. Ibid., 2 July 1940, p5.
117. Maggie Andrews and Janis Lomas, *Hidden Heroines*, Robert Hale, 2018.
118. Anne de Courcy, 'Mosley, Diana, Lady Mosley', *DNB*, January 2011.
119. *The Cornishman*, 4 July 1940, p6.
120. *Daily Mirror*, 26 April 1940, p1
121. *Sunday Pictorial*, 30 June 1940, p8.
122. Ernest Bevin, *Evening Telegraph*, 9 July 1942, p4.
123. *Press and Journal*, 3 June 1942, p1.
124. Juliet Gardiner *Wartime Britain 1939–1945*, Headline, 2004.
125. Ibid., p12.

126. File on Phillis Annie Skinner, National Archives, KV2/685.
127. *Gloucester Citizen*, 9 March 1945, p6.
128. *The Citizen*, 12 March 1945, p5.
129. Ibid.,12 March 1945, p5.
130. *Lancashire Evening Post*, 8 March 1945, p4.
131. *Aberdeen Press and Journal*, 12 March 1945, p4.
132. Gloucester Citizen, 9 March 1945, p6.
133. Florence Horsbrugh, *Evening Express*, 29 May 1945, p2.

CHAPTER 7

The Post-War World: 1945–1960

On 8 May 1945, a carnival spirit swept the country as Britain celebrated the end of the war in Europe. A huge crowd gathered outside Buckingham Palace hoping for a glimpse of the Royal Family; at the VE day celebration in Liverpool, a bonfire was lit with an effigy of Hitler on top; in Wishaw, Motherwell, the whole of Main Street was a blaze of colour, flags from every allied nation flew from lampposts and the streets were crowded with people dressed up for the occasion; in Gloucester, the Duchess wore her Red Cross outfit to welcome a victory parade of nearly 4000 representatives from various organisations, each in their respective uniforms.[1] Meanwhile, women's groups focused on helping the disadvantaged and building for the future. The Women's Institute (WI) set to work knitting jerseys, knickers, vests, cardigans, shawls and scarves for needy children in liberated Europe.[2] A speaker at the Bath National Council of Women (NCW) warned that there would be economic and social chaos 'unless there was a planned restoration of a healthy society all over Europe. … This country could no longer afford to have as low a standard of living as before the war'.[3] The Six Point Group published a new manifesto produced by Dora Russell, Leah Manning and Sybil Morrison which 'was an emotive and dramatically written plea to the women of Britain' asking them to fight for world peace, as all other reforms flowed from this.[4]

Not all women's groups were so sympathetic to change. The Women's League of Empire persuaded 3000 people in Hampstead to sign a petition demanding that refugees be evicted from their homes to 'make room for returning English people'.[5] The arguments of the Women's League were quickly refuted by others who argued that 'these refugees are here, because they were driven out of their own country' and that the campaign by the League was 'an old dodge of diverting the people's resentment away from those really responsible … Hitler used it … Mosley and the British Fascists also attacked the Jews and "aliens" as responsible for unemployment and poverty. … National and race hatred always serve the reactionaries'.[6] It seemed as if the fight against Fascism and racism was not yet ended. Moreover, as the Cold War escalated, many activists abandoned their commitment to pacifism and internationalism and returned to a 'narrower and "safer" domestic agenda'.[7] Subsequently, feminist activists turned to single-issue campaigns such as equal pay, political representation, sex equality, married women's property rights and the marriage bar which prohibited women from working when they married.

During the war, Edith Summerskill had asked the Six Point Group to persuade 100 women to stand at the next General election. Out of this 'Women for Westminster' emerged a group founded to encourage women to become MPs. In the post-war General Election, 87 women stood for Parliament, 24 of these were successful and 21 of them were Labour.[8] Only one Conservative (Lady Frances Davison), one Liberal (Megan Lloyd George) and one Independent (Eleanor Rathbone) were elected. All the significant Conservative women such as Florence Horsbrugh, Thelma Cazalet-Keir, Mavis Tate, and Irene Ward lost their seats or, like Nancy Astor, retired from parliamentary politics.

On 26 July 1945, the Labour Party won a landslide victory. The British electorate, remembering the unremitting poverty and austerity of the 1930s, voted for a British-style socialist revolution. More women than men voted Labour. It was the first time that the Labour Party had governed as a majority, and it took the opportunity to create the National Health Service (NHS), introduce a more comprehensive version of National Insurance, nationalise the Bank of England and other key industries, repeal anti-union laws and reform the education system. Ellen Wilkinson was appointed to the Cabinet as Minister of Education. She was the first woman ever to be appointed to this post, the second woman to become a cabinet minister and the only woman in a cabinet of 20. In this role, she implemented the 1944 Education Act, raised the school-leaving age, introduced free school milk, abolished fees in secondary schools and increased university student numbers by awarding grants. She also helped set up the United Nations Educational, Scientific and Cultural Organisation (UNESCO), the establishment of which had been discussed at the San Francisco conference. When Wilkinson died in 1946, Clement Attlee did not appoint another woman to his Cabinet. Two other women, Edith Summerskill and Jennie Adamson, were appointed parliamentary secretaries, the former to the Ministry of Food, the latter to the Ministry of Pensions. A number of Labour women MPs, who were to be future ministers, were elected: Barbara Castle, Jennie Lee, Margaret Herbison and Alice Bacon.

Just before Labour took power, the women's movement celebrated a success. In February 1943, Eleanor Rathbone had led a deputation to the chancellor to press for family allowances. This time, after years and years of campaigning, she was pushing at an open door. In May 1942, a government White Paper had welcomed the idea, the TUC and Ernest Bevin gave their blessing and William Beveridge approved. They recommended that family allowances were paid to fathers but after threats by Rathbone that women's organisations would mount a challenge to this, the government conceded and mothers received the money instead. In June 1945, the Coalition passed the family allowance bill; on 6 August 1946, the first weekly payments of 5s were paid.

The introduction of family allowances helped to characterise the post-war period, a period that featured a return to traditional family values and of women's place within it. Despite the transformation of Britain by the first majority Labour government, it is often viewed as a time of social and political conservatism. The population was recovering from the devastation of war and desired peace, stability and conformity. Women allegedly were quiescent, glad to return to married life and the home. Moreover, Elizabeth Wilson argues that post-war feminism was 'imprisoned within the constellation of social democratic beliefs',[9] and the arrival of a reforming Labour government lulled many feminists into false sense of well-being. As a consequence, feminism became intertwined with the newly promised Welfare State and all that meant for women's equality. Even so, it was hardly a propitious time for expansion. Britain was on the verge of bankruptcy, had lost approximately one quarter of its wealth, lost many of its overseas assets and was dependent on America for loans.

British Housewives League

On 6 September 1945, the *Daily Mail* reported the death of a 39-year-old housewife and mother of nine. Mrs Alice Robinson of Bassett Road, Friar Park, West Bromwich had put three of her youngest children in a pram, walked to a nearby canal and tipped the pram into a canal near her home before jumping in herself. According to neighbours, her suicide and murder of her babies was the result of 'continuous daily worry of whether she would be too late for the shopping queue'. Rationing was in place, and Mrs Robinson had to queue in several different shops for fish, meat, vegetables, bread, dairy products and sometimes even baby food, all the while trying to look after her children whose ages ranged from a baby to a 17-year-old.[10]

At the time of Mrs Robinson's death, everyone had a ration book. The rationing policy was brought in by the Coalition government to make sure that all British people, regardless of wealth, had enough to eat during the war. Food and other consumer products were rationed, and in short supply. Meat, butter, eggs, tea, cheese, milk, sweets, clothes and petrol were all rationed during the war and continued to be regulated after it. Food shortages and rationing, according to Mass Observation, was the 'top civilian grumble'. Paradoxically, rationing did not affect women equally: the higher-income groups thought themselves disadvantaged because they were unable to buy food, clothes and other consumer goods they could well afford. Ina Zweiniger-Bargielowska points out 'shortages, supplies and rationing' were the most urgent domestic problem facing the post-war Labour government, a government committed to an egalitarian approach to food distribution.[11]

In June 1945, a vicar's wife and mother of three, Mrs Irene Lovelock, walked passed a long line of women queueing for food. Incensed by this, she called a meeting in her husband's Parish Hall. Women, she insisted, would not be beasts of burden indefinitely, queuing for food and goods which were rarely available. Her meeting tapped into a seam of female middle-class anger about the inconvenience of rationing. These housewives were annoyed that they could not buy their sirloin of beef and their fresh lemon sole even though they had the money to do so. Certainly, they did not appreciate Edith Summerskill's attempt to make them buy snoek, a particularly unpalatable species of oily mackerel. As a consequence, the British Housewives League (BHL) was formed. A leading member argued, 'if the miners, the bricklayers, the engineers and all other classes of men' could have a union, why 'can't women have a League to protect their interests'.[12] It was to become a bottom-up rebellion against the Labour government and, as Bea Campbell points out, an assertion of domestic power.[13] Middle-class housewives, frustrated by queuing, food coupons, the shortage of food and other commodities 'and the difficulties of providing family meals out of diminishing rations', became the major opposition group to the austerity imposed by the chancellor, Stafford Cripps.[14]

The aims of the League were threefold: firstly, to provide British housewives with a voice; secondly, to show that 'over-control by the State is not in the interests of a free and happy home life'; and thirdly, to encourage housewives to take their place on local and national bodies.[15] The League was a network of local groups which at its peak claimed 100,000 members, and had an even larger number of sympathisers.

Perhaps not surprisingly, the BHL disapproved of the Welfare State, viewing it as an encroachment on the freedom of the housewife, depriving women of her right to look after her family. It objected to free school milk and the fact that school lunches and cod liver oil were subsidised by the state. The 'lower classes', they argued, were 'being fed at the cost of their independence'.[16] The BHL was avowedly middle class, maintaining that 'the shiftless bad housekeeper who has gained by this communal feeding' would not feel comfortable in their organisation.[17] It campaigned against the forthcoming NHS: Dorothy Crisp threatened to throw Aneurin Bevan off a London bridge if he introduced it. When the NHS was introduced, the League wanted the right of individuals to opt out of it, arguing that it was the essence of a democracy to be able to do so.

In July 1946, when bread joined the list of rationed food, Lovelock stated that 'we are in open revolt against bread rationing', and gathered 600,000 signatures for a petition which they presented to the House of Commons.[18] The BHL led a campaign against the price of vegetables, organising a boycott until prices came down. In June 1947, shouting, 'We're determined to get in', hundreds of women from all over Britain invaded Westminster Hall, hid among the scaffolding and the Members' cloakrooms and, by sheer force of numbers, blocked the entrance to the Chamber in order to protest against food rationing. They demanded a new minister of food and fuel.[19] Special police were used to clear a gangway for the MPs who were being harassed by groups of discontented housewives. Barbara Castle was surrounded and threatened by a large hostile crowd but skilfully managed to argue 'coolly with the women', extricate herself and enter Parliament.[20]

The League's meetings, full of middle-aged, middle-class ladies wearing smart hats and looking fearsomely respectable and self-possessed, were often far from composed. On 6 June 1947, 7000 women crammed into the Albert Hall to hear the Conservative MP Sir David Maxwell Fyfe and the BHL chair, Dorothy Crisp criticise the Labour government's food policy and ask for the removal of the ministers concerned. During the meeting, *Jerusalem, Rule Britannia, Land of Hope and Glory* and *Pomp and Circumstance* were played to a deeply patriotic and nationalistic audience. Not all the women in the audience agreed with the policies and principles of the BHL, and disturbances began soon after the meeting started. Protesters drowned out the speakers by boos and catcalls, shouting out slogans, singing *The Red Flag*, showering water and pamphlets from the balconies and tearing down the League banners, supplanting them with those saying, 'The British Housewives' League does not represent the British working class'. Fights broke out: women were 'seen to tear each other's hair and kick' in a battle of different ideologies.[21] Crisp blew a whistle but the shouts and jeers continued throughout the meeting. Mounted police arrived at the end of the rally, and police escorted several women away in police cars. It had been one paper reported, like the 'explosion of an atom bomb'.[22]

The BHL also suffered from internal wrangles. Many disliked the way that Dorothy Crisp controlled the League, allegedly mismanaged its finance and used the organisation to advance her political career: she was aiming to be an MP and wanted to use the BHL as a launching pad. Her goal was to transform the BHL into a new woman's party, and she spoke of sponsoring 50 candidates at the next election. The executive passed a vote of no confidence in Crisp's leadership, and a number of rank and file members sought to depose her. In September 1947, at a rally in Central Hall, Westminster, the meeting 'staged the biggest pandemonium in its history'.[23] Amid boos and cheers, shouting and hooting, Crisp held on to the microphone, only to have it disconnected by a group of rebels. Dorothy Crisp refused to resign, and the meeting became more and more chaotic and disorderly. One member rushed to grab the microphone from Crisp, who sprang smartly to her feet, 'and trailing a bouquet of red roses' stopped her. All thoughts of sticking to the agenda disappeared as the 'women hurled invective at each other. Fierce raged the battle again, with red-faced women standing up to shout, while others rushed to the platform grabbing microphones. Women yelled and screamed in excitement'.[24] Hats went 'awry, faces flushed, fists shaking, voices screaming, hairpins flying, they trampled over dignity and yelled abuse through hour after hour of unrelieved uproar'.[25] Irene Lovelock fainted (see Fig. 7.1). Police had to be called twice during this stormy meeting, once when the executive tried to expel the four women who led the opposition. It seemed, the Labour-supporting *Daily Herald* argued, that 'women who say they could run the country better than the Government proved themselves incapable of running one of their own

Fig. 7.1 Chaos at the Housewives League Conference (Courtesy of Mary Evans picture library)

meetings'.²⁶ The reports of these meetings gave the average misogynist a reason to revive the old slogan, 'A woman's place is in the home'.

In February 1948, Crisp eventually resigned, citing pregnancy and a prospective tour of the Far East with her husband as the reasons. She had already run twice for Parliament, and each time had been unsuccessful. In August 1948, four days before she was due to give birth, she was widowed when her husband was shot dead in Singapore.²⁷ After his murder, she found it difficult to make ends meet. She went bankrupt and served three prison sentences in Holloway for various attempts to defraud.

In March 1949, in protest against a further cut in meat rations, two members of the League demonstrated outside the House of Commons carrying tea trays on which a week's ration for one person was placed; others gave out leaflets headed 'Bacon and Eggs' campaign.²⁸ Members of the BHL paraded with billboards and banners outside the Colonial Office appealing for increased sugar rations.²⁹ In 1951, four BHL women appeared outside the House of Commons to burn their identity cards and ration books as a protest against an 'outworn and unjust system'. All the books were soaked in paraffin before being set alight on a tin plate, a frying pan and a coffee tin. Unfortunately, it was raining heavily and the wind was strong so only one woman was successful in getting her books to catch fire.³⁰

The BHL claimed to be non-party political—its founder Irene Lovelock had voted Labour in the 1945 election—but its ideas were distinctly conservative.³¹ Its declarations appeared to be straight Conservative propaganda, warning of the dangers of socialism and arguing that control by the state was not in the interests of a 'free and happy home life'.³² In 1946, it passed a vote of no confidence in the Labour Party. The *Sunday Pictorial* insisted that the BFL's claim that it was 'non-party and non-sectarian' was 'clap-trap' because it organised groups to 'pester the life out of Cabinet Ministers' and encouraged its members to march to Food Offices and shout out 'Down with Shinwell—Down with Strachey'. Stafford Cripps insisted that it was a 'political instrument encouraged and misdirected by our opponents'.³³ Nonetheless, the Conservative Party had no desire to be associated with the League, fearing it was too extreme to be acceptable, especially after Lovelock resigned and the leadership was taken over by the extreme right-wing and anti-semitic Dorothy Crisp. Under her aegis, the BHL raged a guerrilla war against Labour, delivering scathing attacks on the socialist government, especially the Ministry of Food. It was a right-wing feminism—Dorothy Crisp advocated gender equality and the organisation encouraged women to become MPs or local councillors—pitched against what was perceived as the male socialist domination of the Labour government.

The BHL showed its political leanings in its support for Conservative parliamentary candidates. In the 1950 General Election, the League urged women not to vote for John Strachey, then Minister of Food, and instead support 'Churchill's man'. It accused the Labour government of being the worst 'in living memory and probably recorded English history', claiming that it had wasted taxpayer's money, had liquidated the empire and had raised the price of food and goods to prohibitive figures.[34] Labour won that election, albeit with a greatly reduced majority.

Meanwhile, the Conservatives spent their time out of office building up party membership. Twice as many women as men joined the Conservative Party: in 1949, there were 2450 women members and 350 men in the Swansea West's Conservative Association alone; in contrast, Labour had 279 women and 417 men. Some of these Conservative women were 'active and vociferous public campaigners'.[35] In Wales, Sam Blaxford argues, women did not just stuff envelopes and organise fundraising parties but were 'vigorous and politically conscious activists' who helped form the policy and practice of the Welsh Conservatives.[36]

A number of leading Conservative women wanted economic justice for women. Evelyn Emmet, chair of the Conservative Women's National Action Committee, campaigned for better maintenance rights for women who had left their husbands. At the time, if a husband reneged on maintenance payments, the former wife had to chase the maintenance through the courts, a complicated and difficult procedure. Emmett was supported by Joan Vickers, who introduced the Maintenance Orders Bill by which maintenance payments were taken directly from the men's wage packet. But Conservative feminism was limited: 3000 women Conservatives said, 'they were truly tired of seeing so much being done for the working classes' at the expense of their own supporters, and urged their government to reduce the cost of living by stopping wage increases.[37]

In 1951, Labour lost the General election, an election fought on rationing and the shortages of consumer goods. It lost because of the female vote: in 1951, an estimated 54% of women voted Conservative. Many were League members, or influenced by its policies: working-class women still tended to vote Labour. It is too simplistic to see the League and its campaigns as a right-wing Conservative front as it drew support across the political spectrum. It may have been organised by the right but it did not speak only for the right. As Elizabeth Wilson points out, the lack of a left-wing feminist response to the problems of the housewife opened up opportunities for a conservative victory, especially when the post-war Labour government 'did not speak adequately to women's needs'.[38] For many, the Welfare State, apart from the NHS, was male in its focus: it cut nursery provision, and the National Insurance Act made married women dependent on their husbands. These policies reflected badly on the Labour government and cast considerable doubt on the ability of the party to deliver women's rights. This perceived rejection of women's concerns was certainly a source of electoral weakness, a weakness compounded by the BHL's campaigning.

The BHL was accused of a 'remarkable silence' after the Conservatives took office, even though the meat allowance was cut further and food bonuses were axed. There were, one reporter noted, 'none of the familiar petitions to Westminster, and not one ration book has been burned in Parliament square'.

The League claimed they were giving the government three months grace.[39] In July 1954, rationing ended. Housewives throughout Britain lit celebration bonfires of ration books to mark the end of over 14 years of rationing. Members of the BHL made a wreath of old ration books and placed photos of all the ministers of food in it before delivering the wreath to the current minister. A rally was held in Trafalgar Square, where women joined in singing 'Roast Beef of Old England'.[40] Women were now free to buy as much meat as they wished—if they had the money. The cost of meat increased.

Meanwhile, the Conservative Party took politics to the housewife by promoting an image of 'the wife as a woman *with rights*' and the party as a protector of law and order. As Campbell argues, Conservative women always 'placed the home at the centre' of their campaigns, believing that women's sphere was domestic, not public.[41] Consequently, Conservative women took their 'womanly matters into the arena of male politics'. In 1950, Margaret Thatcher, then a parliamentary candidate, called for more women to be elected in order to advance women's rights, particularly in the area of housing, shopping and rationing.[42] She was a member of a women's committee which investigated the suitability of high-rise flats for families with young children and which concluded that flats be designed with play areas. Public order was a crucial issue too. At the 1958 women's conference, delegates demanded stricter law enforcement, defended corporal punishment and advocated flogging for adult male offenders, justifying it by a need to protect women and girls.[43] One delegate demanded 'flogging for adults and birching for juveniles'.[44] In this setting, women were viewed as victims, much too weak to defend themselves and requiring all the power of the (male) state to keep them safe. The majority of women at the conference agreed with capital punishment.

In July 1955, Ruth Ellis, a 28-year-old mother with two children, was hanged at Holloway prison for the murder of her lover. An estimated crowd of 1000 stood outside: the women wept and prayed. One woman, Mrs Van Der Elst, wearing a long black coat and black hat walked up and down outside. When police tried to move her on, she replied, 'I will not go. This is my protest against this evil'. The police cleared the path and the road outside the prison so she could continue to walk freely up and down in front of the gates. Anne Clark of the Howard League for Penal Reform led the prayers. The crowd was hushed.[45] Ruth Ellis was the 15th woman to be hanged for murder in the twentieth century: she was also the last. In 1969, capital punishment was finally abolished.

Campaigns for Equal Pay

The Labour government's unwillingness to honour its commitment to equal pay may also have helped the Conservatives regain office. As Beatrix Campbell argues, Labour's 'repudiation of a feminist programme for women left the Tories with the "feminine" political initiative'.[46] In 1946, the Report of the Royal Commission on Equal Pay recommended 'equal pay for commensurate work', but only for teachers, local government officers and certain grades in the civil service. Private sector workers were excluded, a decision probably influenced by the British Employers' Confederation, which insisted that 'women do not make the same contribution as men to the filling of the higher and more responsible posts which are necessary for the efficient conduct of industry'.[47] In June 1947, the Labour Chancellor Hugh Dalton reneged on Labour's electoral promise, telling the House of Commons that the principle of equal pay for equal work could not be made law because the estimated cost would be too high. The recently elected Barbara Castle was not convinced, replying 'that while women fully appreciated the country's economic difficulties they would be deeply disappointed at the suggestion that they alone should be expected to forego any satisfaction of just claims owing to inflationary pressure'.[48] She asked Dalton whether he would make a start in implementing the principle of equal pay in the Civil Service, only to be told 'No. The current economic situation does not admit even a start of the gradual implementation of equal pay for the Civil Service'[49] as it would cost too much. Castle was determined, and tried to drum up support outside Parliament. At a conference lunch of the NCW, she told delegates to organise and 'make the Chancellor of the Exchequer and all the Ministers realise that women were not going to be satisfied with anything less than equal pay'.[50] Women, she argued, wanted action on this, and the only way 'women will get anything is not by sweet reasonableness ... but by making a terrible nuisance of themselves'.[51]

At the same time, Thelma Cazalet-Keir, now chair of the Equal Pay Committee, worked hard to persuade the Conservative Party to embrace the idea of equal pay. It was an uphill battle as the 1949 women's conference protested that equal pay 'would pit the interest of the family man against those of single women, that it would make employers less likely to hire women, and that it would make careers so attractive to women that they would abandon their traditional roles as wives and mothers'.[52] Nevertheless, with the support of the chair of the Conservative Women's National Advisory Committee, Evelyn Emmett, and the indomitable Irene Ward, Cazalet-Keir's view prevailed and the Conservative Party too adopted the principle of equal pay.

Outside Parliament, the Equal Pay Campaign group organised public meetings, distributed pamphlets and wrote to their MPs. In 1951, the group commissioned the feminist campaigner and filmmaker Jill Craigie to make a propaganda film *To be a Woman*, a film that argued that women should not be regarded as cheap labour but be paid the rate for the job.[53] In the early 1950s, Barbara Castle, the Conservative MP Irene Ward, the Ulster Unionist Patricia Ford and Labour's Edith Summerskill 'worked very closely on this matter ... cutting across party lines, concerned not to score party points but to get positive action'.[54] Women's groups like the newly named Fawcett Society gave support.[55] Eventually, the Chancellor Rab Butler gave an assurance that equal pay would be implemented: he was sympathetic to the issue because he believed that it would increase Conservative support among a significant section of working women. Even so, he was reluctant to fulfil his promise, and so a 'massive lobbying campaign' was mounted by women's groups, public service unions and the TUC.[56] Women even threatened to use suffragette tactics to further their cause.[57] In January 1954, the Conservative MP Irene Ward tabled a motion in the House of Commons demanding the government make a definite commitment to equal pay; the Labour MP Barbara Castle also pushed hard, insisting that if women did not obtain equal pay, it 'will stand under the slur of political dishonesty'.[58] On 9 March 1954, four women—Castle, Ford, Summerskill and Ward—presented a petition organised by the Equal Pay Campaign to Parliament. It was signed by 80,000 sympathisers. The women were all inveterate campaigners and knew the importance of attracting publicity. Their arrival to Parliament in three horse-drawn carriages decorated in green-and-white rosettes and streamers ensured that their actions would be widely reported. The women backed up the petition by asking as many questions on equal pay as they dared. Barbara Castle was criticised by other women Labour MPs, notably Alice Bacon and Elaine Burton, for the 'iniquitous action of leading an all-party deputation to the Minister to demand equal pay'.[59] In 1955, the newly elected Conservative government awarded female civil servants equal pay, to be phased in over several years; in 1956, teachers as well as workers in the NHS, the gas and electricity industry gained equal pay; the majority of women had to wait a good deal longer.

Sexual Politics

On 13 December 1950, Barbara Castle introduced a Criminal Law Amendment Bill. She had been persuaded by the Association for Moral and Social Hygiene (AMSH) and the National Council of Women of which she was an honorary executive member to promote the bill in Parliament. It drew support across the benches and was sponsored by Conservative MP Eveline Hill, Labour MP Dorothy Rees and four men. The bill aimed to protect women from being forced by pimps to work as prostitutes. In the previous act (1885) women who were known prostitutes or 'of known immoral character' were exempt from its protective provisions. Pimps could operate without fear of prosecution. Castle urged that prostitutes be given the same legal protection as the so-called innocent women, arguing that it was wrong 'to withhold the protection of the law from any citizen on grounds of his or her moral character'.[60] Behind the scenes, the NCW worked tirelessly in the constituencies to persuade each MP to support Castle. In presenting the bill, 'she showed the poise and timing of a well-rehearsed film star—Mrs Castle's performance … was faultless'.[61] When the bill was debated in the Lords, Lord Chorley remarked that it was an instance 'of the great value of having women members in Parliament' to press for changes to unfair legislation that had been ignored by men.[62] On 22 June 1951, the bill became law.

Other sexual policies were less beneficial to women. In 1954, a committee chaired by Sir John Wolfenden and consisting of 4 women and 11 men was formed to look at the 'problems' of homosexuality and prostitution.[63] Most women's organisations which had been campaigning for the rights of prostitutes were not invited to be on the committee, and thus, as Lesley Hall points out, 'a valuable feminist tradition was excluded from its deliberations'.[64] Only one woman's organisation the NCW gave evidence, and together with the predominantly female AMSH they argued for a single uniform law for men and women. They made the case for the current solicitation laws to be repealed and argued that police officers target men who used prostitutes rather than the women themselves. Wolfenden called AMSH a bunch of eccentric old women who had too much to say for themselves, an indication that he had no wish to take them seriously. Moreover, the term 'Huntley and Palmers'—a well-known biscuit manufacturer of the time—was used for homosexuals and prostitutes respectively, because Wolfenden did not want the (four) women in the room to be embarrassed. Even so, the Wolfenden Report, which followed, is often regarded as a liberalising enquiry. This may have been so in respect of homosexuality—it recommended decriminalising homosexual behaviour between consenting adults—but this was not the case for prostitution: Wolfenden recommended that prostitution be controlled through tighter legislation and policing. In 1959, guided by the Wolfenden Report, the government passed the Street Offences Act, which permitted women to be arrested, prosecuted and sentenced solely on the evidence of a police officer. After two cautions for soliciting, women could be charged as 'common prostitutes', and, if convicted, were liable for imprisonment. As a result of the act, prostitution moved into strip clubs, sex shops, escort agencies and hotels. Only desperate women now walked the streets. The NCW protested vigorously when the Street Offences Bill was presented in Parliament: representatives met with the Home Secretary, drafted amendments to the bill and recommended deleting the words 'common prostitute' and removing the proposed hefty fines and gaol sentences. These amendments were sent to all MPs to little effect. When the bill became law, the NCW commented that it was 'a severe blow to the NCW and those of its Affiliated Societies who have worked for more than forty years for reforms in the law relating to solicitation which would make it more just and equitable'.[65]

Local Activism

Most women were not full-time or seasoned campaigners, nor did they take great interest in national crusades. However, many were involved in local campaigns, sometimes taking action in response to a tragic incident or objecting to a particular state of affairs. Action against a local injustice perhaps, or action to promote change in the place they lived. Frequently, their activities were children or family focused. Such activism did not make the national press, nor did they have national ramifications, yet for the women and those concerned their campaigns made a difference to many lives. They are, for the most part, unsung activists.

In November 1954, six-and-a-half-year-old William Greig drowned in the River Leven. For two days, the police, the boy's relatives and volunteers searched the river trying to locate his body. In the meantime, a group of women from the Co-operative Guild began a petition asking the council to fence the unprotected and dangerous parts of the river near where William fell in. A hundred forms were printed, signatures were made and the petition presented to Buckhaven and Methil Town Council.[66] The Council fenced the river making it 'very difficult for children' to reach it.[67]

Women living in Stanton, Derbyshire, took action against the reopening of an opencast coal mine. The women sent telegrams to the prime minister, the minister of power and a local MP protesting against renewing the mine because the site ran up to the village school and several houses. They stated that they had 'suffered indescribable noise, filth and devastation' from the mining and mothers were worried 'because 15 or 20 of the children have to walk each day along the road which the coal lorries will use, and it has no footpath'. One of the women insisted that if she had 'to stand with a banner in the House of Commons to stop it, I will not mind'.[68]

There are many, many examples of women taking this type of action: 200 women living at a housing estate in Durham protested against the night-time open-cast coalmining taking place near their homes[69]; women in Renfrew objected to the proposed moving of a mother's clinic from the town centre to a mansion up a hill and outside the town, arguing that pregnant women and mothers would not attend the new clinic if they had to struggle, often laden with shopping, and with other children in tow to get there[70]; women in Torquay marched into the United Supporters' Club to protest 'with disgust' against the language used by a footballer'[71]; women in Sunderland complained about the number of nude shows at the local theatre.[72] Following a letter of complaint signed by 22 women, the Maternity Section of the Irvine Central hospital in Ardrossan was given a £3000 makeover which doubled the number of bathrooms and lavatories.[73]

Women in national organisations often worked to improve the day-to-day lives of women in their local area. The Grendon Underwood WI sent a strong protest to the home secretary objecting to a proposed new closed prison because the 'prison population would be bigger than the population of the village'[74]; nearly 250 women representing the Westmoreland WI called for a ban on smoking on the lower decks of local buses;[75] the Women's Section of the Arbroath Labour Party protested against an increase in gas charges, mainly because pensioners already found it difficult to provide food and other necessities from their meagre pensions.[76] Local WIs took on national issues too. At the Staffordshire Federation of Women's Institutes, a resolution was passed overwhelmingly 'deploring the poor quality of material used' in stockings. The member who proposed the resolution quoted instances of her stockings laddering when put on for the first time and suggested that manufacturers be told to improve the quality of their goods.[77] Five thousand delegates at the WI's annual conference unanimously agreed to take action to get rid of the turnstiles in women's public lavatories.⁷⁸ After a long campaign, turnstiles were abolished in 1963.

Three women delegates from Ellesmere Port's Standing Conference of Women's Organisations representing 1000 women met with their Wirral MP, Selwyn Lloyd, to complain of the 'exploitation of sex and brutality in literature, and in the entertainment world and on television'. They argued that the 'amount of flesh exposed by women seemed to be more important than acting, dancing or singing ability' and that this sexual exploitation had a bad effect on the youth of the country.⁷⁹ In their opinion, clubs were also morally wrong to 'cheapen and degrade' women in order to bring in customers. The women of Britain, they believed, should insist on a drastic cleaning up of entertainment and a more rigid censorship of horror and violence.

Keeping the Peace

On 6 August 1946, an atomic bomb was dropped on Hiroshima, killing 75,000 people, injuring many more and obliterating the city. A few days later, Nagasaki was bombed. It ended the war with Japan, at an unfathomable human cost. Unease about the bomb grew as more and more people became aware of its devastating effects, especially when Britain decided it wanted one too. As James Hinton points out 'nuclear weapons rehabilitated the pacifist consensus that Hitler had undermined'.⁸⁰

On International Women's Day 1952, a new women's rights organisation, the National Assembly of Women, was founded. One thousand three hundred and ninety-six women from across Britain and Ireland gathered at St Pancras Town Hall, all united about the need for peace and disarmament. They also spoke out for an increase in women MPs and for equal pay. One delegate 'just listened as woman after woman took the "mike": young women who had lived through the Blitz; young women who had been children in the war and remembered being evacuated … mothers of lads conscripted' to fight in the Korean War.⁸¹ All these women were united in a common purpose: to end wars.

In March 1955, the Golders Green branch of the Co-operative Women's Guild raised concerns about nuclear warfare. Their campaign began slowly, gathering strength at each meeting. On 5 April, 57 women listened to Kikue Ihara, a Japanese primary schoolteacher, talking about the effects of the bomb, holding up photographs of charred bodies and passing around a shadow of a hand on a tile, the hand of a person who had perished.⁸² Two years of resolute campaigning followed leading to the founding of the National Campaign Against Nuclear Weapons Tests, a group which focused on stopping the tests about to take on Christmas Island. On 7 May 1957, 23 women from Hertfordshire dressed in heavy mourning went to Downing Street to deliver a letter to the prime minister, Harold Macmillan. It was taken by Irene Short, then a 38-year-old mother of two children and soon to be an influential Labour MP. The letter said, 'Our survival as a nation … depends on nuclear disarmament. British women are deeply shocked by the dangers of continued experiments of nuclear weapons.' The women were dressed in black, 'mourning for the thousands of people' affected by H-bomb explosions.[83] They asked Macmillan to suspend the tests and to initiate international negotiation on nuclear disarmament. On 12 May 1957, nearly 1000 women marched in a silent procession in the pouring rain from Marble Arch to Trafalgar Square, to protest against the tests. Men were banned from taking part. Again, many were dressed in mourning or else wore black sashes. Some carried banners saying, 'Let those who bear the children of the nation be the conscience of the nation'[84]; some carried banners showing a dead child, with the words 'Please don't let this happen'.[85] The demonstration ended with a meeting in Trafalgar Square, chaired by Diana Collins, wife of the Dean of St Paul's Cathedral who introduced speakers such as leading Labour figures like Edith Summerskill and Joyce Butler and the novelist and pacifist Vera Brittain. The number of campaign groups grew to over a hundred, only to be overtaken a year later by a new organisation: the Campaign for Nuclear Disarmament (CND). The women leaders who had initiated, publicised and campaigned for disarmament faded into the background to be replaced by well-known middle-aged men.[86] Indeed, the image of early CND members as angry, bearded young men wearing anoraks rather than wives and mothers is the one which is often cemented into the British memory. Yet, the organiser of the Aldermaston Marches was a woman, Peggy Duff, who each Easter organised tens of thousands of demonstrators to walk from London to the Atomic Energy Research Establishment in Berkshire. One of the co-founders, Pat Arrowsmith, served 11 prison sentences for her political activities. During one of these, she went on hunger strike and, like the suffragettes before her, was force-fed.

At first, the Women's Freedom League (WFL), the WI, the Six Point Group, the NCW, the International Alliance of Women (formerly the International Alliance for Suffrage) and other women's groups advocated international peace. However, as the Cold War intensified and peace became associated with the British Communist Party and left-wing ideas, these groups—mostly in order to keep their non-partisanship image intact—severed their connections with women's peace movements, reverted to domestic issues and focused on international development.[87]

The NCW Council and the National Women's Citizenship Association agreed that 'poverty constituted the greatest "common enemy on earth"' and worked towards its elimination.[88] In their view, education-centred programmes were the key to international development. Consequently, the NCW worked with UNESCO to set up three-month-long educational courses for Nigerian and Indian Women which emphasised healthcare, nutrition, hygiene and women's political rights. The WI ran a number of exchange programmes for women from the British former colonies to study in Britain. The British government asked the WI to help set up overseas institutes: in the early 1950s, it helped establish WIs in Malaya, Goa and the Philippines and was used as a model for Nigeria's Maendeleo ya Wanawake (Women's Progress). In 1959, the WI provided the Lady Aberdeen Scholarship Fund to train 'country women and home-makers' in developing countries and improve their lives more generally.[89] This concern for international development, Skelton argues, was 'informed by the legacy of European women's missionary work', with all of its assumptions of imperialistic superiority.[90] It was a colonial maternalism, deeply imbedded in notions of cultural condescension, yet for many of the beneficiaries the policy transformed their lives.

The Windrush Generation

On 22 June 1948, the *Empire Windrush* arrived at Tilbury docks carrying 450 Jamaican men, mostly Royal Airforce ex-servicemen who had come to Britain to seek work. Other ships followed. The British Nationality Act 1948 had confirmed citizenship and the right of abode to all members of the British Empire and the country needed workers. The newly created NHS was desperate for staff and sent hospital matrons and other recruiters to the Caribbean to persuade women who were already nurses to emigrate to Britain. Until the early 1960s, thousands of men, women and children emigrated to Britain from the Caribbean. As many have recounted, life in Britain was a disappointment: slum housing cynically overpriced, poor working conditions in jobs well below their capability, low pay, pervasive racism and dismal weather led to widespread disillusionment.

On 23 October 1955, Claudia Jones, a 40-year-old Trinidadian woman and British subject, was released after a year in prison in the Federal Reformatory for Women, Virginia, America.[91] In a trial lasting eight and a half months, she had been accused of 'conspiring to teach and advocate the overthrow of the Federal Government'.[92] In fact, she had been campaigning against racial discrimination and promoting women's rights. Her trial took place at the height of a Red Scare in the United States, led by Senator Joseph McCarthy, who began a series of hostile investigations against people thought to have communist sympathies. It was in this febrile atmosphere that Claudia Jones was found guilty. On release from prison, she was told to leave America but when she was refused entry to her birth country, Trinidad, she embarked on the *Queen Elizabeth* for England.[93] Once in Britain, Claudia Jones started organising again, this time trying to make life better for Caribbean immigrants. In March 1958, Jones founded Britain's first influential black newspaper, *The West Indian Gazette*, a paper that reported on life both in the Caribbean and in Britain and acted as a catalyst for economic, social and political equality. It also reviewed and publicised the work of black artists—writers, musicians, painters—because Jones believed that 'a People's Art is the genesis of their freedom'. Long before the emergence of cultural studies, Jones recognised that culture formed part of our personal identity, and without an acknowledged and celebrated cultural heritage, black identity would be submerged in the mass bundle of a problematic white Britain.

At the time, racism was rife: landlords advertised rooms for rent, saying, 'No Irish, No Coloureds, No Dogs'. And it was legal to do so. Racist violence was common, urged on by the reprehensible Oswald Mosley's Union Movement and Colin Jordan's White Defence League. In September 1958, nine white men, aged between 17 and 20, were sentenced to four years' imprisonment for setting out with iron bars and other weapons on a 'cruel and vicious manhunt' in Notting Hill. The judge, Lord Justice Salmon, commented that their purpose was to 'instil stark terror and inflict as much pain and serious injury as you could'. Summing up, he insisted that 'everyone, irrespective of the colour of their skins, is entitled to walk through our streets in peace, with their heads erect, and free from fear'. It was a right, he declared, 'that these courts will always unfailingly uphold'.[94] He blamed the men for encouraging the racist violence that had erupted in Notting Hill over the recent summer Bank Holiday.

On 30 January 1959, the BBC filmed the Caribbean Carnival at the St Pancras Town Hall, an event promoted by Claudia Jones in response to the previous year's racist riots and the 'face of the hate from the white racists' who had taken part in them. She wanted to 'wash the taste' of Notting Hill away by celebrating the cultural heritage of the Caribbean. Calypso bands, steel bands and singers such as Cleo Laine, Cy Grant and Paul Robeson took part in the various celebrations. Twenty-three-year-old Faye Sparks won the first Carnival Queen beauty contest, a contest which celebrated black is beautiful. No one saw it as sexist. And Sparks was delighted that the reward was a sea trip back home to Jamaica. More than 1000 West Indians participated in the festival; many, many more were unable to get tickets for the celebration. Claudia Jones' Carnival ran for six years, an artistic celebration of Caribbean culture that eventually morphed into the Notting Hill Carnival.

In May 1959, an Antiguan carpenter Kelso Cochrane was murdered by a gang of white men. In response to his murder, Amy Ashwood Garvey, with Claudia Jones and Eleanor Ettlingere as vice chairs, founded a new organisation. This was the Inter-Racial Friendship Co-ordinating Council (IRFCC), and its aims included 'respect for human rights and fundamental freedoms for ALL without distinction as to race, colour, sex, language or religion'. Claudia Jones had a meeting at the Home Office, where she asked for action against racism, more police officers in Notting Hill, an enquiry into the white riots and legislation to make racism illegal.[95] A vigil to commemorate Cochrane's death took place outside 10 Downing Street. A placard reading 'There is only one race, the human race' was held by one participant. The Home Secretary, R. A. Butler promised to 'watch the situation', and later that year the government held an investigation into race relations, chaired by Amy Ashwood Garvey. No one was charged with Cochrane's murder.

Anti-Colonialism

Claudia Jones also joined the Movement for Colonial Freedom (MCF), a political rights group formed in 1954 which campaigned for the end of British colonial rule and gave support to national liberation movements.[96] It was not a woman's organisation but women played a key part in it. On 1 April 1959, women wearing black sashes held a three-day vigil outside 10 Downing Street to protest against the arrest and detention without trial of members of the African Congress, the killing of Africans in Nyasaland and the banning of independence groups in Nyasaland, Northern and Southern Rhodesia.[97]

A significant number of women Labour MPs belonged to the MCF: Barbara Castle was its vice chair, Helen Bastable was its secretary and Lena Jeger and others were active members. Such women activists were subjected to violent protest. The MCF's meetings were often disrupted by Colin Jordan's band of white fascists. At one meeting where Jeger spoke, a number of men broke in and violently disrupted the meeting. Outside there was, according to Jeger, 'the sound of fighting and breaking glass' and racist chants.[98] Barbara Castle, speaking at Central Hall, Westminster, in support of independence for Nyasaland, faced exploding fireworks, dog whistles and shouts of 'Keep Britain White' from the rioters who burst into the meeting.[99]

Castle was a very active member of MCF: there were three key areas in which she played a major part, and helped to change the course of history.[100] The first was in Kenya. In the 1950s, British rule in Kenya was threatened by a wave of nationalism and calls for independence. The British response was repression, the incarceration of its leader Jomo Kenyatta and the imprisonment and maltreatment of thousands of other Africans. There was evidence that the British handled the uprising in a brutal fashion: the Union Jack was called the butchers' apron.[101] Rumours about torture circulated. One of the most infamous was the death of 11 Africans who died in police custody at the Hola prison camp, the prison governor insisting the prisoners died because of drinking water from a contaminated source. Immediately, Barbara Castle sprang into action and asked for the court records. She discovered that 'the European officer in charge of the irrigation scheme at Hola, testified that he personally saw continuous beating of detainees, apparently for refusal to work and not for any disturbance'.[102] Castle brought this injustice to the attention of the House of Commons several times. She told the House about a young man who had had a rope tied to his wrists and was strung up to a crossbeam with his feet two or three feet above the floor, and 'while so suspended he was severely beaten about the body and legs with strips of rubber cut from old motor car tyres. ... He died later of what was described as cerebral haemorrhage. Nobody was charged with murder because it was decided that the prisoner might have hit his head against a door'.[103] Enoch Powell was 'equally outraged. His cold logic clinched our case'.[104] Yet nothing was achieved: the colonial government was not held accountable. It merely changed the name of Hola to Galole in the hope that the massacre would be forgotten. Kenya became independent in 1963 with Jomo Kenyatta as its first prime minister; he changed the name of the town back to Hola. In 2018, after a four-year legal battle, the British government agreed to pay an undisclosed sum to victims who were tortured, maimed or executed by British authorities.

Meanwhile, in January 1958m *The Sunday Pictorial* paid for Barbara Castle to visit South Africa to cover a treason trial where 162 men and women were on trial for their lives. They were members of the African National Congress (ANC), an organisation that campaigned against the segregationist and racist policies of the white government. They were all acquitted. Here Castle met Nelson Mandela, also on trial and also released only to be rearrested, retried and sentenced to life imprisonment. In 1959, the Anti-Apartheid Movement was set up, and Castle set to work organising a boycott of South African goods and trying to force South Africa out of the Commonwealth. In 1961, she became president of the Anti-Apartheid Movement.

Barbara Castle was equally committed to independence for Cyprus, at the time a British Crown colony consisting of 80% Greek Christians or Greek Orthodox and 17% Turkish Muslims. The Turkish Cypriots wanted union with Turkey; the Greek Cypriots led by Archbishop Makarios demanded *enosis*, that is, union with Greece. Britain, both groups insisted, should play no role in its governance. On 1 April 1955, Colonel Grivas, a former army officer, led the National Organisation of Cypriot Fighters (EOKA) in a guerrilla campaign to unite Cyprus with Greece.

The Conservative prime minister, Harold Macmillan, suggested partitioning the island into Greek and Turkish sections: Turkey was seen as a natural ally of the West, despite its deplorable record on human rights, whereas the Greeks were seen as too-communist for comfort. Not surprisingly the Greek Cypriots rejected this proposal. It was against this background that Barbara Castle, now vice chair of the Labour Party, made a speech at the 1957 party conference, outlining her commitment to 'complete this freedom operation for the people of Cyprus' by making it an independent country without partitioning it.[105] In the summer of 1958, Castle received a surprise telephone call from the Greeks inviting her to visit Athens and meet Archbishop Makarios. At the meeting, and after careful and sensitive negotiations, Makarios agreed to drop his long-cherished dream of union with Greece and accepted Castle's proposal for an independent Cyprus: no partition and no union with Greece. Barbara Castle returned to the United Kingdom ecstatic. She had achieved what no other diplomat had: the commitment of Makarios to abandon *enosis*. Unfortunately, the British government declined Markarios' proposals, and the matter was dropped.[106] In 1960, Cyprus was granted independence on the same terms as those negotiated by Barbara Castle two years earlier.

The period between 1945 and 1959 was a great transformative period for Britain. The first majority Labour government introduced a raft of measures to benefit the ordinary man and woman: the National Health Service, the Welfare State; a changed education service; the nationalisation of major industries. Nonetheless, many in Britain also desired to return to the more traditional values of home, hearth and family. Indeed, some female activism—the British Housewives League, the initial Peace Movement, international development, a lot of local protest—was based on traditional notions of woman's place in society. This was challenged, though not undermined, by feminists and their political allies who campaigned for equal pay and women's rights. Some women activists—those such as Claudia Jones—campaigned not just for their own sex but also for justice for their compatriots, or for those in other countries. It is safe to say that this was a period of relative stability in Britain, an equilibrium which was shortly to be shaken up in the 1960s.

Notes

1. *The Citizen*, 14 May 1945, p. 7.
2. *The Chronicle*, 12 May 1945, p. 2.
3. *Bath Weekly Chronicle and Herald*, 12 May 1945, p. 11.
4. Sophie Skelton, *From peace to development: A reconstitution of British women's international politics, c1945–1975*, p. 86, PhD, University of Birmingham, 2014.
5. Pamphlet issued by Hampstead Branch of the Revolutionary Communist Party circa 1945, courtesy of the Modern Records Centre, University of Warwick, online archive.
6. Ibid.
7. Sophie Skelton, *From peace to development: A reconstitution of British women's international politics, c1945–1975*, PhD University of Birmingham, 2014, p. 90.
8. Mrs J. L. Adamson (Dartford), Alice Bacon (Leeds), Bessie Braddock (Liverpool); Miss G. M. Colman (Tyneside); Mrs F. Corbet (Camberwell); Mrs C. S. Ganley (Battersea South); Mrs Barbara Ayrton Gould (Hendon North); Margaret Herbison (Lanark North); Mrs L. Jeger (Holborn and St Pancras); Jennie Lee (Cannock); Mrs Jean Mann (Coatbridge and Airdrie); Mrs E. Leah Manning (Epping); Mrs L. Middleton (Plymouth, Sutton); Mrs M. W. Nichol (Bradford North); Lady Noel-Buxton (Norwich); Mrs F. Paton (Rushcliffe); Jennie Adamson (Dartford); Mrs M. Ridealgh (Ilford North); Mrs C. M. Shaw (Ayr); Dr Edith Summerskill (Fulham West) and Mrs E. A. Wills (Birmingham, Duddeston). Barbara Castle entered Parliament for the first time; Ellen Wilkinson was made a cabinet minister.
9. Elizabeth Wilson, *Only Half-Way to Paradise, Women in Postwar Britain, 1945–1968*, Tavistock Publications, 1980, p. 164.
10. *Daily Mail*, 6 September 1945, p. 3.
11. Ina Zweiniger-Bargielowska, 'Rationing, Austerity and the Conservative Party Recovery after 1945', *The Historical Journal*, Vol 37, No 1, March 1994, pp. 173–197.
12. *The Mercury*, 5 September 1947, p. 3.
13. Beatrix Campbell, *The Iron Ladies*, Virago, 1987, p. 77.
14. Dorothy Crisp, *The Mercury*, 5 September 1947, p. 3.
15. *The Leader*, 14 May 1947, p. 4.
16. *Manchester Evening News*, 17 June 1947, p. 3.
17. Ibid.
18. See 'Ladies from the British Housewives League protest against bread rationing', *British Pathé News*, 21 July 1946.
19. *Manchester Evening News*, 6 June 1947, p. 1.
20. *Belfast Telegraph*, 6 June 1947, p. 7.
21. *The Scotsman*, 7 June 1947, p. 5.
22. *Northern Daily Mail*, 11 September 1947, p. 1.

23. *Sunderland Echo*, 12 September 1947, p. 4.
24. *The Liverpool Echo*, 11 September 1947, p. 4.
25. *Daily Herald*, 12 September 1947, p. 1.
26. Ibid.
27. Gary Love, '"A Mixture of Britannia and Boadicea": Dorothy Crisp's Conservatism and the Limits of Right-Wing Women's Political Activism', *Twentieth Century British History*, Vol 30, Issue 2, June 2019, pp. 174–204.
28. *Lincolnshire Echo*, 29 March 1949, p. 6.
29. *Leicester Mercury*, 26 May 1950, p. 9.
30. *The Courier*, 13 April 1951, p. 5.
31. See James Hinton, 'Militant Housewives: the British Housewives' League and the Attlee Government', *History Workshop Journal*, Issue 38, 1994.
32. Elizabeth A McCarty, 'Irene May Lovelock', *DNB*, 2004.
33. *Sunday Pictorial*, 15 June 1947, p. 3.
34. *Leeds Mercury*, 23 January 1950, p. 4.
35. Sam Blaxland, 'Women in the organisation of the Conservative Party in Wales, 1945–1979, *Women's History Review*, Vol 28, Issue 2, 2019, p. 238.
36. Ibid.
37. *Western Mail*, 22 May 1957, p. 3.
38. Elizabeth Wilson, *Only Halfway to Paradise*, 1980, p. 168.
39. *Evening Herald*, 3 December 1951, p. 4.
40. *Birmingham Post*, 3 July 1954, p. 1.
41. Beatrix Campbell, *The Iron Ladies*, Virago, 1987, p. 83.
42. Krista Cowman, '"The statutory woman whose main task was to explore what women ... were likely to think": Margaret Thatcher and women's politics in the 1950s and 1960s in Clarisse Berthezène and Julie V Gottlieb, *Re-Thinking Right-wing Women, Gender and the Conservative Party, 1880s to the present*, MUP, 2017.
43. Sheila Rowbotham, *A Century of Women*, Viking, 1997, p. 287.
44. Beatrix Campbell, *The Iron Ladies*, Virago, 1987, p. 95.
45. *Evening News*, 13 July 1955, p. 1.
46. Beatrix Campbell, *The Iron Ladies*, Virago, 1987, p. 3.
47. Quoted in *Financial Times*, 17 July 2015.
48. *Western Daily Press*, 12 June 1947, p. 1.
49. *The Northern Whig and Belfast Post*, 25 February 1949, p. 4.
50. *Hastings and St Leonard's Observer*, 16 October 1948.
51. Barbara Castle, HC debates, 16 May 1952, cc1834–1836.
52. Harold Smith, 'The Politics of Conservative Reform: The Equal Pay for Equal Work issue, 1945–1955', *The Historical Journal*, Vol 35, No 2, June 1992, p. 405.
53. This film is available on YouTube.
54. Barbara Castle, HC Debates, 16 May 1952, cc1834–1836.
55. In 1953, the London and National Society for Women's Service was renamed the Fawcett Society in honour of Millicent Fawcett.
56. Harold Smith, 'The Politics of Conservative Reform: The Equal Pay for Equal Work issue, 1945–1955', *The Historical Journal*, Vol 35, No 2, June 1992, p. 408.
57. Ibid., pp. 401–415.
58. Barbara Castle, HC Debates, 2 April 1953 cc1347–1348.

59. Barbara Castle, HC Debates, 16 May 1952, cc1834–1836.
60. HC Debates 13 December 1950, vol 482, cc1175–1178.
61. *The Sunderland Echo*, 20 December 1950, p. 3.
62. HL Debates, 7 June 1951, vol 171, cc1198–1206.
63. See Paula Bartley and Barbara Gwinnett 'Prostitution' in Ina Zweiniger-Bargielowska (ed) *Women in Twentieth Century Britain*, Longman, 2001, Julia Laite, Common Prostitutes and Ordinary Citizens, Commercial Sex in London, 1885–1960, Palgrave Macmillan, 2012 and Helen Self, *Prostitution, Women and the Misuse of the Law: The Fallen Daughters of Eve*, Frank Cass, 2003.
64. Lesley Hall, *Sex, Gender and Social Change in Britain Since 1880*, Macmillan, 2000, p. 161.
65. Daphne Glick, *The National Council of Women of Great Britain*, NCW, 1995, p. 147.
66. *The Leven Mail*, 17 November, 1954, p. 7.
67. *The Fife Free Press*, 22 January 1955, p. 13.
68. *The Birmingham Post*, 25 February 1958, p. 7.
69. *Coventry Evening Telegraph*, 23 September 1953, p. 1.
70. *Port-Glasgow Express*, 2 April 1954, p. 1.
71. *Herald Express*, 10 December 1959, p. 12.
72. *The Stage*, 5 July 1956, p. 3.
73. *Kilmarnock Herald*, 21 September 1951, p. 1.
74. *Buckingham Advertiser*, 12 December 1953, p. 3.
75. *Penrith Observer*, 21 October 1952, p. 1.
76. *The Abroath Herald*, 11 December 1959, p. 4.
77. *Birmingham Gazette*, 19 October 1955, p. 3.
78. *Birmingham Post*, 8 June 1956, p. 5.
79. *Birmingham Post*, 21 April 1958, p. 3.
80. James Hinton, *Protests and Visions*, Hutchinson Radius, 1989, p. 153.
81. Letter to the *Barnoldswick and Earby Times*, 14 March 1952, p. 4.
82. Jill Liddington, *The Long Road to Greenham*, Virago 1989, p. 182.
83. *Lancashire Evening Post*, 8 May 1957, p. 1.
84. *The Birmingham Post*, 13 May 1957, p. 1.
85. *Daily Herald*, 13 May 1957, p. 2.
86. James Hinton, *Protests and Visions*, Hutchinson, 1989, p. 160.
87. Sophie Skelton, *From peace to development: A reconstitution of British women's international politics, c1945–1975*, p. 86, PhD, University of Birmingham, 2014.
88. Ibid., p. 168.
89. Ibid., p. 178.
90. Ibid., p. 143.
91. She was born Cumberbatch, the surname of the slave-owner of her grandparents. See Marika Sherwood, *Claudia Jones, A life in exile*, Lawrence and Wishart, 1999.
92. *The Northern Whig*, 22 January 1953, p. 1.
93. *Evening News*, 10 December 1955, p. 8.
94. *Western Mail*, 16 September 1958, p. 7.
95. Marika Sherwood, *Claudia Jones*, Lawrence and Wishart, 1999, p. 95.
96. At the end of the Second World War, one-fifth of the world was under British sovereignty in one form or the other.
97. *Northern Daily Mail*, 31 March 1959.

98. *The Birmingham Post*, 29 September 1959, p. 1.
99. *Daily Mirror*, 21 March 1959, p. 1.
100. See Paula Bartley, *Labour Women in Power*, Palgrave Macmillan, 2019, for a full discussion of this.
101. Thanks to Janet Anslow, whose grandmother was a chain-maker for this information.
102. Barbara Castle, Hansard, May 1959, cc1428–1433.
103. Barbara Castle, Hansard, 16 June 1959, cc299–312.
104. Barbara Castle, *Fighting All the Way*, 1993, p. 288. See Powell's speech, HC Debates, 27 July 1959, cc232–238.
105. *Birmingham Post*, 5 October 1957, p. 1.
106. Ibid.

CHAPTER 8

The Less-Than-Swinging Sixties: 1960–1970

In the first two months of 1968, three Hull trawlers keeled over in the fierce Atlantic Sea close to Iceland. Hurricane force winds, giant waves and sub-zero temperatures led to the ships icing up, and then submerging in the freezing arctic waters. Fifty-eight men died.[1] Trawler fishing was the most dangerous occupation in Britain—five times more dangerous than coal mining—and these devastating losses hit the close-bound local community particularly hard and prompted women from the fishing industry to take action. Lilian Bilocca, daughter, wife and mother of trawlermen, was outraged by the continuing loss of life and resolved to fight for safer working conditions for those working on the ships.[2] On 2 February 1968, she led hundreds of angry, grief-stricken women to confront the Hull Fishing Vessel Owners' Association and to demand safer ships. No owner would talk to them. A few days later, 'Big Lil', as the 17-stone cod skinner was known, and the other trawler-wives delivered a petition signed by over 10,000 people to the Home Secretary.[3] He and the Labour government were convinced by the suggestions of these 'Headscarf Revolutionaries' and adopted all of the 88 safety measures recommended by the women. It was called the Fisherman's Charter.

Lilian Bilocca personified women's courage but she was not alone. The success of the women's direct action showed once again how community-led organisations could lead to parliamentary change: it was considered one of the biggest and most successful civil society actions of the twentieth century, made headlines in the British press and was filmed by Pathé News.[4] One of the women insisted that 'we have achieved more in six weeks than the politicians and trade unions have in years'.[5] Their success did not meet with universal approval, especially from the 'deeply patriarchal fishing industry',[6] whose 500 trawlermen risked losing their jobs if they did not sail in bad weather.[7] Bilocca received poison pen letters and death threats and was dismissed from her work in a fish factory near the docks. Seen as a dangerous troublemaker, no fish company ever employed her again. By the early 1970s, the Hull fishing

© The Author(s), under exclusive license to Springer Nature Switzerland AG 2022
P. Bartley, *Women's Activism in Twentieth-Century Britain*, Gender and History, https://doi.org/10.1007/978-3-030-92721-9_8

175

industry, whose 150 deepwater trawlers brought in a quarter of the fish sold in Britain, was in decline, a decline exacerbated by the 'Cod Wars' with Iceland, whose government denied access to Hull trawlers. In 1975, St Andrews' Dock, once home to the largest deep-sea fishing trade in the country, was closed. In the early part of the twenty-first century, Hull was the third most deprived area in Britain, largely because the fishing industry was no more. Some blamed Bilocca and the women activists for the decline of the industry and the degeneration of the town. The history of these women disappeared. In 2017, Hull became City of Culture, and there was renewed interest and new interpretations: the local playwright Val Holmes wrote *Lil*,[8] Maxine Peake wrote *The Last Testament of Lilian Bilocca* for the Hull Truck Theatre company,[9] a BBC Documentary *Hull's Headscarf Heroes* was broadcast and a mural was painted on a local community hall. Lilian Bilocca emerged as a heroine.

Local Activism

Lilian Bilocca was neither the first nor the last woman to take direct action against injustice. Women led a range of campaigns, often engaging in protests that were based on domestic concerns yet which challenged traditional notions of passive femininity. Two Birmingham housewives led a sit-down picket outside factories to protest against the intensive farming of chickens. One of the women, Mrs Rosina Roberts, argued that the birds were most cruelly treated: they never saw the light of day nor felt the earth under their feet, but spent their lives in an unnatural factory prison.[10] Moreover, she claimed that the increase in human cancer could be attributed to the use of chemicals to feed factory-reared birds. Other women campaigned for road safety and were not afraid to take direct action when more conventional attempts to effect change had failed. In Tottington, Lancashire, a group of elderly women, some on crutches, went on a march to protest over holes in the road next to their Care Home which prevented them from crossing safely.[11] In Liverpool, hundreds of women blocked a busy road demanding that a zebra crossing be placed there to make it safe for their children to cross. The women, many with children and pushing prams, stood in the middle of the road in a solid mass, chanting and waving banners with slogans such as 'Keep death off Holt Road' written on them. The women threatened to block the road every Saturday until something was done. They had tried all the usual methods of campaigning, sending five petitions to the Council and writing letters of complaint, but had been ignored.[12] In Belfast, 200 housewives formed a human barrier across a busy road and stopped all traffic including trolley buses, heavy lorries as well as cars in their protest against road deaths at that site. Police officers came in their squad cars to remove the women but they refused to budge, saying, 'We intend to stay here all night if necessary'. Some of the women carried placards saying, 'Save our children from death'. All were protesting against the number of road accidents involving their children and called for traffic lights and a zebra crossing.[13] Ever since her four-year old child was killed on the road, Mrs Sarah

Martin had been determined that other mothers should not have to suffer the same way. Nearby in Andersonstown, 30 angry housewives, many sitting on chairs, blocked a street in a housing estate to stop lorries going into a nearby building site. They wanted the builders to construct a temporary road which would bypass their street.[14] The direct action of these women, and of hundreds like them, led to improvements in their local areas.

Other women campaigned for decent living accommodation at reasonable prices. On the 50th anniversary celebrating votes for women, Mrs Roberta Lockhart, a 27-year-old housewife and mother of two, chained herself with a 4 ft chain and a huge padlock to a noticeboard at the council offices in Old Fletton because the council refused to give her a council house.[15] In her hand was a book about women in Parliament which she read while being chained to the railings. Some went on rent strike. At Shrigley, a quiet village in County Down, 100 'angry' women marched to complain about their unfit houses, lack of water, poor roads and lack of sanitation. The villagers had no running water and had to rely on one working water pump for washing, drinking and cooking. A second pump in the village—a 150-year-old well operated by a handle—had been condemned as unfit for drinking. The women were promised a second pump.[16] Running water from a tap at home was not offered. It was 1961.

A number of women focused on righting what were perceived as personal injustices. In April 1960, an 87-year-old grandmother, Mrs Jarvis, won her battle with her town council to keep the home she had lived in for 50 years. The Romford Town Council wanted to build a shopping centre and bought the houses of 20 other residents. Mrs Jarvis refused to sell. For four months, she held out against the entreaties of the council, her fellow houseowners and the firms who wanted to develop the site. She was threatened with a compulsory purchase order. Eventually, it was the council, not Mrs Jarvis, who caved in. Mrs Jarvis commented, 'I love this place and my garden. I find peace as I walk among the flowers. ... They want to build skyscrapers in my garden. That would be terrible.'[17] Others were less successful. Miss Faith Ashford, aged 73, was gaoled in Exeter prison for refusing to obey a judge's order to pull down a wall she had built. She had built a 3 ft high and 15 ft long wall with an ornamental arch outside an Old Smithy that she had converted into a café in the Cornish village of Pentewan. It was admired by holidaymakers who visited the café—but there was a problem. Miss Ashford did not own the land on which the wall was built. On 1 April, 53 days later, she was still in prison insisting that 'it is a beautiful wall and my conscience would not allow me to destroy it'.[18]

CAMPAIGNS FOR EQUAL PAY

In 1968, action taken by another group of women hit the headlines, action which led to widespread change, prompted the Equal Pay Act 1970 and helped give rise to the Women's Liberation Movement (WLM). It was glorified in the film *Made in Dagenham*, and became an iconic part of popular culture. On 7

June 1968, nearly 200 female car seat sewing machinists walked out of the Ford car factory in Dagenham because their work was downgraded to a less skilled category. Soon the strike stopped production leading to 9000 men being laid off. No seats meant no cars: Ford could not sell their cars without the seat covers. The company's loss was estimated at £750,000 a day.[19] The Secretary of State for Employment and Productivity Barbara Castle 'picked up the stitch in time' and encouraged the women to return to work. The Ford women did not have their work regraded but accepted a compromise: a pay rise, an inquiry into their pay scale and the promise of equal pay in the future.

The Ford strike was the most well known of a much larger, often hidden, problem as it soon became evident that other women workers shared the same discontent. Later that year, buoyed up by the success at the Ford plant, Mrs C Page, a union official, insisted at an equal pay conference held in London that women were a powerful force in the country. She warned that if every woman went on strike, the whole of industry and commerce would grind to a halt.[20] The trade union movement responded positively. The third biggest union at the time, the General and Municipal Workers' Union, stated it would give a 'real lead', including strike action, to the campaign for equal pay.[21] At the TUC conference, pressed heavily by the women delegates, unions pledged their commitment to female equality. Women trade unionists also formed the National Joint Action Campaign Committee for Women's Equal Rights to campaign for equal pay.

Strikes for equal pay took place in a number of factories across the United Kingdom. In January 1969, a strike occurred at two factories owned by Renold, a company which made chains for a large number of car firms. Three hundred and fifty women workers at Renold's Manchester factory walked out over a claim for equal bonus payments, followed the next day by 490 women workers at the Coventry factory. The women claimed that they earned 26s 6d a week less than the men because of the company's bonus system.[22] Union officials negotiated a wage increase for the women and tried to persuade them to return to work. The strikers were adamant: they wanted equal bonus payments with men.[23] Eventually, a compromise was reached, and the women returned to work on 13 January. In June, 500 women who worked at the Plessey Telecommunications factory at Sunderland walked out because they wanted the same bonus payments as the men.[24] In November, 230 women from the Pressed Steel Fisher factory at Llanelli, supported by 600 of their male colleagues, came out on strike for equal pay.[25] Employers' liberty to pay women less money was becoming unsustainable.

Labour MP Barbara Castle had been campaigning for equal pay for many years and welcomed the Ford Strike and its subsequent publicity as an opportunity to further her cause. She was now in a position to put pressure on the Labour government to bring it in. In 1970, the Equal Pay Act was passed and came into force in 1975. Women from both major parties supported the bill. Conservative women like Margaret Thatcher, Jill Knight, Mervyn Pike, Sally

Oppenheim, Irene Ward and Evelyn Emmett gave support. Margaret Thatcher 'gladly' welcomed the bill, and joined 'in congratulating the right hon. Lady on having introduced it'.[26] Thatcher commented that 'we should not delude ourselves by thinking that equal pay for women ... necessarily means equal opportunities. There is still a great deal of work to be done in that respect'.[27] Nonetheless, without the long-term commitment of women's organisations and the persistence of Barbara Castle, the Equal Pay Act may have not come to fruition. Undoubtedly, it was an Act won by women for women. It not only represented the end of an almost 50-year campaign but the end of two cherished (largely male) trade union ideals, that of the family wage and that of protective legislation for women.

Some women just asked for wage increases, not complete equality. In Birmingham, about 500 women took part in the first all-women strike at the Joseph Lucas factory. The women, who were employed to assemble car lamps, complained that they were doing complicated machine work at a lower rate of pay than the average unskilled worker in the factory. They wanted an extra 3d an hour, a demand their union official Moss Evans tried to persuade the women against because it might involve pay increases for thousands of other women in the factory grouping.[28] It was tough fighting for women's rights. In September 1960, 32 young women went on one-day strike at the Automobile Association (AA) Birmingham for more money and better conditions. They were promptly dismissed.[29] The Clerical and Administrative Union, which represented the women, asked Prince Philip, as president of the AA, to intervene. The *Daily Mirror* thought it was 'misguided and naïve' to ask him because the Queen's husband could not possibly take sides in a dispute between management and workers.[30] Some women protested about reduced working hours which would result in less pay. In London, 60 women cleaners, waving mops, dusters and home-made banners saying *Justice for Chars* and *Fair Play for Mrs Mopps* massed outside the Law Courts and marched to the Treasury to protest about their new working hours. As they marched into Whitehall, they were heard singing 'Knees Up, Mother Brown' and 'Keep Right on to the End of the Road'. When they reached the Treasury, two of the women went in with a petition signed by 'The Lady Cleaners'.[31]

Not all strikes were about money. In Rugby, a strike at Smith Industries took place when the management restricted women's visits to the lavatory to two a day. One foreman argued that he had noticed that some of the 25 women in his department visited the lavatory eight or nine times a day and production had slumped because of this.[32] In Accrington, a strike of 150 women took place at a textile factory when four teenage girls were suspended for chasing men round the workshop just before their Christmas break. It was, the women argued, just Christmas high spirits.[33] At London airport, 40 ground 'hostesses' decided to 'go slow' in protest at being forced to work a compulsory day's overtime each week by British European Airways. In their view, compulsory overtime would completely ruin their social life as they could not arrange dates with boyfriends and other friends and be sure of keeping them. Other strikes had a nasty rather than a humorous edge. In West Bromwich, 140 women at the Metal Closures went on strike over the employment of a 15-year-old young woman from Jamaica.[34] The teenage Sheila Nelson had arrived as a trainee press worker only to find that white women refused to work with her, complaining that they were not consulted about her appointment and stating that 'if she is allowed to remain more coloured women may be employed'.[35] The union refused to back the strikers, and the young Jamaican teenager returned to work, in what one must judge pretty difficult circumstances.

Black Activism

Meanwhile, Black local activists in London became inspired by international events, particularly the American Black Power movement. In 1968, the British Black Panther movement was founded by Obu Egbuna, Olive Morris and others to fight against 'police brutality, housing discrimination and educational inequalities' in their local area, Notting Hill.[36] A year later, Althea Jones LeCointe became its leader. Under LeCointe's leadership, the group focused on grass-roots organising, tackling racial discrimination in jobs, medical services, housing and social services. One of their high-profile activities centred around the continuing police raids of the Mangrove, a local restaurant popular with the Black community, by staging a demonstration to the police station—only to experience more police brutality. LeCointe and eight others were arrested, charged with conspiracy to incite and put on trial. They were all acquitted, the judge acknowledging that there was 'racial hatred inside the Metropolitan Police'.[37] It was viewed as a landmark legal victory for racial justice. Barbara Beese, one of the accused said 50 years later, 'I am very proud indeed to be one of the Mangrove Nine ... taking on the establishment and winning, exposing its racism and hypocrisy.'[38]

At around the same time, the political activist Jessica Huntley and her husband founded Bogle-L'Ouverture, a radical publishing company named after two Caribbean heroes, Toussaint L'Ouverture and Paul Bogle, and 'which remains one of the foremost Black owned publication houses bringing Black history and culture to a mass audience'.[39] Huntley was committed to educational change, 'particularly cultural education that sought to challenge the Eurocentric and white supremacist narrative that devalued African and Caribbean history and culture'.[40] In 1969, she helped found the Caribbean Education and Community Workers Association, the first specialised Black education group. This led to the publication of *How the West Indian Child is Made Educationally Subnormal in the British School System: The Scandal of the Black Child in Schools in Britain*. Some attempts were made to redress this but it remains an ongoing issue.

Sex, Drugs and Rock and Roll

For some, it was the 'swinging sixties', a time of sexual revolution, of freely available birth control, of legalised abortion, of young people—men and women—with long hair and dressed in colourful clothes, who listened to a new kind of music, watched films like *Rebel Without a Cause* and read books like Shelagh Delaney's *A Taste of Honey*. In 1967, in response to the growing number of young people being charged with possessing drugs, Caroline Coon helped set up Release, a charitable organisation that provided legal advice and legal representation.

Sex was heterosexual: until 1967, homosexuality was illegal. Gay men were prosecuted, given aversion therapy, blackmailed and beaten up. Some committed suicide. In contrast, lesbianism, at least in law, did not exist. Where lesbianism occurred, it was usually on the margins of society, hidden away and unrecognised. In the small town in which I grew up, I knew two young women, one who always masqueraded as a man—in the parlance of the time, a 'butch' lesbian—the other a conventionally dressed woman, known as a 'femme'. Many assumed—or pretended—they were a heterosexual couple; certainly their adopted gender roles were clearly defined, a protection against a largely homophobic community which accepted the couple as long as they adopted 'normal' patterns of behaviour. In London, lesbians could go to *The Gateways*, a club in Chelsea and dance the 'gateways shuffle' to affirm their sexuality and reinforce their self-defined roles as 'butch' or 'femme', but most gay women, like the ones in my home town, were marginalised and isolated. In 1963, a former Auxiliary Territorial Service volunteer, Esme Langley and her friend Diana Chapman, founded the Minorities Research Group to help lesbians cope with the 'difficulties of guilt, isolation and loneliness and to encourage them to come to terms with themselves'.[41] Each month, it published *Arena 3*, a typewritten cyclostyle-copied paper edited by Langley, available only by mail order. It ran until 1972. The paper provided lesbians 'with resources, information and the opportunity to meet other women' and aimed to improve the public image of the lesbian.[42] It was only available by subscription, and only available to married women if their husband signed an agreement: the editors, fully aware of a hostile political climate, feared prosecution for promoting lesbianism.

For many, *Arena 3* was a much-needed lifeline for women like the lesbian who felt 'completely isolated, shut off and abandoned, completely on my own. On reading A3 I feel that there is now hope for the future'.[43] The courage of these early women to 'come out' meant that lesbians began to be noticed, were discussed in the press and interviewed on television programmes. In March 1965, *This Time of Day—Lesbianism*, a BBC television programme in which interviews of women who lived secretly as lesbians, was broadcast. Lesbians began to be featured in plays such as *Trevor*, shown at the Loft Theatre, Leamington Spa, in ballets such as *Francesca,* performed at Sadler's Wells, and in films such as the *Killing of Sister George*, some of which was filmed at *The Gateways*. Edward Bond's play *Early Morning* even argued that Queen Victoria had a relationship with Florence Nightingale. Lesbianism was becoming recognised, if not yet acceptable. The nine men on Coventry Town Council banned *The Killing of Sister George* from being shown in local cinemas: one Councillor argued that it was because it 'had one of the filthiest scenes I have ever seen in my life. Two women making love. And it was in technicolour. That made it worse'.[44]

Undoubtedly, the main focus of sexual protest was hetero, with campaigns concerned with birth control and abortion. In 1964, Leah Manning, no longer a Labour MP, set up a birth control clinic for unmarried women in Harlow because the Family Planning Association (FPA) only offered birth control advice to married women. By this time, about half a million women used the birth control pill, and the FPA was forced to shift its position and allow single women contraception—if they proved they were engaged to be married.

Women still resorted to abortion when faced with giving birth to and bringing up an unwanted child. Women with money could have a relatively safe experience—in the early 1960s, the cost of an illegal abortion by a sympathetic doctor was around £100. Poorer women had no option but to seek out a backstreet abortionist. Some used abortifacients advertised in newspapers as cures for 'menstrual blockage'; others drank bleach, moved heavy furniture, had a hot bath or used a knitting needle to induce a miscarriage. Thousands of women died or else became poisoned by semi-legal medicines. Hospitals would employ extra staff on the A&E wards at the weekends to help women who had been injured by what were termed 'pay-day abortions'.[45] The Abortion Law Reform Association once again sprang into action, led by a new chair, Vera Houghton, and two new members of the Executive, Madeleine Simms and Diane Munday. This time the argument focused on a woman's right to choose, rather than on the unsafe nature of back street abortions. Campaigners claimed that to deny women an abortion was 'to exercise control over women's sexuality and fertility'. Access to abortion was 'advanced as a prerequisite for the full and equal participation of women in society'. [46] This time the campaign was successful, helped not only by the public realisation that abortion was the leading cause of maternal death but by a scandal involving thousands of handicapped babies born because their mothers had taken the thalidomide drug for morning sickness. Mothers who knew they were carrying a physically challenged child and feared the consequences were not allowed to abort the foetus.

There were a few attempts to change the law and make abortion more accessible. Private members' bills were always used because no party wanted to be responsible for advocating such a divisive measure. Bills were put forward: in 1961, by Labour MP Kenneth Robinson; in 1965, by Labour MP Renee Short; in 1966, by Conservative MP Simon Wingfield Digby. All failed. Eventually, in 1966, Liberal MP David Steel introduced a private members' bill to liberalise abortion. The time was propitious: Labour had a big majority; Roy Jenkins was Home Secretary and sympathetic to reform; and Kenneth Robinson was Minister of Health.[47] It helped too that popular female journalists like the widely read *Daily Mirror* journalist Marjorie Proops wrote articles in support, and women's organisations like the Townswomen's Guild circularised its 250,000 members asking them to bring pressure on their MPs to vote for the bill. One female journalist summed up the feeling of many, remarking that 'most of the arguments against abortion law reform are voiced by men' who had no knowledge of the stress and agony that an unwanted child brought to a mother.[48] Parliament, sensing the mood of large parts of the country, was in favour.

Nevertheless, during its second reading on 22 July 1966, David Steel had to fight bitterly over 19 hours and 46 minutes in an all-night sitting. The Roman Catholic and Conservative MP Norman St John-Stevas argued that human life was present from the moment of conception and 'therefore cannot be treated as mere animal matter to be excised from the womb and thrown away in a dustbin or incinerator'.[49] Shirley Williams, also a Roman Catholic, did not speak in the debate and voted against the bill.[50] All MPs were allowed to vote with their conscience: the bill passed with 223 (most MPs were absent) votes to 29, struggled through all the parliamentary stages and became law in 1968 after a 31-year battle. It allowed women in England, Wales and Scotland, but not Northern Ireland, to obtain an abortion provided that two medical doctors decided either that the continuation of the pregnancy would damage the physical or mental health of the pregnant woman or that there was a risk that the child would be born suffering from a physical or mental abnormality. When the Bill passed its third reading, Marjorie Proops remarked that it was a 'small bright sign that the voice of women ... is at last being heard ... by the men who make the laws'.[51] At the time, there were only 25 women Members of Parliament.

However, not all women welcomed abortion rights. In January 1967, the Society for the Protection of the Unborn Child (SPUC) was founded by Elspeth Rhys-Williams and Alan Smith to prevent Steel's Act from becoming law. Aleck Bourne, the gynaecologist who had helped reform the law in 1938, was elected to the Executive. At its first large meeting in Caxton Hall, London speakers argued that it would 'inevitably involve the killing of innocent human beings'[52] and why?—just because it was convenient to do so. Those who opposed abortion used graphic and disturbing language full of gory inaccurate detail, of 'how the limbs of unborn babies can be torn apart during an abortion'.[53] Certainly, the Society's propaganda was high in emotion and low on facts, showing photographs in vibrant colour of six-month foetuses and claiming they were 12-week ones. Undoubtedly, SPUC was a religious-based organisation, but at first Roman Catholics were excluded from its Committee because of their well-known antipathy to both birth control and abortion. Nevertheless, its Executive tended to be active Christians—its Press Officer Phyllis Court, worked for the London Bible Society. The Society organised a petition and asked the 10,000 Anglican vicars to collect signatures—a visiting curate at Kings Norton Parish Church asked his 300 strong congregation to sign it during his sermon.[54] Most vicars refused. Even so SPUC managed to collect 530,000 signatures and took the petition to 10 Downing Street. Meanwhile, the Union of Catholic Mothers urged its members to write to their MPs asking them to oppose abortion. These organisations were unable to stop the bill but they continued their protest against abortion, led protest marches and organised local events to raise money. In November 1968, more than £123 was raised at a bazaar in the church hall at Bedford Park to help SPUC.[55] The Society held demonstrations outside abortion clinics, laying funeral wreaths and intimidating those who entered and who worked there, arguing that 'we do not feel we are interfering with a woman's right to abortion because we don't believe she has that right'.[56] A group of senior gynaecologists in Birmingham refused to perform abortions and set the tone for others in the medical profession.

The New Moral Right

For some women, the right to abortion was associated with a time of depravity and immorality more generally. A new moral authoritarianism asserted itself against what was perceived as a decline in standards, particularly in the fairly new medium of television. Mary Whitehouse, former secondary school art teacher, Christian and fervent anti-communist, led this moral rearmament campaign. In January 1964, she and Nora Buckland, a vicar's wife, launched a campaign which they called *Clean Up TV* with a manifesto aimed at women. Mary Whitehouse was the propelling energy behind the duo, and it is her name which is connected to the movement to censor sex and violence. *Clean Up TV* later changed its name to the *National Viewers and Listeners Association* (NVLA). It was the same overwhelmingly female organisation with the same aim. Its members were usually housewives and retired women in late middle age. Its main target was the BBC. In the opinion of Whitehouse, the BBC was guilty of condoning immorality by programming plays and other entertainments which dealt sympathetically with 'homosexuality, lesbianism, abortion, venereal disease and drug addition'.[57] In June 1965, the NVLA organised a petition signed by 365,000 supporters which a sympathetic MP presented to Parliament. The petition objected to the 'disbelief, doubt and dirt that the BBC pours into millions of homes' by pandering to the 'lowest in human nature, accompanying this with a stream of suggestive and erotic plays which present promiscuity, infidelity and drinking as normal and inevitable'.[58] It asked that the BBC have a radical change of policy and make programmes 'which encourage and sustain faith in God'. [59]

Mary Whitehouse and her colleagues constantly harried the head of the BBC, Sir Hugh Green, and repeatedly tried to have him dismissed. They were 'apt to descend like avenging angels upon anything they consider to have a bad moral influence'.[60] They objected to television films such as Ken Loach's *Up the Junction*, largely because it presented promiscuity as normal and was seen as propaganda for the Abortion Bill that was being discussed in Parliament.[61] Poking fun at Mary Whitehouse and her beliefs became a national sport. She was called Mrs Spitehouse or Mrs Whitewash: one episode from a popular soap of the time, *From Death Us Do Part*, burned her book in front of the cameras while the actors chanted 'unclean'. Whitehouse may have been the butt of salacious jokes and of scornful mockery but she tapped into a national yearning for moral probity. Her six books were popular, her meetings were packed and the right-wing media gave her an extensive platform. Undoubtedly, Mrs Mary Whitehouse was a 'skilled self-promoter' who 'carved out a place for herself on the public stage' and whose popularity tapped deep into the silent majority.[62] Dennis Potter, the radical playwright, argued that Whitehouse stood up for 'all the people ... (who are) laughed at and treated like rubbish by the sophisticated metropolitan minority'.[63]

Undoubtedly, Mary Whitehouse had an overtly right-wing agenda—she won support from Enoch Powell and other members of the Conservative Party who prided themselves on their family values and their moral rectitude. However, within the higher echelons of the party there was a dissonance between theory and practice. At this time, the Conservative government was in trouble, beleaguered by a political scandal involving the secretary of state for war, John Profumo, and his alleged affair with 19-year-old Christine Keeler, who was the lover of a Soviet naval officer. In March 1963, Barbara Castle helped bring the government down by asking whether it was 'true that the Minister of War was involved' with Keeler. Her question brought Profumo to the dispatch box the following day to declare that he 'had been on friendly terms with the girl, but denied any impropriety'.[64] Later, Profumo confessed that he had broken the ministerial code by lying, resigned his cabinet post and left Parliament. The affair severely damaged the Conservative government, and Labour won the next General Election, held in 1964.

Anti-nuclear Protests

In May 1960, Mrs Margaret Prosser, president of the Worthing Women's International League for Peace and Freedom (WLPF) and member of the Direct Action Committee Against Nuclear War, was arrested with five other women for lying down in the road outside the Atomic Weapons Research Establishment at Foulness Island, Essex. Prosser, 70-year-old Mary Poppleton and four other women were put on trial, convicted and imprisoned for seven days in Holloway women's prison. Mrs Prosser was protesting 'to make people think of the evils of this terrible weapon', the atomic bomb. Like the suffragettes before them, the six women refused to pay their fines of £2 and were therefore sentenced to spend time in Holloway.[65] By this time, the WILPF had 'consultative status' at the United Nations; its observers attended all important UN meetings and submitted their views on disarmament, economic development and slavery to various committees. In the WILPF's view, lasting peace could not be attained without social justice and aimed for the 'elimination of all discrimination on grounds of race, sex or creed, and to raise the living standards of under-privileged people'.[66]

Meanwhile, the National Assembly of Women (NAW), an organisation set up in 1952 to work for women's rights, and the Campaign for Nuclear Disarmament (CND) urged its members to campaign against the proposed installation of a Polaris nuclear submarine at the Holy Loch, Scotland by organising meetings, drawing up petitions, writing to their MPs and supporting all groups taking action against nuclear war.[67] Here women activists and MPs worked together to challenge the proliferation of nuclear weapons. The Labour MP for Lanark Judith Hart believed in unilateral nuclear disarmament, joined CND and had walked on the first Aldermaston march, her two young sons in tow. She took the fight to Parliament. In November 1960, Hart spoke out against the citing of a nuclear submarine at the Clyde naval base telling MPs that trade-unionists objected to the siting of the Polaris submarine in Scotland and asking the secretary of state what the effect would be 'of the dropping of a 20-megaton bomb in the vicinity of the proposed Polaris submarine base?'[68] In Judith Hart's opinion: 'submarine warfare tends to induce provocative situations. ... When we are providing money ... for Polaris submarines which are armed with nuclear weapons capable of wreaking the most tremendous damage—it is a killer weapon on a massive scale—then we are likely to increase provocation. ... As soon as a weapon is developed by one side a counter weapon is developed by the other side ... the only way to defend the people of this country in a nuclear age is to prevent the outbreak of war.'[69]

In 1960, the Committee of 100 was founded to organise a mass civil disobedience campaign against nuclear weapons. Another Labour MP and founder of CND, Anne Patricia Kerr, joined the Committee of 100 and also used her parliamentary position to raise the question in the House of Commons. Nineteen other women joined the Committee, including Shelagh Delaney, author of the contemporary play *A Taste of Honey*.[70] On 17 September 1961, members of the Committee of 100 and others blockaded the Holy Loch; others staged a sit-down protest in London. More than 350 were arrested for 'disorderly conduct' during these protests including a number of well-known women such as Vanessa Redgrave, Shelagh Delaney, Pat Arrowsmith, Denise Pyle, Anne Kerr, Jane Noel-Buxton and Dora Russell. One of those arrested, Patricia Raphael, was the wife of a London magistrate and daughter of a former attorney general. The police were accused of behaving brutally, of dragging protestors 'along by their feet with their heads bouncing on the stones'.[71] No officer was charged.

Pat Arrowsmith, vice president of the Campaign for Nuclear Disarmament and leader of the Committee of 100, was given a three-month sentence for 'disorderly conduct' for her part in the anti-Polaris demonstration at Scotland's Holy Loch.[72] She went on hunger strike and was force-fed four times. The National Assembly of Women sent a telegram to the Home Secretary, James Callaghan, protesting against this; Judith Hart visited her in prison and persuaded her to stop her hunger strike.[73] Despite protests and the intervention of MPs, construction of the submarines went ahead, and the first Polaris naval exercise took place two years later; Polaris patrols continued until 1996, when they were replaced by Trident.

Pat Arrowsmith continued protesting. Altogether she served 11 prison sentences for her campaigning, often being physically harmed before being arrested. While demonstrating in Scotland, she had been thrown into the mud, into pools of icy water, hosed down from the side of the Polaris and tossed into the River Clyde. Asked why she was willing to suffer these humiliations, she replied, 'I cannot sit still and be a party to politicians' threats to incinerate a large part of the human race.'[74]

Organisational and Parliamentary Politics

In 1964, women's groups active in Britain had a combined membership of three million. The biggest of these were the Women's Institute (WI), the Women's Co-operative Guild, the Mother's Union, the Townswomen's Guild, the Conservative and the Labour and Liberal women's groups.[75] Only 15 out of these 120 groups considered themselves feminists. Sometimes, the groups focused on minor—yet significant—issues such as the campaign to abolish turnstiles in public lavatories. At the time, several hundred public lavatories had penny-in-the-slot turnstiles at the entrance, making it difficult for pregnant women, disabled women, women with pushchairs, elderly women and larger women to use the facilities. Over a five-year period, at least 150 women had been trapped in them. Male lavatories were free of charge. Barbara Castle sponsored the campaign in Parliament. In 1963, the Public Lavatories (Turnstiles) Act was passed, which abolished the turnstiles and made women's public lavatories free of charge.

Freedom from Hunger Campaign

Sometimes women's groups focused on international change. A number—the National Council of Women, the WI, the Women's International League for Peace, the Townswomen's Guilds and the YWCA—joined the Freedom from Hunger Campaign, a crusade set up by the UN to raise awareness of global hunger and malnutrition and which aimed to eliminate these deficiencies by breaking the cycle of poverty and food shortages. It pioneered a collaboration between non-governmental organisations and government bodies, later recognised to be a key factor in the emergence of an international humanitarian movement, promoting international development programmes.[76]

The Townswomen's Guilds and the WI encouraged their members to study the problem of global hunger and to raise funds for the Freedom from Hunger Campaign. Lectures took place across the country. At Leicester, WI members listened to Mrs Parkes state the 'plain facts', that 'between one-third and one-half of the world's population either has not enough to eat or has the wrong kinds of things to eat and consequently suffers from malnutrition'.[77] Well-used to fundraising, women in the WIs responded positively, and 'sponsored walks, bake sales, coffee mornings, jumble sales, bring and buy sales, raffles, fetes and car boot sales', which together brought in huge sums of money.[78] The Longdon WI held a cheese lunch at Moat House, where 'several varieties of cheese and bread were served with salad and coffee' and raised £37[79]; the Staffordshire WI organised a whist drive which raised £15[80]; the Haswell WI raised £21 from a whist and domino drive[81]; the Mochdre WI raised £20 from a performance of the play 'The Red Cap' in the village hall[82]; the Hanklow WI raised £18 15s 8d from a jumble sale.[83] The Aberdeen branch raised nearly £10,000 from jumble sales, church collections, donations from individuals, organisations such as the Women's Gas Federation and businesses such as the Caledonian Fish Meat Company.[84] Not all WI attempts were so fruitful: the Riley WI only raised £2 12s 6d when they showed a film of a Methodist Guild Holiday in Austria.[85] Nonetheless, all these, and many others—widow's mite and all—added up. The WI pledged to raise £25,750 by 1965 to fund two projects; by 1963, they had raised £180,000, way beyond their goal.

This money, as Skelton points out, allowed the WI to fund training and study courses overseas to remedy the causes of malnutrition, part of which focused on nutrition, part of which 'emphasised new aspects of technical training in agricultural techniques for women, including the use of fertilisers, light machinery and communal ovens'.[86] The WI funded a Karamoja Farm Institute in Uganda and built a co-operative store in Bechuanaland. The Farm taught agricultural techniques to prevent overgrazing and soil erosion, while the Co-op store provided space and encouragement for local women to sell their crops more easily. The profits from the shop funded other projects to help women. The WI also raised sufficient money to support initiatives in Kenya, Ceylon, Rhodesia and Trinidad, all small-scale projects which benefited women. In 1964, the WI enlarged their programme in West Bengal from engaging with 6 villages to working with 18. Their aim was to reduce female illiteracy and provide instruction in healthcare, cookery and handicrafts. Nursery schools were set up so that women could leave their children in care and attend their courses. In 1965, annual leadership courses for women were arranged. A year later, the WI collaborated with the All Pakistan Women's Organisation to set up a scheme in East Pakistan to train local leaders who would then teach 'nutrition, food preservation and preparation, horticulture, maternity and child care, family planning, craftwork and literacy' to other women.[87] Most of the efforts of the WI centred on helping those living in former British colonies, and despite good intentions was generally packed with imperialistic assumptions and strongly held beliefs that the white northern countries were culturally, politically, socially and economically superior to black and brown southern countries. These women may have made a difference to the lives of the women they helped but as Skelton argues, 'the legacies of "imperial maternalism" continued' in a new context of development.[88]

Some commentators have suggested that the women's movement was too amateurish and unfocused and there was an 'unnecessary proliferation of women's organisations, a duplication of aims and methods and far too little co-ordination'.[89] This was set to change. First of all, 15 women's groups joined together to form the Status of Women Committee, whose object was to have a more organised approach to inequality and to work with MPs to secure fairer treatment for women.[90] There were successes: the Divorce Reform Act 1969 enabled couples to divorce after they had been separated for two years if both agreed, or five years if only one wanted a divorce. Neither partner had to prove 'fault'. Even so, the chair of the Committee and Conservative MP, Dame Joan Vickers, declared that 'a lot of legislation might have got through if we had more women in Parliament'. She was particularly annoyed when her Guardianship of Infants Bill, which would provide mothers equal rights of guardianship with fathers, faced 'men's deliberate opposition'.[91] At the time the Bastardy Acts were still in force: in 1969, the Family Law Reform Act gave the same legal rights to children born outside of marriage as those born within it. Other injustices roused the women's groups into joint action. In 1970, Tessa Fothergill set up Gingerbread to help single mothers, and alongside Mothers-in-Action and the renamed National Council for One Parent Families, campaigned for better laws and drew attention to the problems faced by women who brought up their children without a partner.

To effect transformation, as the suffragettes had been only too aware, women needed to be at the centre of power. In 1959, 25 women, 12 Conservative and 13 Labour, were elected to Parliament, the largest number ever, yet still only making up 4% of all MPs. Harold Macmillan became Conservative prime minister, followed by Alec Douglas-Home until 1964. Six women were appointed to ministerial positions during this period: the recently elected 32-year-old Margaret Thatcher, the youngest woman ever to join the front bench,[92] Patricia Hornsby-Smith,[93] Edith Pitt,[94] Mervyn Pike,[95] Patricia Hornsby-Smith[96] and Lady Tweedsmuir.[97] Neither Macmillan nor Hume appointed women to cabinet posts, or indeed to junior ones in the Foreign Office or the Treasury.

In 1964, another Harold, Harold Wilson, took over as prime minister of a Labour government. During his tenure, he awarded official government posts to Margaret Herbison,[98] Alice Bacon,[99] Joan Lester,[100] Gwyneth Dunwoody,[101] Harriet Slater,[102] Eirene White,[103] Shirley Williams,[104] Jennie Lee,[105] Baroness Serota,[106] Baroness Llewelyn-Davies[107] and Baroness Phillips.[108] Wilson also appointed Barbara Castle and Judith Hart to cabinet positions, the first time two women had served in the cabinet at the same time. Individually and collectively, these women made their mark on the political landscape. These women were appointed to a whole range of ministries and departments that had never before had a female minister: the Foreign Office, Overseas Development, Transport, Paymaster General and the Whips Office.

For example, Harriet Slater, National Organiser for the Cooperative-Party and the first woman to be elected in Stoke on Trent, was appointed the first ever female government whip with the formal title of Lord Commissioner of the Treasury. As a whip, she helped steer the Labour government's programme through Parliament with only a majority of three, cajoling, threatening, negotiating with MPs across the political spectrum to effect change.[109] All-night sittings became regular: the Labour government had a whole swathe of social reform waiting, from the legalisation of abortion, to the decriminalisation of homosexuality, the abolition of the death penalty and divorce law reform. Most of these were private member initiatives, allowing MPs to vote with their conscience: Margaret Thatcher voted for the decriminalisation of homosexuality and against the abolition of the death penalty.

Another woman who made a significant impact was Jennie Lee,[110] a well-known left-wing rebel. Wilson appointed her as the first-ever Minister for the Arts, under the aegis of the Department of Education but in charge of her own budget. She thought it a dream job as 'all the others deal with people's sorrows ... But I have been called the minister of the future'.[111] She trebled the Arts Council budget in six years and energised the whole industry, focusing not just on London but also on the provinces. Artists, she insisted, always gave back more than they took, and were 'not essentially takers. They are givers. They want to give us their songs, their poems, their dreams'.[112] Art, she believed, belonged to everyone, not just the elite—she funded it accordingly. Under her guidance and with her financial help, school pupils learned how to play instruments, youth orchestras were founded and youth musical festivals launched. Her department also funded the Young Vic, the National Youth Orchestra, and the National Film School for budding actors, musicians and filmmakers. She was, as her biographer Patricia Hollis argues, 'the first, the longest serving and most loved of all Britain's Ministers for the Arts'.[113]

Jennie Lee's most famous achievement was putting into practice Harold Wilson's dream of an Open University (OU), a university without bricks and mortar which would attract those students who had been denied opportunity to study at a higher level. At the time, only 4% of the population attended university: new ones such as Sussex (1961), Warwick (1965), East Anglia (1963) and York (1963) were built but these offered only full-time courses and remained middle-class territories. Wilson and Lee were both committed to broadening opportunity, increasing social mobility and using television and radio to deliver courses. Lee faced a lack of enthusiasm from every quarter: from ministerial colleagues, from parts of the education sector, from civil servants, from trade unions, sections of the Labour Party and the press as well as from the opposing Conservative Party. But Jennie Lee, backed up by Wilson, was unwavering and tenacious and the Open University was founded. When Labour lost the 1970 election, it was feared that the Open University would disappear. However, Jennie Lee had found a new and unexpected ally in Margaret Thatcher who, as secretary of state for education, defended the OU from attack both in the Cabinet and in the House of Commons. In Thatcher's view, the OU with its low costs and its emphasis on individualised learning, tapped into her beliefs about value for money and self-help. In 1971, the OU admitted its first students, and began its remarkable ascent to become a well-respected, popular institution.

Some, like Eirene White, faced tougher challenges. At the 1966 Labour Party conference, she tried to defend government policy on Rhodesia. At 11 am on 11 November 1965, Ian Smith, the prime minister of Rhodesia ,had declared a Unilateral Declaration of Independence. It was a declaration of bigotry. Ian Smith was a well-known white supremacist who prohibited the majority of Rhodesians—that is, the indigenous black community—from voting. Harold Wilson was expected to take action against this illegal regime, but he prevaricated. Conference delegates demanded tougher sanctions against the Smith regime. White's job was to defend her boss. Her speech, the *Daily Mirror* argued, was 'Disastrous'.[114] She 'clearly lost the sympathy of delegates', who openly talked, laughed and sometimes slow handclapped the minister.[115] Harold Wilson, 'his face dark with anger, listened furiously as Mrs White stumbled from mistake to mistake in her speech'.[116] She was only saved from complete humiliation by the support of the trade union block vote, which voted for the government.

Harold Wilson appointed two women to the most senior ministerial posts of all: to the Cabinet. His first appointment was Barbara Castle, who was to hold four cabinet posts in the Wilson governments, an extraordinary achievement in itself. Her first job was as Minister for Overseas Development. It was a new department allowing Castle to shape it from scratch. Here, Castle set out an ambitious agenda: in June 1965, she announced that all loans to the *poorest* countries would be interest free. In 1965, Wilson promoted Castle to Minister of Transport. Here, she implemented the breathalyser and the 70-hour speed limit, and introduced seat belts. The women across Britain who had campaigned for road safety were undoubtedly pleased.

In April 1968, Barbara Castle was promoted again, this time to secretary of state for employment; in effect, she was the minister of labour. She was now in charge of the most controversial of all government policies, that of reforming the trade unions. At the time, Britain was beleaguered by unofficial strikes, and the Labour government was blamed for being too soft on the trade unions. Castle's white paper *In Place of Strife* proposed to curb their powers. This paper was political dynamite, and she was widely criticized for her proposals. Her image as a left-wing firebrand was damaged, only to be retrieved a little by championing equal pay for women.

The second woman to be appointed to Wilson's Cabinet was Scottish MP Judith Hart, who had earned her parliamentary wings as a junior minister.[117] In 1968—the 50th anniversary of votes for women—Harold Wilson promoted Judith Hart to Paymaster General with a 'rag-bag of responsibilities': to oversee government policy; to make politics seem attractive; to supervise the devolution of powers to Scotland and Wales; to be a 'mini-Minister of Youth'; and, lastly, to promote the equality of women. The new Paymaster General was warned that if she took even half of her workload seriously, she 'risks working herself into a nervous breakdown'.[118] It is safe to say that her contribution as a cabinet minister was limited. After one year in the post, she was moved to become Minister of Overseas Development. This was no longer a cabinet post.[119]

Conclusion

At the beginning of the 1960s, the Women's Freedom League (WFL) was disbanded. The WFL had been founded in 1907 as a militant women's suffrage society and had developed into an organisation which campaigned for women's rights more widely. One of its founders, Teresa Billington-Greig, commented that 'there are still things to be done but our generation has had its day. The new generation has its own problems to solve and must find its own way to do so'.[120] Certainly, there were similar inequalities that had dogged their predecessors which the 1960s generation tried to combat, but there were also new issues and forms of activism which an earlier generation had never addressed, some of which would continue into the next decade. And as the 1960s drew to a close, women's activism was set to change again.

In May 1967, as Britain was discussing joining the Common Market, a campaign was launched by Mrs Joan Debell, a local activist and Conservative Councillor for Pinner North and Hatch End. She organised two petitions, both of which stated that those who had signed them were against unqualified entry into the Common Market and pressed for a national referendum. The first was signed by members of the Conservative Party only, and the second was signed by 'people of all political persuasions. Solid, ordinary people—not kinky'.[121] Thirty-six people signed the Conservative one, and 88 the non-party one. Mrs Debell insisted that it was 'not a backward looking, old-fashioned policy of isolationism' but a feeling that Britain would lose 'its sense of individuality' if it joined the Common Market.[122] The petition was delivered to their MP and a letter sent to Harold Wilson. This local action was replicated across the country. Later that year, Mrs Debell joined forces with the Anti-Common Market League and spent the summer obtaining signatures on a petition to the Queen, asking her to exercise her royal prerogative. The petition argued that it put 'in danger the right of British subjects freely to enjoy those full political and economic liberties which they have inherited from the past'.[123] By 1970, Debell was a leading Anti-Common Market campaigner. When she appeared on an ITV programme in front of an audience of housewives, she suggested that people living in common market countries had a lower standard of living than the British. She told her audience that if people drove through France, they would 'see the shabby public buildings and badly made roads; the old women dressed in black and the middle-aged women drably dressed'.[124] Debell was appointed to the Committee of the Women's Anti-Common Market movement, which the Labour MP Anne Kerr had helped found, to present housewives with the negative side of the Common Market. It organised demonstrations outside large stores using shopping baskets full of goods 'clearly marked with the increased prices they will have to pay'.[125] Mrs Joan Debell was one of many examples of how local actions with small beginnings can develop into national campaigns, leading to changes in the law. It was, she argued, 'simply a question of slogging away—it's nothing dramatic'.

Mrs Debell initiated another campaign, again with future national consequences. In 1974, she caused uproar at a council meeting when she walked to the front of the mayor's bench and dumped a large bag of rubbish onto the carpeted floor of the Chamber. It was from her own house. The indomitable councillor wanted to draw attention to the widespread dumping of rubbish in the area: there were 'screw-top glass jars, plastic containers, tins and two wine bottles … the product of one ordinary household of two adults and two cats'. She implored the Council to introduce a national rubbish campaign in order 'to survive'.[126] The Council took note and implemented a recycling scheme. It would take until the twenty-first century for Debell's campaign to become government policy.

Notes

1. *The Times*, 6 February 1968, p. 1.
2. See Brian W Lavery, *The Headscarf Revolutionary: Lilian Bilocca and the Hull Triple-Trawler Tragedy*, Barbican Press, 2015; Brian W Lavery, 'Bilocca, Lillian', *DNB*, 2013; Tom White, 'Radical Objects: Hull's "Headscarf Revolutionaries" Mural', *History Workshop Journal*, August 2019; BBC *Hull Headscarf Heroes*, broadcast 6 February 2018.
3. The women suggested full crewing of ships, radio operators on every ship, improved weather forecasts, more safety equipment and a ship with medical facilities to accompany the trawlers.
4. Pathé News, *Hull—Trawler Men Aka Three Trawlers Lost at Sea—Wives Demand Stricter Safety Measures* (1968).
5. Hull fishermen's safety campaigner Mary Denness dies, ITV news, 5 March 2017.
6. See Tom White, 'Radical Objects: Hull's "Headscarf Revolutionaries" Mural', *History Workshop Journal*, August 2019, p. 3.
7. *The Times*, 8 February 1968, p. 1.
8. Val Holmes, *Lil*, first performed November 2017.
9. The play, first performed in November 2017 at the Guildhall, Hull, was an immersive piece of theatre written by Maxine Peake, directed by Sarah Frankcom and Imogen Knight, with an original score by The Unthanks and a large cast of amateur actors. There is also a video available at VIMEO.
10. *The Birmingham Post*, 17 July 1963, p. 7.
11. *Coventry Evening Telegraph*, 25 April 1968, p. 52.
12. *Liverpool Echo*, 4 January 1969, p. 1.
13. *Belfast Telegraph*, 22 June 1960, p. 1.
14. *Belfast Telegraph*, 9 February 1967, p. 4.
15. *Coventry Evening Telegraph*, 27 March 1968, p. 1.
16. *Belfast Telegraph*, 6 October 1961, p. 2.
17. *Daily Mail*, 2 April 1960, p. 3.
18. *Daily Mail*, 1 April 1960, p. 7.
19. See *1968: News: Dagenham Women Strike*, BBC Archive.
20. *Daily Mirror*, 22 November 1968, p. 23.
21. Ibid., 23 May 1968, p. 19.

22. *Birmingham Post*, 10 January 1969, p. 3.
23. *Coventry Evening Telegraph*, 7 January 1969, p. 43.
24. *Newcastle Evening Chronicle*, 26 June 1969, p. 13.
25. *Daily Mirror*, 6 November 1969, p. 4.
26. Margaret Thatcher, HC Debates, 9 February 1970, vol 795 cc 913–1038.
27. Ibid.
28. *Birmingham Post*, 26 October 1963, p. 5.
29. *Daily Mail*, 2 September 1960, p. 1.
30. Ibid., 31 August 1960, p. 2.
31. Ibid., 22 April 1960, p. 20.
32. *Birmingham Post*, 12 November 1966, p. 1.
33. *Evening Chronicle*, 22 December 1960, p. 5.
34. *Liverpool Echo*, 22 February 1967, p. 1.
35. *The Birmingham Post*, 22 February 1967, p. 1.
36. See Anne-Marie Angelo, 'The Black Panthers in London, 1967–1972: A Diasporic Struggle Navigates the Black Atlantic', *Radical History Review*, Issue 103, 2009, for a history of the group.
37. See *The Mangrove Nine*, by Steve McQueen, BBC, from a series of films—Small Axe—about the Black British experience.
38. Catherine Baksi, *The Guardian*, 10 November 2020.
39. Hannah Ishmael, *Archival Groundings: The life of Jessica Huntley*, Women's History Network blog, 11 October 2020.
40. Ibid.
41. Quoted in Sue Bruley, *Women in Britain since 1900*, Macmillan, 1999, p. 139.
42. Joanna O'Brien, *On the Cusp of Change: Lesbian Voices from the 60s*, Glasgow Women's Library, internet source, accessed June 2020.
43. *Arena 3*, vol 1, No 9, September 1964, quoted in Joanna O'Brien, *On the Cusp of Change: Lesbian Voices from the 60s* Glasgow Women's Library, internet source, accessed June 2020.
44. *Coventry Evening Telegraph*, 3 October 1969, p. 5.
45. *Independent*, 30 March 2017, internet source.
46. Sally Sheldon "The Abortion Act 1967: A Critical Perspective", in Lee E (eds) *Abortion Law and Politics Today*, Palgrave Macmillan, 1998.
47. C. Francome, *Social forces and the abortion law*, PhD, Middlesex University, 1980.
48. *Reading Evening Post*, 11 January 1967, p. 3.
49. *Aberdeen Press and Journal*, 23 July 1966.
50. HC Debates, 22 July 1966, vol 732, cc 1067–165. Many women spoke in this debate.
51. *Daily Mirror*, 25 October 1967, p. 9.
52. *The Birmingham Post*, 12 January 1967, p. 9.
53. Margarie Proops, *Daily Mirror*, 13 July 1967, p. 7.
54. *Birmingham Post*, 8 May 1967.
55. *Gazette and Post*, 14 November 1968, p. 10.
56. *Birmingham Post*, 27 October 1969, p. 1.
57. Mary Whitehouse, *Mary Whitehouse, 'Who does she think she is?'*, New English Library, 1971, p. 66.
58. Ibid., p. 60.
59. Ibid.

60. *Liverpool Echo*, 10 December 1969, p. 8.
61. Mary Whitehouse, *Mary Whitehouse*, '*Who does she think she is?*', New English Library, 1971.
62. Jessica Prestidge, 'Housewives having a go: Margaret Thatcher, Mary Whitehouse and the appeal of Right Wing Women in late twentieth century Britain', *Women's History Review*, Vol 28, No 2, 2019, p. 278.
63. Ibid., p. 279.
64. *Coventry Evening Telegraph*, 22 March 1963, p. 1.
65. *Worthing Gazette*, 4 May 1960, p. 8.
66. *The Tewkesbury Register*, 24 May 1963, p. 2.
67. *The Birmingham Post*, 17 November 1960, p. 9.
68. HC Debates, 16 November 1960, vol 630, c4700.
69. HC Debates, 2 March 1961, vol 635, cc 1807–919.
70. Clare Annesley, Margaretta Arden, Pat Arrowsmith, Wendy Butlin, Jane Buxton, April Carter, Una Collins, Elizabeth Dales, Shelagh Delaney, Hilda Fitter, Dorothy Glaister, Janet Goodricke, Mary Grigg, Ann Kerr, Isobel Lindsay, Joan Pittock, Heather Richardson, Mary Ringsleben, Edith Russell, Barbara Webb.
71. *The Birmingham Post*, 25 September 1961, P7.
72. She was a public school girl, Cambridge history graduate and daughter of a former Torquay vicar.
73. Arrowsmith had been on hunger strike for 11 days, was forcibly fed and was close to being a martyr for the cause. *The Guardian*, 17 October 1961, p. 2.
74. *Daily Herald*, 30 November 1961, p. 8.
75. Elizabeth Homans, *Visions of Equality, women's rights and political change in 1970s Britain*, PhD, Bangor University, 2015.
76. Matthew Bunch, *The Freedom from Hunger Campaign: Inventing the International Development Movement*, accessed internet, 17 March 2021.
77. *Leicester Evening Mail*, 26 September 1962, p. 3.
78. Skelton, Sophie, *From peace to development: A reconstruction of British women's international politics, c1945–75*, PhD, University of Birmingham, 2014. p. 188.
79. *Rugeley Times*, 13 April 1963, p. 4.
80. Ibid., 27 April 1963, p. 13.
81. *Newcastle Evening Chronicle*, 23 November 1963, p. 9.
82. *North Wales Weekly News*, 28 March 1963, p. 8.
83. *The Crew Chronicle*, 3 November 1962, p. 14.
84. *Aberdeen Evening Express*, 17 April 1963, p. 5.
85. *Long Eaton Advertiser*, 29 March 1963, p. 9.
86. Skelton, Sophie, *From peace to development: A reconstruction of British women's international politics, c1945–75*, PhD, University of Birmingham, 2014, p. 183.
87. Ibid., p. 192.
88. Ibid., p. 196.
89. Elizabeth Homans, *Visions of Equality, women's rights and political change in 1970s Britain*, PhD, Bangor University, 2015, p. 84.
90. *Birmingham Post*, 5 May 1966, p. 10.
91. *The Press and Journal*, 6 March 1968, p. 5.
92. Parliamentary Secretary to the Minister of Pensions, 1961–1964.
93. Parliamentary Secretary, Minister of Pensions, 1959–1961.
94. Parliamentary Secretary, Minister of Health, 1959.

95. Joint Under-Secretary of State at the Home Office, 1963–1964.
96. Joint Under-Secretary of State at the Home Office, 1957–1959.
97. Under-Secretary of State for Scotland, 1962–1964.
98. Minister of Pensions and Social Insurance, 1964–1966; Minister of Social Security, 1966–1967.
99. Minister of State for Home Affairs, 1964; Minister of State for Education and Science, 1967–1970. See Rachel Reeves' biography *Alice in Westminster*, I. B. Tauris, 2016.
100. Under-Secretary of State for Education, 1969–1970
101. Parliamentary Secretary at the Board of Trade 1967–1970.
102. Lord of the Treasury, 1964–1966.
103. Under-Secretary of State for the Colonies 1964–1965; Minister of State for Foreign Affairs, 1966–1967. *Cheshire Observer*, 15 April 1966, p. 9.
104. Minister of State for Education and Science, 1967–1969; Minister of State for Home Affairs, 1969–1970. See Paula Bartley, *Labour Women in Power*, Palgrave Macmillan, 2019 for a fuller discussion of Williams' political life.
105. Minister for the Arts, 1964–1970.
106. Lords in Waiting, 1968–1969; Minister of State for Social Services, 1969–1970.
107. Lords in Waiting, 1969–1970.
108. Lords in Waiting, 1965–1970. She was the first female government whip in the House of Lords. She is the mother of Gwyneth Dunwoody.
109. See the play by James Graham *This House*, which takes place in the Whips Offices.
110. Under-Secretary of State for Education, 1965–1967; Minister of State for the Arts, 1967–1970.
111. Jennie Lee quoted in Rachel Reeves', *Women of Westminster*, I. B. Tauris, 2019, p. 116.
112. Patricia Hollis, *Jennie Lee*, OUP, 1997, p. 252.
113. Ibid.
114. *Daily Mirror*, 8 October 1966, p. 2.
115. *The Coventry Evening Telegraph*, 7 October 1966, p. 1.
116. *Evening Post*, 7 October 1966, p. 1.
117. Under Secretary of State for Scotland, 1964–1966; Minister of State for Commonwealth Affairs, 1966–1967; Minister of Social Security, 1967; Paymaster General, 1968; Minister of Overseas Development, 1969.
118. David Wood, *The Times*, 21 October 1968 HART/13/76.
119. See Paula Bartley, *Labour Women in Power*, Palgrave Macmillan, 2019.
120. Teresa Billington-Greig quoted in Krista Cowman, *Women in British Politics, c1689–1979*, Palgrave, 2010, p. 164.
121. *Harrow Observer*, 11 May 1967, p. 1.
122. Ibid., p. 1.
123. *The Observer and Gazette*, 3 August 1967, p. 2.
124. *The Observer and Gazette*, 10 July 1970, p. 8.
125. *The Observer and Gazette*, 18 December 1970, p. 3.
126. *Harrow Observer*, 12 March 1974, p. 1.

CHAPTER 9

The Selfish Seventies?: 1970–1979

On 27 February 1970, the first-ever Women's Liberation Movement (WLM) conference opened at Ruskin College Oxford. Much to the astonishment of the organisers, 500 women turned up. After much animated discussion, the women participants agreed to four demands: equal pay for equal work, free abortion on demand, equal education and free 24-hour childcare. The WLM helped create a climate conducive to reform which in turn was translated into new laws which benefited women: Guardianship of Minors Act (1973), Matrimonial Causes Act (1973), Sex Discrimination Act (1975), Employment Protection Act (1975), Sexual Offences Act (1976) and Domestic Violence Act (1976).

The WLM began gingerly but this soon changed. In November, a group of WLM women disrupted the Miss World contest, which was being compered by Bob Hope at the Albert Hall. The event was televised, and each year drew an audience of 22 million in Britain and a 100 million worldwide. Like the suffragettes who disrupted events in the early twentieth century, the protestors dressed up for the occasion with smart handbags in which they concealed bombs, plastic mice, leaflets, rattles, rotten tomatoes and smoke bombs. A few women used their rattles as a starting gun for the rest to fire their missiles at the stage. It was a well-regulated chaos: Bob Hope lost his cool—Julia Morley, the wife of the show's organiser, held his ankle to stop him running off. The show was stopped and the live show cancelled. Five women, including Sally Alexander, a future professor of history, were arrested, charged and fined. Their actions were celebrated in the film *Misbehaviour*, starring Keira Knightly.

The next year, on a freezingly cold day, around 3000 women marched on the first-ever Women's Liberation March to celebrate International Women's Day and to publicise the four demands of the WLM. I remember helping to carry an Equal Pay banner, hurriedly created by the Socialist Woman's Group

© The Author(s), under exclusive license to Springer Nature
Switzerland AG 2022
P. Bartley, *Women's Activism in Twentieth-Century Britain*, Gender and History, https://doi.org/10.1007/978-3-030-92721-9_9

of which I was a member. Jill Tweedie, the *Guardian* columnist, pointed out that the demonstrators were a mixed bag of 'long and short and thin and fat, quiet, middle-aged ladies in careful make-up, bare-faced girls with voices loud as crows. ... Professionals, manual workers, spinsters, wives, widows, mothers' all bound together by a commitment to eradicate, or at least undermine, patriarchy. It was not such a diverse group as Tweedie suggested as the class and ethnicity of the women was uniform.

The march was great fun. And a great spectacle, imitating the suffragette demonstrations with music, singing and even street theatre. Women dressed up as brides, as Miss Behave or Miss Stress (who was pulled along in a cage), and we all sang *Keep Young and Beautiful if you want to be loved*, only too aware that we were singing it ironically—the double irony that we were in fact mostly young and beautiful was lost on us.

Women's Liberation activists were criticised in the press for being dour, hard-faced and unfriendly, accusations that echo across the centuries whenever women have taken action against injustice. Women's Liberation was blamed for 'producing a new breed of hard-drinking' female gangsters,[1] and for the breakup of families. Even those allegedly sympathetic argued that much of feminist activity was 'counter-productive because it is too strident and too earnest'.[2] In her book *The Female Woman*, Arianna Stassinopoulous accused women's liberation of wanting to turn Britain into an orphanage by its demand for 24-hour nurseries. Women's Liberation, she insisted, was an attack on the very nature of women.

I remember the WLM being friendly, joyful and innovative. Women created slogans which neatly encapsulated their politics. Some were humorous: a woman needs a man like a fish needs a bicycle; a woman needs a man like a moose needs a hatrack; lesbians ignite; marriage is an institution, but who wants to live in an institution? Others were more serious: women hold up half the sky; the hand that rocks the cradle can rock the boat; the personal is the political; there will be no women's liberation without revolution—there will be no revolution without women's liberation; the future is female; women of the world unite.

At first, the WLM was open to men. In fact, the 1971 conference was organised with the help of a husband-and-wife team, both of whom were Maoists. The two—who intimidatingly sat on the stage as the conference participants entered the room—proposed that men take a leading role in the organisation and that a formal leadership team be established. This idea was anathema to the non-hierarchical beliefs of the female delegates who had no wish to have their movement dictated to by a bunch of Maoists. The couple were asked to leave the stage. And refused. They had not reckoned on the power of women, particularly lesbian women. I remember watching a group of women from the Gay Liberation Front storm the platform, grab the microphone and tackle the Maoists. As a conference, we all left the room and left the Maoists to it. Men were later banned from the WLM. After a negative press conference in 1970, reporters had not been allowed into the conference: the confrontation was never reported. The conference participants decided not to mention it publicly either.

Journalists may have been banned but some sneaked in, pretending to be feminists. Maureen Cozens, women's editor of the *Sunday Sun*, attended the WLM 1976 national conference incognito and reported that 'the lesbians were all *visible* and vociferous, bottles of brown ale, butch haircuts, unmade up faces and bouncing breasts abounded'. She spoke of chaos, disorganisation, shouting matches and 'one big unhappy family of sisters'.[3] The fears of feminists that the press would regard them as an object of ridicule were confirmed. Conferences continued until 1978, with more demands added on each year. By this time, the women's movement had multiplied and developed into diverse campaign groups (abortion rights, women's refuges, violence against women) and a variety of feminisms (socialist feminism, radical feminism and revolutionary feminism). Black and Asian women, who experienced different kinds of sexism, often combined with racism and who felt marginalised in what was in effect a white movement, set up their own groups. Women's liberation spread everywhere. It even invaded 'one of the sacred male strongholds'—the independent private Warwick School, which was established for the 'sons of gentlemen'—for a debate on the WLM phenomenon.[4] And, as the advert from the *Coventry Evening Telegraph* below shows, shopkeepers recognised that it served a useful purpose for them[5] (Fig. 9.1).

Nonetheless, like the suffrage movement before them, the WLM was a minority, and largely white movement. When she launched her first naval frigate—the HMS Amazon—Princess Anne assured the press that she would never join the Women's Liberation Movement because she had no sympathy with it.[6]

Spurred on by the WLM, there was an explosion of feminist literature. A range of journals, newsletters and papers with evocative and sardonic titles like *Spare Rib, Speak Out, Socialist Woman, Women's Voice, Scarlet Women, Bloody Woman, Red Rag, Shrew, FOWAAD*, all offered women a fresh perspective and a new way of looking at the world. *Socialist Woman* was a front for the International Marxist Group (IMG), a Trotskyist organisation. Generally, it reported on strikes, working-class women, trade union activity and other worthy stuff. In 1973, its editor—an IMG member—joined with radical feminist activists to produce something quite different: a paper which focused on other areas of women's experience like sexuality. It even had a section on self-examination, with details drawn by one of the collective. The front cover itself was provocative: posing the idea that men, not just capitalism, were holding women back. Its editorial was written by Carol Riddell, who had had sex reassignment surgery and had recently become a woman. The editor and the other IMG women were thrown out of the organisation and *Socialist Woman* reverted to its usual format (Fig. 9.2).

Teacher activists worked to challenge the sexism prevalent in 1970s Britain. They accused school textbook writers of keeping girls out of the story. In a survey of 100 science textbooks, only boys were shown doing experiments.

> **JOIN THE DEMONSTRATION FOR WOMEN'S LIBERATION**
>
> On FRIDAY, SATURDAY AND MONDAY
>
> 16th, 17th and 18th APRIL
>
> AT
>
> **MARSONS**
>
> **9, BULL YARD, COVENTRY,**
>
> when ELIZABETH REEVES, the Bendix
>
> Home Economist, will be giving continuous
>
> Demonstrations of the NEW
>
> 10 full place setting
>
> **BENDIX AUTOMATIC DISHWASHER**

Fig. 9.1 Advert from *Coventry Evening Telegraph*, 6 April 1971 (Courtesy of author)

There was only one picture of a girl: she was blowing bubbles.[7] To counteract this, women wrote books of their own: in 1975, Carol Adams and Rae Laurikietis' *The Gender Trap* was published. One of the books examined 'language and the way we use words and images in jokes, cartoons, picture postcards, pop lyrics, books and films, showing how this underlines and sometimes creates stereotypes'. In a rather chilling extract, the authors reported how Jimmy Saville claimed that being famous enabled him to have his 'crumpet', that is, sexually assault women. He boasted that there had been incidents 'on trains and boats and planes and bushes and fields, corridors, doorways, floors, chairs, slag heaps, desks and probably everything except the celebrated chandelier. But you never see Jimmy's love life plastered across the newspapers'.[8] At the time, Saville was a very popular media figure—it would take another generation of women to demolish his reputation, and only after he had died.

Fig. 9.2 Front cover of *Socialist Woman* 1973 created by a feminist collective (Courtesy of author)

'BLACK WOMEN TOGETHER'

At the same time, Black women were organising separately, influenced more by Samora Michel and Angela Davies than Germaine Greer or Shulamith Firestone.[9] In 1973, a Black Women's Group was formed in Brixton, London, 'in response to the lack of interest in women's issues displayed by male-dominated Black organisations' such as the Black Panther movement and the Black Liberation Front.[10] Other groups were founded across England: the United Black Women's Action Group in Tottenham, North London, the Liverpool Black Sisters and the Manchester Black Women's Co-operative. As Natalie Thomlinson points out, 'Black women's activism developed out of the

Black left at the same time as white feminism developed out of the white left.'[11] Black women objected to the fact that they were expected to be 'coffee-makers, cooks, fundraisers and, of course, willing sexual partners' in the Black struggle rather than equal partners. They were not expected to talk about the oppression even though they 'suffered as women at the hands of black men, who saw women's liberation strictly ... "a white girl's problem"'.[12] In fact, as the Black paper *Speak Out* argued, Black women were placed at the 'intersection of all forms of subjugation in society—racial oppression, sexual oppression and economic exploitation'. As a result, they were a 'natural part of many different struggles—both as black people and as women.'[13]

Racism meant that Black women's priorities were sometimes different from those of white women. As Beverley Bryan, Stella Dadzie and Suzanne Scafe argue 'it just didn't make sense for us to be talking about changing lifestyles and attitudes, when we were dealing with issues of survival, like housing, education and police brutality'.[14] Amrit Wilson commented that 'very few white women can know or imagine what a battle with racist society means. In Britain racism is like a cage, a system of bars which defines the position of black women and men, limiting their freedom, their choice of jobs, cutting down their aspirations, attacking them and their children emotionally and physically. It is these bars that black women have to break'.[15] Contraceptive rights, for example, were different for Black women, who faced pressure to use dangerous birth control methods by less-than-well-meaning doctors.

The Brixton group was active on a number of fronts: working with teenagers to combat racism; campaigning against the 'SUS' (Stop Under Suspicion) laws where young Black men were too often 'picked up, beaten and locked away' if they were suspected of 'loitering with intent' to break the law; helping to organise Black People Against State Brutality; setting up the Mary Seacole Craft Centre; creating study programmes; and campaigning against a damaging contraceptive injection mainly used on Black women. Another group, the United Black Women's Action Group, focused on similar issues but also drew attention to the exclusion of Black students from school and the prevalence of sickle cell anaemia, a hereditary blood disease affecting Black people.[16]

In February 1978, the Organisation of Women of Asian and African Descent (OWAAD) was formed, which, like Claudia Jones before, promoted Black culture. It aimed to establish a national Black women's umbrella organisation composed of groups and individuals active in anti-racist campaigns. On 18 March 1979, nearly 300 Black women from across England attended the first National Black Women's Conference at the Abeng Centre in Brixton, the first ever conference to bring together 'Asian, Afro- and Indo-Caribbean, African and Black sisters born and brought up in Britain'. It marked, according to one delegate, 'an important stage in the development of an autonomous Black Women's Movement', whereby the voices of Black women would be heard. Black women, they argued, suffered a triple oppression 'by male dominated Black groups; by white dominated women's groups; and by middle-class dominated left groups'.[17] Delegates listened to talks on racism and sexism in immigration laws, the racist use of Depo-Provera and other birth control injections, campaigns against the 'SUS' laws, the suffering caused by sickle cell anaemia, and the setting up of refuges and supplementary schools for Black women.[18]

On 3 June 1979, the Brixton Black Women's Group and AWAZ organised a demonstration against police brutality and the harassment of immigrants. It was precipitated by the reaction of the police to a previous peaceful protest a couple of months before. On 23 April 1979, in a deliberate act of provocation, the National Front (NF) had held an election meeting in Southall Town Hall, an area with a significant south Asian population. In response, the women of Southall organised a sit-down outside the Hall in an attempt to stop the NF from holding their meeting. An estimated 5000 turned up to support. The police decided to give support to the NF, not to the Black community which lived there. In the early evening, the police, mounted police and the Special Patrol Group used dogs, riot shields and truncheons to force the protestors into a nearby park. Women suffered racial and sexist abuse.[19] Blair Peach, a teacher in his 20s, was attacked and later died of head injuries.

Asian women had to deal with particular racist issues. Most British Asians came from Pakistan, Bangladesh and India. Some came from East Africa, having been expelled by the Ugandan and Kenyan governments. The Asian Women's Movement (AWAZ) campaigned against 'state racism', particularly against passport raids, deportations, police brutality and the demeaning treatment of women. In February 1979, a *Guardian* journalist, Melanie Phillips, uncovered a scandal whereby Asian women travelling to meet their fiancés in Britain were subjected to a humiliating invasive physical examination to see if they were virgins—the common sexist and racist belief was that all Asian women were virgins before marriage. On 10 February, the Asian women's group AWAZ organised a sit-in and a picket at Heathrow airport which morphed into a demonstration in central London. More than three years earlier, the immigration minister Alex Lyon had sent an instruction to all immigration officers forbidding the internal examination. Unfortunately, he was sacked by Jim Callaghan, and the practice continued.[20] Shortly after Phillips' article, the invasive examination policy was officially discontinued.

In 1974, a group of Asian women set up a Women's Association to help integrate women into British society and to protect their heritage. Many feared that their culture would be lost in the future because of Western influence and the tensions developing between older and younger generations of the Asian community.[21] They reached out to the white community. At a joint meeting with the Harrow Housewives' Register, Asian women spoke of 'loneliness, language difficulties, conflicting life-styles, tiredness' as common problems. The Mid-Warwickshire Federation of Townswomen's Guilds urged its members to interact with the Asian community so 'we could give each other mutual help' and avoid the parochialism that often beset the Guild. It was believed that the 'friendships formed in the guild … are so valuable to all women, particularly those coming to a new town' like Coventry.[22] Some Asian refugees from

Uganda had lost everything: their home, their money, their possessions. The Bracknell branch of the Women's Royal Voluntary Service provided household furnishings to displaced Asians fleeing from the Ugandan tyrannical regime and helped them build up their new homes.[23] Here were conventionally white middle-class women trying to make a difference to Asian women's lives, even though today their efforts might seem somewhat condescending.

Occasionally, the workplace was the site of the disconnectedness between race, gender and class. For example, the Leicester branch of Imperial Typewriters, which had a workforce of 1600 of whom 1100 were Asian, paid white workers more. In 1974, Asian women workers went on strike for equal pay. The picket line 'was not like a normal picket line with a couple of placards and a half a dozen men turning back the lorries'.[24] It was said to have a 'vivacity and style' that made it unique because it was made up largely of women— 'young, long-haired, golden-earringed, bedenimed and brown-skinned', who set up a 'fearful yowling and hollering' when a management representative came by.[25]

The management repudiated the Asian women's claim and was disgracefully backed up by the white workers and the Transport and General Workers' Union, which refused to give the 500 strikers any support. It was institutional racism, this time one of the institutions being a trade union organisation that supposedly protected workers. Eventually, the strikers received help from Black groups, the women's movement and a European Workers' Committee. It was not sufficient and the strikers returned to work without winning their case. The Race Relations Board inquired into the racial discrimination suffered by the women from both the trade union and the management, but little was done.[26] But as Amrit Wilson points out, the women strikers had few regrets, as one striker confirmed when she said that she 'had gained lots of things ... I had learned to fight' and would not be pushed around again.[27] In 1975, the factory closed.

'Strikers in Saris': 20 August 1976–14 July 1978

It was the hottest summer on record. On 20 August 1976, Jayaben Desai encouraged her colleagues, mostly East African Asian women, to go on strike at the Grunwick film-processing plant at Dollis Hill in North West London. One hundred and thirty-seven women, fed up with pay inequality, degrading racist practices, compulsory overtime and the anti-union principles of the management, refused to work unless the management changed its policies.[28] Here was a group of marginalised Asian women, many of them recent immigrants, refusing to conform to the negative stereotype of docile and subservient victims by taking on the stubborn owner of a firm who preferred Asian women workers to white women because he could pay them less and treat them worse.

The second surprise was that this diminutive Asian woman—Jayaben Desai was only 4 ft 11″—garnered support from the predominantly white male trade unions, many of whom burned with resentment that the Grunwick owner was exploiting newly arrived immigrants by undercutting wages. Jayaben Desai was one of the growing number of South Asian women who came to Britain to work in the factories, office and service sectors, some fleeing persecution, some expelled from Uganda and other newly independent African countries, all just trying to make a better life for themselves and their families. The Cricklewood Post Office workers, who serviced the area, sprang to the women's defence by refusing to deliver films to the processing plant. Other trade unions followed: miners, steel workers, factory hands, dockers and others of the big battalions gave support by helping to picket the factory and raise money for the strikers. The dispute was widely reported. On 11 July 1977, the unions called for a mass picket, and again women like me answered that call. Arthur Scargill and the mining unions, representatives from nearly every trade union, virtually all the left-wing political organisations, members of the Labour Party including Shirley Williams as well as women's liberation groups—around 20,000 people—all packed into the small streets around Grunwick. There were constant clashes between the police who had been brought in from around the country and those who picketed the factory. The Anglo-Indian owner of Grunwick tried to discredit Desai by painting her as a loose woman, but while he was unsuccessful, his relentless obstinacy was to prove unassailable.

The Labour government, in an attempt to end the strike, called in the Advisory and Arbitration Service (ACAS) and set up a government enquiry led by Lord Scarman. The Grunwick firm refused to implement the recommendations. The strike lasted for two years and ended with a hunger strike by Desai, desperate to keep the protest going. On 14 July 1978, the strike was called off. The strikers had lost. Even so, it was viewed as a unique and transformative moment for all, an 'iconic moment in the history of the labour movement: the moment when trade unions recognised the rights of women and minority workers as equal to those of white working class men'.[29] Some argued that 'the greater victory was arguably the message it sent about immigrant workers' place in society and their determination to stand up for their rights'.[30] Amrit Wilson notes that the strike proved that Asian women workers could be 'strong, resourceful and courageous, that they can stand up, face the world and demand their rights'.[31] In 2016, a BBC radio programme argued that the involvement of white working-class men in support of Asian women was a turning point in race relations.[32] Certainly the image of a burly white male trade unionist standing in solidarity with the diminutive Jayaben Desai was a powerful one. However, and more tragically for the trade union movement itself, the solidarity of the trade union movement in defending unjust working practices led to the banning of secondary picketing by Margaret Thatcher's government.

These strikes predated the industrial turbulence that in late 1978 and early 1979 spread across Britain during a particularly cold winter. It became known as the 'Winter of Discontent'.[33] A period of high inflation worldwide led to the value of wages dropping. As Tara Martin points out, 'female-dominated, service-sector unions, many of the largest in the nation at that time, also led strikes across Britain'.[34] Some of this was about equal pay, better working conditions and trade union recognition. Strikes led by women broke out in different parts of Great Britain and in a variety of industries: in Basingstoke, Birmingham, Dundee, Elland, Glasgow, Havant, Liverpool, Loughborough, Oxford, Paisley Stirmur, Rochdale, Rugby, Sheffield, Southall, South Shields, Wigan and Wolverhampton. Cleaners, clerical workers, laundry workers, textile workers, hosiery workers, office workers, shop assistants, football pool administrative staff, shellfish packers, teachers and even nurses went on strike. The National Union of Public Employees (NUPE) led many of them: in the North East of England, 90,000 hospital workers went on strike for better pay, resulting in six major hospitals in the area ceasing to function.[35]

Sexual Politics

Abortion: A Woman's Right to Choose vs the Sanctity of Life

In 1972, the Reading women's liberation group did a survey of women who had had abortions, or had been refused one, in order to compile a list of sympathetic GPs as a work of reference for other women.[36] They were all too aware that some doctors still objected to abortion, even though it was legal within certain constraints. Sheila Rowbotham wrote of one woman who asked her doctor to recommend an abortion only to be 'marched back into the reception room and in front of the patients the doctor said "So you want an abortion do you? Well just lie down and open your legs and I'll do it here and now"'.[37]

Two organisations, the Society for the Protection of the Unborn Child (SPUC) and Life both were fiercely against abortion and led campaigns to repeal the 1968 Act. For them, the sanctity of life overrode all other rights. The right to life was viewed as a fundamental human right, a right which attached itself to an embryo from the moment of conception, a right which should be protected and defended at all times.[38] Both groups fought hard to overturn the 1968 Abortion Act.

The SPUC argued that the right to life overrode a woman's right to choose. Indeed, the unborn child was seen to have the same rights as an infant or an adult basically because Roman Catholics, who now formed the majority of members, believed life began at conception. In 1971, around 8000 people took part in an anti-abortion march in Birmingham, the centre of the opposition to abortion. This was followed by demonstrations in Liverpool, Manchester and London. At the end of each march, every demonstrator placed a white paper daisy representing the death of an unborn baby in a large container. One SPUC member felt that 'abortion is being used as a means of contraception and this I find abominable. Abortion has given a greater freedom to some—a freedom to be sexually promiscuous'.[39]

The organisation Life, which was founded in 1970 as a breakaway group from SPUC, took a tougher stance than its progenitor and was opposed to all abortions, 'regardless of when it is done, how and by whom'.[40] Abortion was thought to be part of a decline in moral order, an indication of a 'rising tide of permissiveness' and 'contemporary sexual freedom ... the (sexual) revolution has ... gone hand in hand with the dehumanisation of sex ... the cult of nudity and the outpouring of pornography all make abortion less abhorrent'.[41] Life took a fundamentalist line and argued that all abortion should be banned because it took away potential human life. Its president, a male Roman Catholic, Lord Scarisbrick, stated that Life 'wants to see abortion repudiated as uncompromisingly as are, say racialism and robbery with violence'.[42] Emotions ran high, and with it emotionally charged language. Abortion, in Life's view, was little more than child murder, as the most basic human right, the right to life, was arbitrarily denied to the unborn. One woman insisted that 'if you are going to destroy foetuses it is not a long shot from saying that ... once a child is born with a particular deformity or defect we'll also destroy that'. Another argued that 'abortion will weaken respect for all human life and could lead to "mercy" killing, euthanasia and the killing of "sub-standard" members of humanity—a Nazi philosophy'.[43] They maintained that women who wanted an abortion were helped along by 'negligent and unscrupulous professionals; misguided counsellors and misinformed politicians; feckless and irresponsible women' within a dominant culture of too much sexual permissiveness.[44]

Both SPUC and Life shared a belief that the 1968 Abortion Act should be repealed to prevent further moral decay, to save the unborn child, to protect women from male pressure to have unprotected sex and to halt the profiteering of abortion clinics. Both groups tended to be dominated by active members of Christian religious groups, mainly Roman Catholics. One SPUC member, a married mother and college lecturer in her 30s argued that there was a 'general decline in moral standards, a diminution in the importance of family life, a lack of integrity of politicians and increasing selfishness and materialism amongst the community in general'.[45] It campaigned hard to repeal the act. Roman Catholic schools organised coaches to take their girl pupils to demonstrations to swell the numbers on anti-abortion marches.[46] Joan McKenna remembers her school, St Joseph's Catholic Comprehensive, Newcastle, organising a coach to Manchester to take part in an anti-abortion march: sex was never mentioned, and for most girls, it was a chance of a day out to a city they had never visited. Both SPUC and LIFE unashamedly drew on its Catholic captive audience. In 1970, 500 teenagers, led by two young Catholics who had founded the National Youth Right to Life Campaign, marched in protest against abortion and laid a wreath on Manchester's cenotaph which said 'in remembrance of 85,000 babies aborted in 1970, R.I.P'.[47] On 20 June 1971, coachloads—from Glasgow, Leeds, Manchester, Bristol and Devon—came to Birmingham to demonstrate against abortion. It attracted a gathering of approximately 8000 marchers: nuns, priests, parents and young people. The first speaker at the rally was Jean Lynch, an 18-year-old sixth former who had originated the anti-abortion campaign in Birmingham[48] (Fig. 9.3).

Anti-abortion groups had the *News of the World* on their side. In February 1974, two of its journalists—Michael Lichfield and Susan Kentish—wrote an

Fig. 9.3 Anti-abortion rally marching down Digbeth, Birmingham 20 June 1971, *Birmingham Post* (Courtesy of Mirror/Reach Licensing)

article 'Phantom Babies Sensation', which allegedly was the result of an investigation by them both. The two later co-authored *Babies for Burning*, an horrific—and false—account which alleged that doctors sold aborted babies alive for experiments or sold foetuses to be made into soap.[49] The book was widely condemned for its attempt to terrify people by its inaccurate, fabricated stories. It showed, insisted the pro-abortion Labour MP Maureen Colquohoun, 'the extent to which anti-abortionists will go' to achieve their goal.[50] In her opinion, anti-abortionists would flagrantly and unashamedly lie and lie about abortion practices to strengthen their case for preventing abortion at all cost. It was fake news.

Anti-abortion activists gathered sympathy from a number of parliamentarians. In the 1970s, three parliamentary Bills put forward by individual MPs to limit women's right to abortion gained a second reading. The first attempt took place in 1975 when a Labour MP James White introduced a Private Members Bill, which recommended that the time limit for abortion be reduced from 28 to 20 weeks, and that abortion should be made more difficult for women. His bill passed by 115 votes, was referred to a Select Committee and disappeared. Two years after White's bill was defeated, William Benyon, a Conservative MP and member of SPUC, brought in another Private Members' Bill. It obtained a second reading by a majority of 38 votes but was defeated because parliamentary time ran out, largely because MPs made a determined effort to fight the bill. The third attempt was in 1979 when the Conservative

MP John Corrie tried to reduce the upper time limit for abortion from 28 to 20 weeks and curtail the actions of private abortion clinics and counselling services.

The first attempt to restrict access to abortion led in March 1975 to the formation of the National Abortion Campaign (NAC). The NAC had its roots in the Women's Liberation Movement (WLM): the right to abortion was one of the first four demands of the WLM, a central and fundamental tenet of white feminists. The NAC stated categorically that abortion was a woman's right to choose—she alone had the right to control her own body and her own life. It adopted the policy of 'Free abortion on demand—a woman's right to choose'. This was in contrast to previous abortion campaigns which focused on health and social issues such as rape and incest, whether the foetus had birth defects and the dangers of illegal abortions. Indeed, feminists objected to the fact that in order to obtain an abortion each woman had to convince two doctors to support it. Moreover, abortions were usually only granted to women who met certain clinical, medical or social criteria such as a malformed foetus or an inability to look after a future child because of her psychological, social or material circumstances. The power to decide was in the hands of the medical profession; feminists argued that the decision should be the woman's in whom the foetus resided. It was a woman's right to decide what to do with her body, a principle of self-determination, a basic human right.

The NAC campaigned against each attempt to limit women's rights to abortion. Groups all around Britain organised local protests as well as participating in the big national demonstrations. On 21 June 1975, NAC held a mass demonstration in London which attracted over 20,000 women, the biggest women's demonstration since the suffragettes. This was followed in October by a conference to fight against the proposed restrictions on abortion and to campaign for 'free abortion on demand—a woman's right to choose'. The conference was attended by over 1000 women and developed a programme of actions focusing on the need for women to have control over their own fertility. Small groups of women made their own protests: six women carrying pro-abortion placards chained themselves in front of the altar at Westminster Roman Catholic Cathedral in protest against the Catholic churches campaign to restrict abortions.[51] All over Britain, women organised to protect their abortion rights: in Bristol, they set up stalls in shopping centres; in Cambridge and Chippenham, they wrote to every GP; in Liverpool, they persuaded their local Trades Council to support abortion which was 'quite an achievement as it's predominantly male and the area's so Catholic'; in London, the South London group wrote a 15-minute play which they performed on the streets; in Oxford, they lobbied their two MPs.[52]

For the campaign against the Benyon Bill, the Harrow NAC marched behind a car with a coffin on top which commemorated the women who died as a result of backstreet abortions.[53] On 14 May 1977, over 10,000 women marched in London behind a float carrying the all-women rock band *Jam Today*, and sang to the tune of Bill Bailey, 'Won't you drop dead, Bill Benyon, won't you drop dead. You know you've done us wrong', and held banners saying, '*No to the Knitting Needle*'.[54] Marchers carried placards saying *Not the Church, Not the State, Women must decide their fate*. For the march against the Corrie Bill, Jane Clarke remembers Jeremy Corbyn marching with his dog, who wore a placard saying, *Crap on Corrie*. Women carried banners which read *Keep Your Rosaries Off Our Ovaries* and *If men got pregnant Abortion would be a sacrament*.[55]

The NAC worked closely with sympathetic Labour figures like Joyce Gould, chief women's officer and MPs such as Oonagh McDonald, Renée Short, Audrey Wise and Jo Richardson—these acted as a conduit between the NAC, the Labour Party and Parliament. By the time of the Corrie Bill, women MPs had organised themselves into an effective group and collectively they mounted a counter-attack against the restrictive bills put forward respectively by White, Benyon and Corrie. They helped 'arrange the marches and compose the petitions and collect the signatures, to say nothing of the time taken up in committee.'[56] Not all MPs were supportive. Some were absent whenever abortion was debated. Others voted against. In each debate, nearly 600 men discussed the right of women to control their own bodies: on average, there were fewer than 30 female MPs. On the second reading of White's Bill, 12 women voted for and 4 against.[57] Labour MP Renée Short implored the House not to have 'more lurid propaganda about babies crying on the way to the incinerator, as was mentioned in that disgusting little book by two gutter journalists … the results have been checked and checked again and found to be absolutely false'.[58] During the second reading of Benyon's Bill, 15 women voted against and 7 voted for the bill.[59] Maureen Colquhon complained that 'we seem to be considering constantly anti-women measures, which preoccupy this male-dominated Chamber'.[60] It is time, she urged, 'that they accepted the fact that women, and only women have the right to decide what is to happen to their bodies'.[61] Once more, the bill was sent to a Committee. In July 1979, John Corrie put forward a Third Bill to restrict abortion.[62] Betty Boothroyd and Jo Richardson spoke against; five women voted for and five against the bill.[63] All the bills failed.

Abortion was the last resort of desperate women. One of the continuous calls of women across the century was the right to birth control. In the 1960s, 'the pill' was introduced and became a popular contraceptive device. In 1976, a new drug, an injectable birth control drug called Depo-Provera, which gave contraceptive protection for over three months, came on to the British market. Soon it faced criticism because of the increased risk of breast cancer and cancer of the cervix to those injected with the contraceptive treatment. It also had unpleasant non-life-threatening side effects like heavy menstrual bleeding, weight gain, dizziness, nausea, extreme tiredness, aches and pains, blood pressure changes and depression. One health visitor justified these side effects by saying, 'better a woman gets cancer in 30-years-time than gets pregnant now.'[64] Unlike other forms of contraception, it was administered by GPs at surgeries and Family Planning Clinics. More egregiously, it was disproportionately given to working-class, Black and Asian women, often without their consent, and allegedly often because of class and racial prejudices on the part of the medical profession.

In 1978, against this racist and eugenicist background, white activist Janet Hadley helped set up the Campaign against Depo-Provera (CDP), a movement sparked off by the contribution of a number of Black women at a socialist women's conference.[65] Stella Dadzie, a radical Black activist, became involved, and articles on Depo-Provera and the campaigns against its use appeared regularly in Black feminist magazines. Dadzie and the CDP aimed to force the withdrawal of Depo-Provera by exposing the way it was used on women without their consent.[66] They drew attention to the racist nature of the birth control movement and condemned the Family Planning Association as a 'consciously and conspiratorially racist operation with avowedly genocidal intentions'.[67] Its catchy slogan 'Ban the Jab', its distribution of leaflets in Asian languages warning of the dangers of Depo-Provera, its publication of a report outlining the side effects of the drug and its clever media strategy led to widespread condemnation. In 1979, a Panorama documentary focused on the negative aspects of the drug; a Labour MP raised the issue in the House of Commons, and in 1982 the new secretary of state for health, Ken Clarke, revoked Depo-Provera's licence. However, pressure by the powerful drugs company proved too strong and Depo-Provera was eventually relicensed as a suitable contraceptive drug.

In its newsletter *Speak Out*, black activists reported that another newer contraceptive injection—Noresthisterone—was being used at two London hospitals. This had various uncomfortable side effects such as 'headaches, dizziness, putting on a lot of weight ... scant and irregular periods or no periods at all'. It was felt that the women who were given the drug were being 'experimented on' just as the women who had been given the Depo-Provera contraceptive were treated as guinea pigs.[68]

Domestic Violence

In the summer of 1971, 500 women, a cow and a Co-op milk float marched down Chiswick High Road. They were protesting against the School Milk Act put forward by the secretary of state for education and science, Margaret Thatcher, which stopped free school milk being given to pupils.[69] The demonstration had been organised by the Chiswick Women's Liberation group. This group later formed what was to become Women's Aid, a charity working to end domestic violence which took forward one of the WLM's demands. At the time, battered women were the subject of mirth rather than concern: most seaside resorts had their Punch and Judy shows, and comedians joked about women being beaten by their male partners. It was thought to be a working-class problem, 'a plague of the ghetto', not to be found in genteel middle- or upper-class circles. Moreover, women were seen to provoke the beatings by 'nagging' their husbands and even to enjoy—like Judy—being punched around. It took a long time to stop the jokes, but women's liberationists organised to provide protection for women who were abused by their partners.

The Chiswick group set up the first refuge in a derelict house they had bought with money borrowed from Erin Pizzey's husband and the 'generosity of groups like the Mothers' Union, Ladies Circles and the National Council of Women'.[70] Erin Pizzey became the public voice of Women's Aid, interviewed by newspapers, the radio and television. Documentaries were made about her work. Her book *Scream Quietly or the Neighbours Will Hear* documented the experiences of battered women. In her book, she told stories of how women were hit with brooms, kicked around, beaten, punched and sometimes strangled. One 'policeman's wife appeared at the door with six broken ribs, burns on her thighs from boiling water, and bruises all over her face'.[71] It was hard for these women, especially those with children, to escape. There was nowhere for them to go. The Women's Aid Refuges were 'one of the most notable and innovative forms of voluntary action', action that had strong links with the Women's Liberation Movement, in terms of both its ideas and the people involved.[72] Refuges were run by the women collectively, all taking responsibility for its management.

The Chiswick campaign helped start an international movement. In 1975, the first women's refuge in Northern Ireland was opened in Belfast by Women's Aid, offering women and children a safe and protective home away from domestic abuse. It was set up by a group of social workers, police, the NSPCC and feminists. At first, it was run on authoritarian lines—with more men than women on the committee—until a group of feminists took control and changed the culture. It was a distinctly feminist approach, the 'mental, physical and sexual abuse of women by their partners is about male power and male control. … Battered women experience male power and male violence in its most overt form'.[73] Their aim was to help women take control of their own lives, build up self-respect and encourage self-determination in women whose experiences had been shaped by their powerlessness.

By the end of the 1970s, Women's Aid sponsored shelters all over Britain. In 1976, Scottish Women's Aid was established to provide a national voice and co-ordinating body for regional groups like the one in Clackmannanshire which had set up a refuge and operated a 24-hour telephone helpline.[74] Groups of feminists—like me—from across the political and social spectrum often squatted in unoccupied houses to use them as safe spaces for women at risk: squatting was much easier in the 1970s—all you had to do was break in, change the locks, pay the rates at the local council office and make sure that someone stayed in the squat until it was secured. These were desolate, desperate places for desolate, desperate women. In Chiswick, any woman who needed refuge was accepted. The result was overcrowding: the home was legally suitable for 36 people but 110 women and children lived there at one time. Rather than offer alternative accommodation, the local authority prosecuted Pizzey for allowing too many women and children to stay there.

On 1 June 1976, as a result of the actions of feminists and sympathetic politicians, the Domestic Violence and Matrimonial Proceedings Act came into law, which gave women better legal protection against the violence of their husbands or cohabiting partners. Even so, men could legally rape their wives. In 1989, Scotland made marital rape illegal, and after a Rape in Marriage Campaign orchestrated by Women's Aid, Rape Crisis Centres and Women Against Violence Against Women, the rest of the United Kingdom followed five years later.[75]

'We Will Walk Without Fear': Women Against Violence Against Women

Every woman I know has experienced some form of unwelcome attention from men: wolf whistles, sexist remarks, being followed by strangers, having bottoms or breasts squeezed in crowded places, being sexually harassed and seeing unknown men expose themselves. Some women have been raped. Some women have been murdered. Most women fear being in an isolated place. Night-time brings out the worst behaviour. Some men believe 'respectable' women should not be on the streets after dark and that women were 'fair game' if they dared to be there. One of the most frightening cities was Leeds—in three and a half years, a serial killer known as the Yorkshire Ripper murdered 11 women, 7 of whom lived in the city. He was later arrested, tried and imprisoned.

All across the United Kingdom, groups of women decided to take action to establish their right to walk freely in the streets at night. In 1977, a group of Edinburgh women held the first Reclaim the Night March. It was Halloween. Dressed as witches, women 'swarmed across' a park notorious for sexual assault.[76] Women tried to make the 'night safe by their togetherness' and show that women had the right to be on the streets. About 60 women marched through Coventry protesting about the number of sexual assaults and attacks on women; in Liverpool, 300 women marched into the city centre following a route past pubs, clubs and cinemas protesting against street violence and kerb crawling and using cymbals, tambourines and rattles to announce their arrival.[77] The Plymouth Women's Liberation group marched through areas where sailors congregated and where drunken violence was common, reacting to abusive comments by chanting even louder and drowning out the voices of men.[78] One hundred and thirty women met in Leeds City Square, 'torch lit figures shouting in the windy darkness, and suddenly we're in a big circle holding hands. ... City Square is wild, a spontaneous women's take-over'.[79] In Liverpool, police tried to stop the women's march, allegedly because they were concerned about the safety of the women, thus unwittingly endorsing the fact that women were unsafe on the streets.

In London, hundreds of women 'wailing and dancing' marched through the streets of Soho, 'humming, buzzing, shouting. A real woman's march, a rampage. Surging, droning, chanting. "Women Fight Rape." "Yes means yes,

No means No, However we Dress, wherever we go."'[80] On Halloween, 31 October 1978, women, wearing fancy dress and masks, again tried to 'Reclaim the Night' along the Soho streets of strip clubs and porn shops. This time, the police responded brutally. Women were dragged to the ground, kicked, held by the throat, pulled by the hair, had their arms twisted behind their backs and were thrust to the ground—simply for challenging the pornography capital of Britain. Sixteen women were arrested, illegally fingerprinted, refused permission to call their solicitors, slapped across the face and locked into cells until 4 am.[81] The first six to be prosecuted were defended by the feminist barrister Marguerite Russell and were acquitted by the magistrate, who accused one policeman of having 'deliberately lied'. The rest of the women asked for their cases to be dropped and called for an enquiry into police behaviour on the night, an enquiry supported by Labour MP Jo Richardson.[82]

However, Reclaim the Night marches caused some concern in Black communities, especially when women marched through mixed-race areas. As Thomlinson points out, 'the prospect of white women marching through Black areas calling for an end to male violence raised the uncomfortable spectre of the myth of the Black rapist whose primary victims were white women.'[83] Equally, calling for increased police presence in areas with a significant Black population, a group with a history of being harassed and beaten up was seen as racist, and at best insensitive. Many Black women felt angry and offended by these marches, and an opportunity of Black and white women to unite against male violence was missed.

At the same time, the WLM made rape a public issue. Rape Crisis Centres were founded to help women who had been raped and to campaign for a change in the law. In 1976, the Sexual Offences (Amendment) Act guaranteed anonymity for victims alleging rape. However, like domestic violence, the rape of women did not cease, and it proved exceedingly difficult to gain a conviction.

Moreover, there was a backlash against the freedoms advocated by WLM and others, particularly sexual freedom. Mary Whitehouse, who continued to be one of the leading figures of the National Viewers' and Listeners' Association (NVLA), continued to campaign against the commercialisation of sex and violence, and what she thought of as sexual libertarianism. In 1976, she successfully prosecuted *Gay News* for blasphemous libel and regularly clashed with the editor of OZ, an underground counterculture magazine. She was bombarded with hate mail and threatening letters and was humiliated on some broadcasting programmes, but the silent majority were listening. In 1973, she presented a petition signed by 1.35 million to Prime Minister Edward Heath protesting against the decline in public decency. It is a grotesque irony that in 1974 her organisation, the NVLA, gave an award to Jimmy Savile for his 'wholesome family entertainment'.

Local Activism

Much of women's local activism remains absent from the historical record. So many women across Britain wanted to improve their neighbourhood. Housewives in a small Cheshire village blocked a road with their prams in protest at heavy goods vehicles driving through their streets[84]; a group of mothers waved banners asking for better nursery provision stood outside the Gloucestershire County Council offices before handing in a petition signed by 1000 women.[85] One of the most moving and inspiring stories is that of *The Dolly Mixtures*, 'a group of ordinary women who did extraordinary things'.[86] These were eight women who performed in the North East working men's clubs in order to raise money for a hospital dartboard and pool table: Margaret Graham (now Fleck), Hilda Joyce, Sylvia Nichols, Doris Ashcroft, Betty Dickinson, Jean Smith, Liz Errington and Joan Lumsdale. It started off 'in a very small way' and with a 'bit of sadness'.[87] In 1972, Margaret Graham's husband Ken was in hospital enduring chemotherapy for bowel cancer. He, and the other men in the ward, were bored. Margaret and Ken's sister Hilda decided to raise a bit of money to buy a dart board or a pool table to alleviate the mind-numbing and dispiriting tedium of hospital life and to raise the spirits of the men. To do so, they formed an all-woman entertainment group which performed at first to all-women audiences, but when they developed a bit more confidence, they took their act to working-men's clubs and extended their campaign to raise money for cancer research. By this time, 34-year-old Ken had died, and Margaret wanted to help raise money for this important research.

The women entered a man's world: apart from strippers, women were not allowed into male clubs. *The Dolly Mixtures* were unique. As Betty says, 'we were the only female group on the circuit and we were viewed with suspicion when we walked in.'[88] The eight women sang, danced and told jokes. They dressed in chicken costumes, in gingham dresses with pigtail wigs, in Carmen Miranda outfits with fruits on their heads (see Fig. 9.4), all made by the women. For a saucy song about pheasant pluckers, they wore smocks and put straw in their hair.

It was challenging performing in all-male clubs: during the interval, they had to leave the clubroom because women were not allowed to be there unless they were on stage; they often had to change costumes in the corridor, a cupboard or a very smelly dressing room, a difficult task for eight women all trying to get ready at the same time. Once, when Margaret's sister dared to enter the bar, a burly man put her over his shoulder and carried her out. Sexual innuendos, lewdness and harassment was common with shouts of 'get 'em off' when they performed. Men accosted them saying, 'you're bloody lovely you, can I have a snog?' or 'Do you want a quickie?' They frequently had their bottoms pinched or slapped. It was a rough way to earn money, with clubs often seeming like a 'war zone', especially when it was a stag night and fights broke out. *The Dolly Mixtures* responded with laughter rather than argue or challenge: their goal of raising as much money as possible was their priority. It was a close

Fig. 9.4 *The Dolly Mixtures* in their Carmen Miranda costumes (Courtesy of Margaret Fleck)

group, the women all 'bonded together' and supported each other against bad male behaviour. Only once in 14 years did the group walk out: at a business men's club in Newcastle when the men constantly called out, 'get em off'. The women decided that 'they had had enough' and left in the interval. As Margaret points out, 'they were supposed to be gentlemen.'[89] It was 'the way of the world then, men felt able to treat you like that'.

In 1988, *The Dolly Mixtures* stopped performing largely because the working men's clubs were closing—there were 12 working men's clubs in South Shields of which only one was left in the twenty-first century. During this time, the group raised more than £100,000, a considerable amount of money at the time. Half-way through their fundraising, the Cancer Research team wrote to them saying that the continuous flow of money raised by *The Dolly Mixtures* had helped them make a breakthrough in the treatment for colon cancer.[90] In 1984, the women's group refocused their campaign to collect money for the miners and their families during the strike. Tom Kelly and John Miles wrote a musical, *The Dolly Mixtures*, about their lives which was first performed at the Customs House, South Shields, in 2016, and has had several revivals[91] (Fig. 9.5).

Some local activists had wider agendas. Three women chained themselves to railings outside the Canadian High Commission in protest against the annual seal hunt in Canada.[92] In 1973, about 60 women protested at the Coliseum theatre, where the Georgian State Dance Company was performing. At the

Fig. 9.5 Five surviving members of *The Dolly Mixtures*—Hilda Joyce, Sylvia Nichols, Doris Ashcroft, Margaret Fleck and Betty Dickenson with Tom Kelly (sitting R) (Courtesy of Leah Strug)

time, a Leningrad court had found nine Jewish men guilty of 'organised anti-soviet activity' and sentenced them to prison camp for between one and ten years. The accused were charged with maintaining illegal ties with the Israeli government and sending it 'information containing vicious slander about the position of Jews in the Soviet Union'.[93] As the orchestra started to play, one protester stood up and blew on a hunting horn, symbolising the 4 am whistle used to wake prisoners in the labour camps; others opened umbrellas displaying slogans; yet others jumped on to the stage to interrupt the dancers.[94]

There were also protests against the violence of the British state. On 3 July 1970, the British government imposed a curfew on the Falls Road, a Catholic area in Belfast. Two days later, over a thousand women, some pushing prams, some with young children clutching their hands, and all carrying bread, bottles of milk and shopping bags full with food marched into the Falls Road. Some had come straight from church and were wearing their Sunday best. They had heard rumours that because of the curfew families were unable to buy food and were going hungry. Troops at the barricades watched in astonishment as the women came towards them chanting, singing and sometimes yelling. The army looked the other way and let the women through. One of the leaders of the march, 61-year-old Dolly Monaghan said, 'They couldn't mow us down, could they? And they couldn't trap us all in jail. There wouldn't be the room.' She told reporters that the women had told their menfolk to stay away because they feared the police force would be more likely to attack them, than attack women. The men obeyed.⁹⁵

It got worse. In January 1972, 13 civil rights demonstrators were shot on the streets of Derry/Londonderry: Bloody Sunday. This, the curfew and the violence of the army led to a further rise of support for the Irish Republican Army (IRA) and further resistance by the Catholic population. On 10 August 1976, three children were killed by a car careering down the road after the driver had been shot dead by British soldiers. Two women, one the aunt of the murdered children, Máiread Maguire, and the other, Betty Williams, who had arrived at the scene shortly after, founded the Peace People to combat the ever-increasing violence in the community. It drew a huge following—more than 100,000 signed their declaration, peace protests followed and the death rate from sectarian violence declined by 70%. In 1976, the two women were awarded the Nobel Peace Prize. Nevertheless, violence and internment continued. In 1978, Women Against Imperialism was founded to combat the violence of the British state and to fight for women's equality. It arranged pickets outside Armagh prison, gave talks at Republican venues on domestic violence, campaigned for better living conditions and encouraged the IRA to stop the practice of tying women to a lamppost and tarring and feathering them because they had fraternised with British soldiers.⁹⁶

Campaigning for Disability Rights⁹⁷

In 1970, Susan Masham, aged 34, became the youngest Life Peer when Harold Wilson added her name to his New Years Honours List for her work for 'social services and her work for the handicapped'.⁹⁸ She was now a member of the House of Lords, a baroness in her own right, sitting as a crossbench member. She was three times a minority: a woman in a male House; a young woman in an institution full of ageing peers; and a wheelchair user in a House of largely able-bodied colleagues. In 1958, Susan had been left disabled by a riding accident, married her aristocratic fiancée a year later and became Lady Masham, then Countess of Swinton. In 1960, she went to Rome to take part in Olympics, where she won a gold and four silver medals.

She made her maiden speech at the same time as three other peers with mobility difficulties. The three had decided to make their speech on the Chronic, Sick and Disabled Persons Act. As a consequence, 'we brought all sort of things in to make life easier for disabled people such as housing, such as telephones. …we had quite a lot of first-hand experience that we could give for that legislation'.⁹⁹ Lord Longford, who sponsored the Bill in the Lords, insisted that they were determined that the 'disabled shall not feel second-class citizens in their own country'.¹⁰⁰

There was a lot to reform. Two years later, Marsham spoke of the continued humiliations suffered by less able individuals: those needing assistance had to pay £10 fee for transport to disembark from any aeroplane. She told the story of a 60-year-old woman with multiple sclerosis who had 'been deeply shocked and horrified when she was forced to bump her way down the aircraft steps on her behind'.[101] In some cases, a 'rattly old van with no proper heating' was used to take people to and from the aircraft. Catching a train was no easier as wheelchair users were put in the guards van: there were no places at all in the passenger sections for those in wheelchairs. Gradually, and with a lot of pressure from outside Parliament, reforms helped to ease the difficulties faced by those in need of physical assistance.

In 1974, Baroness Masham founded the Spinal Injuries Association (SIA) because of her concern about the 'lack of specialist medical care available to all newly injured people, and the dearth of information and advice available ... once discharged from hospital'. She had come across several paraplegics and tetraplegics whose treatment in various hospitals had led to 'disastrous results'[102] and realised that people who had suffered spinal cord injury needed a specialist organisation. In 1976, she was the subject of *This is Your Life*, a very popular programme hosted by Eamonn Andrews, for her work in championing disability causes. In the same year, the SIA published *So You're Paralysed?*, a book which told the stories of people living with a spinal injury, drew attention to the association and its aims, and to the fact that spinal injury needed a special type of treatment.

Lady Masham was not the first activist to campaign for disability rights. In 1964, the Disablement Income Group (DIG) was founded by two English women, Megan Du Boisson and Berit Thornberry, followed a year later by Dr Margaret Blackwood, who founded DIG, Scotland. In 1976, a group of women founded GEMMA to help disabled lesbian and bisexual women. It organised lots of social activities: picnics, swimming sessions, and wheelchair friendly discos, all of which helped end the isolation felt by many disabled women. Susan Masham was newsworthy: an aristocratic, physically attractive woman who knew a number of influential individuals but together, she and these organisations confirmed the fact that some individuals needed specialised help to make their lives as good as possible.

Conclusion

At the start of the 1970s, women were barred from going into Wimpy bars on their own after midnight. Feminists challenged this and the discrimination ended. Moreover, the campaigns of WLM, a change in public mood and the election of sympathetic governments led to a number of legal reforms that benefitted women. In 1971, judges could no longer assess a widow's damages based on a judgement as to whether she might remarry; in 1972, unmarried mothers were given the same rights as married ones to pursue maintenance orders; in 1973, the Guardianship of Infants Act gave mothers equal rights regarding decisions about the children. In March 1974, the Labour government returned to power with Harold Wilson as prime minister once more. Sue Bruley argues that the commitment of women Labour MPs and the support of a sympathetic prime minister were key factors behind the raft of legislation which was passed in the 1970s.[103] For example, Barbara Castle, who was appointed secretary of state for social services, her fourth post as cabinet minister, put forward her Child Benefit Act, which reformed the way in which child benefit was awarding the allowance directly to mothers rather than as a tax break to fathers. In the same year, the Employment Protection Act gave women the rights to six weeks maternity pay and maternity leave up to 29 weeks. In addition, the Sex Discrimination Act (1975) made it illegal for women to be discriminated against in housing, employment, education, training and the provision of goods and services. Before the act, married women were not allowed to buy goods on credit. When the Sex Discrimination Bill was discussed in the House of Lords, Lord Monson told the Peers that British Rail would have to advertise for 'signal persons'; the Post Office for 'post persons'; councils for 'dust persons'; and pubs for 'buxom bar persons'.[104]

Women—as individuals or in groups—had led a number of initiatives such as setting up women's refuges to help vulnerable women escape male violence. However, women did not always agree as evidenced in the abortion campaigns and over the issue of sexual freedoms; neither were women as united against patriarchy as some hoped, particularly when Black feminists challenged the basis of many white campaigns.

In 1975, Margaret Thatcher was elected leader of the Conservative Party, the first woman to lead a major political party. Just before the 1979 General Election, the feminist journal *Spare Rib* discussed whether or not a victory for Margaret Thatcher would be a victory for women. The authors felt that 'as feminists the issue is not the success or failure of one individual woman, but whether the actual polices of Thatcher, and of the party she represents, can promote the interest of women generally'.[105] They concluded that Thatcher's commitment to shrinking the state would be detrimental to most women. On 4 May 1979, Margaret Thatcher became the first female prime minister of Britain and set about transforming the country.

Notes

1. *Evening Express*, 9 September 1972, p. 5.
2. *The Wicklow People*, 25 January 1974, p. 6.
3. *The Journal*, 26 April 1976, p. 3.
4. *Coventry Evening Telegraph*, 17 January 1972, p. 9.
5. Advert from *Coventry Evening Telegraph*, 16 April 1971, p. 23.
6. *Daily Mirror*, 27 April 1971, p. 3.
7. Ibid., 27 November 1972, p. 11.
8. Unknown newspaper quoted in Carol Adams, Laurikietis, *Messages and Images*, Virago, 1976, p. 30.
9. See Beverley Bryan, Stella Dadzie and Suzanne Scafe, *Heart of the Race*, republished Verso, 2018, p. 149.
10. *Spare Rib*, October 1979.
11. Natalie Thomlinson, *Race, Ethnicity and the Women's Movement in England, 1968–1993*, Palgrave Macmillan, 2016, p. 65.
12. *Speak Out*, No 4, circa 1980, p. 4.
13. Ibid.

14. Beverley Bryan, Stella Dadzie and Suzanne Scafe, *Heart of the Race*, republished Verso, 2018, p. 149.
15. *Spare Rib*, November 1975.
16. Ibid., October 1979.
17. Ibid.
18. Ibid., June 1979.
19. Ibid., July 1979.
20. Alex Lyon had been vociferous in his support of Asians who were fleeing from repressive regimes. In April 1976, he was sacked by Jim Callaghan when he became prime minister.
21. *Harrow Observer*, 30 January 1976, p. 12.
22. *The Birmingham Post*, 14 July 1978, p. 3.
23. *Reading Evening Post*, 16 October 1972, p. 3.
24. *Race Today*, July 1974 in Paul Field (ed) *Here to Stay, here to Fight*, Pluto, 2019, p. 125.
25. Ibid.
26. Ibid.
27. Amrit Wilson, *Finding a Voice*, Virago, 1978, p. 58.
28. See *Stand Together!*, a film on the 'mass day of solidarity' on 11 July 1977, made by Grunwick Strike Committee, available online University of Warwick.
29. *Striking Women: Voices of South Asian women workers* from Grunwick and Gate Gourmet, exhibition in Women's Library, 2009–2010.
30. BBC news, *Grunwick dispute: what did the 'strikers in saris; achieve?* 10 September 2016
31. Amrit Wilson, *Finding a Voice*, Virago, 1978.
32. *Grunwick Changed Me*, BBC, 17 August 2016.
33. See Tara Martin, 'The Beginning of Labor's End? Britain's "Winter of Discontent" and Working-class Women's Activism, *International Labor and Working-Class History*, No 75, Spring, 2009.
34. Ibid., p. 52.
35. Ibid.
36. *Evening Post*, 23 June 1972, p. 9.
37. Sheila Rowbotham, *The Past is Before Us, Feminism in Action since the 1960s*, Penguin 1989, p. 69.
38. Alan Henry Clarke, *The Abortion Campaign: A Study of Moral Reform and Status Protest*, PhD, University of Nottingham, 1984.
39. Ibid., p. 178.
40. Ibid., p. 243.
41. A pamphlet from LIFE quoted in Alan Henry Clarke, *The Abortion Campaign: A Study of Moral Reform and Status Protest*, PhD, University of Nottingham, 1984, p. 66.
42. Scarisbrick quoted in Alan Henry Clarke, *The Abortion Campaign: A Study of Moral Reform and Status Protest*, PhD, University of Nottingham, 1984, p. 77.
43. Alan Henry Clarke, *The Abortion Campaign: A Study of Moral Reform and Status Protest*, PhD, University of Nottingham, 1984, p. 185.
44. Ibid., p. 86.
45. Ibid., p. 175.
46. Thanks to Joan McKenna for this information.
47. *Daily Mirror*, 29 December 1970, p. 7.

48. *Birmingham Post*, 21 June 1971, p. 1.
49. David Marsh and Joanna Chambers, *Abortion Politics*, Junction Books, 1981.
50. *The Press and Journal*, 31 March 1975, p. 2.
51. Daily Mirror, 20 October 1975, p. 2.
52. *Spare Rib*, July 1975, p. 27.
53. *Observer and Gazette*, 25 February 1977, p. 8.
54. *Spare Rib*, July 1977.
55. Thanks to Jane Clarke for this information.
56. Patricia Vallance, *Women in the House*, Athlone Press, 1979, p. 88.
57. Only three women (Renée Short, Helene Hayman and Lena Jeger) spoke against White's Bill.
58. Renee Short, Maureen Colquhon and Jo Richardson spoke against and Elaine Kellett-Bowman and Jill Knight spoke in favour of the bill. The MPs who voted against were Joyce Butler, Maureen Colquhoun, Renée Short, Gwyneth Dunwoody, Helene Hayman, Margaret Jackson (later Beckett), Lena Jeger, Shirley Summerskill, Ann Taylor, Joan Lestor, Millie Miller and Jo Richardson. Margaret Bain, Harvie Anderson, Carol Mather, Lynda Chalker voted in favour (HC Debate, 7 February 1975, vol 885, cc1757–868). A number of women MPs like Labour's Judith Hart, Betty Boothroyd and Conservative's Janet Fookes and Sally Oppenheim-Baines were absent from the count.
59. Betty Boothroyd, Joyce Butler, Barbara Castle, Maureen Colquhoun, Gwyneth Dunwoody, Helene Hayman, Margaret Jackson, Lena Jeger, Oonagh McDonald, Millie Miller, Jo Richardson, Renee Short, Ann Taylor, and Audrey Wise voted against; Margaret Bain, Jill Knight, Carol Mather, Sally Oppenheim, Janet Fookes, Harvie Anderson, Elaine Kellett-Bowman voted for. Again, some women were absent, often for political reasons. (HC Debates 25 February 1977, vol 926 cc1783–895).
60. HC Debates 25 February 1977, vol 926 cc1783–895.
61. Ibid.
62. HC Debates 13 July 1979, vol 970 cc 891–983.
63. Jill Knight, Carol Mather, Sally Oppenheim, Janet Fookes, Margaret Thatcher voted for; Betty Boothroyd, Joan Lestor, Jo Richardson, Ann Taylor, Sheila Wright voted against.
64. *Spare Rib*, April 1978, p. 28.
65. See Caitlin Lambert, '"The Objectionable injectable": recovering the lost history of the WLM through the Campaign against Depo-Provera', *Women's History Review*, 2020, Vol 29, No 3, pp. 520–539, for an examination of white women's contribution to the campaigns against this drug.
66. Keith Joseph, quoted in Caitlin Lambert, '"The Objectionable injectable": recovering the lost history of the WLM through the Campaign against Depo-Provera', *Women's History Review*, 2020, Vol 29, No 3, p. 524.
67. Janet Hadley quoted in Caitlin Lambert, '"The Objectionable injectable": recovering the lost history of the WLM through the Campaign against Depo-Provera', *Women's History Review*, 2020, Vol 29, No 3, p. 532.
68. *Speak Out* Issue No 1, circa 1979.
69. *Spare Rib*, June 1972, p. 8.
70. Erin Pizzey, quoted in *The Liverpool Echo*, 2 November 1974, p. 5.
71. *New York Times*, 29 November 1975, p. 17.

72. Jan Pahl, 'Refuges for Battered Women: Ideology and Action', *Feminist Review*, Spring 1985, p. 25.
73. Karen McMinn, 'Women's Aid: Feminism at the Grass Roots', *Fortnight*, 27 May–9 June 1985, p. 13.
74. See Scottish Women's Aid at womensaid.scot. The group have recorded oral history interviews and have made a documentary film called *Speaking Out, Recalling women's aid in Scotland*, which charts the experiences of eight women who were involved in Women's Aid.
75. See Adrian Williamson, 'The Law and Politics of Marital Rape in England, 1945–1994, *Women's History Review*, Vol 26 No 3, 2017.
76. *Spare Rib*, January 1979, p. 9.
77. *Liverpool Echo*, 30 March 1979, p. 18.
78. *Spare Rib*, May 1978.
79. Ibid., January 1978.
80. Ibid., January 1978.
81. Ibid., January 1979.
82. Ibid., June 1979.
83. Natalie Thomlinson, *Race, Ethnicity and the Women's Movement in England, 1968–1993*, Palgrave Macmillan, 2016, p. 169.
84. *The Liverpool Echo*, 20 July 1978, p. 3.
85. *The Birmingham Post*, 9 November 1978, p. 3.
86. Ray Spencer, the director of the Customs House, Youtube.
87. Interview with Margaret Fleck, 21 September 2020.
88. *Sunderland Echo*, 20 June 2019.
89. Interview with Margaret Fleck, 21 September 2020.
90. Ibid., 21 September 2020.
91. The *Dolly Mixtures Musical*, August 2019. https://www.bing.com/videos/search?
92. *Belfast Telegraph*, 29 March 1978, p. 9.
93. *New York Times*, 21 May 1971, p. 1.
94. *Observer and Gazette*, 8 June 1973, p. 6.
95. *Daily Mail*, 6 July 1970, p. 2.
96. Theresa O'Keefe, '"Mother Ireland, Get Off Our Backs": Republican Feminist Resistance in the North of Ireland', in Lorenzo Bosi et al, *The Troubles in Northern Ireland and Theories of Social Movements*, Amsterdam University Press, 2017.
97. See Jameel Hampton, *Disability and the Welfare State in Britain, Change in Perception and Policy, 1948–1979*, Policy Press, 2016.
98. *Belfast Telegraph*, 1 January 1970, p. 8.
99. Interview by Jon Newman with Baroness Masham, August 30th 2012, accessed internet 23 July 2020.
100. *The Birmingham Post*, 10 April 1970, p. 1.
101. Ibid., 4 February 1972, p. 2.
102. Spinal Injuries Association website, accessed 24 July 2020. You can donate directly to the organisation from their website.
103. Sue Bruley, *Women in Britain Since 1900*, p. 158.
104. *Daily Mail*, 2 July 1975, p. 3.
105. *Spare Rib*, May 1979, pp. 3–4.

CHAPTER 10

Margaret Thatcher's Age and After: 1979–2000

On 4 May 1979, Margaret Thatcher became the first female prime minister of Britain. She loathed feminism, believing it to be 'poison'. In 1982, Thatcher pronounced that 'the battle for women's rights has largely been won. ... I hate those strident tones we hear from some Women's Libbers'.[1] She presented herself as a housewife and mother who happened to be a politician and, as G. E. Maguire points out, used her femininity as part of a carefully cultivated image, an image which she strategically mixed up with a ferocious cold-bloodedness. Francois Mitterrand commented that she had 'eyes like Stalin and the mouth of Marilyn Monroe'.[2] Her nicknames Attila the Hen and the Iron Lady reflect the ambivalence of her personality. She did not, as Beatrix Campbell argues, feminise politics but 'offered feminine endorsement to patriarchal power and principles'.[3] As prime minister, she did not promote women's issues, appointed only one woman to her cabinet and did not encourage women to stand for Parliament. Under her watch, feminism came under attack. Even so, Thatcher became a role model and icon for many women like the Spice Girls, whose mantra of Girl Power swept them to the top of the pops. Mary Stott, the *Guardian*'s feminist women's editor, believed that Thatcher 'represented a fundamental and unalterable shift in the gender dynamics of the nation ... things (couldn't) be quite the same again, because a basic brick (had) been removed from the edifice of beliefs and prejudices about the role of women'.[4] Both her admirers and detractors agree that the 1980s and most of the 1990s were framed by the first woman prime minister and her government.[5]

Sexual Politics: Victoria Gillick, Mary Whitehouse and Feminists

Right-wing women gained courage from the election of a woman committed to upholding family values, a mythologised version of Victorian ideals and reverence for the former British Empire. In 1980, a new moral crusade was triggered by Victoria Gillick. This Roman Catholic mother of ten was outraged by a Department of Health and Social Services' (DHSS) circular, which allowed doctors to prescribe contraceptive pills to girls under 16 without the permission of their parents. Victoria Gillick argued that doctors would be complicit in a criminal act because it was illegal for someone to have sex with a girl under the age of 16. Moreover, it would be treatment without consent, since the teenager was underage and came under the authority of her parents.

Victoria Gillick presented herself as an ordinary wife and mother but she was a political activist, a former member of a racist anti-immigration group which maintained that 'it is so wrong to tell us, who have lived in these isles for thousands of years, that we must not have any more of the children we want, because Parliament is allowing more immigrants in … these immigrants must be repatriated'.[6]

Mrs Gillick launched a one-woman crusade against the state. She took the matter to court and lost; she appealed against the decision to the Court of Appeal and won when the court ruled that girls under 16 should not be given contraception without parental consent; the House of Lords reversed this by stating that if a young girl was deemed to be competent to consent to her own medical treatment, then she did not need parental permission.

Her campaign, according to Beatrix Campbell 'touched the raw nerves of the permissive era and the hard edge of patriarchal sex'.[7] Moreover, Gillick drew support from a number of Black organisations such as the Afro-Caribbean Standing Committee, the Union of Muslim Organisations, the West Indian Standing Conference and the Confederation of Indian Organisations, members of whom were ignorant of Gillick's fascist sympathies but who shared some of her conservative values.[8] In the twenty-first century, what became known as 'The Gillick Competence' was to have unforeseen consequences for young people.

Meanwhile, Mary Whitehouse and her National Viewers' and Listeners' Association (NVLA) continued to push for a clean-up of television, film and video.[9] Whitehouse was condemned by the liberal establishment and often called a fascist; supporters of *Gay News* held posters of her alongside Adolf Hitler and chanted 'Whitehouse—Kill, Kill, Kill' on their demonstrations. She received death threats.[10] The BBC controller had a distorted image of Whitehouse with five breasts hanging on his walls and apparently used to throw darts at it.[11] Whitehouse presented herself as the voice of the 'silent majority'. In fact, the NVLA was mainly a woman's organisation, consisting largely of housewives who rejected the permissive culture and were sympathetic to the moralistic views of Mary Whitehouse. It was a foretaste of Brexit: here was a populist who spoke plainly and simply to people's prejudices, 'a champion of the under-represented, and anti-intellectual everyman'.[12]

Margaret Thatcher's moral compass, her particular brand of Christianity and her traditional values, as Jessica Prestidge points out, fitted well with Whitehouse's view of the world. Both women 'reflected a tradition of "militant" domesticity associated with the … British Housewives League'.[13]

Undoubtedly, Whitehouse was delighted by Thatcher's premiership and wrote to her that 'it was a wonderful thing to have a Prime Minister utter those marvellous words of St Francis'.[14] Thatcher responded by hoping that the two would 'continue to communicate with one another over those issues about which we both feel so strongly'.[15] Indeed, Thatcher presented an award at the NVLA ceremony where she praised Whitehouse by saying, 'Let no-one ever again say "what can one person do?" Look at Mrs Whitehouse and see the answer.'[16] In 1980, Thatcher awarded her a CBE. Even so, Thatcher generally kept her at a political distance.[17]

In the 1960s and 1970s, Mary Whitehouse's warnings about sexual debasement seemed old-fashioned, out of tune with the liberated time. She was repeatedly denounced as a repressive, repressed figure. However, in the 1980s, Mary Whitehouse's opinions began to be reassessed. A decade earlier, her critique of Linda Lovelace's performance in *Deep Throat* and Lovelace's autobiography *Inside Linda Lovelace*—a book which was acquitted in an obscenity trial—was ridiculed. However, her views were later seen as prescient when it emerged that Lovelace was coerced into performing sexual acts, kept as a slave and forced to 'perform' at gunpoint. Moreover, Whitehouse began to gain support from unexpected quarters when feminists voiced concern about pornography. In 1980, Women Against Violence Against Women was formed. This group picketed sex shops and lobbied local authorities to refuse to give them licenses. At the same time, a group called Angry Women 'carried out nineteen arson attacks on Leeds sex shops, with results ranging from causing minimal damage to shops being completely gutted.'[18] In 1987, Labour MP Clare Short founded the Campaign against Pornography (CAP), sparked off by her Ten Minute Rule Bill to take pornographic images out of newspapers like the photographs of topless models in page 3 of the *Sun*. Largely because of Clare Short, the group secured funding, established a high public profile, organised conferences and a campaigning network to take 'soft' pornography off the shelves of newsagents—the 'Off the Shelf' campaign.[19] In 1989, Catherine Itzin founded the Campaign Against Pornography and Censorship, a smaller and less influential group with a radical feminist agenda.

Both Short and Itzin wanted to refocus anti-pornography campaigns through a feminist narrative by arguing that it objectified and degraded women and contributed to sex discrimination, sexual inequality, sexual violence and sexism. In contrast, Mary Whitehouse argued that pornography was simply immoral because of its depiction of sex outside marriage. The two organisations campaigned separately. Even so, CAP accepted support from well-known right-wingers such as Jill Knight, a Birmingham MP who opposed abortion and supported the restriction of gay and homosexual rights. Clare Short defended this by stating, 'I know all about her terrible attitudes on everything. But this is a hegemonic project and … we will make alliances with people that we don't always agree with because … we want to win.'[20] Here, feminist and conservative activism shared a common purpose, even though their reasoning was dissimilar. Their alliance was, in the words of Nancy Whittier, a 'collaborative adversarial relationship' as each group 'explicitly opposed each others' larger social movements, ideologies and agendas' but were willing to co-operate on single issues.[21] For instance, although both were opposed to pornography, they took different approaches to abortion and gay rights: CAP in favour; Mary Whitehouse firmly opposed.

Another area in which both Mary Whitehouse and feminists agreed was over child sexual abuse. Mary Whitehouse's NVLA set up Action to Ban Sexual Exploitation of Children (ABUSE), bombarding MPs and newspapers with letters and organising a petition against child abuse. This petition was signed by one and a half million people and had led to the Protection of Children Act 1978, which criminalised child pornography. Whitehouse's attack on 'kiddie porn' took place at a time when paedophilia was viewed by a small vocal minority as a valid sexual practice—the National Council for Civil Liberties allowed the Paedophile Information Exchange to become affiliated to it. Academics joined in: Cecil Greek and William Thompson criticised Whitehouse's campaigns to restrict erotic visual materials, and their article makes for chillingly uncomfortable reading today, particularly when they seem to defend child sexual abuse.[22] At first, Mary Whitehouse's campaigns drew support from religious conservatives and those of a right-wing persuasion but in the 1980s her views on pornography and child sexual abuse were endorsed by feminists, though once again from a completely different perspective. In 1984, Margaret Thatcher's government, guided and persuaded by Whitehouse's NVLA, passed the Video Recordings Act, which made it illegal to sell or rent 'adult videos' to children and banned all those not approved by the censors. In 1986, Esther Rantzen set up ChildLine to help children report abuse and to support them when they did.

Feminists believe in women's equality but they differ over its interpretation. One of the most acrimonious disagreements in this period took place in the London Lesbian and Gay Centre. This had been set up in 1985 with funding of three quarters of a million pounds from Ken Livingstone's Greater London Council (GLC), which was committed to financing unrepresented, oppressed and vulnerable groups. The centre provided 'office space, meeting rooms and a bar for lesbian and gay community groups',[23] and a safe place with electronic locks, panic buttons and other monitoring devices in place to protect the women from unwanted visitors. Almost immediately, the centre was embroiled in an argument over whether S&M (sado-masochist) lesbians should be allowed to use the centre, particularly when some wore Nazi uniforms and insignia. On the one hand, those in favour of this, and of allowing women to walk around the centre being pulled by a chain around their neck, cited the need for sexual freedom and the right of women to self-identify as SM. On the other hand, lesbian feminists argued that SM 'simply reproduced all the elements of heterosexual sex ... dominance, submission and violence' and had no place in a lesbian feminist world which sought to give same-sex relationships a political meaning.[24] After a series of angry and aggressive meetings, the SM section of the lesbian community won the right to use the centre. In 1986, Margaret

Thatcher abolished the GLC and the future of the centre was endangered: it closed five years later.

Black women's organisations, like their white counterparts, were also divided over sexual policy. At its annual conference in 1981, Black lesbianism was rejected by the Organisation of Women of African and Asian Descent (OWAAD), leading to Black lesbians forming their own organisations. Julia Sudbury notes that Black lesbian groups were formed in most cities with a Black population, only to disappear when the government directed its malevolent gaze over gay and lesbian organisations.[25] Local authorities refused to allow Black lesbians to use their premises and libraries banned any literature which a advertised any gay organisation. One exception was London's Camden Council. On 31 October 1987, largely because of funding and support from the Council, the Camden Lesbian Centre and Black Lesbian Group opened its centre in Phoenix Road. It housed a number of groups such as the Lesbian Disability Group, GEMMA and Zamimass, a Black socialist lesbian organisation. In 1985, Zami—a French-creole word that came to mean lesbian—had held its first conference, attracting over 200 women from across the United Kingdom. Zami members were keen to 'distance themselves from white feminists' preoccupations with the concerns of middle-class women' and focused primarily on what they termed 'racialised class exploitation' (Fig. 10.1).[26]

Meanwhile, the Conservative government threatened gay and lesbian rights. In 1988, it passed a Local Government Act (Section 28), which stated that local authorities should not 'a) intentionally promote homosexuality or publish material with the intention of promoting homosexuality and b) forbade the teaching in any maintained school of the acceptability of homosexuality as a pretended family relationship'. In 1987, at the Conservative Party conference, Margaret Thatcher had told her audience that 'children need to be taught to respect traditional moral values', not that 'they have an inalienable right to be gay'. In one sweep of an unjust law, countless numbers of gay and lesbian young people had their sense of self undermined and their mental health compromised. There were protests: three lesbians 'brought turmoil' to the House of Lords when they threw ropes over the public gallery and abseiled down into the Chamber during a debate on the proposed Act;[27] five lesbians, some wearing Edwardian costumes, chained themselves to the gates in front of Buckingham Palace; others burst into the BBC during a live broadcast of the Six O'Clock News and chained themselves to the newsreaders' chairs. Nicholas Witchell, who was co-presenting the news with Sue Lawley, sat on one of the demonstrators and tried to silence her by putting his hand over her mouth.[28] Sympathetic MPs gave the women support. Mark Fisher, Labour MP for Stoke on Trent Central, was the first to sign a petition urging the Council 'to support non-compliance with Section 28' and urged Parliament to repeal the act. He opened a gay and lesbian exhibition which was hosted by Peter Cheeseman, director of the New Vic Theatre in Stoke.[29]

During the 1980s and 1990s, Adam Lent argues, activists joined or worked with the Labour Party in increasing numbers. Local authorities, especially the

Fig. 10.1 Advert for Centre (Courtesy of Women's Library, Glasgow)

large Greater London Council, set up Women's Committees. These employed a 'sizeable proportion of core activists'[30] who were previously voluntary, unpaid campaigners. Unfortunately, Thatcherite ideologists, whipped up by the tabloid press, accused those who advocated equality measures as being part of the 'loony left'. In the first half of the 1980s, local left-wing councils provided funding to a variety of women's groups: in London, 400 or so women's groups—300 of them were Black organisations—were awarded grants by the Greater London Council Women's Committee set up by the Labour-controlled Greater London Council (GLC) run by Ken Livingstone. Valerie Wise, the daughter of Labour MP, feminist and equal rights activist Audrey Wise, was chair of the Women's Committee. In an interview, Valerie Wise stated: 'You name it, we funded it. We funded everything in London. I mean, we just—it was—it was absolutely fantastic because we had this money.'[31] In the growing hostile political environment of the 1980s, where councils were accused of being part of the 'loony left', these grants diminished and disappeared. Activists soon found that their well-paid jobs as equal opportunities, anti-racist, lesbian and gay rights officers vanished too. Adam Lent argues, 'In a head-on crash with the combined weight of a Conservative government at the peak of its popularity and a ruthless, reactionary tabloid press, they stood little chance of survival.'[32] Moreover, because of the generous funding, a number of activist groups had become professionalised and were not staffed by unpaid activists.[33] When funding dried up, these organisations no longer enjoyed a volunteer base, and many were forced to close.

For the most part, feminists were on the defensive, trying to stave off a continuous attack by a Conservative government headed by an unsympathetic woman. Public spending cuts, increasing unemployment and demonisation by the media put feminism on the defensive. Moreover, in the 1980s the white—and largely middle-class—Women's Liberation Movement, which had prided itself on the shared nature of women's experience, broke into fractious and occasionally peevish splinters. The spirit of supportive sisterhood disappeared. For the majority of women in the country, some of the newer feminisms seemed somewhat absurd, exclusive and completely outside their lived experience.[34] At the beginning, feminists seemed united against inequalities, oppression and patriarchal capitalism. As the 1980s progressed, white feminism split into socialist feminism, radical feminism, revolutionary feminism, all arguing with each other about whether patriarchy or men were to blame, and which was the purest form of progressive politics. In many ways, feminism was saved by Black women who reconfigured politics by putting forward a new theoretical framework—that of intersectionality.

BLACK LIVES MATTER

Sometimes women were forced into activism by tragic events. On 2 March 1981, more than 20,000 Afro-Caribbean demonstrators marched across London, protesting against the lack of justice for the teenage victims of a house fire. Many carried placards saying, *Thirteen dead and nothing said* and *No Police Cover-up*. Six weeks previously, 13 Black youngsters aged between 14 and 22[35] had died in a fire at Yvonne Ruddock's 16th and Angela Jackson's 18th joint birthday party at 439 New Cross Road, South London. The parents, grandparents, relatives and friends of the young people who died suspected a racially motivated arson attack. There was a heightened awareness of racism—the area was a stronghold of the National Front, a fascist group, which was implicated in an earlier arson attack on a Black club in the area and several intimidatory attacks. The police, media and the government ignored the violence and the fire. Relations between the police and the local Black community were strained before the fire, and the death of so many teenagers acted as a catalyst for the local community to confront the daily instances of prejudice and racial aggravation. It was, as Leila Hassan Howe points out, 'a response to the urgent need to take a stand and transform a Britain in which, for years, the black community had felt under attack'.[36]

Leila Hassan Howe, one of the organisers, later stated that the aim of the marchers was to 'cause maximum disruption' by walking through the capital city.[37] It was called the National Black People's Day of Action. Police changed their assessment of the fire, said they suspected arson and launched a murder enquiry after survivors told them that they had seen a white Austin Princess car drive off soon after the fire started. No one was ever charged, and later the police retracted their suspicion and declared it to be an accidental fire, a view confirmed by two inquests. The grieving families never received a satisfactory answer: the exact cause of the fire was never established. The legacy of the fire, the grief of the friends and relatives, the demonstration and the lack of empathy by white authorities helped 'create a black British voice with a politicised identity'.[38] Certainly, it was a defining moment in the life of Black Britons, a time when the structural racism endemic in the United Kingdom was challenged by a group which found its voice through personal tragedy.

A month later, a wave of riots took place across cities in Britain, mostly led by young Black people who were angry at persistent harassment by the police who constantly used the 'SUS' laws to stop and search young Black men. In addition, unemployment had greatly increased as Mrs Thatcher's economic reforms rolled out. The New Cross Fire and the later riots arguably signalled a turning point in the movement towards race equality and racial justice. Certainly, it symbolised 'public indifference to the plight and problems' of Black British people.[39] And the racist violence continued, and with it police reluctance to prosecute. On the night of the anniversary of the New Cross Fire, Maurice and Jannette Marius woke up at 2 am to find the front room of their house full of poisonous smoke with a bottle full of petrol on the floor. If the petrol bomb had gone off, the family of 11 would have died. The police insisted that they were 'not treating it as a racial incident'.[40]

In April 1993, one of the most egregious racist attacks took place in South East London. Britain was shocked by the racist murder of Stephen Lawrence, a Black teenager from Plumstead who was waiting at a bus stop in Eltham when he was attacked by a gang of white youths and stabbed to death. Five young white men were arrested but not charged. Stephen's parents, Doreen and Neville Lawrence, refused to let the murder of their son go unchallenged. The Lawrences were to wait several years before they saw a modicum of justice for their son. They accused the Metropolitan Police of incompetence, unprofessional conduct and racism and brought a private prosecution against the suspects. Indeed, the police's reaction was 'not to catch the five youths whose names were being handed to them by dozens of sources, but to ask the Lawrences what a black youth was doing at a bus stop … From that moment they had to live with the awful truth that their son … was treated as a criminal by a racist police force for merely being black'.[41]

In April 1996, three of the men were brought to trial, only to be acquitted by a jury. A year later, an inquest into Stephen's death returned a verdict of murder 'in a completely unprovoked racist attack by five white youths'. In an unprecedented and surprising front page, the usually high-Tory *Daily Mail* ran a headline which said, **MURDERERS. The Mail accuses these men of killing. If we are wrong, let them sue us**. It also posted photos of the five murderers.[42] Legally, it was contempt of court of a cosmic order, and the *Mail*'s editor Paul Dacre was liable to be tried and imprisoned. Newspapers had no authority to be judge and jury. They did so, because 'after a criminal case, a private prosecution and an inquest, there has still been no justice for Stephen'.[43] The headline generated the publicity needed for politicians to take note: the Conservative Prime Minister John Major publicly backed justice for the Lawrence family, as did Nicholas Lyell, the Attorney General. Eventually, after years of campaigning, media support and the election of a Labour government, the Home Secretary set up a judicial enquiry chaired by Sir William MacPherson. Its summary offered some solace to the family when it concluded that the Met was 'institutionally racist' and that this racism was a primary reason why they had failed to solve the case. In 2012, two of the murderers were finally convicted. Doreen Lawrence continued to campaign for justice not just for her son, but for other victims of racist crime. In 2003, she was awarded an OBE, in 2013 she became Baroness Lawrence of Clarendon.

Meanwhile, Leila Hassan Howe along with her husband Darcus Howe and Ambalavaner Sivanandan took over the Institute of Race Relations and its paper, *Race Today*. Under their aegis, both the organisation and the journal took a radical turn becoming 'a beacon of the black radical thought and practice'.[44] Black feminist organisations flourished. A number of activist groups— Akina Mama Wa Afrika, Black Lesbian Group; Black Women for Wages for Housework, Black Women's Resource Centre, Cambridge Black Women's Support Group, Liverpool Black Sisters, Muslim Women's Helpline, Onyx, Osaba Women's Centre, Panahghar, Shakti Women's Aid and Wai Yin Chinese Women's Society—were founded in the 1980s, inspired by the creation of the Organisation of Women of African and Asian Descent (OWAAD) in the late 1970s.[45]

Some focused on improving the opportunities for Black women. In 1985, Dr Wanjiru Kihoro, an economist and feminist in exile from Kenya, founded Akina Mama Wa Afrika (AMwA), Swahili for 'African Sisterhood', the first to focus on African women, many of whom were refugees fleeing from oppressive regimes. At first, AMwA's volunteers worked in an office in Covent Garden, but in 1997 it transferred its headquarters to Kampala, Uganda. It was both a 'transnational and pan-African … unapologetically feminist' organisation, with a commitment to improving the position of African women.[46]

The Southall Black Sisters

The Southall Black Sisters (SBS), which was affiliated to OWAAD, was active on a number of fronts, helping individual women, lobbying politicians, pressurising the media and campaigning. They published articles and spoke in public, particularly where it concerned violence against women.[47] In 1982, they set up the first Black women's service. The group found their time taken up by case work—they dealt with approximately 1000 enquiries a year—simply because of the number of women facing racial harassment and domestic violence. The SBS 'broke the silence' on domestic violence within the Black and

Asian communities, particularly their protest against the murder of Mrs Dhillon and her three daughters: Mr Dhillon had set them all on fire because he did not have a son.[48] The SBS organised pickets outside the houses of other violent men like Chandra Mohan Sharma, whose wife hanged herself because of his continuing violence.[49]

One of their notable successes was their campaign to release Kiranjit Ahluwalia from prison. In December 1989, Mrs Ahluwalia, a 35-year-old devout Sikh from Crawley, was convicted and sentenced to life imprisonment for the murder of her brutally violent husband. She had doused him in petrol and set fire to him while he slept.[50] During her ten-year marriage, her husband Deepak 'beat her, tried to strangle her, threatened her with knives, pushed her downstairs, tried to run her over in a car and raped her'.[51] He also ripped out handfuls of her hair, cut her with knives, broke her fingers, drenched her with boiling tea and tried to break her legs and burn her face with a hot iron. Unlike men who killed their wives, pleaded provocation and received a much-reduced sentence, Mrs Ahluwalia was found guilty of murder, not manslaughter, because her crime was premeditated. She appealed, helped by women's groups like the Southall Black Sisters. On 25 September 1992, three judges at the Court of Appeal, Old Bailey, accepted her plea of guilty of manslaughter, imposed a sentence of three years and four months—the exact time she had spent in prison. She was free. The trial 'was a turning point for battered women who kill their tormentors' by recognising that women suffered from 'battered wives' syndrome'.[52] A legal precedent had been set. In March 1993, Diana, Princess of Wales, visited the Chiswick Women's Refuge where Mrs Ahluwalia lived, told her she was 'very brave and a symbol for other women suffering from domestic violence' and urged her to write a book about her experiences.[53] In 1992, Jack Ashley introduced a Homicide Bill that would force courts to take a history of domestic violence into account when judging those who had murdered an abusive partner. It was passed unopposed, a result, commented SBS' Pragna Patel because of 'overwhelming public pressure to reform the law'.[54]

Another case taken up by SBS was that of Zoora Shah, who in 1993 was sentenced for 20 years in prison. She had arrived in Britain in the 1970s from rural Pakistan through an arranged marriage. She was illiterate and could not speak English, making her especially vulnerable. During the marriage, her husband was violent and abusive, and when she was pregnant with her fourth child, he abandoned her. She became homeless, destitute and isolated—there were no women's refuges where she lived in Bradford, and her community gave her no support. As with other helpless and defenceless women, she was befriended by a criminal, in her case a disreputable character called Mohammad Azam, a married drug dealer who groomed her, sexually abused her and forced her into prostitution. In her own words, she was 'used as a mattress by all the men in her community'. When Azam threatened to abuse her daughters, Zoora poisoned him with arsenic, and he died. In 1993, she was given a 20-year sentence. It took a concerted campaign by the SBS to have her sentence commuted to 12 years.⁵⁵ And as with other fights against sexual abuse, the SBS had to fight against the cultural relativism of white Britain and the criticism of some in the Asian community for bringing 'shame' and 'dishonour' to the group. Zoora was released in 2006.

Despite the efforts of the SBS and other women's groups, the murder of women continued. In 1995, 42% of women who were killed were killed by a male partner—statistics showed that only 26.6% of men were convicted of murder; many received short sentences, or sometimes just a community order.

Domestic violence, the SBS insisted, had no boundaries, cutting across class, race, religion and nationality. Nonetheless, they were among the first to recognise that though women from different classes and different races had a 'commonality of experience', it was crucial to recognise that women were not an homogenous group, and not all women's needs were the same.⁵⁶ Refuges for Black women were opened across the United Kingdom: on International Women's Day 1991, Amadudu (a Nigerian word for women of colour) opened in Toxteth, Liverpool, for Black women and white women with Black children 'to escape the misery suffered at the hands of brutal boyfriends and husbands'.⁵⁷ It was the first Black refuge in Liverpool, able to house six families with a dormitory for emergencies. It had a garden, a children's playroom and bright cheerful rooms—the organisers were keen to maintain a family atmosphere, rather than an institutional one. Amadu provided moral support and practical help with housing, legal and cash problems.

A number of Asian men and sections of the left were hostile to raising the issue of violence against women in their community. The SBS were 'accused of being home wreckers and of destroying families' as well as being labelled 'as a Westernised force, something alien to Asian culture' by right-wing Asian men who were threatened by their challenge to male authority. Male white leftwingers accused the SBS of fuelling racism.⁵⁸ Asian community leaders in Southall petitioned the local authority to cut off funding to their refuge, a threat averted only by a vigorous campaigning to keep it open. In Birmingham, Asian men unsuccessfully demonstrated against Asian women's refuges: in 1989, the first Muslim refuge opened in a converted mosque run by a broadbased committee from different women's groups.

Throughout the 1980s, the SBS focused its energies in trying to make the state legislate to protect women and not hide behind a principle of 'cultural sensitivity' whereby police, law and local authorities declined to intervene in the domestic abuse of women in Black and Asian areas. In 1999, SBS joined a working group on forced marriages set up by the Home Office. The Home Office minister, Mike O'Brian, wanted the state to recognise that gender-based violence and forced marriage was an abuse of women's human rights. This, as SBS stated, 'was a historical and potentially liberating announcement for South Asian women' who had been subjected to abuse.⁵⁹

Meanwhile, women activists in the Catholic Church were raising the issue of sexual harassment by priests. In 1995, Sister Maura O'Donaghue, medical doctor and AIDS co-ordinator for the Catholic Fund for Overseas Development, went to Rome to brief the Cardinal responsible for those in religious life, on the alleged sexual abuse of nuns in 'Botswana, Burundi, Columbia, Ghana, India, Ireland, Italy, Kenya, Lesotho, Malawi, Nigeria, Papua New Guinea, the Philippines, South Africa, Sierra Leone, Tanzania, Tonga, Uganda, the United States, Zambia, Zaire and Zimbabwe'. It was, she argued, a cruelty based on the 'economic and sexual powerlessness of women'.[60] The Catholic Church was not alone. This type of harassment, activists began to realise, was prevalent across class, religions and regions.

Black vs White Feminism

Black feminists challenged the predominantly white and middle-class WLM. A number of Black feminists felt that white women paid 'lip service to Black issues without truly incorporating their concerns into their own feminist programme'.[61] White British women were accused of ignoring the ways in which 'racism profoundly structured' the lives of Black British women and of making little effort in understanding Black women's needs. For instance, white feminist opposition to marriage ignored the fact that immigration laws prevented Black women from marrying their choice.[62] In 1985, a Black feminist newsletter accused the WLM of racism because it ignored the experience of non-white women. They argued that the white feminist claim of universal sisterhood was a racist sham because white women represented their own cultural experiences as common to all women, when they patently were not.

In *Feminist Review*, a journal edited and largely read by white women, Black female activists were offered the chance to edit a 1984 issue of the journal. In an excoriating review, Valerie Amos and Pratibha Parma maintained that 'white, mainstream feminist theory … does not speak to the experiences of Black women and where it attempts to do so it is often from a racist perspective and reasoning.'[63] Mostly, they argued, Black women remained invisible within a feminist and Eurocentric discourse, often hidden under an umbrella of patriarchy or a parasol of capitalism. Moreover, they argued, white women gained their own modicum of equality at the expense of Black women. Ignored, patronised and/or undermined by white feminists who failed to acknowledge their lived experience, Black women queried the very basis of feminism. Racial justice, they insisted, must be added to both feminism and socialism not only to bring in women across the social, economic and racial spectrum but also to make sense of the totality of women's oppression. In so doing, Black women established a new theoretical principle, that of intersectionality, an analytical framework whereby interlocking sections of power (e.g. gender, class, sex, race, sexuality, religion and disability) intersect to either oppress or privilege.[64] White feminists could thus no longer presume that their experience of sexism was universal and found that their theoretical models were inadequate. A new way of looking at the world, this time through the eyes of Black women, was to emerge. It was a holistic, rather than a sectional approach to inequality and oppression, and in so doing stimulated new versions of feminisms.

Gradually, and often pressurised by Black women activists and theoreticians, there was a paradigm shift as white feminists began to reject 'essentialism', to acknowledge the specificity of 'white feminism' and to admit the existence of white privilege. As Sudbury points out, 'black women's experiences of racism are always gendered and therefore differ from those of black men. Similarly, our experiences of sexism are always racialised and therefore differ from those of white women.' Black feminists called for an awareness of 'gendered racism and racialised sexism'.[65] They argued that 'anybody who proposes gender identity politics or race identity politics as sufficient' is mistaken because 'every single one of us is more than whatever race we represent ... and more than whatever gender category we fall into'.[66] It came to be called intersectionality. Nonetheless, building sisterhood between Black women was an uphill task, as, like white women, the Black community was divided by class, education, sexuality and so on.[67]

Even so, as Tomlinson points out, during the 1980s there were 'heightened levels of interaction between Black and white feminists' even though that interaction 'resulted in both animosity and progress'.[68] In 1982, the feminist journal *Spare Rib*'s editorial committee consisted of an equal number of women of colour and white women. Gradually, Black and white feminists worked together. One successful collaboration began in 1989 when the Southall Black Sisters founded Women Against Fundamentalism (WAF) to fight the threat posed to women by the rise of rigid and conservative interpretations of religious texts. It began as a protest against the supreme leader of Iran Ayatolla Khomeini's *fatwa* authorising the murder of Salman Rushdie because of the alleged blasphemy in his book *The Satanic Verses*. Khomeini declared that defenders of the *fatwa* would be revered as 'martyrs', which in effect was an incitement to murder. Muslim fundamentalists tried to get the book banned, staged demonstrations and book burnings. Salman Rushdie, fearful of his life, was forced into hiding.

On 8 March, the Southall Black Sisters and the Southall Labour Party Women's Section co-organised an International Women's Day event at which over 200 women attended. The topic was, 'The Resurgence of Religion: What Price do Women Pay?'. It was here that the SBS issued a defence of Salman Rushdie as well as the right to free speech, the right to dissent and doubt and the right not to have their lives controlled by the leaders of their respective communities. The Southall Black Sisters recognised this as part of a global resurgence of repression and wanted to counter 'both the religious fundamentalisms and the racisms' that surrounded the debate.[69] The British male left was silent, fearful of inflaming racism against Muslims.

On 27 May 1989, Muslims and their supporters marched from Hyde Park to Downing Street to protest against Rushdie and his novel. More than 20,000 demonstrators, some holding effigies of Rushdie hanging from the gallows, marched across London. Violence erupted as demonstrators clashed with the police and the National Front. The SBS staged a counterprotest against the march. One 65-year-old woman, Barbara Smoker, president of the Secular

Society was surrounded by demonstrators who chanted 'Kill, kill, kill' when they spotted her banner calling for free speech.[70]

The Women Against Freedom (WAF) encompassed a range of individuals and groups from a variety of ethnic and religious backgrounds. It was a broad political alliance which revealed the links between the fundamentalists in Muslim mosques, Jewish synagogues, Hindu temples, Sikh gurdwaras and Christian churches. All fundamentalists, whatever their religion, had one thing in common—they used God as an excuse to control women. The WAF focused on three key areas of fundamentalism which particularly affected women: education, women's refuges and the anti-abortion campaign.[71] They opposed faith-based schools, campaigned for women's refuges and clearly saw that the campaigns against abortion—like that of SPUC—were based on Christian fundamentalism. Over the years, it organised seminars and public meetings, produced a journal and created a website. Moreover, WAF became the exemplar for 'transversal politics', that is politics that focus on shared political values rather than politics which assumed a common identity like that of woman, or Black, or lesbian.[72]

Peace and War: Greenham Common Women's Peace Camp 1981–1990

On 27 August 1981, a group of 36 women, 4 men and 3 children walked 120 miles from Cardiff to the RAF Greenham Common base in protest against the decision to store 96 American cruise missiles there. They were from the newly created *Women for Life on Earth: Women's Action for Disarmament*. When they arrived on 5 September, they delivered a letter to the commander of the base and asked to meet him. When the letter and their request for a meeting was ignored by the camp commander, four of the women chained themselves to the perimeter fence. They decided to be as determined as the suffragettes before them, and indeed later mirrored some of their other tactics such as defacing property, getting arrested and being imprisoned.[73] A peace camp was set up outside the fence which grew into nine different camps, named initially after the colours of the rainbow, at various gates around the base: Yellow Gate, Blue Gate, Turquoise Gate, Indigo Gate, Violet Gate, Red Gate, Orange Gate, Emerald Gate and Green Gate. There was also one called Pedestrian Gate. Stopping the cruise missiles became a way of life. Men had once left home for war; now women left home for peace.

At first, a few men were involved, but in 1982 the Greenham women decided to make the camp women-only. It became, as Margaret Laware argues, 'a feminist space of public action and self-discovery for women who sought to challenge the course of nuclear strategy and military policy and wider systems of patriarchal control'.[74] Militarism was equated with men, and men were equated with violence against women more generally. Slogans such as 'Take the toys from the boys', 'Arms are for linking' and 'War is Menstruation Envy' summed up such attitudes.⁷⁵ As Suzanne Moore points out, the women peace activists 'weaponised traditional notions of femininity' by using 'their identity as carers and mothers to say, this is about the future safety of our children'.⁷⁶

Greenham women, like the suffragettes before them, used unconventional and imaginative methods of protest, which subverted conventional ideas of femininity. On New Year's Eve 1982, 44 women mounted ladders to break into the base, clambered on top of the silos and danced in a circle on top of them. On the anniversary of the Nagasaki nuclear bombing, a group of women broke into the base and presented Japanese lanterns to the soldiers. On 1 April 1983, 200 women dressed up as teddy bears covered themselves with sticky honey and entered the camp for a picnic—a teddy bear's picnic, acting out the classic children's rhyme. Suzanne Moore notes the brilliant absurdity of 'heavily armed soldiers against teddy bears'.⁷⁷

The camp grew organically as more and more women pitched their tents, built bivouacs of plastic sheeting draped around trees and bushes, or placed their caravans on the common. Living conditions were harsh, especially in winter. There was no electricity, fresh running water or basic sanitation. Moreover, the Greenham women were not made welcome by local people: pubs refused to serve them; vigilante groups attacked them; police officers arrested them and released them in the middle of the night several miles outside the Greenham base; the local authorities repeatedly evicted them. Some people were distinctly unpleasant, attacking the women with maggots and pig shit, slashing their tents with knives.⁷⁸ On one occasion, the women were 'woken by vigilantes urinating on their tents and masturbating in front of them'.⁷⁹ Women were constantly harassed, arrested for obstruction, put on trial and convicted. On 5 August 1989, a 22-year-old Welsh activist, Helen Wynne Thomas, died from head injuries after being hit by a West Midlands police horsebox while crossing a busy road outside the military base. An inquest returned a verdict of accidental death. Over the years, numerous attempts were made to evict the women and bust up the camp. Each time the Greenham Common women returned.

There were several pleas for help and support. In December 1982, I went with a group of women friends to '*Embrace The Base*', responding to a call by the Greenham Women to come and join our hands together and encircle the camp. We travelled in a rented minibus and were made very welcome when we stopped off for a coffee and a loo break at a house near the airbase. The house belonged to Helen Leigh's parents whose father worked at the Atomic Weapons Research Establishment as a nuclear scientist. Both Helen's mother and father were warm and friendly to this rather scruffy bunch of young women, all dressed in the warmest clothes we possessed. Helen's father, who had been part of the team at the first nuclear test on Christmas Island, was later awarded an MBE for his work in negotiating the US test ban treaty.⁸⁰ Our band of women joined 30,000 others who had come for the day to link arms and pin photos of family, of friends, flowers and love tokens. As *Spare Rib* reported 'Webs of wool, a woman's diary, doves, recipes, women's and peace symbols made from ferns … an empty Bacardi bottle, thousands of balloons … an inexplicable postcard of the Royal Family and hundreds of tampons dipped in red'.[81] One woman pinned an entire tea set to the fence. The decoration of a masculine military base with feminine emblems and the symbols of domestic life emphasised the silliness as well as the violence of war. And then we embraced the army camp. The enfolding of the nine-mile fence by women's hands was a powerful image, challenging the brute force of male power by a circle of female love. One woman commented that 'for nine miles we formed a living chain to lock in the horrors of war, to stand between them and our world and to say: we will meet your violence with a loving embrace' (Figs. 10.2 and 10.3).[82]

In November 1983, the first of the Cruise missiles arrived at the base. On Sunday 11 December 1983, around 50,000 women came to the base and were encouraged to hold up mirrors to reflect the evil of the base onto itself. At 2 pm, 'women created a wall of sound with voices and musical instruments'.[83] The sound of women keening was startling. This time large numbers of women took wire cutters and cut the fence; others pulled the fence down leading to hundreds of arrests and hundreds more being injured by police. Later that night, two women who were found inside the base were wrapped in barbed wire, beaten up, tied to the concrete fence posts where soldiers masturbated in

Fig. 10.2 Decorating the fence at Greenham Common (Courtesy of author)

Fig. 10.3 Embracing the Base at Greenham Common (Courtesy of author)

front of them.[84] Despite police and legal efforts to contain them, the women had undermined the idea that a military base was secure—'a military base easily penetrated by a group of non-violent women was no longer a military base.'[85] Such actions touched a military nerve, making the military seem vulnerable.

In December 1987, the US president, Ronald Reagan, and the Soviet leader, Michael Gorbachev, signed the Intermediate-Range Nuclear Forces Treaty in which both countries agreed to scrap many of its missiles, including the 96 at Greenham. In 2000, the camp was closed; in 2002, the camp became a commemorative and historic site.

The Greenham women were part of an international movement for peace: camps were set up in America, Australia, Italy and elsewhere. Support came from all over the world. Yoko Ono visited and donated enough money to enable the Greenham women to buy some land next to the base where they could keep their caravans. A group of Australian women brought quick drying cement and blocked all the army camp's sewage outlets.

The Greenham Common protest has become a powerful image of female action. However, as pointed out by black feminists, it was largely a white and middle-class movement—the photograph which I took above illustrates this. Amos and Parmar accuse peace activists of focusing on the Cruise missile base alone and 'not exposing, campaigning or mobilising against Britain's role in illegal mining for uranium in Namibia for fuel for its Trident submarines'.[86] Only when the women at Greenham cared less about the national and more about the international dimensions of the armament trade, they argued, would it attract Black women. Greenham Common remained predominantly white.

Civil War in Ireland

Meanwhile, civil war raged in the United Kingdom. On 12 October 1984, the IRA tried to assassinate Margaret Thatcher by planting a bomb at the Grand Hotel in Brighton where she was staying. It caused a massive explosion, leaving a gaping hole in the façade of the building, killing 5 people and injuring 31 more. It was one of several attempts by the IRA to force the government to change policy by bombing civilian targets in Britain in an effort to end the oppression of nationalists in the North and unite the island of Ireland. Republican feminists supported these strategies, believing that the British occupation of the North was the 'main source of women's oppression as it shapes all political, economic and social structures'. One member of the Provisional IRA, Mairéad Farrell, insisted that she was doubly oppressed, one for being a woman, one for being Irish.[87] She was imprisoned for 14 years for trying to plant a bomb in a Belfast hotel used by British soldiers. In prison, she and other women joined the 'dirty protest' taking place in male prisons as part of a demand for political status, smearing excrement and menstrual blood on their cell walls. For over a year, she and around 30 women continued their 'no-wash' protest. In 1986, Farrell was released. She travelled to Gibraltar to plant another bomb, this time targeting the Royal Anglian Regiment, and was shot in the back by plainclothes soldiers. In 1980, Sinn Féin set up a Women's Department to ensure that women had a political voice in the organisation; a year later, the Falls Road Woman's Centre was opened to provide advice for women on abortion (illegal in Ireland), birth control, domestic violence and childcare. In 1994, when the Hume-Adams talks were going on, Clár na mBan was formed to make sure that women's needs were taken into account in the peace process: their recommendations became part of the Good Friday Agreement. It was the diplomacy of another woman, Mo Mowlam, who, as secretary of state for Northern Ireland, helped to bring about a ceasefire and the signing of the Good Friday agreement which eventually brought peace to the island of Ireland.

WOMEN AGAINST PIT CLOSURES: REALITY AND MYTH[88]

On 12 March 1984, in what would turn out to be a long and bitter year-long strike, the miners' leader Arthur Scargill called for national action against the closing of pits across Britain. Margaret Thatcher's government and the National Coal Board had recommended a cut in coal production which would mean the loss of 20,000 jobs and the closure of 20 mines. Meanwhile, the government had stockpiled coal, banned secondary picketing, cut welfare payments and restricted benefits to the families of the strikers. The strike is remembered for its length, the battle between Scargill and Thatcher, and the participation of women in the mining communities. It is also remembered for the stories that emerged, namely that women in the mining community created a working-class women's liberation movement and, in so doing, changed their lives dramatically.

All across the country, miners' support groups were formed, pickets arranged, meetings held and demonstrations organised. On 18 March 1984, Betty Cook and a number of Barnsley women organised a women's meeting at which over 100 attended. These women were encouraged to form groups in their local towns. A later rally, on 12 May, organised by the Barnsley Miners' Support Group attracted 10,000 women from the surrounding mining areas. It was a woman's march, organised by women, led by women. Gradually, these local groups joined together to become Women Against Pit Closures (WACP). It was a radical grass-roots organisation of working-class women, the first of its kind, an autonomous group of women from the mining communities of Britain. Some call it the working-class women's liberation movement.

Within a couple of weeks, women in the miners' support groups set up communal kitchens, distributed food parcels to help feed the children and their families, held parties and outings for children and lobbied gas and electricity companies to be sympathetic to strikers who could not pay their bills. They also provided prams, nappies, children's clothing and shoes, tampons, soap, washing powder and anything else that was needed by the women in the mining communities.[89] Soon the women participated in more political action, joined picket lines, spoke in public, collected money for the strike fund, and organised meetings and demonstrations. It was not always easy. When the women joined picket lines, they faced abuse from unsympathetic police officers who called them 'Scargill's slags', and when the women sang protest songs loudly, they commented, 'the cows are in good voice this morning'.[90]

On 11 August 1984, there was a 15,000-strong mass meeting and march in London, an indication of the strong level of support by the wives, daughters, sisters and mothers of striking miners. Consequently, the belief that an 'army of women working collectively' gained traction, as did the conviction that WACP was part of a huge movement of self-activating, working-class women' who would be in the vanguard of campaigns for socialism.[91] However, as Mary McIntyre points out, the women who boarded the buses for 'an eventful, exciting, free out "with the lasses"' did not necessarily become involved in the day-to-day work of helping the striking miners.[92] In fact, she points out that the vast majority 'would come for a meal but they weren't willing to do anything. When you asked them, they said "Oh, I don't want to be involved"'.[93] In the Seaham support group which fed over 200 families, only 12 women turned up on a regular basis. The same occurred right across the pit towns. In reality, McIntyre concludes, it was a small number of women who did a disproportionate amount of work to help feed the families of striking miners. Other studies support her analysis and suggest that only 25% of women were active in WACP.[94]

Of course, activism, from the suffragettes to the women at Greenham Common—has only ever attracted a minority of women. Moreover, in every social or political movement there will be numbers of sympathisers who—for all kinds of reasons—do not want to be full-time activists themselves but who will attend meetings, join marches, go on demonstrations, thereby giving encouragement to those who can or want to spend more time campaigning. As a result of the combination of full-time activists and their part-time supporters, the WAPC achieved an unprecedented level of support. The Durham CLP Miners' Families Support group alone, a group of mainly women, helped to raise a total of £93,724.01, food with a collective value of £20,146.79 as well as donations of clothes and children's toys.[95] Rich individuals were moved by the women: Bruce Springsteen invited six miners' wives who were active in WAPC to his concert in Newcastle, where he presented them with a cheque for $20,000 (£16,000). He told the group that he especially wanted to meet them 'because he thought the women were the backbone of the miners' struggle';[96] oil millionaire John Paul Getty donated £100,000 to the miners' fund which WAPC distributed.[97]

Another impression of the strike was that women in the fight against pit closures were politically inexperienced.[98] Much was made of the fact that they were housewives and mothers, not trade union members or radical activists. It was, as the founder of the Barnsley women's group Betty Cook said, an extension of their domestic role, only gradually morphing into something more political as women became involved in picketing and raising money.[99] It worked. The generally unsympathetic press looked kindly on these groups of working-class women who were desperately trying to feed their families.

However, as Sutcliffe-Braithwaite and Thomlinson argue, the image of 'politically naïve miners' wives', who only took action because they were forced to do so was a carefully constructed one.[100] Many women in the WAPC 'sought to legitimise their political activities through a rhetorical strategy of "ordinariness"'. In reality, many of the women were not so 'ordinary' as they were already active in a range of other organisations such as trade unions, the Labour Party and the women's co-operative movement, or else belonged to families who were politically engaged. Indeed, as McIntyre points out, the miners' support groups were not set up by 'political novices' but by political and trade union activists, certainly in the Durham coalfields. In an oral history of the WACP, 28 out of the 45 women interviewed took part in some form of activism before the strike.[101] In Wales too, the women's support groups were set up by experienced activists, well versed in how to run a successful campaign.

Nonetheless, it is important to remember that the women who had been activists before the strike were facing new and complex challenges: public speaking, writing articles, raising money, organising meetings and orchestrating demonstrations. Moreover, although the regional and national groups were run by women who had been political activists, most of the local groups were managed by local women, many of whom were unused to taking part in any type of protest. Even when local groups were set up by politically experienced women, they attracted 'ordinary housewives' who took on more roles as they gained experience.

The traditional narrative that women 'underwent a metamorphosis from housewife to political activist' because of their engagement with the men's struggle has validity.[102] For the women, the strike was a crucial turning point in their own personal and political development. One WACP member, Yvonne

Woodhead, insisted that she had changed so much, and that she 'used to think that politics was for politicians ...I was not involved except just to vote at election time. ... But in the strike I saw for myself how facts can be used ... twisted round and round ... as lies'.[103] Through helping the coal miners, the women in these communities came to be aware of their own strength, their own abilities and their own potential. It was, claimed many women, a transformative experience. The strike increased their political awareness more generally. Bridget Bell, the secretary of *Women Against Pit Closures* insisted that 'the strike absolutely changed our lives in understanding the power of collective action as women'.[104]

Certainly, the strike brought the miners' wives into contact with a range of women outside their social circle. Their world 'got bigger—professionals, feminists, punks, lesbians and gays, black people and Asians, we met them all and we stopped judging people by how they looked or how they spoke'.[105] Women travelled beyond their local area, some to Europe, some a lot further. The National Chairperson of WAPC, Ann Lilburn, was a 45-year-old housewife who had 'flown for the first time, attended and spoken at my first international conference, and addressed rallies big and small ... if someone had told me a year ago I would be doing this, I would've said they were stark raving mad'.[106]

Women in the mining communities lived in a heterosexual world, based on rigid definitions of masculinity and femininity, rarely meeting a gay man or a lesbian. This changed, as lesbian and gay communities in London showed support for the striking miners and their families. The Lesbian and Gays Support the Miners group (LGSM) collected around £20,000 from street donations, raffles and events. The 'Pits and Perverts' concert on 10 December at the Electric Ballroom in Camden Town alone raised £5000 for the South Wales mining community.[107] One group bought a van for the women to drive around the Welsh valleys—it was bright pink with the words 'Lesbians and Gays Support the Miners'. In so doing, the Lesbians and Gays Support the Miners (LGSM) group brought sexual politics into trade unionism, and socialism into the gay and lesbian community.[108] Miners' families hosted gay and lesbians when they came to stay: it could have provoked a clash of cultures; instead, it led to a mingling, breaking down the respective stereotypes held by the miners of gays and lesbians as 'weirdos' and lesbians and gays of miners as 'sexists'. In 1985, a miners' brass band led the Gay Pride March. Two years later, the Labour Party included gay and lesbian rights in its manifesto, encouraged to do so by the block vote of the National Union of Miners.

For Black and white feminist activists, the miners' strike 'represented a moment in history that was pregnant with the possibilities of forging unity between black and white people against inequality and injustice'.[109] One unifying link was over police brutality. In June, the first official Black delegation organised by the Southall Black Sisters, the Brixton Black Women's Group and others travelled to Kent to present a coachload of food—from tins of baked beans and crates of samosas to bottles of whisky—and £400 to the Dover Miners Wives Group for the Kent miners on strike. As Pragna Patel comments, 'the arrival of coach loads of black people, including Asian women, with our food and our music, in mining communities where few had encountered black people or eaten Asian food before, must have been a sight to behold. Sitting in their working men's clubs, drinking and chatting, both sides were acutely conscious of the fact that we had occupied parallel worlds until that point.'[110] Wilmett Brown, on behalf of the Black delegation, spoke at the rally, stressing the 'need for solidarity' and the need to boycott the scab coal coming from South Africa. Later that day, Pragna Patel from Southall Black sisters spoke at a special meeting organised by Elvington Miners' Wives, saying that the mining communities had not 'always been forthcoming in their support of Black communities' when they faced police harassment and 'expressed hopes that there would now be a more concrete unity … based on their shared experiences of policing methods'. One of the miners replied, acknowledged their communities' culpability and promised to support the Black community in future.[111] For Pragna Patel, who had hoped to demonstrate that issues of police brutality, racism, women's rights and employment were all part of the same struggle, and who had hoped to form a progressive alliance, these were welcome words of solidarity.

On 3 March, the anniversary of the start of the strike, the miners returned to work without a settlement. It had been momentous year-long struggle which was life-changing for many women. After a year of constant activity, their life 'stopped dead.' Some found it difficult to adjust and women complained of 'boredom, 'feeling unsettled' as well as 'being down in the dumps'.[112] The WAPC gradually faded away as women left the organisation. However, women maintained that they would never again be the 'little woman at home', tied to the kitchen sink, with their world revolving around 'tea for hubby and the two kids'. One woman insisted that her sons treat her as an equal and not just the 'dishwasher indoors'. The strike may have been lost, but the women in the WAPC believed that the 'wives have all become richer, because our lives are fuller'.[113]

The story of the WAPC may have been 'beset with contradictions' but nonetheless it is an inspiring one. Despite the constant interference and monitoring by the leaders of the NUM, it remained a grass-roots movement of women who fed, clothed, and encouraged their husbands, sons and family members not to give up the struggle.[114] Women's activism not only put them on the 'national stage as an autonomous women's movement' but challenged gender relationships and conventional ways of organising. It is held that miners, caricatured as misogynistic macho men, only reluctantly welcomed the support of their wives. However, some miners reacted positively right from the beginning. The leaders of the miners' strike, Arthur Scargill, welcomed women's participation on the picket lines. His wife, Anne, became a leading figure in the WAPC, and was called 'King Arthur's Queen', her husband's secret weapon. She hit the headlines when she was arrested and charged with obstruction when picketing outside a Nottinghamshire coal mine. Anne Scargill defended her action by drawing upon the image of a dutiful wife saying, 'I have always supported my husband, but I felt this time I had to speak out for the women of our community'. For the first time in the history of the miners' union, she insisted, women have taken 'action on their own account to save pits and jobs, and preserve the mining community in which they live'. Arthur publicly claimed he was 'proud of her involvement and of the role that all the women active in the miners' support group are playing in this dispute'.[115] Arthur Scargill's view was not unanimous. At one mine, the men were 'horrified' that the women had come to picket. The believed that women's place was—and should be—firmly in the home.

Unquestionably, the women activists helped the strike continue, raising vast sums of money, feeding families and generating more positive media coverage.[116] In return, they asked to be respected. One of their requests was to affiliate to the National Union of Miners, an honorary, symbolic membership which would convey the appreciation of the miners towards the WAPC. At first, the Miners Union voted against giving women associate membership, merely proving how temporary and flimsy their admiration for women had been.[117]

In 1992, the secretary of state of the department of trade and industry announced that Britain would close 31 of the remaining 50 coal mines. The government also insisted that any miners who went on strike against this would lose their redundancy payments. Once again, Women Against Pit Closures sprang into action. On 15 January 1993, the Lancashire WAPC, led by Mrs Sylvia Pye, reorganised itself at a pub in Earlestown, Newton-Le-Willows.[118] It was the only pit left in Lancashire, a modern, efficient and profitable colliery employing about 800 miners and many others in associated work. The group, as Karen Beckwith points out, 'was white; everyone was working-class, and everyone lived in Lancashire' with many women activists from the 1984–1985 strike.[119] Women set up camps outside seven pits, modelling themselves on the Greenham Common camp. The Parkside Pit Camp was set up on 18 January 1993, when a group of men and women moved a caravan to the pit entrance. Another caravan for men and a portacabin followed. The women's caravan 'had extensive tea and coffee making facilities, a telephone, a small television, a radio, and a tape deck. The camp had cold running water, mail delivery, daily milk delivery, portable toilets, food and a means by which donations to the camp were accepted'.[120] For 17 months, at least two women were present 24 hours a day to keep the camp operating, offering tea to visitors and answering questions. They staged events: Anne Scargill and three other women went down the Parkside mineshaft and staged a sit-in; some chained themselves to railings; a few climbed the tall winding tower, stood on top with banners and refused to budge. Several women set up a 'pit camp' outside the offices of the Board of Trade. As before, the women drew support from unexpected quarters: the violinist Nigel Kennedy contributed to a miners' benefit gala to help the campaign; the North Staffordshire Sikh community helped the Hem Heath pit; a local GP brought champagne and whisky to the Parkside camp at Christmas. The resistance of the women proved futile: at Parkside, the women were evicted, the colliery was closed, the shafts sealed with bricks and the mine buildings razed to the ground. It took 'just seconds to wipe decades of industrial history' when the concrete towers were blown up.[121] Many people who gathered to watch the destruction wept as 450 years of mining were brought to a close when the towers crumbled to the ground.[122] They were only too aware that their communities, not just their jobs, were being destroyed. Many saw it as a deliberate vindictive act, an intentional retaliation by the Tory government for the miners' strikes in the 1970s and 1980s.[123] Their worst fears were realised: at the start of the strike, there were 174 mines; by 2015, they had all closed.

Nonetheless, a number of women who participated in the WAPC continued to take part in other struggles. Some established a Rape Crisis Centre in Barnsley, some became involved in peace campaigning, some supported other strikes, some campaigned against apartheid in South Africa.[124] For example, when Asian workers went on strike at a clothing factory in Smethwick, 150 women and miners joined them on the picket line.[125] Sian James, a leading member of the Welsh WAPC, began her political journey when she joined the Welsh women's miners' support networks. After the strike, she became involved in women's rights and later became Labour MP for Swansea East, the first woman to be elected to that seat. Others—including Anne Scargill and Betty Cook—divorced their husbands.

Women had begun to take a more active role in trade unions overall. The National Union of Public Employees (NUPE) saw a marked increase in women shop stewards, and by 1983 women formed 44% of all the shop stewards in the union.[126] In the early 1980s, women NUPE members, who worked in the NHS catering and laundry services, found their pay and conditions threatened by privatisation. Seventy thousand Afro Caribbean and Asian workers would be affected across the NHS by Thatcher's government's attempts to cut service provision. In 1983, the general secretary of NUPE Rodney Bickerstaffe urged the Labour Party to support the minimum wage, a policy which would be of particular benefit to low-paid women. Supported by Clare Short, Bickerstaffe eventually pushed the Labour party to adopt the principle of the minimum wage. When the Labour Party was elected in 1997, the minimum wage policy became law.

It had taken feminists and their allies over 80 years to achieve equal pay for women. The battle was won in 1970, took five years to come into effect, only to be ignored in practice. It would take a woman activist—Julie Hayward— from Liverpool to make it work. Hayward was a cook at the Cammell Laird shipyard in Liverpool whose work had been valued as less skilled than her colleagues. On 31 October 1984, the 25-year-old cook won her three-year battle over equal pay when an industrial tribunal ruled that Hayward's job was just as skilled as the painters, joiners and insulation engineers at the plant.[127] She was the first woman to win a case under the Equal Pay Act. The decision gave hope to thousands and thousands of underpaid women across the country. However, the company resisted the ruling and turned to the Court of Appeal—which overturned the Industrial Tribunal's ruling. Hayward's case seemed lost, and with it the hopes of women workers across Britain fighting for equal pay.

Backed by her union, Hayward's case reached the House of Lords, which upheld her claim for 'equal pay for work of equal value'. The five (male) law Lords remarked that 'the decision may have the salutary effect of drawing to the attention of employers and trade unions the absolute need for ensuring that the pay structures of various groups of employees do not contain any element of sex discrimination, direct or indirect'.[128] The company threatened to take the case to the European Courts; the CBI urged the government to change the law in the shipyard's favour.[129] Nevertheless, no one could doubt the ruling. After a 12-year struggle, Julie Hayward's perseverance was rewarded. She had achieved a legal victory, a historical battle painstakingly won by the courage of one woman helped by her union and a campaign to support her. Her test case victory would pave the way for other women to make similar claims. There were times, she said, 'when I just felt like packing the whole thing in. But this was about the principle, not money. In the end I've helped other women, and that's really gratifying'.[130] The female shipyard cook was seen to have 'served up the right ingredients for hundreds of women'.[131]

THE ROAD TO POWER

There may have been a female prime minister but there were few women MPs. In 1980, the women's rights activist Lesley Abdela set up the 300 Group, a cross-party organisation dedicated to getting women into Parliament. The group put on staged debates in the House of Commons and ran courses around the country to help train women in public speaking. In 1987, the number of women MPs increased to 41, and in 1992 to 60. It was still not enough—women remained grossly underrepresented in the House of Commons. The Labour Party decided to 'give immediate attention to developing a strategy' for women.[132] At the 1982 Party Conference, women delegates proposed that each constituency be compelled to include at least one woman on their shortlist for the selection of its parliamentary candidate: the bigger trade unions voted against and the motion failed. At the end of the 1987 conference, when delegates were singing the Red Flag, about 30 women cut in and held up placards saying, 'one woman on every shortlist'.[133]

After yet another defeat in 1987, Clare Short initiated 'a quiet revolution … inspired by the need for Labour to win more women's votes, the need to regenerate the party and to improve women's representation in public life'.[134] The Labour leadership set about introducing quota systems to select women at local party and executive levels. In 1992, following another electoral defeat, the Women's Committee recommended that all-women shortlists be adopted so that winnable seats were paired in each area, and half required to draw up all women shortlists: a resolution which was passed a year later at the Labour Party conference with the strong support of the then leader John Smith and many women trade unionists. 'It is clear', Short argued, in her *Briefing for MPs*, 'that the selection process so far has excluded women, especially in the most winnable seats. Increasing women's representation in parliament is essential if we are to build a House of Commons which more truly represents the whole population. As more women come into the Commons, the culture will change, the agenda of politics will broaden, and the institution itself will be transformed'.[135] In the same year, Diane Abbott, one of four ethnic minority MPs, was elected and became the first Black female MP: she had achieved a number of firsts—the first Black woman to study at the University of Cambridge, the first Black woman to work at the Home Office and the first Black woman to be employed by the National Council of Civil Liberties. The sexist and racist abuse faced by this first Black female MP is frightening.

Meanwhile, the Woman's Committee and the Woman's Officer of the Labour Party, having gone through an acrimonious fight to gain all-women shortlists, were equally determined to get a 50% representation in the newly devolved Welsh and Scottish Parliaments using different means. They were aware that more women are normally elected in a proportional representation system and persuaded the Labour government to institute this in the two countries. In the first Welsh Assembly, women constituted 41.7% of those elected; in Scotland, 37.2% of those elected were women.

In addition, Labour women MPs pressed for a minimum of four women to be elected by the Parliamentary Labour Party to serve in the Shadow Cabinet. Critics within the party called their proposal a 'tart's charter', a 'skirt too far', and fiercely opposed it. In 1993, the policy was adopted and MPs were required to vote for at least four women to the Shadow Cabinet. In July 1996, just one year before the General Election, expectations were surpassed when five women were elected: Margaret Beckett, Ann Taylor and Clare Short came top of the polls, beating all the men on a list which included Robin Cook, Gordon Brown and David Blunkett. Mo Mowlam and Harriet Harman were also elected.

In 1997, Labour won the election. The quota system had worked: 120 women were elected: 101 Labour, 13 Conservative and 3 Liberal Democrat. Moreover, the new Prime Minister Tony Blair was obliged to promote the five women elected as shadow cabinet ministers to secretaries of state: Margaret Beckett,[136] Harriet Harman,[137] Mo Mowlam,[138] Clare Short[139] and Ann Taylor.[140] Those early twentieth-century suffrage activists would have been delighted, for sure.

Once in power, women could make a difference: Clare Short, secretary of state for international development (DfID), was one cabinet minister set to do so internationally by pointing British development policy in a new direction. Her ambition to reduce and even eradicate poverty in the poorest countries of the world through sustainable development could not be done alone. In the same year as Short's appointment, Hilde F Johnson was appointed Minister for International Development for Norway; a year later, Eveline Herfkens became Minister for Development Cooperation in the Netherlands, and Heidemarie Wieczorek-Zeul became Federal Minister of Economic Cooperation and Development in Germany.[141] In the summer of 1999, the four met at Utstein Abbey, a thirteenth-century Abbey built by Irish and Augustinian monks on a small island off the coast of Norway. Here they forged an alliance to change the way that aid was distributed and used. They became known as the Utstein 4.

All four women had promoted women's rights before they became ministers; all four were committed to empower women; all four were aware that women and children constitute the vast majority of the world's poor and that poverty eradication programmes needed to target them particularly. Moreover, they believed that conflict, violence and civil unrest was inextricably linked to poverty and that in turn war exacerbated deprivation. One of their challenges was to help end the conflict in Sierra Leone, where a brutal civil war was destroying the country: within two years, peace was established, the rebels were disarmed and the country held democratic elections, helped by the judicious application of aid.

To be effective, the four women had to convince other aid agencies, the World Bank, the International Monetary Fund, the United Nations, the OECD and others to support their approach. Over several years, the Utstein 4 encouraged the World Bank and the IMF to shift to focus on poverty reduction. A senior World Bank official credited the U4 for 'helping to ensure that within the Bank, poverty became … the overarching objective of all the Bank's programmes'.[142] Under Short's direction, DfID became a highly regarded organisation internationally.[143]

As the century drew to a close, there was renewed optimism among activists on the left and centre of politics. A newly elected Labour government promised a fresh sense of direction, and set out to reverse a long-time historical trend that rewarded the rich—mostly white men—rather than those who were poorer. By this time, feminists recognised that the idea of universal sisterhood was a myth rather than a reality, and that the theoretical position of comprehensive female victimhood could not be sustained. Women are not, and never were, a homogenous group. They are, and always were, divided by class, race, ethnicity, sexual identification, national identity, political persuasion and so much more. Even so, this does not mean that women cannot work together in harmony when fights against common injustices call upon them to do so.

Notes

1. *New Statesman*, 8 April 2013.
2. G. E. Maguire, *Conservative Women*, Palgrave Macmillan, 1998, p188.
3. Beatrix Campbell, *The Iron Ladies*, Virago, 1987, p246.
4. Jessica Dawn Prestidge, *Margaret Thatcher's politics: the cultural and ideological forces of domestic femininity*, PhD, University of Durham, 2017.
5. Ibid.
6. *Spare Rib*, March 1984, p17. Her husband became a UKIP councillor. Later, Gillick joined LIFE, the anti-abortion group.
7. Beatrix Campbell, *The Iron Ladies*, Virago, 1987, p197.
8. Martin Durham, *Moral Crusades, Family and Morality in the Thatcher Years*, New York University Press, 1991.
9. Ibid.

10. Mary Kenny, 'In Defence of Mary Whitehouse', *The Spectator*, June 2010.
11. Jessica Prestidge, 'Housewives having a go: Margaret Thatcher, Mary Whitehouse and the appeal of Right Wing Women in late twentieth century Britain', *Women's History Review*, Vol 28, No 2, 2019, p279.
12. Jessica Dawn Prestidge, *Margaret Thatcher's politics: the cultural and ideological forces of domestic femininity*, PhD, University of Durham, 2017, p78.
13. Jessica Prestidge, 'Housewives having a go: Margaret Thatcher, Mary Whitehouse and the appeal of Right Wing Women in late twentieth century Britain', *Women's History Review*, Vol 28, No 2, 2019, p286.
14. Ibid, p280.
15. Jessica Dawn Prestidge, *Margaret Thatcher's politics: the cultural and ideological forces of domestic femininity*, PhD, University of Durham, 2017, p75.
16. Ibid.
17. Ibid.
18. Julia Maria Long, *OBJECT!: The Re-emergence of Feminist Anti-pornography activism in the UK*, PhD, London South Bank University, 2011.
19. Ibid, p81.
20. See Barbara Norden, 'Campaign Against Pornography', *Feminist Review*, No 35, Summer, 1990, p3.
21. Nancy Whittier, 'Re-thinking Coalitions: Anti-Pornography Feminists, Conservatives, and Relationships between Collaborative Adversarial Movements, *Social Problems*, Vol 61, No 2, May 2014, p176.
22. Greek, Cecil E. and William Thompson, *International Journal of Politics, Culture and Society*, Summer 1992, Vol 5, No 4, p601.
23. Adam Lent, *British Social Movements since 1945*, Palgrave Macmillan, 2019, p159.
24. Ibid, p160.
25. Akina Mama Wa Afrika internet site, November 2020.
26. Julia Sudbury, '*Other Kinds of Dreams': black women's organisations and the politics of transformation*, Routledge, 1998, p164.
27. *Irish Independent*, 4 February 1988, p22.
28. *Evening Post*, 24 May 1988, p4.
29. *Evening Sentinel*, 20 June 1988, p3.
30. Adam Lent, *British Social Movements Since 1945*, Palgrave, 2001, p180.
31. Margarete Jolly, *Sisterhood and After*, OUP, 2020, p128.
32. Adam Lent, *British Social Movements since 1945*, Palgrave Macmillan, 2019, p198.
33. Ibid.
34. See George Stevenson, *The Women's Liberation Movement and the Politics of Class in Britain*, Bloomsbury, 2019, for an analysis of working-class women's response in north-east England to the WLM.
35. Humphrey Brown, 18; Peter Campbell, 18; Steve Collins, 17; Patrick Cummings, 16; Gerry Francis, 17; Andrew Gooding, 14; Lloyd Richard Hall, 20; Patricia Johnston, 15; Rosalind Henry, 16; Glenton Powell, 15; Paul Ruddock, 22; Yvonne Ruddock, 16; Owen Thompson, 16.
36. Leila Hassan Howe, *Guardian*, 8 October 2020.
37. Ibid.
38. BBC Caribbean news, 18 January 2011.
39. *Daily Mirror*, 5 March 1981, p10.

40. Ibid, 3 February 1982, p9.
41. Ibid, 19 February 1999, p11.
42. See interview with Paul Dacre, *Daily Mail* on-line video, 12 January 2012.
43. *Daily Mail*, 14 February 1997, p1.
44. Leila Hassan Howe, *Guardian*, 8 October 2020.
45. See Julia Sudbury, '*Other Kinds of Dreams*': *black women's organisations and the politics of transformation*, Routledge, 1998.
46. Akina Mama Wa Afrika internet site, November 2020.
47. Purna Sen, 'Domestic Violence, Deportation and Women's Resistance: Notes on Managing Intersectionality', *Development in Practice*, February 1999, vol 9, No 1/2.
48. Pragna Patel and Hannana Siddique, 'Standing in the Same Dream: Black and Minority Women's Struggles against Gender-Based Violence and for Equality in the UK', in Stephanie Condon et al *Violence against Women and Ethnicity: Commonalities and Differences across Europe*, Saint Philip Street Press, 2020, p260.
49. *Spare Rib*, July 1984, p9.
50. *Aberdeen Press and Journal*, 23 March, 1993, p13.
51. *Irish Independent*, 26 September 1992, p30.
52. *Spare Rib*, October 1992, p45.
53. *Crawley News*, 31 March 1993, p10.
54. *The Leader*, 3 January 1992, p8.
55. Hannana Siddiqui, 'Black Women's Activism: Coming of Age?', *Feminist Review*, No 64 Spring, 2000
56. Hanana Siddiqui, 'Fundamentalism, Racism, and Violence Against Women, The Southall Black Sisters Experience,' *Socialist Lawyer*, Spring 1996, p10.
57. *Liverpool Echo*, 26 August 1991, p9.
58. Hanana Siddiqui, 'Fundamentalism, Racism, and Violence Against Women, The Southall Black Sisters Experience,' *Socialist Lawyer*, Spring 1996, p10.
59. Pragna Patel and Hannana Siddique, 'Standing in the Same Dream: Black and Minority Women's Struggles against Gender-Based Violence and for Equality in the UK', in Stephanie Condon et al *Violence against Women and Ethnicity: Commonalities and Differences across Europe*, Saint Philip Street Press, 2020.
60. *The Irish Times*, 10 February 2019. I am grateful to Julian Filowchowski, former for this reference.
61. Natalie Thomlinson, *Race, Ethnicity and the Women's Movement in England*, 1968–1993, Palgrave Macmillan, 2016, p164.
62. Kum Kum Bhavnani, 'Racist Acts', *Spare Rib*, April 1982.
63. *Feminist Review*, No 17, July 1984, quoted in Natalie Thomlinson, *Race, Ethnicity and the Women's Movement in England*, 1968–1993, Palgrave Macmillan, 2016, p164.
64. The term was coined by Kimberlé Williams Crenshaw in 1989 in which she identified various factors of advantage and disadvantage.
65. Julia Sudbury, '*Other Kinds of Dreams*': *black women's organisations and the politics of transformation*, Routledge, 1998, p225.
66. Ibid, p177.
67. Julia Sudbury, '*Other Kinds of Dreams*': *black women's organisations and the politics of transformation*, Routledge, 1998.

68. Natalie Thomlinson, *Race, Ethnicity and the Women's Movement in England, 1968–1993*, Palgrave Macmillan, 2016, p192.
69. Submission by Women Against Fundamentalism and Southall Black Sisters to the Commission on Integration and Cohesion, 2007.
70. *Sunday Mirror*, 28 May 1989, p2.
71. Gita Sahgal and Nira Yuval-Davis, 'Refusing Holy Orders', *Women Against Fundamentalism*, November 1990, Newsletter No 1.
72. See Sukhwant Dhaliwal and Nira Yuval-Davis, *Women against Fundamentalism*, Lawrence and Wishart, 2014.
73. Elaine Titcombe, 'Women Activists: rewriting Greenham's History, *Women's History Review*, Volume 22, 2013, Issue 2, pp310–329.
74. Margaret L. Laware, 'Circling the Missiles and Staining them Red: Feminist Rhetorical Invention and Strategies of Resistance at the Women's Peace Camp at Greenham Common', *NWSA Journal*, Vol 16 No 3 2004, p20.
75. See Jill Liddington, *The Long Road to Greenham*, Virago, 1989.
76. Suzanne Moore, *The Guardian*, 20 March 2017.
77. Ibid.
78. Mary Millington, *The Guardian*, 20 March 2017.
79. *Spare Rib*, September 1988, p43.
80. Thanks to Helen Leigh's late parents for their kindness and hospitality.
81. *Spare Rib*, February 1983, p18.
82. Quoted in Margaret L. Laware, 'Circling the Missiles and Staining them Red: Feminist Rhetorical Invention and Strategies of Resistance at the Women's Peace Camp at Greenham Common', *NWSA Journal*, Vol 16 No 3 2004, p29.
83. *Spare Rib*, February 1984, p9.
84. Ibid.
85. Quoted in Margaret L. Laware, 'Circling the Missiles and Staining them Red: Feminist Rhetorical Invention and Strategies of Resistance at the Women's Peace Camp at Greenham Common', *NWSA Journal*, Vol 16 No 3 2004, p31.
86. Valeria Amos and Prathiba Parmar. 'Challenging Imperial Feminism', in Sue Morgan, *The Feminist History Reader*, Routledge, 2006, p293.
87. Theresa O'Keefe, '"Mother Ireland, Get Off Our Backs": Republican Feminist Resistance in the North of Ireland', in Lorenzo Bosi et al., *The Troubles in Northern Ireland and Theories of Social Movements*, Amsterdam University Press, 2017, p 167.
88. See Jean Stead, *Never the Same Again, Women and the Miners' Strike*, The Women's Press, 1987.
89. Meg Allen, *Carrying on the Strike: The Politics of Women Against Pit Closures*, PhD, University of Manchester, 2001.
90. *Guardian*, 10 May 2004.
91. Mary McIntyre, *The Response to the 1984–5 Miners' Strike in Durham County: Women, the Labour Party and Community*, PhD, University of Durham, 1992, p69.
92. Mary McIntyre, *The Response to the 1984–5 Miners' Strike in Durham County: Women, the Labour Party and Community*, PhD, University of Durham, 1992, p50.
93. Ibid, p53.
94. Meg Allen, *Carrying on the Strike: The Politics of Women Against Pit Closures*, PhD, University of Manchester, 2001, p 24.

95. Record of cash donations to Durham CLP Miners Families Support Group, quoted Mary McIntyre, *The Response to the 1984–5 Miners' Strike in Durham County: Women, the Labour Party and Community*, PhD, University of Durham, 1992, p256.
96. *Sunday Mirror*, 9 June 1985, p1–2.
97. *Daily Mirror*, 28 November 1984, p4.
98. Florence Sutcliffe-Braithwaite, and Natalie Thomlinson, "National Women Against Pit Closures: gender, trade unionism and community activism in the miners' strike, 1984–5, *Contemporary British History*, Vol 32, Issue 1, 2018.
99. Ibid, p85.
100. Ibid, p79.
101. Meg Allen, *Carrying on the Strike: The Politics of Women Against Pit Closures*, PhD, University of Manchester, 2001, p67.
102. Jean Spence, and Carol Stephenson, '"Side by side with our Men?" Women's Activism, Community and Gender in the 1984–5 Miners' Strike', *International labour and working-class history*, 75 (1), 2009, p73.
103. Quoted in Meg Allen, *Carrying on the Strike: The Politics of Women Against Pit Closures*, PhD, University of Manchester, 2001, p31.
104. *Guardian*, 10 May 2004.
105. Quoted in Meg Allen, Meg, *Carrying on the Strike: The Politics of Women Against Pit Closures*, PhD, University of Manchester, 2001, p13.
106. *Newcastle Journal*, 6 March 1985, p6.
107. Dairmaid Kelliher, 'Solidarity and Sexuality: Lesbians and Gays Support the Miners, 1984–5, *History Workshop Journal*, Spring, Vol 77, Issue 1, 1974. See also the 2014 film *PRIDE*.
108. Ibid.
109. Pragna Patel, 'Southall: solidarity with samosas', *Socialist Lawyer*, June 2009, No 52, p22.
110. Ibid, p23.
111. *Spare Rib*, August 1984, p11.
112. Monica Patricia Shaw, *Women in protest and beyond: Greenham common and mining support groups*, PhD, University of Durham, 1993.
113. Ibid.
114. Florence Sutcliffe-Braithwaite, and Natalie Thomlinson, "National Women Against Pit Closures: gender, trade unionism and community activism in the miners' strike, 1984–5, *Contemporary British History*, Vol 32, Issue 1, 2018, p90.
115. *Liverpool Echo*, 26 June 1984, p10.
116. Loretta Loach, 'We'll Be Here Right to the End … and After', in *Digging Deeper: issues in the Miners' strike*, Verso, 1985, p172.
117. *Liverpool Echo*, 11 March 1985, p4.
118. Karen Beckwith, 'Lancashire Women Against Pit Closures: Women's Standing in a Men's Movement, *Signs*, Vol 21, No 4, Summer 1996.
119. Ibid, p1043.
120. Ibid, p1044.
121. Simon Caldwell, *A Glorious Past Bites the Dust*, internet site accessed 1 December 2020.
122. *Liverpool Echo*, 4 October 1993, p9.
123. *The Kerryman*, 23 October 1992, p8.

124. Meg Allen, Meg, *Carrying on the Strike: The Politics of Women Against Pit Closures*, PhD, University of Manchester, 2001.
125. *Guardian*, 12 March 2014.
126. Tara Martin, 'The Beginning of Labor's End? Britain's "Winter of Discontent" and Working-class Women's Activism, *International Labor and Working-Class History*, No 75, Spring, 2009.
127. *Daily Mirror*, 31 October 1984, p11.
128. Quoted in *Liverpool Echo*, 5 May 1988, p8.
129. The Equal Opportunities Commission, an all-female body set up under the Sex Discrimination Act, supported Julie Hayward's case.
130. *The Daily Mirror*, 26 October 1999, p6.
131. *Liverpool Echo*, 6 May 1988, p5.
132. *Women Candidates May 1979—General Election*, Private and Confidential Memo, NEC 25 July 1979.
133. *Press and Journal*, 3 October 1987, p5.
134. Clare Short, 'Women and the Labour Party' in Joni Lovenduski and Pippa Norris, *Women in Politics*, 1997.
135. Judith Squires 'Quotas for Women: Fair Representation' in Joni Lovenduski and Pippa Norris, *Women in Politics*, 1997.
136. As secretary of state for trade and industry and president of the Board of Trade (later Lord President of the Council and leader of the House of Commons).
137. As secretary of state for social security and minister for women.
138. As secretary of state for Northern Ireland (later Cabinet Office minister and chancellor of the Duchy of Lancaster).
139. As secretary of state for international development.
140. As Lord President of the Council and leader of the House of Commons (later chief whip).
141. Constantine Michalopolous, *Ending Global Poverty: Four Women's Noble Conspiracy*, OUP, 2020.
142. Constantine Michalopolous, *Ending Global Poverty: Four Women's Noble Conspiracy*, OUP, 2020, p1. Constantine Michalopolous, *Ending Global Poverty: Four Women's Noble Conspiracy*, OUP, 2020, p78.
143. In 2020, it ceased to be an independent department when PM Boris Johnson merged it with the Foreign Office, and an honourable chapter in British history closed.

CHAPTER 11

Conclusion: Change and Continuities

After a hundred years of women's activism, what has changed? In 2018, the *Financial Times* exposed the illegal pay and conditions in a number of Leicester factories which made clothes for New Look, River Island, Boohoo and Missguided, popular brands in Britain. Leicester's garment industry was allegedly detached from UK law, 'a country within a country' where Asian-heritage women machinists worked long hours. At the time, the minimum wage was £8.72 an hour but the workers were being paid £3.50, with no holiday or sick pay. It was modern slavery. In one dilapidated building, where broken windows were patched up with cardboard boxes, where walls were crumbling and electrical wires dangled dangerously from the ceiling, textile workers were expected to work a 40-hour week with no breaks.[1] The Covid crisis exacerbated this: women were told to come to work even when they showed symptoms of the virus. Meg Lewis, the campaign manager of Labour Behind the Label, commented that it was 'heart-breaking to see grotesque inequality when some people profit so much while there are workers at the bottom of the chain whose lives are being put at risk'.[2] In 2019, Boohoo recorded profits of £59.9 million.

In April 2021, the *Financial Times* commented 'we are two nations …about one in four workers in the UK is on "contingent" work: zero-hours contracts, short-term contracts, gig work, solo self-employment'.[3] The Living Wage Foundation (LWF) discovered that two-fifths of working adults in full- or part-time employment were given less than a week's notice of their shifts. Of those who suffered from uncertainties like this, the hardest hit were low-paid workers from Black, Asian and minority ethnic backgrounds, those with children and those working in the hospitality, retail and leisure industries.[4] These least regarded, often-invisible workers were mostly women. Very many of them relied on food banks, a twenty-first-century charitable response to desperation. In the 1900s, as *Women and Activism* has shown, Margaret Bondfield, Olivia Malvery, Mary Macarthur, Margaret MacDonald and other activists were all too familiar with these kinds of inequalities. A hundred years later, the endeavours of those activists who had steadfastly campaigned for equal pay, for maternity leave and for an end to sex discrimination at work disappeared in the time it took to sign a zero-hours contract. In the early 2020s, after the advances from 1945 to 1979, inequality and the unequal distribution of wealth were prevalent throughout the United Kingdom—one of the richest economies in the world. Those from poorer socio-economic backgrounds were more likely to suffer from the COVID pandemic and the deleterious health conditions associated with poverty.

The story is complicated. During the twentieth-century, middle-class women successfully fought for the right to work in a range of occupations previously barred to the female sex: for example, as solicitors, barristers, politicians, stockbrokers and company directors. In 1997, American-born Marjorie Scardino became the first woman CEO of a FTSE 100 company; in 2017, Cressida Dick became the first woman commissioner of police of the Metropolis; in 2020, Dame Sharon White, whose parents were part of the Windrush generation, became the first woman to be appointed chair of the John Lewis partnership. For women like Scardino, Dick and White, who worked in lucrative, highly satisfying occupations, the activism of twentieth-century women made a significant difference; for those in deskilled, dead-end and poorly paid jobs, the difference was negligible. Moreover, the unity of women—only ever an idealistic dream held by some feminists—splintered further when well-educated, professional women took high-earning jobs and relied on working-class women to clean their houses and look after their children, often on a minimum wage. The servant class was reinvented.

The gains of a number of privileged women coincided with feminism becoming (almost) respectable, quite disassociated from its socialist beginnings. Margaret Thatcher and other female Conservatives had disavowed feminism. Yet when Theresa May was leader of the Conservatives, she was photographed wearing a T-shirt which read, 'this is what a feminist looks like'. It had been designed by the Fawcett Society in an attempt to destigmatise the word and to celebrate the diversity of feminists and feminism. Other Conservative women—Amber Rudd, Anna Soubry and Nicky Morgan—identified with the message and expressed their approval. In 2010, *Harvard International Review* published Teresa May's article 'Woman of the House: Standing for Gender Equality in British Politics', in which she argued, 'for fair representation at the heart of politics in order that we are represented by a true cross section of society rather than the white, middle-class men that still dominate the House of Commons'.[5] As an MP and then party leader and prime minister, Theresa May championed opportunities for women and was known for being supportive and encouraging to women in her party; moreover, she spoke up against domestic violence, female genital mutilation and the sexual trafficking of women.

Which Conservative woman was the anomaly? Margaret Thatcher or Teresa May? As this book has shown, the Conservative Party has always had a share of feminist mavericks: Nancy Astor worked with Labour's Ellen Wilkinson on a range of women's rights; the Duchess of Atholl worked with the Independent

MP Eleanor Rathbone on preventing genital mutilation; Mavis Tate chaired the cross-party Woman's Power Committee; and Irene Ward campaigned with Labour's Barbara Castle for equal pay. Nonetheless, in the latter part of the twentieth century, women's rights was rarely an important issue for Margaret Thatcher and female Conservatives. In the first half of the twenty-first century, this changed. From 2005 onwards, Conservative women were more eager to proclaim themselves as feminists, even though their feminism was not focused on creating a more egalitarian society, but about fighting for parity with men. It is, as David Swift argues, 'a neo-liberal, anti-statist, anti-Left feminism', an individualistic feminism under the banner of which women should have the same opportunities as men to exploit others. This type of feminism 'is free— they do not have to spend, nor undermine systematic privilege'.[6] Class inequality and the reasons for its continuance were ignored. In the view of Teresa May and other Conservative women, feminism meant equality and equal rights with men, not equality across the board.

For the most part, a woman's rights to free contraception and to abortion were realised in England, Scotland and Wales but not Northern Ireland. In 1998, the Portuguese-born London-based artist, feminist and anti-fascist Dame Paula Rego RA used her talent to paint women shortly after and illegal abortion. Her powerful, visceral and unsettling series of ten images, called *Untitled: The Abortion Pastels*, 'highlights the fear and pain and danger of illegal abortion … making abortions illegal is forcing women to the backstreet solution'.[7] She had painted the images after a failed referendum in her home country but her work had resonance elsewhere. It was art as activism. In October 2020, after years of campaigning, abortion in Northern Ireland was decriminalised. Until then, abortion was illegal unless a woman's life was at risk: there were no exceptions for rape, incest or foetal abnormalities. Here the Protestant and Catholic conservative male hierarchy were united, forcing women who wanted an abortion to either use backstreet abortionists or travel to England.

During the Covid pandemic, when non-essential health services were limited and waiting times soared, women across Britain feared that there would be restricted access to abortions. However, on 20 March 2020, the Department of Health empowered GPs and health providers to make abortion pills available to women in the first ten weeks of pregnancy. The appropriate medication was delivered by post after a detailed telephone assessment and counselling. Prior to this 'telemedicine' service, women had been required to attend a clinic for an ultrasound and take a first pill under supervision. The second pill, which would trigger a miscarriage, was to be taken at home. The introduction of telemedicine, according to an analysis of 50,000 abortions that took place in England, Scotland and Wales between January and June 2020, provided a safe, effective and more accessible service.[8] Telemedicine was not made available in Northern Ireland.

As in the twentieth century, there was a backlash from religious groups. Immediately after the telemedicine abortions had been approved, Christian

Concern sought a judicial review against the DHSS. Its aim is to 'herald the dignity and worth of every human person, and campaign against experimentation on, or eradication of, unborn children' and uses 'legal, policy and media expertise to seek justice and protect the vulnerable ... we also work to protect families, unborn children, disabled and elderly people, and those who want to leave Islam, for example'.[9] Christian Concern took the case to the High Court, claimed that the government contravened the 1967 Abortion Act and (wrongly) cited that two deaths had occurred because of the telemedicine abortions. They lost the case, took it to the Court of Appeal and lost again.[10]

Pornography endured. A new wave of feminist anti-pornography campaigners emerged at the beginning of the twenty-first century. As Julia Long points out, young activists—like those in the 1970s—put stickers on pornographic adverts, called for tougher licensing laws on lap dancing clubs, tried to restrict access to literature which portrayed women in various states of nudity and set up anti-porn blogs.[11] In 2004, the London Feminist Network was established. This had a radical feminist agenda, a policy that excluded men, and a focus on campaigning against male violence, pornography and prostitution—in 2010, membership was around 1500. Similar groups were founded across Britain in all the major cities. In 2010, UK Feminista was set up to co-ordinate and facilitate feminist activism.[12] Younger feminists used a technology not available to their older colleagues: social networking. By using Twitter, WhatsApp, Facebook, blogs, e-zines, e-lists and websites, they could create new local, national and international communities committed to their dedicated feminist agenda.[13]

Meanwhile, the London-based OBJECT! was set up to challenge the 'sexual objectification of women in the media and popular culture'. Working with the Fawcett Society, OBJECT! campaigned to remove sexist advertising, to stop licensing lap dancing clubs and tackle prostitution. It was a challenge to stop the spread of pornography—the female body was a valuable sexual commodity, a marketable product in an industry that in 2007 was estimated to be worth over £69 billion. Moreover, pornographic and sexualised images were normalised: bikini waxes, breast enhancement and labia surgery were used by 'ordinary' women who were neither prostitutes nor porn stars. There were some successes: in 2009, the Policing and Crime Act, an act which restricted the licensing of lap dancing clubs and made it an offence to pay for someone who had been forced or coerced into providing a sexual service was passed; in 2009, the Playboy store in Oxford Street closed down, edged on by the 'Bin the Bunny' campaign of Anti-Porn London; in 2010, the group Mumsnet launched a campaign to persuade Primark to stop selling padded bikini tops to seven-year-old girls.[14]

In 2006, the *#MeToo Movement*, a movement against sexual abuse and sexual harassment was initiated by an American Black woman who had been raped and sexually assaulted as a child. It swept across the world and achieved headline status when accusations were made against the movie baron Harvey Weinstein. In 2017, British male MPs were accused of sexual harassment by female junior staff employed in the UK Parliament. Theresa May, by now prime minister, proposed that an independent grievance procedure be set up. Cabinet members resigned; Labour MPs were suspended from the party; and a former SNP leader was charged with sexually assaulting nine women.

Despite the campaigns of twentieth-century activists, violence against women continued. Each year, the Femicide Census, Counting Dead Women and other organisations record the names of women killed in the United Kingdom by men who have been charged or convicted of murder. Since 2016, Labour MP Jess Phillips, Shadow Minister for Domestic Violence and Safeguarding, has read out the names of these women in the House of Commons to ensure the murdered women are remembered. Between 2009 and 2015, 1425 women across the racial spectrum were murdered, 92% by men known to them. Every three days a woman was killed.[15] The murders of Sarah Everard, murdered by a police officer, and Julia James in early 2021 were stark reminders of the vulnerability of women's lives.

In 2000, Southall Black Sisters (SBS) celebrated their twenty-first anniversary. For two decades, SBS had led the Black feminist movement, running a 'resource centre providing information, advice advocacy, counselling and support to women on domestic violence and related issues'.[16] They were unable to stop all violence. In 2002, a young 16-year-old Iraqi Kurdish woman, Heshu Yonis, was murdered by her father for having a Lebanese Christian boyfriend. It was called an 'honour killing', a phrase criticised by the SBS because it 'exoticised' what in effect was gender-related murder. There were successes: their campaign to free Kiranjit Aluwalia led to a change in the law, so too did their campaigns to have gender persecution to be recognised as a reason for women to be granted asylum. In 2007, the Forced Marriage Act was passed. However, as SBS observed, 'honour killings' continued, and with it a growth in fundamentalist beliefs.

Nonetheless, as the twenty-first century began, Black and minority women were hopeful that the government was becoming more sympathetic to women trapped in violent marriage, especially to those who were scared to leave their abusive husbands because of their fragile immigration status.[17] The election of feminist MPs also appeared to help the status of women. The Labour government introduced a number of reforms like the 2004 Domestic Violence Crime and Victims Act as well as a series of non-legislative measures.[18] In 2009, the Scottish government published its governmental policy, *Safer Lives, Changed Lives: A shared approach to tackling violence against women in Scotland*. It adopted a definition of violence against women which included pornography, prostitution, stripping, lap dancing, pole dancing and table dancing, all of which were considered commercial sexual exploitation.[19] In 2010, when Theresa May was Home Secretary, the British government published *Our Call to End Violence against Women and Girls* and strengthened the legislative framework further. It introduced new laws against stalking, made it a criminal offence to force women into marriage and to use coercive and controlling behaviour. The Domestic Violence Disclosure Scheme, known as Clare's Law after Clare Wood, who was murdered by her partner, gave women the right to know if their partner had a violent past. In addition, new protective orders for domestic violence, sexual violence and female genital mutilation gave local authorities the right to take protective action.[20] In 2019, 'upskirting' was made a criminal offence: offenders faced up to two years in prison for taking an image under a woman's skirt or dress.[21]

There were international successes too. In wartime, men's sexual violence had been regarded as a 'weapon of war'. In 2002, when the International Criminal Court was established, the then secretary of state for international development, Clare Short, and her Norwegian colleague, Hilde F Johnson, worked together to make sure that sexual violence was included in the definition of war crimes and that it was seen as a grave breach of the Geneva Convention. In 2002, this became international law after 66 member states ratified the agreement.

There were many missed opportunities. As the journalist and activist Joan Smith points out, 'many academics, police officers, and members of the security services have a professional interest in terrorism. Yet few have ever remarked on one of its most significant features, which is that it is overwhelmingly carried out by men. ... all six of the men who were directly involved (at Westminster Bridge, Manchester Arena, London Bridge and Finsbury Park) had histories of misogyny and abusing women.'[22] In 1999, a white supremacist planted three nail bombs in London which targeted Black people, Asians and gays. Three died, and more than 140 were injured. The murderer had had sadomasochistic dreams that he was an SS officer who had women as slaves. The murderer of Jo Cox, Labour MP for Batley and Spen was a fascist whose 'premeditated crimes were nothing less than acts of terrorism designed to advance his twisted ideology'.[23] Both men were sympathetic to Nazism, the Ku Klux Klan and other misanthropic and misogynistic organisations.

The global pandemic also led to setbacks. According to the Office for National Statistics, police-recorded crime data show a significant increase in domestic abuse. Domestic abuse occurs in all social classes, racial and sociocultural groups, and calls to the United Kingdom's domestic abuse helpline have surged by more than a third. A spokeswoman for Women's Aid reported a similar rise in cases, and that 'lockdown has shut down routes to support and safety for women and children experiencing abuse'. Similarly, Refuge reported that 'lockdown restrictions have given perpetrators of abuse unprecedented power and control'. Meanwhile, cash-strapped refuges have had to turn away victims attempting to escape from the violence of abusive partners.[24]

In the twenty-first century, identity politics surged in popularity, and with it came disagreements as various groups asserted the primacy of their own entitlements. One of the issues dividing feminists relates to transgender politics. In 2004, the government passed the Gender Recognition Act whereby people who had transitioned, had had a medical diagnosis of 'gender dysphoria' and had lived in their chosen gender for two years were reassigned their sex. In 2013, Paris Lees a journalist and transgender rights activist came top of the

Independent's Pink List. Growing up in Nottinghamshire, Lees had first identified as a gay man before transitioning to become a woman. In 2018, she became the first openly transgender woman featured in *Vogue*: hers was a success story. In 2019, the British Social Attitudes survey suggested that 'public attitudes to transgender people are broadly positive' and that the 'public sees transphobia as wrong'.[25]

However, a number of transgender people questioned the sex-gender-sexuality system, arguing that it 'produces gendered and sexed bodies and identities in a binary and hierarchical manner'.[26] Stonewall, the LGBT charity, campaigned for a system of 'self-ID' whereby individuals can pick their gender. Public health bodies swapped words for 'women' and 'girls' and started to use 'cervix havers' and 'menstruators' to comply with these demands.

A number of feminists feared that, as biological sex began to be questioned, the notion of womanhood was being erased. They objected to trans activists calling women 'people who menstruate' 'people with vulvas', and were concerned that women's rights and resources were 'at grave risk, not only from the effects of "austerity" but also from an extreme trans activism seeking to silence women and assail feminist organisations'.[27] Others, like Dame Jenni Murray, argued that upbringing is essential in the determination of 'real womanhood' as those who had been brought up male and had previously lived as men enjoyed a number of privileges not enjoyed by those born and brought up as women.[28] In 2018, David Lewis stood for a women's officer role in the Labour Party, claiming that he identified as a woman. But only on Wednesdays. He had wanted to draw attention to 'what happens when you say that someone's gender depends only on what they say and nothing else'.[29] He was suspended from Labour.

Unfortunately, the debate around transgender became toxic, far more acrimonious than any previous disagreements that have beset women activists. Lesbians, radical feminists and other women who challenged Stonewall's narrative were targeted by trans activists. One young lesbian, who believed in the importance of biological sex, and detested lesbians being called bigots for not dating transwomen with penises suffered widespread abuse on social media. For supporting her and defending a woman's right to define herself as a woman, the successful novelist J. K. Rowling was called 'cunt', 'bitch' and TERF (trans-exclusionary radical feminist) and accused of 'literally killing transpeople with hate'. She received rape and death threats on a daily basis.[30] Feminist academics and journalists who agreed with J. K. Rowling's thinking on this matter were publicly hounded, humiliated and threatened with dismissal. There was, the *Spectator* pointed out, 'evidence that the targeting of female academics is fuelled by misogyny … the new face of sexual harassment'.[31] The suppression and silencing of women's voices is worrying.

In 2020, three senior judges ruled that children under the age of 16 were unlikely to be mature enough to make a decision on whether to go forward with gender-reassignment. A case had been brought before them by a 22-year-old woman who had earlier transitioned to a man but had reverted to being female. Previously, the Tavistock clinic had been providing puberty blockers for those who thought they suffered from gender dysphoria, sometimes to those as young as ten years old. The court ruling was a reversal of the Gillick ruling that permitted children under 16 to decide whether or not they could be prescribed birth control devices without parental consent. A representative from the trans children's charity Mermaids argued that the decision was a 'potential catastrophe for trans young people'; in contrast, a leading psychiatrist at the Tavistock advised caution when treating young people for gender dysphoria and criticised the 'weaponisation of victimhood, the fact that the fear of being seen to be transphobic now overrides everything.'[32]

For some women, persistent racial discrimination rather than sexual politics overshadowed their lives. In 2013, three Black American women created #BlackLivesMatter 'as an ideological and political intervention in a world where Black lives are systematically and intentionally targeted for demise'.[33] After the murder of George Floyd in 2020, it became a global network. Rebecca Achieng Ajula-Bushell, a former British swimmer and now filmmaker, helped set up a race equality group to draw attention to racism in rural Gloucestershire where she lived. In her view, there was a 'horrific divide between the moneyed people who come in from London and live in big stone houses and the sprawling estates that are under-funded'. She believed that in areas such as the Cotswolds, communities needed a 'sense of unity and camaraderie between white working class and black and ethnic minority working groups. Economic justice is a real hallmark of the BLM movement'.[34]

Doreen Lawrence has waited a great many years for justice. In November 2020, she and her husband Neville gave evidence to a public enquiry set up by Theresa May to examine how undercover police officers had spied on them when they were trying to persuade the police to investigate the murder of their son Stephen. Only two of the five suspects had been jailed for the murder. Their lawyer stated that it was an 'utter disgrace' that the Lawrences were still fighting for justice. 'For any parent to have to outlive their child is unimaginable—to lose their child in such circumstances is inconceivable; to still be fighting for justice 27 years on is unacceptable; and for those parents to be fighting for justice while being spied upon by the police, whose very role was to support and protect them, is simply unforgivable.'[35] Doreen Lawrence wrote to the court that she 'now leads a completely different life—one that I never imagined I would have or wanted. For years I have felt like an only soul in a sea of millions'.

Certainly, it seemed as if twenty-first-century women activists were much too divided across the class, gender and race continuum to work together. However, an issue that unites activists is the danger to our planet. As Bayard Rustin, a Black gay activist remarked, 'political alliances are not based on love. They are based on mutual interest'.[36] But while climate change affects us all and brings together activists in a common goal, it is not class-, race- or gender neutral. The impact of climate change is not felt equally, for it is the poor and marginalised groups who suffer more. Marina Andrijevic points out that women and girls in the global south are disproportionately vulnerable to the effects of the climate catastrophe, 'not because there is something inherently vulnerable about women, but because of socio-cultural structures that deprive women'.[37] For example, water scarcity affects the largely female agricultural workforce in Africa, making it tough to grow crops and thereby lead a healthy life.

In March 2021, the charity LGBTQ1 set up a fund to support those whose 'vulnerability to climate change is worsened by poverty and discrimination'.[38] *Woman's Hour* put forward a Power List of 30 women activists committed to environmental action.[39] The Forbes List put forward 100 names.[40] These are women across the class, ethnic, sexual and political spectrum, united in one cause. Among these are Deirdre Wood, who founded a Community Kitchen Co-operative in Kilburn London to grow and provide sustainable food; two teenage sisters Amy and Ella Meek, who have picked up over 60,000 pieces of plastic litter and organised a team of others—Kids Against Plastic—to tackle plastic pollution; Fatima-Zarha Ibrahim, who is Co-Director of Green New Deal and a Justice Campaigner; Juliet Davenport, who founded Good Energy, a company which is a 100% renewable electricity supplier; Bea Johnson, who pioneered a zero-waste lifestyle; Rowena Bird, who co-founded Lush Cosmetics, a company which sells package-free products; Alexandra Wanjiku Kelber, an activist with Black Lives Matter who is interested in the 'politics of food, gender, social change, race and environmental justice'; Gail Bradbrook, who is co-founder of Extinction Rebellion and Caroline Lucas, a Green MP who has fought all her life on this issue.[41] Meanwhile, the government fielded an all-male team to host COP26.

In 1935, the novelist Winifred Holtby wrote, 'the march of women is never regular, consistent or universal … it advances in one place while it retreats in others. One individual looks forward, another backward, and the notions of which is "forward" and which is "backward" differ widely'.[42] As *Women and Activism* argues, there is no one unswerving story of women united in struggle. The progress towards equality is certainly patchy: the benefits won in the twentieth century for disadvantaged women are often no longer available, while privileged groups benefit from opportunities not available to Holtby and her generation. Moreover, the newer challenges around gender identification faced by twenty-first-century women are ones that might surprise earlier activists.

Raphael Samuel pointed out that history is 'an active relationship between the past and present'. When I was at school, there was no women's history. History was a white man's story of high politics, war and diplomacy. Women activists questioned this, discovered new sources and created new ways of viewing the past. They were helped by the creation of the Library of the London Society for Women's Service in 1926 which preserved the history of the women's suffragist movement and collected the papers of newer campaigns. In 1957, the library was renamed the Fawcett Library and, in 2002, renamed the Women's Library, now housed at the LSE. The suffragette collection is at the

London Museum. Despite these rich collections, there were problems. Firstly, and all too frequently, the stories of the least-powerful, often poor and marginalised groups were not recorded. To make sure that twentieth- and twenty-first-century women's activism did not disappear into historical thin air, the Women's Resource Centre set up *Sisters Doing It for Themselves*. This is an oral history project which looks at the pioneering women who made/make a difference in the women's voluntary and community sector. Some of them appear in this book.[43] Secondly, there is no denying that twentieth-century women's historians in the United Kingdom told a predominantly white story. The founder of OWAAD, Stella Dadzie, drew attention to the fact that Black people had been 'airbrushed out of history'.[44] It was crucial, she argued, to decolonise the curriculum.[45]

Without new research and these fresh interpretations, there is a real danger that history itself—not just the people in the past—will perish.

Notes

1. *Financial Times*, 17 May 2018. Thanks to Clare Short for this reference.
2. *Independent*, 5 July 2020.
3. *Financial Times*, 16 April 2021.
4. Living Wage Organisation web site, accessed 20 April 1921.
5. *Harvard International Review*, Spring 2010, p40.
6. David Swift, 'From "I'm not a feminist, but …" to "Call me an old-fashioned feminist…" conservative women in parliament and feminism', *Women's History Review*, Volume 28, Issue 2, 2019, p335.
7. Paula Rego. A major retrospective exhibition of her work appeared at the Tate Britain in 2021.
8. Royal College of Obstetricians and Gynaecologists, 19 February 2021.
9. Christian Concern website, accessed 20 March 2021.
10. *The Guardian*, 21 April 2021.
11. Julia Long, *OBJECT!: The Re-emergence of Feminist Anti-Pornography Activism in the UK*, PhD, London South Bank University, 2011, p10.
12. Ibid.
13. Ibid.
14. Ibid.
15. *Femicide Census*, 2009–2018, online report. The report lists and is dedicated to all the women killed by men.
16. Hannana Siddiqui, 'Black Women's Activism: Coming of Age?', *Feminist Review*, No 64 Spring, 2000, p83.
17. Pragna Patel and Hannana Siddique, 'Standing in the Same Dream: Black and Minority Women's Struggles against Gender-Based Violence and for Equality in the UK', in Stephanie Condon et al *Violence against Women and Ethnicity: Commonalities and Differences across Europe*, Saint Philip Street Press, 2020, p266.
18. See *Labour Policy on Domestic Violence, 1999–2010*, 22 May 2012.
19. Julia Long, *OBJECT!: The Re-emergence of Feminist Anti-Pornography Activism in the UK*, PhD, London South Bank University, 2011.

20. *Ending Violence against Women and Girls, Strategy 2016–2020*, HM Government report, March 2016.
21. I am grateful to Rosie Keep for this information.
22. *Femicide Census*, 2009–2018, p25.
23. Sue Hemmings, Crown Prosecution Service quoted in *The Guardian*, 23 November 2016.
24. *Independent*, 3 February 2021.
25. *Attitudes to transgender people*, Equality and Human Rights Commission, 2019, p3.
26. OpenDemocracy, 31 March 2021.
27. Quoted *The Scotsman*, 11 July 2020.
28. Kathleen Stock, Material Girls, *Why Reality Matters for Feminism*, Fleet, 2021.
29. *The Guardian*, 23 May 2018.
30. For the full article, see J. K. Rowling *Writes about her Reasons for Speaking out on Sex and Gender Issues*, jkrowling.com.
31. Julie Bindel, *Spectator*, 4 May 2021.
32. *The Guardian*, 2 May 2021.
33. Black Lives Matter website, accessed 24 April 2021.
34. BBC News, 22 July 2020.
35. *The Guardian*, 10 November 2020.
36. Quoted in 'Why Liberals Make Everything About Race' with Touré Reed, The Jacobin Show, YouTube.
37. Carbon Brief, 15 December 2020, accessed 24 April 2021.
38. Hugo Greenhalgh, Reuters, 11 March 2021.
39. Caroline Lucas, Farhana Yamin, Rosamund Kissi-Debrah, Mya-Rose Craig, Sophie Howe, Ella Daish, Joanna Haigh, Beccy Speight, Minette Batters, Carolyn Cobbold, Gail Bradbrook, Judy Ling-Wong, Franny Armstrong, Brenda Boardman, Diane Gilpin, Caroline Mason, Miranda Lowe, Zarina Ahmad, Holly Gillibrand, Amanda Absalom-Lowe, Catherine Howarth, Rebecca Willis, Kate Humble, Fiona Harvey, Judy Webb, Yvonne Witter, Mikaela Loach, Safia Minney, Mandi Roberts, Christine Grosart.
40. Solitaire Townshend, 100 UK Leading Environmentalists (who happen to be women), 16 November 2020.
41. Ibid.
42. Quoted in Elizabeth Homans, *Visions of Equality, women's rights and political change in 1970s Britain*, PhD, Bangor University, 2015, p30.
43. Of all references in this book, the one I recommend the most is *Sisters Doing it for Themselves: an introduction*. It is an oral record of a remarkable group of women activists who make/made a significant difference to the lives of other women. Set up by the Women's Resource Centre and hosted by the LSE library, it was introduced on 16 July 2020 and launched on 28 April 2021 and is available online.
44. *The Guardian*, 21 November 2020.
45. Stella Dadzie, internet talk at the Institute of Historical Research, 26 April 2021. In 2020, she published *A Kick in the Belly: Women, Slavery and Resistance*, which explored how enslaved women in the Caribbean fought back against the cruel system.

BIBLIOGRAPHY

Adams, Carol and Laurikietis, *Message and Images*, Virago, 1976.
Alexander, Sally and Davin, Anna, 'Feminist History', *History Workshop*, Spring 1976.
Allen, Meg, *Carrying on the Strike: The Politics of Women Against Pit Closures*, PhD, University of Manchester, 2001.
Anderson, Gerald D, *Fascists, Communists and the National Government*, University of Missouri Press, 1983.
Andrews, Maggie, *The Acceptable Face of Feminism*, Lawrence and Wishart, 2015 (2nd edition).
Andrews, Maggie and Lomas, Janis, *The Home Front in Britain, Myths and Forgotten Experiences since 1914*, Palgrave Macmillan, 2014.
Andrews, Maggie and Lomas, Janis, *Hidden Heroines*, Robert Hale, 2018.
Andrews, Maggie *Women and Evacuation in the Second World War*, Bloomsbury, 2019.
Angelo, Anne-Marie, 'The Black Panthers in London, 1967–1972: A Diasporic Struggle Navigates the Black Atlantic', *Radical History Review*, Issue 103, 2009.
Arnot, Julie, *Women workers and Trade Union participation in Scotland, 1919–1939*, DPhil, 1999.
Atkinson, Diane, *Elsie and Mari Go to War*, Preface, 2009.
Atkinson, Diane, *Rise up Women, the Remarkable Lives of the Suffragettes*, Bloomsbury, 2018.
Atwood, Kathryn, *Women Heroines of World War 1: 16 Remarkable Resisters, Soldiers, Spies and Medics*, Chicago Review Press, 2014.
Baillie, *The Women of Red Clydeside: Munition Workers in the West of Scotland During the First World War*, DPhil, McMaster University, 2002.
Baldwin, M Page, 'Subject to Empire: Married Women and the British Nationality and Status of Aliens Act', *Journal of British Studies*, Vol 40, October 2001.
Ball, Stuart, 'The Politics of Appeasement: the Fall of the Duchess of Atholl and the Kinross and West Perth by-election, December 1938', *The Scottish Historical Review*, Vol 69, April 1990.
Banks, Olive, *Faces of Feminism*, Basil Blackwell, 1986.
Bartley, Paula, *Emmeline Pankhurst*, Routledge 2002.

Bartley, Paula, 'Suffragettes, class and pit-brow women', *History Review*, December 1999.
Bartley, Paula, *Ellen Wilkinson: From Red Suffragist to Government Minister*, Pluto, 2015.
Bartley, Paula, *Labour Women in Power: Cabinet Ministers in the 20th century*, Palgrave Macmillan, 2019.
Beaumont, Catrina, 'Citizens not feminists: the boundary between negotiated citizenship and feminism by mainstream women's organisations in England, 1938–1939', *Women's History Review*, Vol 9, Issue 2, 2000.
Beckwith, Karen, 'Lancashire Women Against Pit Closures: Women's Standing in a Men's Movement', *Signs*, Vol 21, No 4, Summer 1996.
Berthezène, Clarisse and Gottlieb, Julie, *Re-Thinking right-wing women, Gender and the Conservative Party, 1880s to the present*, MUP, 2017.
Bickerstaffe, Elizabeth Pearl, *A Spanish Civil War Scrapbook*, International Brigade Memorial Trust and Lawrence and Wishart, 2015.
Blaxland, Sam, 'Women in the organisation of the Conservative Party in Wales, 1945–1979', *Women's History Review*, Volume 28, No 2, 2019.
Bondfield, Margaret, *Shop Workers and the Vote*, People's Suffrage Federation, 1911.
Bondfield, Margaret, 'Women and the Factory System, Conditions – Past and Present', *Labour*, July 1934.
Bondfield, Margaret, *A Life's Work*, Hutchinson, 1948.
Bosi, Lorenzo, et al. (ed) *The Troubles in Northern Ireland and Theories of Social Movements*, Amsterdam University Press, 2017.
Braybon Gail and Summerfield Penny, *Out of the Cage, Women's Experiences in Two World Wars*, Pandora, 1987.
Breitenbach, Esther and Wright Valerie, 'Women as Active Citizens: Glasgow and Edinburgh, c1918–1939', *Women's History Review*, Volume 23, Issue 3, 2014.
Brodie, Marc, 'Boyle, Constance Antonia', *DNB*, 2004.
Brookes, Barbara, *Abortion in England 1900–1967*, Routledge, 2012.
Brookes, Pamela, *Women at Westminster*, Peter Davies, 1967.
Brooke, Stephen 'The Body and Socialism: Dora Russell in the 1920s', *Past and Present*, November 2005.
Brookes, Stephen, '"A New World for Women", Abortion Law Reform in Britain during the 1930s', *The American Historical Review*, April 2001.
Bruley, Sue, *Women in Britain since 1900*, Macmillan, 1999.
Bruley, Sue, Beatrice Green and the unsung heroines behind 1926's Lockout, Walesonline.
Bryan, Beverly, Dadzie, Stella and Scarfe, Suzanne, *Heart of the Race*, Verso, 2018.
Bush, Julia, 'British Women's Anti-Suffragism and the Forward Policy, 1908–1914', *Women's History Review*, Vol 11, Number 3, 2002.
Butcher, Deborah, *Ladies of the Lodge: a history of Scottish Orangewomen, c1900–2013*, PhD, London Metropolitan University, 2014.
Caine, Barbara, *English Feminism*, OUP, 1997.
Caldicott, Rosemary, Lady Blackshirts, Bristol Radical Pamphleteer, 2917.
Campbell, Beatrix, *The Iron Ladies, Why do Women Vote Tory?*, Virago, 1987.
Carroll, David, *Dad's Army: The Home Guard 1940–1944*, The History Press, 2002.
Caslin, Samantha, *Save the Womanhood*, Liverpool University Press, 2019.
Castle, Barbara, *Fighting All The Way*, Pan, 1993.
Cawston, Amanda, 'The feminist case against pornography: a review and re-evaluation', *Inquiry*, July 2018.

Clarke, Alan Henry, *The Abortion Campaign: A Study of Moral Reform and Status Protest*, PhD, University of Nottingham, 1984.
Clements, Samantha, *Feminism, citizenship and social activity: The role and importance of local women's organisations, Nottingham, 1938–1969*, PhD, University of Nottingham, 2008.
Cohen, Susan, *Eleanor Rathbone and the Refugees*, Vallentine Mitchell, 2010.
Collette, Christine, *The Newer Eve, Women, Feminists and the Labour Party*, Palgrave Macmillan, 2009.
Condon, Stephanie, Thiara, Ravi K., Schroettle, Monika, *Violence Against women and Ethnicity: Commonalities and Differences Across Europe*, Saint Philip Street Press, 2020.
Coote, Anna and Campbell, Beatrix, *Sweet Freedom: The Struggle for Women's Liberation*, Wiley-Blackwell, 1982.
Cowman, Krista, *'Mrs Brown is a Man and a Brother', Women in Merseyside's Political Organisations, 1890–1920*, Liverpool University Press, 2004.
Cox, Pamela and Hobley, Annabel, *Shopgirls*, Arrow Books, 2014.
Crawford, Elizabeth, *The Women's Suffrage Movement, a reference guide 1866–1928*, UCL, 1999.
Cullen, Stephen, 'Four Women for Mosley: Women in the British Union of Fascists, 1932–1940', *Oral History*, Spring 1996.
Currell, Melville, *Political Woman*, Rowman and Littlefield, 1974.
Davies, Mary *Sylvia Pankhurst, A Life in Radical Politics*, Pluto Press, 1999
D'Cruze, Shani, *Everyday Violence in Britain*, 1850–1950, Pearson, 2000.
Debenham, Clare, *Grassroots feminism: a study of the campaign of the Society for the Provision of Birth Control Clinics, 1924–1938*, PhD, University of Manchester 2010.
Debenham, Clare, *Birth Control and the Rights of Women: post-suffrage feminism in the early twentieth century*, Tauris, 2014.
Dee, Olivia, *The Anti-Abortion Campaign in England, 1966–1989*, Routledge, 2019.
Derry, Caroline 'Lesbianism and Feminist Legislation in 1921: the Age of Consent and "Gross Indecency between Women"', *History Workshop Journal*, Volume 86, Autumn 2018.
Dhaliwal, Sukhwant and Yuval-Davis, Nira, *Women against Fundamentalism*, Lawrence and Wishart, 2014.
Durham, Martin, 'Gender and the British Union of Fascists', *Journal of Contemporary History*, July 1992.
Durham, Martin, *Women and Fascism*, Routledge, 2006.
Durham, Martin, *Moral Crusades, Family and Morality in the Thatcher Years*, New York University Press, 1991.
Eustance Claire et al., *A Suffrage Reader*, Leicester University Press, 2000.
Faraut, Martine, 'Women resisting the vote: a case of anti-feminism?', *Women's History Review*, September 2007.
Fernandez-Armesto, Felipe (ed) *England 1945–50*, Folio Society, 2001.
Field, Paul et al. (editors), *Here To Stay, Here To Fight*, Pluto, 2019.
Francome, C, *Social forces and the abortion law*, PhD, Middlesex University, 1980.
Fryth, Jim, *The Signal Was Spain*, Lawrence and Wishart, 1986.
Gardiner, Juliet, *Wartime Britain 1939–1945*, Headline, 2004.
Gazeley, Ian. 'Women's Pay in British Industry during the Second World War', *The Economic History Review*, Vol 61, No 3, August 2008.
Gifford, Lewis, *Eva Gore Booth and Esther Roper*, Pandora Press, 1988.

Glick, Daphne, *The National Council of Women of Great Britain, The First One Hundred Years*, NCW, 1995.
Gottlieb, Julie V *Feminine Fascism: Women in Britain's Fascist Movement*, I B Tauris, 2003.
Gottlieb, Julie, 'Rotha Beryl Lintorn-Orman', *DNB*, 2008.
Gottlieb, Julie V and Toye, Richard (editors), *The Aftermath of Suffrage*, Palgrave Macmillan, 2013.
Gottlieb, Julie V, *'Guilty Women', Foreign Policy and Appeasement in Inter-War Britain*, Palgrave Macmillan, 2015.
Gullace, Nicolette F, 'Christabel Pankhurst and the Smethwick election: right-wing feminism, the Great War and the ideology of consumption', *Women's History Review*, Volume 23, Issue 3, 2014.
Graves, Pamela M, *Labour Women, Women in British Working-Class Politics 1918–1939*, CUP, 1994.
Greek, Cecil E and William Thompson, 'Saving the Family in America and England', *International Journal of Politics, Culture and Society*, Summer 1992, Vol 5, No 4.
Grey, Daniel J R, 'Women's Policy Networks and the Infanticide Act 1922', *Twentieth Century British History*, Vol 21, No 4, 2010.
Groot, de Gertjan and Marlou Schrover, *Women Workers and Technological Change in Europe in the nineteenth and twentieth centuries*, Taylor and Francis, 1995.
Haessley, Kate, *British Conservative Women MPs and 'Women's Issues'*, 1950–1979, PhD, University of Nottingham, 2010.
Hall, Lesley, 'Articulating Abortion in Inter-War Britain', *Women's History Magazine*, Issue 70, Autumn 2012.
Hall, Lesley, *The Life and Times of Stella Browne*, I B Tauris, 2011.
Hall, Lesley, *Sex, Gender and Social Change in Britain Since 1880*, Macmillan, 2000.
Hamilton, Agnes Mary, *Margaret Bondfield*, Leonard Parsons, 1924.
Hannam, June and Hunt, Karen, *Socialist Women*, Routledge, 2001.
Harris, Carol, *Women at War in Uniform, 1939–45*, Sutton Publishing, 2003.
Harrison, Brian 'Women in a Men's House: the Women MPs, 1919–1945', *The Historical Journal*, September 1986.
Harrison, Brian, *Prudent Revolutionaries: Portraits of British Feminists between the Wars*, OUP, 1987.
Hilson, Mary, 'Women Voters and the rhetoric of patriotism in the British General Election of 1918', *Women's History Review*, Vol 10, 2, 2001.
Hinton, James, *Protests and Visions*, Hutchinson Radius, 1989.
Hollis, Patricia, *Jennie Lee, A Life*, OUP 1997.
Holmes, Rose, *A Moral Business: British Quaker work with Refugees from Fascism, 1933–1939*, PhD, University of Sussex, 2013.
Holton, Sandra Stanley, *Feminism and Democracy: Women's Suffrage and Reform Politics in Britain*, 1900–1918, CUP, 1986,
Homans, Elizabeth, *Visions of Equality, women's rights and political change in 1970s Britain*, PhD, Bangor University, 2015.
Hunt, Cathy, *Righting the Wrong, Mary Macarthur 1880–1921, The Working Woman's Champion*, West Midlands History, 2019.
Ibberson, D, *Our Towns, A Close-up*, OUP, 1943.
Jeffreys, Sheila, *The Sexuality Debates*, Routledge and Kegan Paul, 1987.
Jolly, Margaretta, *Sisterhood and After*, OUP, 2020.
John, Angela V, *Turning the Tide: The Life of Lady Rhondda*, Parthian, 2013.

Kelliher, Dairmaid, 'Solidarity and Sexuality: Lesbians and Gays Support the Miners, 1984–5', *History Workshop Journal*, Spring 1974 Vol 77 Issue 1.

Laite, Julia, *Common Prostitutes and Ordinary Citizens, Commercial Sex in London, 1885–1960*, Palgrave Macmillan, 2012.

Lambert, Caitlin, "'The objectionable injectable'; recovering the lost history of the WLM through the Campaign Against Depo-Provera", *Women's History Review*, 2020, Vol 29, No 3.

Langley, Helen, 'Ward, Irene Mary Bewick, Baroness Ward of North Tyneside', *DNB*, 2004.

Laware, Margaret, 'Circling the Missiles and Staining them Red: Feminist Rhetorical Invention and Strategies of Resistance at the Women's Peace Camp at Greenham Common', *NWSA Journal*, Vol 16, No 3, 2004a.

Lavery, Brian, *The Headscarf Revolutionary: Lilian Bilocca and the Hull Triple-Trawler Tragedy*, Barbican Press, 2015.

Lavery, Brian, 'Bilocca, Lilian', *DNB*, 2013.

Law, Cheryl, *Suffrage and Power, The Women's Movement, 1918–1928*, I B Tauris, 1997.

Laware, Margaret L, 'Circling the Missiles and Staining Them Red: Feminist Rhetorical Invention and Strategies of Resistance at the Women's Peace Camp at Greenham Common', *NWSA Journal*, Vol 16 No 3 2004b.

Lee, Ellie, *Abortion Law and Politics Today*, Palgrave Macmillan, 1998.

Lent, Adam *British Social Movements Since 1945*, Palgrave, 2001.

Levine, Philippa, '"Walking the Streets in a Way No Decent Woman Should": Women Police in World War 1', *The Journal of Modern History*, Vol 66, March 1994.

Lewenhak, Sheila, *Women and Trade Unions*, Ernest Benn, 1977.

Lewis, Gifford, *Eva Gore Booth and Esther Roper*, Pandora Press, 1988.

Lewis, Helen, *Difficult Women*, Vintage, 2019.

Liddington, Jill, *The Long Road to Greenham, Feminism and Anti-Militarism in Britain since 1820*, Virago, 1989.

Loach, Loretta, 'We'll Be Here Right to the End … and After', *Digging Deeper: issues in the Miners' strike*, Verso, 1985.

Logan, Anne, 'In Search of Equal Citizenship: the campaign for women magistrates in England and Wales, 1910–1939', *Women's History Review*, Vol 16, Issue 4, 2017.

Long, Julia, *OBJECT!: The Re-emergence of Feminist Anti-Pornography Activism in the UK*, PhD, South Bank University, 2011.

Love, Gary, '"A Mixture of Britannia and Boadicea": Dorothy Crisp's Conservatism and the Limits of Right-Wing Women's Political Activism', *Twentieth Century British History*, Vol 30, Issue 2, June 2019, pp. 174–204.

Lovenduski, Joni and Randall, Vicky, *Contemporary Feminist Politics: Women and Power in Britain*, OUP 1993.

Lovenduski, Joni and Norris, Pippa, *Women in Politics*, OUP, 1996.

Lugard, Lady, 'The Work of the War Refugee Committee', *Journal of the Society of Arts*, March 1915.

Martin, Tara, 'The Beginning of Labor's End? Britain's "Winter of Discontent" and Working-class Women's Activism, *International Labor and Working-Class History*, No 75, Spring, 2009a.

McCarthy, Helen, 'Parties, Voluntary Associations, and Democratic Politics in Interwar Britain', *The Historical Journal*, Vol 50, No 4, 2007.

McCarty, Elizabeth A, 'Irene May Lovelock', *DNB*, 2004.

MacPherson, D A J, 'The Emergence of Women's Orange Lodges in Scotland: gender, ethnicity and women's activism, 1909–1940', *Women's History Review*, Vol 22 Issue 1, 2013.

Maguire, G E, *Conservative Women, A History of Women and the Conservative Party, 1874–1997*, Palgrave Macmillan, 1998.

Malvery, Olive, *The Soul Market*, Hutchinson, 1907.

Malvery, Olive, *The White Slave Trade*, 1912.

Manning, Leah, *A Life for Education*, Garden City Press, 1970.

Marsh, David and Chambers, Joanna, *Abortion Politics*, Junction Books, 1981.

Martin, Tara, 'The Beginning of Labor's End? Britain's "Winter of Discontent" and Working-class Women's Activism', *International Labor and Working-Class History*, No 75, Spring, 2009b.

Mayall, Laura, 'Suffrage and Political Activity', *Women, War And Society, 1914–1918*, Imperial War Museum, internet accessed January 17, 2020.

Mayer, Annette, *Women in Britain, 1900–2000*, Hodder and Stoughton, 2002.

McMinn, Karen, 'Women's Aid: Feminism at the Grass Roots', *Fortnight*, May 27th–June 9th 1985.

McIntyre, Mary, *The Response to the 1984–5 Miners' Strike in Durham County: Women, The Labour Party and Community*, PhD, University of Durham, 1992.

Michalopolous, Constantine, *Ending Global Poverty: Four Women's Noble Conspiracy*, OUP, 2020.

Morgan, Sue (ed) *The Feminist Reader*, Routledge, 2006.

Morley, Edith, *Before and After, Reminiscences of a Working Life*, Two Rivers Press, 2016.

Moss, Jonathan, *Women, Workplace Protest and Political Identity in England, 1968–85*, MUP, 2019.

Moulton, Mo, '"You Have Votes and Power': Women's Political Engagement with the Irish Question in Britain, 1919–23", *Journal of British Studies*, Vol 52, No 1, 2013.

Noakes, Lucy, 'Women's Military Service in the First World War', Women, War and Society, 1914–1918, Imperial War Museum.

Nicolson, Harold, *Diaries and Letters, 1930–39*, Collins, 1966. Norden, Barbara "Campaign Against Pornography", *Feminist Review*, No 35, Summer, 1990.

Norden, Barbara, 'Campaign Against Pornography', *Feminist Review*, No 35, Summer 1990.

O'Coín, Sean, *The Forgotten Volunteers*, Belfast Cultural and Local History Group, 2020.

Page Baldwin, M, 'Subject to Empire: Married Women and the British Nationality and Status of Aliens Act', *Journal of British Studies*, Vol 40, October 2001.

Page, Michael, *Dora Black: a volunteer with the Women's Emergency Corps*, Surrey Heritage, June 27, 2007.

Pahl, Jan, 'Refuges for Battered Women: Ideology and Action', *Feminist Review*, Spring 1985.

Pankhurst, Richard, *Sylvia Pankhurst, Artist and Crusader*, Paddington Press, 1979

Patel, Pregna, 'Southall: solidarity with samosas', *Socialist Lawyer*, June 2009, No 52.

Pennington, Shelley and Westover, Belinda *A Hidden Workforce, Homeworkers in England, 1850–1985*, Macmillan Education, 1989.

Phillips, Melanie, *The Divided House*, Sidgwick and Jackson, 1980.

Prestidge, Jessica, *Margaret Thatcher's politics: the cultural and ideological forces of domestic femininity*, PhD, University of Durham, 2017.

Prestidge, Jessica, '"Housewives having a go": Margaret Thatcher, Mary Whitehouse and the appeal of Right Wing Women in late twentieth century Britain', *Women's History Review*, Vol 28, No 2, 2019.
Pugh, Martin, 'Horsbrugh, Florence Gertrude', *DNB*, September 2004.
Pugh, Martin, *Women and the Women's Movement in Britain*, Palgrave Macmillan, 2000.
Pugh, Martin, Liberals and Women, website of the Liberal Democrat History Group.
Purvis, June, *Emmeline Pankhurst*, Routledge, 2002.
Purvis, June, 'What Was Margaret Thatcher's Legacy for Women?', *Women's History Review*, May 2013, Volume 22, Issue 6.
Randall Vicky, *Women in Politics*, Macmillan, 1987.
Rachel Reeves, *Women of Westminster*, I B Tauris, 2019.
Rowbotham, Sheila, *A Century of Women*, Viking, 1997.
Rowbotham, Sheila, *The Past is Before Us, Feminism in Action since the 1960s*, Penguin 1989.
Rowbotham, Sheila, *Dreamers of a New Day*, Verso, 2011.
Gita Sahgal and Yuval-Davis, Nira, 'Refusing Holy Orders', *Women Against Fundamentalism*, November 1990, Newsletter No 1.
Sandbrook, Dominic State of Emergency, *The Way We Were: Britain 1970–1974*, Penguin, 2010.
Sebestyen, Amanda, *68, 78, 88: From Women's Liberation to Feminism*, Prism Press, 1988.
Self, Helen, *Prostitution, Women and the Misuse of the Law: The Fallen Daughters of Eve*, Frank Cass, 2003.
Sen, Purna, 'Domestic Violence, Deportation and Women's Resistance: Notes on Managing Intersectionality', *Development in Practice*, February 1999, vol 9, No 1/2.
Shaw, Monica Patricia, *Women in protest and beyond: Greenham Common and mining support groups*, PhD, University of Durham, 1993.
Sheridan, Dorothy, *Wartime Women, a Mass-Observation Anthology*, Phoenix Press, 1990.
Sherwood, Marika, *Claudia Jones, A life in exile*, Lawrence and Wishart, 1999.
Short, Clare, *An Honourable Deception? New Labour, Iraq, and the Misuse of Power*, Free Press, 2004.
Siddiqui, Hannana, 'Fundamentalism, Racism, and Violence Against Women, the Southall Black Sisters Experience, *Socialist Lawyer*, Spring 1996.
Siddiqui, Hannana, 'Black Women's Activism: Coming of Age?', *Feminist Review*, No 64 Spring, 2000.
Skelton, Sophie, *From peace to development: a reconstruction of British women's international politics, c1945–1975*, PhD, University of Birmingham, 2014.
Sloane, Nan, *The Women in the Room, Labour's Forgotten History*, I B Tauris, 2018.
Smith, Angela K, *Suffrage Discourse in Britain during the First World War*, Ashgate, 2005.
Smith, Harold, 'The Womanpower Problem in Britain during the Second World War', *The Historical Journal*, Vol 27, No 4, 1984.
Smith, Harold, 'British Feminism and the Equal Pay Issue in the 1930s', *Women's History Review*, Vol 5, Number 1, 1996.
Smith, Harold (ed), *British Feminism in the Twentieth Century*, Edward Elgar, 1990.
Spence, Jean and Stephenson, Carol, '"Side by side with our Men?" Women's Activism, Community and Gender in the 1984–5 Miners' Strike', *International labour and working-class history*, 75 (1), 2009.
Srebnik, Henry, 'Class, ethnicity and gender intertwined: Jewish women and the East London Rent Strikes, 1935–1940', *Women's History Review*, Vol 4, Number 3, 1995.

Stead, Jean, *Never the Same Again, Women and the Miner's Strike*, The Women's Press, 1987.
Stock, Kathleen, *Material Girls, Why Reality Matters for Feminism*, Fleet, 2021.
Strachey, Ray, *Women's Suffrage and Women's Service*, London and National Society for Women's Service, 1927.
Sudbury, Julia, *'Other Kinds of Dreams': black women's organisations and the politics of transformation*, Routledge, 1998.
Summerfield, Penny, *Women Workers in the Second World War*, Routledge 1984.
Sutcliffe-Braithwaite, Florence and Thomlinson, Natalie, "National Women Against Pit Closures: gender, trade unionism and community activism in the miners' strike", 1984–5, *Contemporary British History*, Vol 32, Issue 1, 2018.
Swift, David, 'From "I'm not a feminist but …" to "Call me an old-fashioned feminist…" conservative women in parliament and feminism', *Women's History Review*, Vol 28, Issue 2, 2019.
Tagayanaki, Mari, *Parliament and Women c1900–1945*, PhD, King's College London, 2012.
Takayanagi, Mari, Unwin Melanie and Seaward, Paul, *Voice and Vote, celebrating 100 years of votes for women*, Regal Press, 2018.
Tagayanaki, Mari, '"Does the right hon. Gentlemen mean equal votes at 21?", Conservative women and equal franchise, 1919–1928', *Women's History Review*, Vol 28, Issue 2, 2019.
Thackeray, David, "Home and Politics: Women and Conservative Activism in Early-Twentieth Century Britain", *Journal of British Studies*, Vol 49, No 4, 2010.
Thom, Deborah, *Nice Girls and Rude Girls. Women Workers in World War 1*, I B Tauris, 1998.
Thomas, Gill, *Life on All Fronts, Women in the First World War*, Cambridge University Press, 1989.
Thomas, James and Williams Susan A, 'Women and Abortion in 1930s Britain', *Social History of Medicine*, Vol 11, August 1998.
Thomlinson, Natalie, *Race, Ethnicity and the Women's Movement in England, 1968–1993*, Palgrave Macmillan, 2016.
Thompson, Dorothy (ed) *Over Our Dead Bodies, Women Against the Bomb*, Virago, 1983.
Thunberg, Greta, *No One is Too Small to Make a Difference*, Penguin, 2019.
Titcombe, Elaine, 'Women Activists: rewriting Greenham's History', *Women's History Review*, 2013 Volume 22, 2013, Issue 2.
Vallance, Elizabeth, *Women in the House*, Athlone Press, 1979.
Visram, Rozina, *Ayahs, Lascars and Princes*, Pluto, 1986.
Visram, Rozina, *Asians in Britain, 400 years of History*, Pluto, 2002.
Williams, Susan, *Ladies of Influence*, Penguin Books, 2001.
Williamson, Adrian, 'The Law and Politics of Marital Rape in England, 1945–1994', *Women's History Review*, Vol 26, No 3, 2017.
Wilson, Amrit, *Finding a Voice, Asian Women in Britain*, Virago 1978.
Wilson, Elizabeth, *Only Half-Way to Paradise, Women in Postwar Britain, 1945–1968*, Tavistock Publications, 1980.
White, Tom, 'Radical Objects: Hull's "Headscarf Revolutionaries" Mural', *History Workshop* Journal, August 2019.
Whitehouse, Mary *Mary Whitehouse, 'Who does she think she is?'*, New English Library, 1971.

Whittier, Nancy, 'Re-thinking Coalitions: Anti-Pornography Feminists, Conservatives, and Relationships between Collaborative Adversarial Movements', *Social Problems*, Vol 61, No 2 May 2014.
Women and Socialism Conference Paper 3, Birmingham September 1974.
Zweiniger-Bargielowska, Ina, "Rationing, Austerity and the Conservative Party Recovery after 1945", *The Historical Journal*, Vol 37, No 1, March 1994
Zweiniger-Bargielowska, Ina (ed) *Women in 20th century Britain*, Longman, 2001.

Index[1]

A

Abortion, 3, 7, 8, 96–99, 181–184, 189, 197, 199, 206–211, 220, 227, 228, 238, 242, 259, 260
Abortion law reform, 97, 99, 183
Abortion Law Reform Society, 98
Action to Ban Sexual Exploitation of Children (ABUSE), 228
Actresses' Franchise League, 21, 91n118
Adams, Carol, 31n16, 200
Adult suffrage, 22, 23, 31n6
African National Congress (ANC), 169
Age of marriage, 79
Ahluwalia, Kiranjit, 234
Air Raid Protection (ARP), 135
Air Transport Auxiliary (ATA), 135, 138
Alexander, Sally, 6, 197
Aliens, 71, 99, 100, 143, 151, 235
Allen, Mary, 52, 78, 102, 143
Amazon Defence Corps, 133, 134
Amos, Valerie, 236, 241
Andrews, Maggie, 50, 130
Anti-Apartheid Movement, 169
Anti-fascism, 5
Anti-nuclear protests, 185–187
Anti-Suffrage League (ASL), 22
Anti-Sweating League, 15, 16
Appeasement, 112–116

Arena 3, 181
Arrowsmith, Pat, 165, 186, 195n73
Artists Suffrage Franchise League, 21
Asian Women's Movement (AWAZ), 203
Association for Moral and Social Hygiene (AMSH), 51, 78, 81, 90n83, 161, 162
Astor, Nancy, 8, 9, 42, 65–69, 78–81, 84, 85, 89n66, 93, 94, 99, 100, 106, 114–116, 116n1, 123–125, 127, 129, 152, 258
Atholl, Kathleen, Duchess of, 5, 68, 69, 85, 93, 96, 100, 105, 107, 109, 110, 114, 116n1, 258

B

Baldwin, Stanley, 85, 86, 100, 109, 113
Barmaids, 24, 25, 34n64
Barmaids Political Defence League, 25
Basque Children's Committee, 107, 109
Bastardy Act, 189
Beese, Barbara, 180
Belgian refugees, 38, 44–45
Benyon, William, 208
Bickerstaffe, Elizabeth Pearl, 106–108
Bickerstaffe, Rodney, 107, 119n75, 248
Billington-Greig, Teresa, 23, 192

---

[1] Note: Page numbers followed by 'n' refer to notes.

© The Author(s), under exclusive license to Springer Nature Switzerland AG 2022
P. Bartley, *Women's Activism in Twentieth-Century Britain*, Gender and History, https://doi.org/10.1007/978-3-030-92721-9

Bilocca, Lilian, 175, 176
Birth control, 3, 4, 27, 71, 81, 83–84, 97, 98, 181–183, 202, 203, 210, 211, 242, 264
Black activism, 180
Black, Dora, *see* Russell, Dora
Black Friday, 21, 103
Black Lives Matter, 7, 231–236, 265
Black Women's Group, 201
Bloody Sunday, 218
Bogle-L'Ouverture, 180
Bondfield, Margaret, 15–19, 22–24, 32n31, 32n33, 40–43, 55, 56, 64, 66, 68, 69, 76, 83, 87n33, 89n71, 93, 94, 118n36, 132, 257
Bonham Carter, Violet, 105, 107, 113, 116
Bourne, Aleck, 98, 99, 183
Boyle, Nina, 52, 53
Bridgeman, Caroline, 70
British Fascisti, 71
British Housewives' League, 155
British Union of Fascists (BUF), 9, 101–103, 109, 115, 143
British Union of Fascists Women's Corp, 101
Brittain, Vera, 89n66, 103, 104, 113, 144, 165
Brixton Black Women's Group, 203, 245
Brown, Stella, 97, 98
Bryan, Beverly, 7, 202

C
Campaign Against Pornography and Censorship, 227
Campaign for Nuclear Disarmament (CND), 165, 185, 186
Campbell, Beatrix, 6, 9, 159, 225, 226
Canary Girls, 41
Caribbean Carnival, 167
Castle, Barbara, 152, 154, 160, 161, 168, 169, 178, 179, 185, 187, 189, 191, 219, 259
Cat and Mouse Act (Prisoners Temporary Discharge for Ill-Health Act), 21
Catering trade, 64
Catholic Church, 72, 83, 209, 235, 236
Cavell, Edith, 48

Cazalet, Thelma, 99, 107, 116n1, 123, 125–127, 152, 160
Chain makers, 15, 16, 31n18, 173n101
Chamberlain, Neville, 65, 79, 112–115, 124
Chisholm, Mairi, 45
Churchill, Winston, 25, 86, 105, 114, 124, 126, 127, 133, 136, 138, 157
Committee of 100, 186
Common Cause, 19, 67, 78, 113
Communist Party, 71
Conservative Party, 8, 9, 29, 30, 69, 70, 108, 114, 157–160, 185, 190, 192, 220, 229, 258
Conservative women, 4, 8, 9, 70, 96, 114, 115, 125, 152, 158, 159, 178, 258, 259, 266n6
Conservative Women's Advisory Committee, 85, 106
Conservative Women's Association (CWA), 114, 115
Corrie, John, 209, 210
Cradley Heath, 16, 31n18
Criminal Law Amendment Act 1922, 78
Crisp, Dorothy, 154, 155, 157
Cumann na mBan, 72
Cyprus, 169

D
Dadzie, Stella, 7, 202, 211, 266, 267n45
Davin, Anna, 6
Dawson, Margaret, 52
Debenham, Clare, 8, 83
Defence of the Realm Act (DORA), 42, 50, 56
Denman, Lady Gertrude, 77, 140
Depo-Provera, 4, 203, 210, 211
Desai, Jayaben, 7, 204, 205
Despard, Charlotte, 37, 54, 56, 67, 75, 85, 103
Disability rights, 218–219
Divisions in feminism, 83
Divorce and divorce law, 71, 80, 189
Dolly Mixtures, The, 5, 215–217
Domestic violence, 211–214, 218, 233–235, 242, 258, 261, 262
Drummond, Flora, 65, 105

E

Equal compensation, 125–127
Equal franchise, 3, 4, 83, 85, 93, 100
Equal opportunities, 3, 179, 230
Equal pay, 3, 9, 42, 43, 71, 89n65, 97, 100, 125–128, 144, 145, 152, 159–161, 164, 170, 177–180, 191, 197, 204, 205, 248, 249, 258, 259
Equal Pay Act 1970, 177, 178
Equal Pay Committee, 160
Ethiopia, 104
Evacuation, 98, 109, 123, 124, 129–133

F

Fabian Women's Group, 18
Family allowances, 71, 81–82, 97, 152, 153
Family wage, 82, 128, 179
Fascists and fascism, 5, 9, 71, 93, 101–113, 115, 116, 124, 138, 143, 144, 152, 168, 226, 231, 262
Fawcett, Millicent, 19, 23, 27, 37, 55, 76, 81, 82, 85, 93, 171n55
Feminism and feminists, 4, 6–9, 22, 29, 31n7, 52, 56, 57, 61n107, 66, 68, 71, 74, 75, 79–83, 86, 89n65, 89n66, 94, 96–100, 102, 105, 115, 116, 123, 126, 127, 129, 138, 142, 147n64, 152, 153, 157–160, 162, 169, 187, 198, 199, 201, 202, 209, 211–214, 219, 220, 225–231, 233, 236–238, 241, 242, 245, 248, 251, 258–263, 266n6
First World War, 3, 42, 50, 63, 71, 78, 127, 133, 144
Flying Ambulance Corps, 45
Forcible feeding, 20, 52
Ford strike, Dagenham, 178
Freedom from Hunger campaign, 187–191

G

Garrett Anderson, Louisa, 46
Gays, 3, 5, 65, 104, 181, 227–230, 245, 262–264
General strike, 65, 66, 70, 71, 75

Germany, 30, 37, 38, 49, 55, 56, 61n107, 75, 101–106, 112–116, 123, 141, 143, 144, 250
Gillick, Victoria, 225–231, 264
Glasgow, 17, 24, 31n6, 39, 43, 54–56, 64, 72, 74, 83, 95, 108, 128, 206, 207, 230
Gleichen, Helena, 48, 59n67, 133
Gore-Booth, Constance, 25
  See also Markievicz, Constance
Gore-Booth, Eva, 19, 24, 67
Gottlieb, Julie, 9, 103, 106, 114, 171n42
Graves, Pamela, 8, 74, 83, 84
Greenham Common, 7, 238–243, 247

H

Hall, Lesley, 97, 98, 162
Hannam, June, 7, 8
Harrison, Brian, 6
Hart, Judith, 186, 189, 191, 222n58
Haverfield, Evelina, 43, 47, 48, 59n66
Hollings, Nina, 48, 133
Holmes, Vera, 47
Home Guard, 133, 134
Homeworkers, 13, 15, 16
Homosexuality, 3, 5, 27, 161, 162, 181, 184, 189, 190, 229
Horsbrugh, Florence, 100, 113, 114, 116n1, 123–127, 133, 145, 152
Howe, Leila Hassan, 231, 233
Hull, 3, 109, 134, 138, 175, 176, 193n5, 193n9
Hunger Marches, 95
Hunger strikes, 20, 37, 52, 165, 186, 195n73, 205
Hunt, Karen, 7, 8

I

Immigrants and immigration, 141, 203–205, 226, 236, 261
Infanticide, 80
Inghinidhe na hÉireann, 29
Inglis, Elsie, 46, 47, 59n66
International Women's Day, 144, 164, 197, 235, 237

Internees, 142
Ireland, 2, 17, 29, 35n86, 52, 67, 71, 72, 75, 90n83, 164, 236, 242
Italy, 48, 56, 101, 103, 104, 133, 140, 142, 236, 241

J

Jarrow Crusade, 96
Jewson, Dorothy, 68, 69, 83
Johnson, Amy, 138
Jones, Claudia, 7, 167, 170, 202
Jones, LeCointe Althea, 180

K

Kean, Hilda, 102, 118n52
Kenney, Annie, 24, 27
Kenya, 168, 188, 233, 236
Khan, Inayat Noor, 138, 139
Knocker, Elsie, 45, 59n56

L

Labour Party, 8, 18, 25, 32n33, 65, 70, 71, 82–85, 95, 101, 104, 107, 111, 152, 157, 190, 205, 210, 229, 244, 245, 248, 249, 263
Lancashire and Cheshire Women Textile and Other Workers' Representation Committee (LCWT), 19, 27, 34n64, 34n65
Land Army, 49, 106, 135, 136, 140
Langley, Esme, 181
Laundry Board, 63
Laundry workers, 15, 63, 206
Lawrence, Doreen, 7, 232, 233, 264
Lawrence, Susan, 40, 66, 68–70, 73, 74, 87n33, 94
Lee, Jenny, 8, 66, 87n33, 94, 152, 189, 190, 196n111
Lesbian and Gays Support the Miners group (LGSM), 245
Lesbians and lesbianism, 3, 5, 78, 181, 182, 184, 198, 199, 219, 228–230, 238, 245, 263
Lewis, John, 64, 65

LGBTQ1, 265
Liberal Party, 2, 16, 23
Liddington, Jill, 8, 56
Life, 206, 207
Lintorn-Orman, Rotha, 9, 71
Living Wage Foundation (LWF), 257
Lloyd-George, Megan, 114, 116n1, 124
Local activism, 2, 162–164, 176–177, 215–218
Londonderry, Lady, 49, 58n35, 106, 115
London Society for Women's Service, 90n83, 91n118, 265
Lovelock, Irene, 153–155, 157
Lowndes, Mary, 38
Lowther, May, 46

M

Macarthur, Mary, 15–17, 31n6, 31n18, 40, 42, 67, 70, 257
MacDonald, Margaret, 15, 22–24, 257
MacDonald, Ramsay, 25, 31n7, 93, 94, 96
Malvery, Olive, 1, 7, 14, 15, 29, 31n5, 257
Manning, Leah, 94, 107, 109, 111, 151, 170n8, 182
Marion, Kitty, 20
Markievicz, Constance, 29, 57
See also Gore-Booth, Constance
Married Women's Property Act, 77
Masham, Susan, 218, 219
Matrimonial Causes Act, 77, 80, 197
Maxse, Margorie, 30, 70
Means Test, 94, 95
Miss World, 4, 197
Mitford, Diana (Mosley), 98, 101, 102, 143
Mitford, Unity, 102, 115, 116, 143
Mosley, Cynthia, 94, 101, 102
Mosley, Diana (Mitford), 103, 143
Mosley, Oswald, 9, 98, 101–103
Movement for Colonial Freedom (MCF), 167, 168
Much Markle Watchers, 133
Munich agreement, 113–116
Munition workers, 41–43, 54, 55

N

National Abortion Campaign (NAC), 209, 210
National Assembly of Women (NAW), 164, 185, 186
National Black People's Day of Action, 231
National Committee for Rescue from Nazi Terror, 142
National Council for Equal Citizenship (NCEC), 82, 97, 116, 123
National Council of Women (NCW), 74, 91n118, 97, 98, 117n23, 117n25, 123, 132, 151, 161, 187, 212
National Federation of Women Workers (NFWW), 15–17, 41–43, 64
Nationality laws, 97, 99–100
National Joint Committee for Spanish Relief (NJC), 107, 110
National Unemployed Workers' Movement (NUWM), 95, 107
National Union of Societies for Equal Citizenship (NUSEC), 2, 68, 69, 74–85, 90n83, 91n118, 93, 95, 96, 99, 110, 111, 117n24
National Union of Women's Suffrage Societies (NUWSS), 19, 21, 22, 27, 33n42, 33n43, 33n45, 37–39, 46, 55, 57, 68, 77, 87n32
National Union of Women Workers (NUWW), 31n6, 44, 52, 89n65, 117n23, 117n25
See also National Council of Women (NCW)
National Viewers and Listeners Association (NVLA), 184, 214, 226–228
National Vigilance Association, 28
Nevinson, Margaret Wynne, 77, 79
New Cross Fire, 232

O

OBJECT!, 260
Open University (OU), 190
Opposition to war, 143–144
Orange Order, Ladies of, 72
Organisation of Women of Asian and African Descent (OWAAD), 202

P

Pacifism and pacifists, 55, 56, 66, 102, 105, 113, 115, 144, 152, 164, 165
Pankhurst, Christabel, 27, 28, 38, 66, 67, 115
Pankhurst, Emmeline, 18, 20, 21, 28, 32n33, 37, 38, 41, 46, 47, 53, 85
Pankhurst, Sylvia, 37, 40, 54, 103, 104
Parliamentary Committee on Refugees, 105, 141
Parma, Pratibha, 236
Peace movements, 8, 55–57, 115, 165, 169
Peace People the, 218
Peace Pilgrimage, 75
Peace Pledge Union, 115, 144
Pethick-Lawrence, Emmeline, 56, 67, 76, 94, 116, 131
Phillips, Jess, 261
Phillips, Marion, 8, 40, 43, 66, 70, 80, 82, 84, 87n33, 203
Philipson, Mabel Hilton, 68, 69, 78, 85
Picton-Turbervill, Edith, 87n33, 116, 123
Pitbrow women, 26–27, 34n64
Pizzey, Erin, 212
Pornography, 5, 207, 214, 227, 228, 260, 261
Prostitution, 25, 28, 77, 81, 161, 162, 172n63, 234, 260, 261
Protective legislation, 1, 23–27, 81–83, 179
Pugh, Martin, 6, 60n89, 71, 124

Q

Queen Mary, 40, 65, 73, 136

R

Racism, 7, 152, 180, 199, 202, 204, 231–233, 235–237, 246, 264
Rape Crisis Centres, 213, 214
Rathbone, Eleanor, 69, 78, 81–83, 87n33, 94, 105–107, 109–111, 113, 114, 116, 116n1, 124–126, 141–143, 152, 259
Rationing, 123, 130, 131, 153, 154, 158, 159, 170n18

Reclaim The Night, 214
Refugees, 29, 38, 44–45, 52, 106, 109–111, 113, 116, 136, 141–143, 151, 203, 233
Rent strikes, 54–55, 96, 177
Representation of the People Acts 1918, 1928, 57, 77
Rhodesia, 188, 190
Rhondda, Lady Margaret, 85, 89n66, 95, 105, 114
Richardson, Mary, 102, 103
Right to Serve March, 38
Roper, Esther, 19, 24–27, 34n65
Rowbotham, Sheila, 5, 6, 115, 206
Royden, Maud, 27, 52, 56, 66, 104, 111, 113, 115, 116
Russell, Dora, 44, 83, 84, 98, 116, 151, 186

S

Scafe, Suzanne, 7, 202
Scargill, Anne, 246–248
Scottish Women's Hospitals (SWH), 46, 47, 71
Second World War, 104, 123–145
Section 28, 229
Separation allowances, 53, 54
Sex Disqualification Removal Act, 77
Sexual politics, 3, 27–29, 50–54, 77–81, 161–162, 225–231, 245, 264
Shah, Zoora, 234
Shop assistants, 18, 23, 64, 65, 85, 206
Shop Assistants Union, 64
Short, Clare, 3, 227, 248–251, 262
Singh, Duleep, 20, 50
Single mothers, 28, 53, 79, 189
Sinn Féin, 29, 67, 242
Six Point Group (SPG), 74, 77, 78, 84, 85, 89n66, 90n83, 91n118, 97, 104, 105, 127, 131, 151, 152, 165
Snowden, Ethel, 70, 75
Society for the Protection of the Unborn Child (SPUC), 183, 184, 206–208, 238
Soul Market, The, 1, 14
Southall Black Sisters (SBS), 233–237, 245, 246, 261

Spanish Civil War, 106, 107, 112, 115–116, 124
Spanish Medical Aid Committee (SMA), 111
Spanish Relief Committee, 107, 108
Standing Joint Committee of Industrial Women's Organisations (SJC), 2, 43, 108
Status of Women Committee, 188
Stopes, Marie, 83, 98
Strachey, Ray, 10n9, 39, 67
Strikes, 16, 17, 20, 37, 42, 43, 52–55, 63–65, 70, 104, 115, 127, 128, 165, 178–180, 186, 191, 199, 204–206, 216, 242–248
Suffragettes, 5, 16, 17, 20, 21, 23, 24, 27, 37, 38, 43, 44, 46, 48, 50, 52–56, 78, 80, 81, 89n66, 100, 102, 103, 109, 115, 116, 126, 131, 143, 161, 165, 185, 189, 197, 198, 209, 238, 239, 243, 265
Suffragists, 22–24, 27–29, 33n49, 34n64, 37, 42, 46, 53–56, 66–68, 72, 77, 81, 89n66, 97, 99, 113, 123, 125, 129, 140, 265
Summerskill, Edith, 116, 116n1, 124–129, 133–134, 152, 154, 160, 161, 165
Sweated Industries Exhibition, 15

T

Tate, Mavis, 77, 98, 100, 105, 116n1, 124–127, 142, 152, 259
Thatcher, Margaret, 8, 159, 171n42, 178, 179, 189, 190, 205, 211, 220, 222n63, 225–251, 258, 259
Thorndike, Sybil, 66, 103, 113
Tomlinson, Natalie, 7, 237
Townswomen's Guilds, 2, 82, 97, 106, 110, 132, 183, 187, 203
Trades Boards Acts, 16
Trades Union Congress (TUC), 65, 152, 161, 178
Trade unions, 15, 41–43, 63–66, 68, 125, 127, 128, 175, 178, 179, 191, 199, 204–206, 244, 248, 249
Transgender politics, 262
Tuckwell, Gertrude, 15, 16, 77, 80

U

Ulster Unionists, 29, 72
Ulster Women's Unionist Council (UWUC), 72
Unemployment, 40, 65, 94–96, 151, 231, 232
United Nations Educational, Scientific and Cultural Organisation (UNESCO), 152, 165

V

Varley, Julia, 16
Venereal disease (VD), 28, 50, 128, 184
Visram, Rozina, 7
Voluntary Aid Attachments, 50
Voluntary Women Patrols, 78
Votes for women, 3, 9, 22–23, 28, 29, 33n43, 33n50, 57, 85, 177, 191

W

Waitresses, 1, 50, 64
Wall Street Crash, 93–96
Ward, Irene, 9, 94, 107, 116n1, 124, 125, 127, 152, 160, 161, 179, 259
War Refugees Committee, 44
White, James, 208
White slavery, 28
Whitehouse, Mary, 3, 184, 185, 214, 225–231
Wilkinson, Ellen, 5, 8, 32n33, 39, 42, 63, 66, 68, 69, 75, 76, 78, 82, 84, 85, 89n66, 89n71, 94–96, 99, 100, 103–105, 107, 110, 111, 116, 116n1, 124–127, 136, 145, 152, 170n8, 258
Wilson, Amrit, 7, 202, 204, 205
Wilson, Harold, 189–192, 218, 219
Windrush, 258
Wintringham, Margaret, 66, 68, 69, 76, 77, 80, 81, 85
Wise, Valerie, 230
Wolfenden Report, 162
Woman Power Committee (WPC), 125
Women Against Fundamentalism (WAF), 237, 238
Women Against Imperialism, 7, 218
Women Against Pit Closures (WAPC), 242–249
Women Against Violence Against Women, 213–214, 227
Women for Westminster, 152
Women's Aid, 211–213, 262
Women's Ambulance Service, 71
Women's Auxiliary Air Force (WAAF), 135, 137, 138
Women's Auxiliary Army Corps (WAAC), 50
Women's Committee against War and Fascism, 107
Women's Committee for the Relief of Miners' Wives and Children, 66
Women's Co-operative League, 43
Women's Emergency Corps, 43–49
Women's Freedom League (WFL), 21, 23, 27, 37, 52, 55, 57, 67, 77–80, 84, 86, 90n83, 90n87, 91n118, 97, 127, 165, 192
Women's Guild of Empire, 65, 90n83
Women's History Network, 6, 194n39
Women's Home Defence (WHD), 133, 134
Women's Hospital Corps, 46
Women's Industrial Council, 17
Women's Institute (WI), 2, 50, 74, 83, 88n65, 97, 110, 123, 129–132, 140, 151, 163, 165, 187, 188
Women's International League for Peace and Freedom (WILPF), 55, 75, 112, 185
Women's Labour League (WLL), 2, 43, 70
Women's Land Army, 106, 135
Women's League of Empire, 151
Women's Liberal Federation, 2, 52, 91n118, 123
Women's Liberation Movement (WLM), 6, 7, 10n9, 177, 197–199, 209, 211, 212, 214, 219, 231, 236, 242, 243
Women's National Liberal Federation (WNLF), 68, 71, 90n83
Women's Police Service, 52, 143
Women's refuges, 7, 199, 212, 220, 234, 235, 238

Women's Royal Air Force (WRAFS), 50, 51
Women's Royal Naval Service, 50, 135, 140
Women's Service Bureau, 38, 39
Women's Social and Political Union (WSPU), 2, 20–22, 27, 33n43, 33n44, 33n45, 38, 43, 55, 65, 66, 89n65, 89n66, 106
Women's Unionist and Tariff Reform Association (WUTRA), 2, 29, 30, 69
Women's Voluntary Services (WVS), 129, 131, 132, 135, 137
Women's World Committee against War and Fascism (WWC), 103
Workers' Birth Control Group, 83, 84, 91n107

The manufacturer's authorised representative in the EU is Springer Nature Customer Service Centre GmbH, Europaplatz 3, 69115 Heidelberg, Germany. If you have any concerns regarding our products, please contact ProductSafety@springernature.com

Printed and bound by CPI Group (UK) Ltd, Croydon, CR0 4YY
25/03/2026
02078196-0016